"And Martha Served"

History of the Sisters of St. Martha, Antigonish, Nova Scotia

James D. Cameron

Nimbus Publishing Limited
PO Box 9301, Station A
Halifax, NS B3K 5N5
(902) 455-4286

Design: Joan Sinclair

Cover: Chapel stained-glass window by Rambusch of Canada Ltd., logo of the fifteen founding Sisters designed by Sister Irene Doyle.

Printed and bound in Canada

Canadian Cataloguing in Publication Data
Cameron, James D., 1953–
"And Martha Served"
ISBN 1-55109-328-6

1. Sisters of St. Martha -- History. 2. Nuns -- Nova Scotia -- Antigonish -- History. I. Title.

BX4490.98.C36 2000 271'.975 C99-950270-0

Canada

Nimbus Publishing acknowledges the financial support of the Canada Council and the Department of Canadian Heritage.

Table of Contents

This volume is respectfully dedicated to those extraordinary women of the Congregation of the Sisters of St. Martha, Antigonish, on the occasion of their centennial celebration in the year 2000

List of Illustrations

Unless otherwise noted, all photographs are included by the kind permission of the Congregation of the Sisters of St. Martha Archives, Bethany, Antigonish.

List of Appendices

Foreword

In preparation for the jubilee year 2000, Pope John Paul II in his apostolic letter *Tertio Millennio Adventiente* speaks of a jubilee as a time of grace, a day blessed by the Lord.

As we Sisters of Saint Martha begin our jubilee celebration of foundation, these words of our Holy Father remind us that the time of grace, the day of blessing, is upon us. Among the many graces and blessings is the publication of this story of Martha life. Between the covers of this book lies a faithful documentation of God's grace made visible throughout a century of relationships of the sisters with God and with the people.

We are deeply indebted to Dr. James Cameron, author of this popular history. Through his scholarly skill, reflective spirit, and fidelity to truth, we have a concise document recording what lies at the heart of the Sisters of Saint. Martha. It is the story of ordinary women who became religious in the service of the Church, supported by their faith in God, and their openness to the people who collaborated with them, especially when other resources were absent.

Throughout the ages, peasants and scholars alike have wondered at the mystery of grace as seen in the everyday relationships and activities of people with their God. As you read this story of life, may you pause often, as we have done throughout this past century, to wonder and to give thanks for the revelation of God's unconditional love through the lives of the Sisters of Saint Martha.

At this time of grace and this day of blessing, I ask you to join us in a prayer of thanksgiving for every person who has walked with us, bringing us to this place of jubilee.

Sister Yvonne Vigneault
Congregation Leader
Congregation of the Sisters of Saint Martha
Antigonish, 1999

Preface

In 1996, congregation leader Sister Yvonne Vigneault and her council commissioned me to write the history of the Congregation of the Sisters of St. Martha (CSM), Antigonish, for their centennial celebration in 1999–2000. With pleasure I present this first published narrative history of the congregation's pilgrimage from the 1890s to 1981. Over six hundred women have served as Marthas. Although they have recorded their past and have produced several valuable, unpublished histories for internal use, modesty and humility have inhibited them from trumpeting from the housetops their marvellous contributions in household services, health care, teaching, social work, pastoral services and spiritual development. Moreover, until recent decades, Canadian religious and secular historians have neglected to record women's contribution to the development of Canada. It is a happy, appropriate coincidence that the Sisters of St. Martha celebrate one hundred years of accomplishment on the occasion of the country's millennium celebration of its heritage. The congregation's published history will allow the public to recognize and celebrate the Martha contribution to Canada's development.

This study is a popular, narrative meditation on Martha history, unencumbered by extensive scholarly notes but constructed on a solid documentary foundation. It strives for balance, fairness, and honesty while recognizing the sisters' aims and devout Christian faith as members of a Roman Catholic congregation of religious women. The narrative covers the origins of the sisterhood in the 1890s at a small college in eastern Nova Scotia, and its growth and expanding responsibilities in household services, health care, teaching, social work, and pastoral and spiritual services. As well, it examines the sisters' community and spiritual life, constitutions and government, membership features, and external relations. The congregation spread across Canada to British Columbia, south into Massachusetts and more recently to the Caribbean. During the 1950s and 1960s, Martha numbers and missions expanded. The 1960s also witnessed revolutionary upheavals and the beginning of a massive renewal and updating program that extends to the present. Given the constraints of length, time, and propriety, this study could not be a detailed history of the many individual missions established by the Marthas. The appendices include key historical documents and other important statistical and historical information about the congregation.

The history of the Antigonish Marthas demonstrates the space Roman Catholicism has provided for celibate women to follow careers alternative to marriage and motherhood. Throughout their history, the Marthas have operated with considerable independence but within the general boundaries established by male authority within the Church and by popular Canadian sentiment about the appropriate roles for women. In the process, they have ministered personally to countless people, helped to develop Catholic institutions within Canada, and furthered the ends of social Catholicism.

Service appears central to the Martha experience. This congregational life-thrust is modelled after their biblical patroness, St. Martha, the hospitable, devoted friend and servant of Christ. Actually, the title "And Martha Served" was suggested by the title of a 1940s vocation pamphlet written by Sister Irene Doyle. The phrase comes from John 12:2, the Confraternity text of the New Testament (the Catholica Press, 1950) that recounts Martha's service when Jesus visited her home in Bethany. Marthas are religious women who devote themselves to the service of God. Their evolving constitutions from 1897 to 1983 capture this primary commitment in the perennial phrase "a generous love for God." Their 1983 constitutions affirm that, "The spirit of the Sisters of St. Martha is a generous love for God, a gift which leads and inspires us in all our relationships and activities." Second, the Marthas are warm, unassuming human beings who identify closely with other people and their needs. Thus they are the "people's sisters" and are devoted to serving them. Their solidarity with people is anchored in the congregation's Christian conviction that all people are made in God's image and are thus of value. It also flows from their obedience to Christ's command to love others, and from their shared cultural background with many of those whom they served. As well, this solidarity is revealed in their sacrificial and diverse services to people at the point of greatest need.

The following history is based on archival sources, most found in the CSM Archives, but others from the St. Francis Xavier University Archives, the Antigonish Diocesan Archives, the Public Archives of Nova Scotia, and diocesan archives in Halifax, Ottawa, Regina, Calgary, and Kamloops. I have also made use of oral sources and closely consulted Sister May Mulvihill's unpublished, encyclopaedic, and faithful multi-volume history completed in 1980. The bibliography provides a list of the sources used.

Since sisters were given religious names before the 1960s and afterwards frequently reverted to their baptismal names, naming sisters in a history creates problems. In order to reflect historical usage, while keeping identities clear, I've adopted this policy: (1) at first mention of a sister's name, to state her religious name followed by her baptismal name in brackets and then her surname; (2) at subsequent mention, to use only her religious name; and (3) after 1967, and only if the sister reverted to her baptismal name, to use at first mention her baptismal name followed by her religious name in brackets, and thereafter only her baptismal name.

The happy duty remains for me to acknowledge gratefully those persons closely associated with this project. First, the CSM advisory committee–Sister Josephine Keyzer (chair), Sister Joan Fultz, Sister Irene Doyle, and Sister M. Simone Roach–provided perceptive advice and patient direction throughout. They saved me from a multitude of sins and helped me substantially improve the manuscript. Sister Irene also permitted me access to selected materials from the CSM Oral History Project. Sister Mary Roderick MacMullin, CSM Archivist, and her successor, Sister Marie Raymond MacDonald, willingly contributed in countless ways. The congregation's documentary heritage is wonderfully preserved and organized, thanks largely to the competent, conscientious labours of Sister Mary Roderick. Christa King was a great help as research assistant during the summer of 1998.

Bishop Colin Campbell allowed me to use sources in the Antigonish Diocesan Archives. Kathleen MacKenzie, St. Francis

Xavier University Archivist, granted me access to useful documents in that institution's archival collection. And the archivists at the diocesan archives in Halifax, Calgary, Regina, Kamloops, and Ottawa also provided me with relevant materials. Dr. Hugh Gillis, former academic vice-president of St. Francis Xavier University, kindly provided office and computing facilities for the duration of the history project. Dr. Raymond MacLean, Father R.B. MacDonald and Sister Yvonne Vigneault read the manuscript and made helpful suggestions for its improvement.
I'm thankful also to the staff at Nimbus Publishing–Dorothy Blythe, Amy Black and others–for their expertise in design and editorial work.

Finally, I thank those many hospitable and delightful Marthas who cheerfully submitted to my prying interrogations in the quiet halls and dining room at Bethany, and oftentimes shared openly with me their rich memories of experiences, both serious and humorous. I have acknowledged their contributions in Appendix IX.

The Sisters of St. Martha largely funded this project. However, they gratefully acknowledge financial support from the Government of Canada, through its Millennium Partnership Program, the Centre for Regional Studies at St. Francis Xavier University, the Social Sciences and Humanities Research Council of Canada, and the Jackman Foundation of Toronto.

While acknowledging the wonderful and willing assistance of so many Marthas and others, I alone remain responsible for the following narrative, along with any errors and omissions.

James D. Cameron

St. Martha, Patroness of the Sisters of St. Martha, Antigonish

Chapter One

Martha Origins

Antigonish was enjoying a summer day in late July 1897 when the daily eastbound Intercolonial train chugged into the station of this eastern Nova Scotia town of about eighteen hundred souls. Thirteen Roman Catholic sisters in distinctive black habits disembarked. After assembling their minimal belongings on the station platform, the travel-weary sisters trekked along the dirt road, their destination the College of St. Francis Xavier on St. Ninian Street, beside the impressive St. Ninian's Cathedral. The rector, Rev. Dr. Daniel Chisholm, and other college officials happily received these young, energetic sisters, whose new assignment was to manage the domestic affairs of the bustling institution. The college had prepared for their arrival, and a handsome two-storey, red brick convent stood ready for them. The town's local newspaper, *The Casket*, later succinctly reported: "The Sisters of Charity and of St. Martha came to the College last week. They are very much pleased with the residence prepared for them."[1] Thus began the fascinating and remarkable odyssey of a small band of Canadian religious women.

The Roman Catholic College of St. Francis Xavier was nearly fifty years old but had lacked efficient, competent household management. Its rector and bishop had decided to attack this obstinate problem by securing a community of sisters who would become responsible for the institution's domestic needs. The Sisters of Charity (SC, or the Charities) in Halifax, who had recently established an auxiliary order of Sisters of St. Martha to do the domestic work in their institutions, generously agreed to train sisters for the work.

However, by 1900, church and college authorities in Antigonish were dissatisfied with the small numbers the Sisters of Charity had sent to the college. That year, therefore, the Bishop of Antigonish took a decisive step to create a new congregation. Thus was born the congregation of the Sisters of St. Martha, Antigonish.

Needy College

The sisters' new home, St. Francis Xavier College (St.F.X.), had been established in 1853 by Bishop Colin Francis MacKinnon (d. 1879) to satisfy the higher educational needs of his Diocese of Antigonish, which had been established in 1844. He had been especially anxious to secure dependable native-born priests; a college would permit him to develop a home-grown priesthood, as well as Catholic lay leaders. The bishop's diocese embraced the largely rural counties of eastern Nova Scotia and Cape Breton Island–Inverness, Victoria, Richmond, Cape Breton, Guysborough, Pictou, and Antigonish. The Roman Catholic faithful of this extensive territory were ethnically diverse and included Micmac, Scottish Highlanders, Irish, Acadians, and English. Most of the flock were mothers and housewives, children, farmers, fishermen, or tradesmen, and all were of modest means. By 1891, the diocese boasted more than 73,000 faithful and at least eighty-five churches and seven convents.

Bishop MacKinnon's college had grown with his diocese. By 1891 St.F.X. registered about 108 students in its high school/academy and college programs. The faculty, almost all priest-professors, totalled five. A period of steady advance and building expansion had begun in 1880 that included a three-storey brick classroom/residence building (1880), college incorporation (1882), an addition of two large brick wings (1888), an adjacent female school (1883) run by the Montreal-based Congregation of the Sisters of Notre Dame, and a college rink (1887).

This growth continued under the rectorship of Rev. Dr. Daniel Chisholm (1891–1898), a thirty-two-year-old native of North Intervale, Guysborough County, and a St.F.X. alumnus.

"Dr. Dan," as the students called him, was a conscientious, unassuming, practical, and physically delicate administrator/disciplinarian. According to *The Casket*, St.F.X. was in a "flourishing condition" at the start of his rectorship.[2] As student enrolments increased, Dr. Dan expanded the college program and improved and enlarged its facilities. Masters and honours programs were initiated (1890, 1897), electricity was installed in the college corridors and study hall (1892), an alumni organization was formed (1893), and an affiliation was struck with neighbouring St. Bernard's Academy (1894). In this heady, expansive atmosphere, Dr. Dan, in 1894, successfully urged the St.F.X. board of governors to adopt a five-year building plan. It called for an enlarged kitchen, a third story for thc college building, and a convent for sisters who would be responsible for the institution's household management.

Rev. Dr. Daniel A. Chisholm, Rector of St. Francis Xavier University, 1891–1898.

The rector's vision for St.F.X. was no doubt molded by the industrialization and urbanization visible in the region, especially in places such as Cape Breton and Pictou counties. In Cape Breton the Bostonian, Henry Whitney, had formed the Dominion Coal Company in 1893. Towns and cities, especially those on the Intercolonial Railway, were growing. One effect was to heighten class differences, along with other existing social distinctions, such as those between Protestant and Catholics and among ethnic groups. Calls for reform–poor relief, women's rights, and temperance and prohibition–also intensified. And Liberal governments remained entrenched in Halifax with W.S. Fielding serving from 1884 to 1896 and then G.H. Murray from 1896 to 1923.

Dr. Dan's plan for a convent and resident sisters to undertake household management aimed to resolve the college's perennial problem of unsatisfactory domestic help. As St.F.X. expanded, its cleaning, food preparation, and laundry needs became evermore burdensome. The domestic services of local women generally proved inadequate.[3] A student at St.F.X. in the 1890s recalled: "During the incumbency of Rev. Dr. Chisholm as Rector … the domestic problem had become very acute. In the kitchen ruled four or five old ladies … qualified for old age pension …."[4] Other Catholic colleges had faced the same difficulty, and some of them had solved it very satisfactorily by forming communities of religious women to perform household duties. Hence, the following Canadian congregations dedicated to domestic work had been founded by 1900: Little Daughters of St. Joseph, Montreal (1857); Little Sisters of the Holy Family, Memramcook, New Brunswick (1880); Sisters of St. Martha, St. Hyacinthe, Quebec (1883); and the Little Daughters of St. Francis, Quebec (1891).[5] Rector Chisholm and his bishop tried in 1893, but unsuccessfully, to obtain sister domestic workers from other colleges, such as St. Hyacinthe College, Quebec. Instead, their correspondents urged them to establish their own community of sisters to take on the domestic needs of St.F.X.[6]

Bishop John Cameron, ever solicitous for the needs of his diocesan college, heeded this advice. As a young priest, he had been rector during St.F.X.'s founding years (1854–1858), and he had become its chancellor at his appointment to the episcopacy in 1877. Conveniently, the Antigonish County native knew a congregation of women in Halifax: the Sisters of Charity. Indeed, they were indebted to him, for during a most unpleasant dispute with their archbishop, Rome had placed the Charities under the jurisdiction of Bishop Cameron from 1880 to 1882.[7] The Charities had been serving in the bustling Halifax seaport since 1849; Bishop William Walsh had invited them there to teach and care for orphans. Their New York motherhouse had granted them independence in 1856, and then in 1873 they had moved to the Rockingham property on Bedford Basin where they had opened a new motherhouse called Mount Saint Vincent. By 1893, the

Most Rev. John Cameron, third Bishop of the Diocese of Antigonish, 1877-1910.

Charities had even opened teaching missions in Bishop Cameron's diocese at Stellarton, Pictou County (1882), North Sydney (1883), and Havre Boucher (1891).[8]

So, in 1894, when Bishop Cameron asked their superior general, Mother Mary Bonaventure Kennedy, if she would train novices for a housekeeping mission at his college in Antigonish, she felt obligated to help.[9] She had witnessed Bishop Cameron's loyalty to her congregation during its difficulties with Archbishop Michael Hannan; furthermore, she was a close friend of the Canadian Conservative prime minister, John S.D. Thompson (d. 12 December 1894), an intimate associate of Bishop Cameron, and had served in the bishop's diocese at Stellarton from 1882 to 1886. In fact, this was the first mission of the Sisters of Charity within the Diocese of Antigonish.[10] So the two religious leaders struck a deal: Bishop Cameron would send young female candidates from the Diocese of Antigonish to be trained in the Charities' novitiate of their recently established auxiliary order of Marthas. Within two years these religious women would return to found a mission at St.F.X. College, Antigonish, and would care for its considerable domestic needs.

Formation in Halifax

Bishop Cameron enlisted the aid of his diocesan clergy for this project. He sent them an important circular on 22 May 1894 that reported:

> *The need for a change in the domestic service of St. Francis Xavier's College has long been felt and steps have of late been taken to supply it in a permanent way. After much casting about, we have at length, through the large-hearted and broad-minded kindness of the Reverend Mother M. Bonaventure, Superior of the Sisters of Charity, settled upon a plan that, with God's blessing, will answer our purpose most satisfactorily.*[11]

His plan was, of course, for Mother Bonaventure to train candidates from the Diocese of Antigonish "to perform the domestic duties of educational and charitable institutions,our College to be given a preferential place."[12] The novitiate was to open in September, and Bishop Cameron expected, about two years hence, "a colony of the Sisters of St. Martha duly trained for every kind of domestic service, and under the charge of one or more Sisters of Charity so long as this may be required." He urged his priests to comb their congregations "for such persons as may be fit to join the new order, and to point out to them the great spiritual and even temporal advantages of the life to be led by the Sisters of St. Martha." [13] Recruits had to be virtuous, robust, and industrious; generally, only those between eighteen and twenty-six years of age would be accepted. During the two-year novitiate in Halifax, each would be responsible for her own clothes, bedding, and doctor's bills.

The bishop's and rector's scheme was certainly a prudent one given their circumstances. The domestic service problems of St. F.X. would be permanently solved by having on campus a group of religious women completely responsible for its household management. Their vowed lifestyle would ensure: first, selfless dedication to collaborate with the priests in the cause of Christian education; second, an edifying religious example for the young Catholic students, and third, minimal expense for St.F.X. The college's constituency was generally poor, and hence the college, whose income came largely from tuition fees, had modest economic resources. From its inauguration, the college's central purpose had been the encouragement and early formation of candidates for the priesthood. Celibate religious women on campus, along with the priests, would model and no doubt encourage careers dedicated to the mission of the Roman Catholic Church in eastern Nova Scotia.

Bishop Cameron's circular of 22 May 1894 initiated the search for young women candidates for the proposed community. Soon Dr. Dan, rector of the college, began to receive names of promising candidates from diocesan pastors and letters of inquiry from interested young women.[14] He carefully investigated the parentage and character of each applicant and then forwarded this information, usually provided by parish priests, to the Sisters of Charity in Halifax. In the fall of 1894, Caroline McNamara, later Mother Innocentia, corresponded with Rector Chisholm and stated her resolve to enter after Christmas. One young woman correspondent confessed to trepidation at the thought of travelling by train all the way from eastern Nova Scotia to join the new order in Halifax. The Antigonish *Casket* on 20 September 1894 gave the earliest clear report of movement toward Halifax: "The first of the recruits from Antigonish for the Sisterhood of St. Martha lately founded under the auspices of the Sisters of Charity left town yesterday. It is understood that a number of others from different parts of the Diocese have joined or are preparing to join the new Sisterhood." The first woman to join from the Diocese of Antigonish was Elizabeth MacAdam of Eskasoni, Cape Breton; she became Sister Mary Francis in religion.

In Halifax the young candidates entered the novitiate of the recently founded Martha auxiliary order. This new community, under the close supervision of the Charities, had its own rule and duties. Mother Bonaventure, reports her biographer, "entrusted the formation of the young religious to reliable Sisters in her own community, and she always showed them great consideration and respect. Indeed, she once severely chided a Sister of Charity who was heard to remark disparagingly about these 'uneducated young ladies'" from eastern Nova Scotia.[15] The Martha novices wore a distinctive habit and followed a rigorous daily schedule: 5 A.M., rise; 5:30, prayer, followed by meditation and mass; 7 A.M., domestic duties, cleaning, laundry, sewing, care of the sacristy, and cooking; 12 noon, lunch; 1–3 P.M., domestic duties again; 3–4 P.M., daily walk and recreation; 4–5 P.M., duties; 5 P.M., supper; 6:45, rosary; 7 P.M., evening recreation; and 8:10, penance, points of meditation, night prayers, and then retire. Like all other religious, the novices observed periods of silence, went on periodic retreats, participated in spiritual conferences, observed holy days and received religious instruction. Their training with the Charities included domestic service at the Mount Saint Vincent motherhouse and on various missions within Halifax, in Wellesley, Massachusetts, and on Cape Breton Island.

Preparations at St.F.X.

While the Charities trained an expanding band of Martha novices at Mount Saint Vincent, Dr. Dan pressed on with his expansion program at St.F.X. and prepared for their arrival. The first phase, completed in 1895, was a new two-storey brick wing (sixty feet by forty feet), aligned east to west and housing a basement, kitchen facility, bakery, small dining room, laundry, pharmacy, and infirmary. The next stage included a convent for the

First CSM convent (1897–1900) and then CSM Motherhouse (1900–1921) on St.F.X. campus. Now Augustine Hall.

sisters. By the summer of 1897, a three-storey brick residence, about forty-eight-feet square and designed to accommodate twenty-five Sisters of St. Martha, had been finished at a cost of $25,000. This "handsome structure" on St. Ninian's Street was placed directly west of the new St.F.X. kitchen facility and connected to it by a structure thirty-four by twenty-four feet. A *Casket* reporter commented on the attractive altar built by Angus D. Chisholm for the convent's chapel: "It is really a gem and speaks volumes for his taste and skill as a workman."[16] Other general college improvements completed by the fall of 1897 that would be important for the Marthas' domestic work included arrangements for water from the town system, full electrification, plumbing and hot water heating, and a laundry plant. Contemplating the new building additions and improvements, the same reporter judged St.F.X. to be "the foremost Catholic centre of advanced education in the Maritime provinces."

The rector's efforts to improve the college were admirable, and his work certainly bettered the living conditions for students and professors alike. Dr. Dan hoped that the Sisters of St. Martha, then in training at Halifax, would manage the new facilities efficiently. However, for reasons beyond his control, his plan went a little askew. Mother Bonaventure had completed her term as superior general on 8 December 1895, and had been replaced by Mother Mary Fidelis Eustace, a forty-five-year-old native of Halifax who, unlike her predecessor, had no obvious connection with the Diocese of Antigonish or its bishop, and was less enthused than Mother Bonaventure about training a sizeable number of her Marthas for a mission at St.F.X. Mother Fidelis sent no Marthas there in the fall of 1896, contrary to what college officials had originally hoped.[17] Then, when she did send sisters in 1897, Dr. Dan received from her fewer than desired–only thirteen. He was disappointed and reminded her that he had erected a convent, at the urging of Mother Bonaventure, to accommodate twenty-five sisters.[18]

Mother Fidelis replied, "Of the eight young girls you sent, some of them are not yet fit for the work. The ten I proposed to send you are the best members of the sisterhood, but even their services would be of little value without direction, hence the necessity of sending three of our Sisters."[19] The Charities, who had trained the Marthas at their own expense and laboured under financial burdens,[20] found the Marthas a useful auxiliary order at the motherhouse and on their missions. Moreover, they were dissatisfied with the snail's pace of vocations. On this last point, Dr. Dan confidently assured Mother Fidelis that once the new sisterhood had seized the "popular imagination" there would be an avalanche of postulants. He painted a rosy picture:

> *When your Sisters find out how pleasant everything is made for them–a bright, well-ventilated residence, containing every convenience conducive to comfort, not a particle of heavy work–all that will be done by machinery–a beautiful chapel with a gem of an altar, etc. they will vie with each other in their desire to be here and will not find anything at all discouraging in our work.*[21]

True, Chisholm had purchased a steam laundry equipped with a mangle and washer, and the bakery had a bread mixer, but the remainder of the work was to be done by hand. For example, the ironing was to be done with manual irons heated on a Beehive stove. And there were, of course, no electric vacuum cleaners or floor polishers. His optimistic prediction of light labour and an avalanche of candidates was soon put to the test.

Establishment of the St.F.X. Mission

Mother Fidelis upheld her end of the deal with Antigonish, but on her own terms. Thus ten young Sisters of St. Martha and three Sisters of Charity arrived in Antigonish on the eastbound Intercolonial in July 1897 and trekked up to the college with its "bright, well-ventilated residence, containing every convenience conducive" to the comfort of the new arrivals. The ten Marthas were: Sister M. Francis (Elizabeth) MacAdam, Sister M. Dorothy (Isabel) Beaton, Sister M. Thecla (Bridget Ellen) Chisholm, Sister M. Ninian (Agnes) Beaton, Sister M. Cecilia Dugas, Sister M. Dominica, all professed; and Sister M. Simeon MacKinnon, Sister M. Theodore (Julia) Sampson, Sister M. Andrew (Margaret) MacDonald, and Sister M. Lucy Maillet, all novices. As Mother Fidelis promised, these neophyte religious were accompanied by three Sisters of Charity: superior Sister M. Rita Jones, nurse Sister M. Gregory Lyons, and cook Sister M. Borromeo. The college calendar stated, "The Superioress and Assistant Superioress of the Convent will, for some time at least, be Sisters of Charity of long experience in religion and in the management of domestic affairs."[22] Three years after Bishop Cameron's announcement, St.F.X. finally had its small band of sisters who were expected to eliminate the college's domestic disorder.[23]

In the tradition of the Church, the college Marthas lived under a rule, or constitutions. On the eve of their departure for Antigonish, the Charities had produced for them a handwritten rule based on that of the Sisters of St. Martha, St. Hyacinthe, Quebec,[24] and approved by Archbishop Cornelius O'Brien, Halifax. It set forth two fundamental aims for the young sisters: (1) "to become true spouses of Jesus Christ, and to aid one another in the work of their perfection; and (2) "to aid … good works undertaken by the Community of the Sisters of Charity." The Marthas' true spirit was to be "a generous love for God which prompts them to spend and immolate themselves for works so dear to the heart of God." The rule elaborated on the vows of poverty, chastity, and obedience, and advised that hard manual labour was to be accepted "as the chastisement of sin and in expiation of their faults." The life of each sister was regulated from rising to retiring, and her behaviour was to be carefully supervised by her superior, whose commands were to be obeyed as those of God Himself. Honour and obedience were to be rendered to the Sisters of Charity "in the persons of those who are appointed to direct and govern" the Marthas. The rule directed the sisters to practise "the greatest respect" for the priests and to be "extremely reserved with men employed about the College." The Marthas' new constitutions outlined a scrupulously regulated and ordered life. Working under it at St.F.X. would be training for spiritual Olympians.[25]

The tasks facing the occupants of the new convent were legion and exhausting; contrary to the rector's expectation, most were done by hand and much of the work was heavy. The thirteen sisters were immediately called upon to cook, serve, clean, sweep, scrub, wash, polish, sew, darn, and iron. One pioneer sister recalled:

> *The Sisters swept and dusted all the classrooms three times a week, the corridors daily. They did all the bed-making in dormitories and private rooms. They emptied the washbasins in the students' rooms, cleaned out their bathrooms, and toilets (and a sorry mess these were, at times). Every day, except Mondays and Saturdays (on which days the beds were aired and turned down), white bedspreads and starched pillow shams were placed on all beds in the students' dormitories in the mornings and in the evenings, they were folded nicely and put away.*[26]

Nursing sick students in the infirmary and looking after the chapel sacristy were also Martha responsibilities. And for youths in residence at the college high school, the sisters acted as surrogate mothers. Their rule called them "to have a maternal care of the small pupils of the College, without however showing any familiarity." In 1899 a grateful parent wrote the rector: "I am also very thankfull [sic] to his teachers and dear Sr. Gregory who was the first who showed Jack that he could allways [sic] relie [sic] on Her as Mother, and I am glad to say that he respects her as mother."[27]

The entry of the small community of Marthas certainly marked a new era in the health, hygiene, and comfort of the St.F.X. faculty and students. The Marthas dramatically transformed the domestic regimen and atmosphere. The "neatness and home-like appearance of the dormitories" and the refectory's "excellent table" revealed their dedication and skill.[28] One person remembered, "Eventually the college, from being a little better than a barracks, became more homelike, more orderly and by far a better place to live.... On the whole there was a striking contrast between the 'old order' and the 'new.'"[29] The new order was immediately appreciated by all Xaverians. In a letter to Mother Fidelis, the rector was lavish in his praise: "I am so content with the work that has been done by your excellent religious that my only regret is that I am not in a position to offer you more than you received yearly from us. The revd. clergy now in retreat speak in most glowing terms of the superior accommodations offered them this year by your good Sisters."[30]

The life and routine of the St.F.X. sisters remained relatively undisturbed for the first three years. Their work was exhausting, endless, but these were "hard and happy years."[31] The happiness, however, was twice tempered by sorrow, for the grim reaper visited the little pioneer community. The first superior, Sister Rita Jones, SC, died in 1898, and then Sister Lucy Maillet, a Martha novice, passed away in March 1899, stricken by tuberculosis. The two sister superiors who succeeded Sister Rita were Sister Anina (1898) and Sister Mary Clare (1899). The foundling community was also saddened by the departure in February 1898 of its friend Dr. Dan. Strenuous work had undermined his delicate constitution; at his premature death in 1905, a student remarked that Dr. Dan had left St.F.X. "already marked for the tomb."[32] In his place Bishop Cameron appointed the former vice-rector, Rev. Dr. Alexander M. Thompson. Only thirty-two at the time, he had already served at the college for seven years and had gratefully witnessed the highly desirable changes effected by the sisters.

Toward Independence

The young common life of the Marthas at St.F.X. was forever altered in the summer of 1900 by a permanent rupture in their relations with the Sisters of Charity. The decisive event was a watershed for the Marthas of Antigonish Diocese, as it established them as a separate and distinct congregation. From the accession of Mother Fidelis in 1895, both parties to the agreement–St.F.X. and the Charities–had expressed considerable dissatisfaction with how it was working out in practice. Mother Fidelis had complained of the expense and inconvenience of training sisters for the college, and she had repeatedly accused the Antigonish Diocesan clergy of not doing their part of sending candidates to join her auxiliary order. She warned the new rector,

Rev. Dr. Thompson, in August 1899: "I take this opportunity therefore, dear Rev. Father, of asking you to remind them of this duty, if they wish our services to continue."[33] Even though many had entered from the Diocese of Antigonish and perhaps as many as twenty-five from elsewhere,[34] Mother Fidelis considered the number of entrants abysmally low.

For their part, St.F.X. college officials and the bishop-chancellor were disgruntled by Mother Fidelis' apparent miserly stance toward Antigonish. Some of her subordinates likewise thought she should have been more generous.[35] By February 1900, increased domestic demand at the college had even required Rector Thompson once again to hire workers from the town.[36] This was a troubling regression toward the pre-Martha arrangements at St.F.X. and utterly unacceptable to Bishop Cameron; therefore, he decided to take matters into his own hands. He would establish a congregation independent from the Charities' auxiliary group of Marthas, and the convent at St.F.X. would become, instead of a mission, a motherhouse with its own novitiate drawing young women directly from the Diocese of Antigonish. He arranged for Archbishop O'Brien of Halifax to meet with the Sisters of St. Martha during their annual July retreat at Mount Saint Vincent and convey to them the new plan.

Rev. Dr. Alexander M. Thompson, Rector of St. Francis Xavier University, 1898–1906
(courtesy of the St. F.X. Archives)

On the final day of their retreat, 12 July 1900, Archbishop O'Brien summoned the Marthas from the Diocese of Antigonish to the motherhouse assembly hall. Not all, but at least twenty of them, were present.[37] A sister described the proceedings:

> *His Grace placed before them the purpose of calling the meeting. He informed the Sisters of St. Martha who had come from the Diocese of Antigonish that their Bishop was prepared to receive them and establish them into a diocesan Congregation. If any of them were unwilling to assume this undertaking, they were left perfectly free to remain with the Sisters of Charity. In one word, he simply called for volunteers.*

Said Archbishop O'Brien in his closing remarks: "I give my blessing to those who go to Antigonish and to those who choose to remain with the Sisters of Charity."[38]

The archbishop allowed a short pause for reflection and then asked that volunteers for Bishop Cameron's proposed new congregation stand up. Unfortunately, the sisters had been ill-informed of their pending, momentous choice.[39] In the cold, intimidating presence of Mother Fidelis who, for good and evident reasons, did not want to lose these sisters, thirteen young Marthas courageously rose to their feet. This was a pivotal moment in the history of the Sisters of St. Martha. Sister M. Faustina (Mary) MacArthur, later a superior general of the Antigonish Marthas, recollected, "I said the Memorare and Come Holy Ghost. I just felt I had to get up."[40] The decision made by each volunteer was personally troublesome, for the young sisters were caught between two commanding, wily administrators Mother Fidelis and Bishop Cameron–and between deep, conflicting loyalties–to the Sisters of Charity to whom the professed had made commitments, and to the Diocese of Antigonish from whence they came.

Mother Fidelis, who recorded the names of those who stood at the fateful meeting, was incensed that certain sisters had decided in favour of exodus to the promised land in Antigonish.[41] She segregated these volunteers and pressured each one to reverse her decision and remain with the Charities.[42] Sister Faustina remembered, "We were bewildered, feeling like rebels, the Sisters of Charity were not allowed to speak to us, we were off retreat but we were just stunned." In spite of Mother Fidelis's entreaties and tactics, Sister Faustina and the others were convinced God was calling them to form a new foundation in Antigonish. Sister Faustina and her own blood sister, Sister M. Remegius, did return to the Mount motherhouse for several more weeks, where Mother Fidelis made special efforts to convince them to stay. However, ultimately, all the volunteers for Antigonish remained faithful to their original, agonized choice.[43]

The thirteen resolute pioneers who volunteered for Antigonish were Sister Thecla Chisholm, Sister M. Innocentia MacNamara, Sister M. Dorothy Beaton, Sister M. Theodore Sampson, Sister M. Ninian Beaton, Sister M. Andrew MacDonald, Sister M. Faustina MacArthur, Sister M. Remegius (Laura) MacArthur, Sister M. Marcella (Leah) Beaton, Sister M. Anne MacAdam, Sister M. Benjamina (Mary Bell) Beaton, Sister M.

Potens (Mary Anastasia) Landry, and Sister Joseph Agnes (Janet) MacDonald (the last five were still novices). These sisters left for Antigonish in small groups until, by early September, all had arrived, including two more–Sister M. Francis MacAdam and Sister M. Jovita (Margaret) MacArthur (blood sister to Sister Faustina and Sister M. Remegius)–who, while absent from the retreat on July 12, had subsequently decided for St.F.X. This brought the founding number of plucky Martha pioneers to fifteen.[44] The first novice to enter Bishop Cameron's new congregation, Sister Joseph Agatha (Mary Joseph) Hines, had a particularly vivid memory of the arrival of the three MacArthur sisters at the convent in Antigonish:

> *One day about the middle of September, while helping with the refectory tables in preparation of the boys coming, I glanced out the window and behold three sisters, all dressed up, coming up the walk to the convent. I dropped the dishes and called to everyone within hearing. At the front door we met Sister M. Faustina, Sister Remegius and Sister Jovita. They had arrived on the 2:30 train and no one to meet them, so it had to be shank's mare. I do not think they received such a welcome this side of heaven before or since. So we were increasing very fast and we were very, very happy.*

By July 24, the Sisters of Charity earlier assigned to Antigonish for supervising the young and inexperienced Marthas had returned to the motherhouse in Halifax. Those Marthas who had not decided for Antigonish were absorbed over the next four years into the Sisters of Charity.[45] Bishop Cameron and the rector of St.F.X., Dr. Thompson, were elated with the arrival of the volunteers for the new congregation. The bishop had orchestrated this development and, by doing so, had struck a mortal blow to the Charities' auxiliary order of Marthas. Rector Thompson was angered to learn that some volunteers had been pressured to stay with the Charities; he stingingly informed Mother Fidelis of his displeasure. The choice offered the sisters by the archbishop "belongs by a sacred and inalienable right to themselves individually, and to no other mortal," he asserted. In his view, it was "diabolical," "vicious and unwarranted" that certain Charities had told Sister Faustina and others that God would not bless their decision to go to Antigonish; he urged Mother Fidelis forthwith to undo any harm that had been done. However,

The Founding Sisters of St. Martha

Sister M. Innocentia (Caroline) MacNamara, 1871–1909

Sister M. Faustina (Mary) MacArthur, 1873–1954

Sister M. Dorothy (Isabel) Beaton, 1870–1949

Sister M. Andrew (Margaret) MacDonald, 1873–1937

Sister M. Ninian (Agnes) Beaton, 1876–1956. To Poor Clares in 1912.

Sister Joseph Agnes (Janet) MacDonald, 1877–1929

Sister M. Marcella (Leah) Beaton, 1878–1957

Sister M. Remegius (Laura) MacArthur. 1875–1927

Sister M. Theodore (Julia) Sampson, 1867–1950

Antigonish, Nova Scotia – 1900

Sister M. Thecla (Bridget Ellen) Chisholm, 1872-1902

Sister M. Potens (Mary Anastasia) Landry, 1870–1967

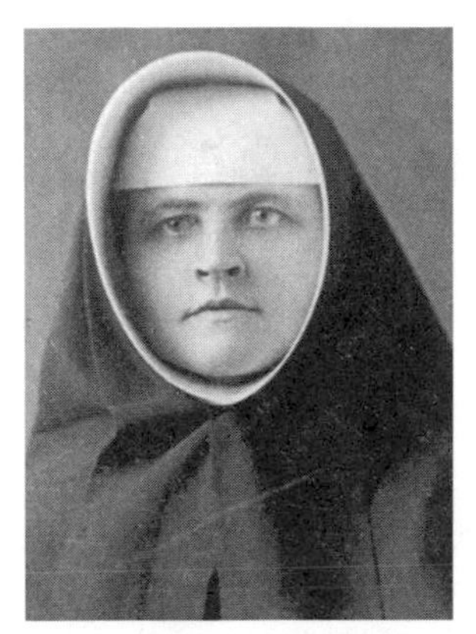

Sister M. Francis (Elizabeth) MacAdam, 1869–1942

Sister M. Benjamina (Mary Bell) Beaton, 1880–1934

Sister M. Anne (Katie) MacAdam, 1871–withdrew 1907

Sister M. Jovita (Margaret) MacArthur, 1878–1957

he also wanted her to know that his college recognized its debt to her congregation: "I cannot allow the occasion to pass without thanking you and your assistants for having sent to preside over the domestic affairs of this College for the last three years such holy and zealous women as those with whom we have been favoured."[46]

The Marthas' voluntary withdrawal from the jurisdiction of the Charities rendered obsolete parts of their rule drafted in 1897. So authorities in Antigonish (especially Rev. Alexander MacDonald, vicar general), with the help of Canon O'Donnell of St. Hyacinthe, Quebec, produced revised constitutions to suit the new circumstances.[47] Instead of assisting and obeying the Sisters of Charity, the Marthas were now required to assist and obey the college authorities. The second aim of the revised rule directed them to help those devoted to "the Christian education of youth and the training of young men for the priesthood." As well, it placed the community, in temporal matters, under the authority of the St.F.X. board of governors and the bishop of Antigonish; a council, composed of the rector, the vice-rector, and another college priest, were granted the power to decide the eligibility of applicants to the community and to give permission for novices to make first profession. For its part, the college was responsible for the full financial support of the community–food, clothing, lodging, health care, and funeral expenses. Each sister was allowed a monthly wage of $2. Evidently, by volunteering for Antigonish, the Marthas had exchanged the maternalism of the Charities for the paternalism of St.F.X.; they had surrendered their role of auxiliary for a sisterhood and found themselves instead as an auxiliary for a priesthood.

The sisters in Antigonish not only required a revised rule; they also needed a new superior, for the Charities had returned to Halifax. As the Marthas had no experience in self-government and only seven of them were professed, Bishop Cameron arranged for the provisional election of a superior for one year. Appropriately, the election was held on 29 July 1900, the Feast of St. Martha, and subsequently celebrated as the founding date of the community. The sisters chose Sister M. Innocentia MacNamara, a twenty-nine-year-old native of Lower River Inhabitants, Richmond County, who had entered the Martha auxiliary order in Halifax, 28 December 1894. Mother Innocentia[48] was a hardworker and a dedicated religious, with a good sense of humour and a retiring disposition. Her subordinates, who by October numbered fourteen, were young: their average age was twenty-seven, the youngest being twenty-one and the oldest thirty-two. All but two were of Scottish descent and their counties of origin were: Antigonish (five), Pictou (three), Inverness (four), Richmond (one), and Cape Breton

Mother M. Innocentia MacNamara, superior general, 1900–1901

(two). Sister M. Ninian Beaton was also elected that day as mistress of novices to direct those who had not completed the novitiate program in Halifax and those who would enter the community in Antigonish.

From a worldly viewpoint, the congregation of the Sisters of St. Martha had been created to fulfil the domestic needs of a small Roman Catholic residential college in eastern Nova Scotia. St.F.X. was the "Cradle of the Congregation" and its first beneficiary.[49] Unlike congregations such as the Sisters of Charity and the Sisters of Notre Dame, the Marthas had no single foundress; instead, they were founded cooperatively by a college rector Rev. Dr. Daniel Chisholm, Bishop John Cameron, the Sisters of Charity of Halifax, and the fifteen pioneer Marthas who had volunteered for Antigonish. Of course, from a spiritual perspective, which was that of the sisters themselves, the founding was the work of God alone.[50] At the pivotal retreat in Halifax, God had inspired the Marthas to volunteer for Antigonish and had granted them the grace to face an unknown future. From the ecclesiastical standpoint, the new congregation was the first surviving homegrown sisterhood in the Diocese of Antigonish.[51] It was not, however, the first to have established missions there, for others such as the Congregation of the Sisters of Notre Dame, the Sisters of Charity, and the Daughters of Jesus had earlier established diocesan missions, even in the town of Antigonish itself. But their members, in contrast to the Marthas, were not exclusively from families within the diocese.

The year 1900 was a promising time for the Marthas to begin their pilgrimage as a new religious community. Only thirty-three years before, the Dominion of Canada had been founded. Prime Minister Sir Wilfrid Laurier had optimistically prophesied that the twentieth century belonged to Canada, for the young nation of about 5.3 million appeared to be in an expansive mode. Locations in the Maritimes, for example, Sydney, New Glasgow, Amherst, and Moncton, and others in central Canada, witnessed the rapid construction of factories which functioned like powerful magnets drawing country folk into the cities. And the gargantuan and open land resources in western Canada lured countless domestic and foreign immigrants to settle the prairies. All this restless growth, development, and movement created urgent social and spiritual needs both within the Maritimes and across the young country, and congregations of religious, such as the Sisters of St. Martha, were being called on to meet those urgent needs. The Antigonish Marthas were well-equipped to meet the challenges ahead, with their youthful energy, selflessness, religious discipline, dedication, and high motivation inspired by true spirit, "a generous love for God which prompted them to spend and immolate themselves" for others.[52] In meeting those challenges, they would become part of the powerful national network of English-speaking Catholic religious, educational, and philanthropic institutions that Canadian Roman Catholics had been constructing since even before Confederation in 1867.

Notes

1 *The Casket*, 29 July 1897, p. 8.
2 *The Casket*, 13 August 1891.
3 Rev. Duncan J. Rankin, "Rev. Dr. Dan. A. Chisholm," (1949), F1,S1,SS1,f2,b1, St. Francis Xavier University Archives (STFXUA) Antigonish, and Sr. John Baptist Cameron, "History of the Sisters of St. Martha," p. 5, Congregation of the Sisters of St. Martha Archives, (CSMA) Antigonish. Unless otherwise indicated, all documented sources are located in the CSMA.
4 Quoted in Rankin, "Rev. Dr. Dan. A. Chisholm," p. 7.
5 Claude Auger, "'To Sacrifice Herself to Jesus in His Priests': Religious Congregations for the Service of the Clergy," unpub, 1996.
6 Very Rev. Canon O'Donnell to Bishop John Cameron, 5 May 1893, and Rev. Louis A. Paquet to Rev. Dr. Daniel Chisholm, 6 January 1894, F1,S1,SS2,f1,b1.
7 R.A. MacLean, *Bishop John Cameron: Piety and Politics* (Antigonish: The Casket Printing and Publishing Co, 1991), pp. 80–85.
8 Sister Mary Olga McKenna, "The Sisters of Charity, Halifax: Their Legacy of Service to the Diocese of Antigonish, 1882–1994," pp. 4–5. Paper presented at the Reverend A.A. Johnston Memorial Conference, St Francis Xavier University, 19 August 1994.
9 Maria Constance, SC, *Mother Mary Bonaventure* (Wellesley Hills, Mass.: Mount Saint Vincent, 1972), p. 44.

10 Sister Mary Olga McKenna, *Charity Alive: Sisters of Charity of Saint Vincent de Paul, Halifax, 1950–1980* (Lanham, MD: University Press of America, 1998), p. 53.
11 Bishop John Cameron to the Reverend Clergy, 22 May 1894. For the complete text, see Appendix I.
12 Ibid.
13 Ibid.
14 The recruitment process described in this paragraph is based on Rev. Dr. Daniel Chisholm's correspondence, 1894–1897 in F1,S1,SS2,f1,b1.
15 Maria Constance, SC, *Mother Mary Bonaventure*, p. 45.
16 *The Casket*, 8 July 1897.
17 Bishop Cameron and the college officials expected the first Marthas to come in the fall of 1896 (see *The Casket*, 14 March 1895, p. 8, 6 February and 5 March 1896, p. 8), but I could find no information explaining the delay.
18 Rev. Dr. Daniel Chisholm to Mother Fidelis, 2 July 1897, MG 45/2/247a,b,b79/2, Father Edwards Papers, STFXUA.
19 Mother Fidelis to Rev. Dr. Daniel Chisholm, 15 July 1897, F1,S1,SS2,f1,b1.
20 See Eileen Ryan, *Mother Mary Fidelis Eustace* (Dorval, Quebec: Saint Veronica Convent, 1972), p. 15.
21 Rev. Dr. Daniel Chisholm to Mother Fidelis, 2 July 1897, MG 45/2/247a,b,b79/2, Father Edwards Papers, STFXUA.
22 *St.F.X. Calendar, 1897–1898*, STFXUA.
23 For a complete chronological list of missions established by the Marthas during their history to 1998, see Appendix IV: Chronological list of CSM missions. See the map for the geographical location of their missions.
24 See correspondence, 5 January to 9 August 1901, F25,S1,SS3,f1,b205.
25 This paragraph is based on "First Rules and Constitutions of the Sisters of St. Martha," 1897, F5,S2,SS1,f1,b254.
26 Sister John Baptist Cameron, "History of the Sisters of St. Martha, 1894–1948," p. 12.
27 Mrs. R.F. Hayes to Rector Thompson, 29 June 1899, RG 5/8/2092, President Thompson Papers (PTP), STFXUA.
28 *Calendar of the Collegiate School of St John the Baptist, 1902–1903*, p. 5, STFXUA.
29 Sister John Baptist Cameron, "History of the Sisters of St. Martha, 1894–1948," p. 6.
30 Rev. Dr. A.M. Thompson to Mother Fidelis, 11 August 1899, RG5/8/306a,b, PTP, STFXUA.

31 Sister John Baptist Cameron, "History of the Sisters of St. Martha, 1894–1948," p. 6.
32 *The Casket*, 16 March 1905, p. 2.
33 Mother Fidelis to Rev. Dr. A.M. Thompson, 17 August 1899, RG 5/8/306cm, PTP, STFXUA.
34 Sister May Mulvihill, "History of the Sisters of St. Martha, I:1894–1900," (1980), chap. 1:9–10 claims 31 had entered from the Diocese of Antigonish. The loss by fire of Mount Saint Vincent's records makes it impossible to verify these figures.
35 Sister Mary de Sales, SC, wrote Bishop Cameron, 20 June 1902: "The request that you made a couple of years ago for more help should have been responded to at once, I mean help for the college, and every Sister in the Community would agree in this." F1,S1,SS1,f1,b1. See also Sister Mary Regis,SC, to Bishop Cameron, 6 July 1900, ibid.
36 Mother Fidelis to Rev. Dr. A.M. Thompson, 27 February 1900, RG 5/8/308, PTP, STFXUA.
37 See Interview with Sister Bibiana, SC, 15 July 1965, Mount Saint Vincent, F1,S2,SS1,f2,b1, and Questionnaire to Pioneers, 1946, F1,S2,SS1,f1,b1.
38 Quoted in Sister May Mulvihill, "History of the Sisters of St. Martha," I:1:32.
39 Some sisters recollected that Mother Fidelis wanted the matter kept under wraps until the meeting with the archbishop, but that certain sisters knew what was up and let the cat out of the bag. Ibid.
40 Quoted in Sister Yvonne Vigneault, "Grace and an Unvarnished Woman," p. 7.
41 The analogy with the Israelite exodus from ancient Egypt was made by Sister Irene Doyle in the pamphlet, "Creation, Mission, and Spirit," n.d., p. 22.
42 Questionnaire to Pioneer: Sr. M. Jovita MacArthur, 1946, F1,S2,SS1,f1,b1.
43 Interview with Mother Faustina in Sister Yvonne Vigneault, "Grace and the Unvarnished Woman," p. 9.
44 See Appendix II for further details on the identities of the founding sisters.
45 Interview with Sister Bibiana, SC, 15 July 1965, Mount Saint Vincent, F1,S2,SS1,f2,b1.
46 Rev. Dr. A.M. Thompson to Mother Fidelis, 24 July 1900, RG 5/8/309-13, PTP, STFXUA.
47 Canon O'Donnell spent a few weeks with Bishop Cameron in July 1900. His College of St. Hyacinthe had established a congregation of Marthas nearly two decades before. *Casket*, 26 July 1900, p. 8.

48 Before 1967, the title "mother" was automatically given to a superior general and she retained that title even after she had completed her term of office.

49 This was stated by Bishop James Boyle at the congregation's jubilee in 1950. See sermon by Most Rev. James Boyle, 1 August 1950, in Commemorative booklet, 1950, n.p., F1,S5,SS1,f2,b2.

50 Sister John Baptist Cameron noted that, unlike many congregations, the Marthas could not claim a foundress; therefore "the Sisters are content to consider it the work of God alone." "History of the Sisters of St. Martha," p. 1.

51 Father Vincent de Paul had established at Pomquet in August 1823 Sisters of the Third Order of La Trappe. The last Trappistine died in 1917. See A.A. Johnston, *A History of the Catholic Church in Eastern Nova Scotia,* 2 vols. (Antigonish: St. Francis Xavier University Press, 1960, 1971), I:374–5, II:549.

52 "First Rules and Constitutions of The Sisters of St. Martha," 1897, FS,S2,SS1,f1,b254.

Mother M. Faustina (Mary) MacArthur, superior general 1901–1910, 1916–1922

Chapter Two

Forging a New Congregation

By July 1900, Mother Innocentia McNamara and her sisters had commenced their pilgrimage through the tentieth century. It had been a courageous, audacious start, for their numbers were small, their experience limited, their future uncertain, and their supports few. One sister, Mother Faustina, later reflected on their pioneering difficulties:

> *We were obliged to pass the first ten years of our existence with little or no ecclesiastical supervision, as our late Bishop was too advanced in years to take an active interest in our infant Community. During the first few years it was predicted on more than one occasion that our Community could not long exist.*[1]

However, the infant community did survive, expand, and prosper. Within ten years their numbers grew from fifteen to about forty-two professed sisters.[2] The pronouncement of permanent vows by nine sisters on 22 July 1905 in the little motherhouse chapel signified increased permanency and stability for the new congregation. And the Marthas' exclusive commitment to a single institution–St.F.X.–was short-lived, as urgent calls for their assistance came from within the Diocese of Antigonish and from elsewhere.

Caring for the domestic needs of the students and priest professors at the college was demanding, relentless, and poorly rewarded work. A sister recalled, "We were very poor in these early days. I remember Mother M. Innocentia buying a pair of shoes. Sister M. Potens wore them in the forenoon, while she worked in the College, and Mother wore them in the afternoon if she had to go downtown shopping."[3] In addition, the Marthas supplemented St.F.X.'s meagre income through small enterprises, for example, preparing altar bread and sewing priestly vestments for the parishes. Over and above these daily duties, the sisters had to create a new religious congregation. They needed an appropriate rule, proper governance, and a novitiate; they needed to devise religious ceremonies, to encourage vocations to their new community, to define a dress code, and to forge their own unique identity and spirit.

True, they did not start from scratch in developing their community and spiritual life. The rich resources of the Roman Catholic faith with its centuries-old congregations, its numerous holy days, its elaborate ritual and doctrine, and its vast array of spiritual manuals, disciplines, and prayers provided much of the substance for life in the new Martha community. Moreover, the fifteen founding sisters of St. Martha had received training through the generosity of the Sisters of Charity, Halifax, who had also produced the Marthas' first constitutions.

In 1901 the congregation had its handwritten constitutions of 1900 slightly revised and then printed under the imprimatur of Bishop Cameron.[4] It provided for the election of a mother superior every three years from among the professed sisters who were at least thirty years old and of prudent, discreet, gentle yet firm, and dedicated character. Under the pioneering circumstances, the age regulation was dispensable, for the professed Marthas selected Sister M. Faustina MacArthur, a twenty-eight-year-old native of Pine Tree, Pictou County, born of devout Catholic parents who had also given two other daughters–Sisters M. Remegius and M. Jovita–to the Marthas. Mother Faustina had entered the auxiliary order at Mount Saint Vincent, Halifax, with her sister, Sister M. Remegius, on 16 November 1896. Before entering, she had worked as a dressmaker. Her superior, Mother Fidelis, had been keenly disappointed by the departure for Antigonish of this capable young woman.[5] In her own community, Mother Faustina became known as a competent, desirable superior, for her congregation would entrust its leadership to her from 1901 to 1910 and again from 1916 to 1922. Others described her as gentle, kind, and humble; one remembered that she often advised her Martha sisters, "Keep your feet on the ground, the ground is the place for us." In retrospect, she confided that the young Marthas were ill-prepared for self-government: "We made many mistakes and I made most of them," she confessed.[6] However, she was a creative individual who quickly developed strong administrative abilities. The anxieties that sprang from her willingness to confront male authority, as well as her deep commitment to her community, occasionally undermined her health.

Mother Faustina led through a formative period when her sisters defined their customs, practices, and ideals.[7] They relaxed the rule of silence on Thursdays (a college holiday), Sundays, holy days of obligation, and summer holidays (mid-June through mid-September). Their "praiseworthy customs" included rising at the first sound of the bell, dressing quickly, keeping habits, veils, capes, and other garments in perfect order, observing silence, and avoiding waste, tangled thread, and breakage. Of course, each sister was diligently to observe the vows of poverty, chastity, and obedience. Though forbidden to speak to the students because of the monastic, semi-cloistered model that almost all women religious were required to follow–a rule probably breached more often than obeyed–the sisters were also directed to always be kind and courteous to them. Anything that undermined their community's common life, such as gossip, backbiting, special or exclusive friendships, disobedience, or complaining, was to be strictly avoided. On the form of greeting one another, the constitutions stated: "In passing through the house the Sisters will bow and salute one another with the aspiration, 'Praise be to Jesus,' the saluted one answering 'Amen.'" For obvious reasons, the first Marthas believed it important to protect the good name of their young community. They promoted work of the highest standards and treated "externs," people outside of the congregation, with great respect.

Through time, the congregation defined the specific duties of each position within it; for example, superior general, mistress of novices, infirmarian, sacristan, portress, kitchen supervisor, and clothes-room supervisor. The mistress of novices was a key elected position. The 1901 constitutions gave five pages of directives for this role and affirmed that "the spiritual conduct of a Professed Sister and the future of a Religious Order depends in a great measure upon the training of the Novitiate." The novice mistress supervised those in the novitiate–the segregated, two-year basic training program for candidates hoping to become professed members of the congregation–and was directed to break their self-will and "to train them in the practice of holy obedience and humility." Postulants (new applicants) were to participate in the novitiate community and examine their own vocation through a period of six months before becoming novices. The congregation preferred applicants between sixteen and thirty years of age, in good health and with a sound character reference. For example, Sister Mary Benedict (Mary) MacDougall's character certificate, signed by Father Alexander MacPherson of Broad Cove Chapel and dated 30 April 1912, stated, "I hereby beg to recommend Miss Mary MacDougall of this Parish, as, to the best of my judgment, a fit and proper subject for the Congregation of St. Martha. The bearer is of good moral character, religiously inclined. She is of a family that is good, having no moral or physical taint or defect."[8] Of course, such candidates had to be approved, according to the sisters' constitutions, by the college council. Sometimes they either left the postulancy on their own or were dismissed. The postulant register reported varied reasons for dismissal: "no vocation to the religious life," "curved spine and ribs out of place," "stubborn and childish," "parents needed help and sent for her," "history not good," and "very poor health and lacking in frankness."[9] For the postulant who persisted to become a novice and receive the "holy habit," the novitiate offered instruction in religion, domestic work, and the rules of the congregation for a further eighteen months; then those who persevered made first or temporary vows. A worthy candidate could make perpetual or permanent vows only after five years. The first novice mistress was Sister M. Ninian Beaton of Inverness County, Cape Breton, who had entered in 1896.

Young Catholic women of the diocese were attracted to the Marthas for different reasons. The most common was personal conviction of a calling or vocation to the religious life. This seed had been frequently planted by a parish priest, a teaching or nursing sister, or a family member or relative. Regularly, diocesan priests, who considered the Marthas "our own sisters," directed young women to the community. The religious life offered a surer path to salvation, an opportunity to gratify high idealism and radical commitment, and an assurance of economic security. For some, it offered an escape route from an intimidating world. During a time when educational and work opportunities for women were severely limited in Canadian society, "joining a religious order meant an opportunity to gain an education and to have a meaningful career.... Becoming a nun, therefore, was a highly acceptable and rewarded option for girls who had completed grammar school."[10] At that time, denominational identities and boundaries were firmly etched, and Canadians took for granted denominationally distinct educational and health care institutions. Hencc work opportunities for Catholic religious women were legion, especially during the early twentieth-century era of nation-building.

By 1910 the congregation of Marthas was composed of about forty-two young women from mainland eastern Nova Scotia and Cape Breton Island. Most who appeared at the convent door with trunk and suitcase in hand were of Scottish background–although a minority came from Irish or Acadian homes–and originated among "the poorer class."[11] Generally, they had reached their twenties, but some teenagers also entered. The first congregational register has a series of entries such as this:

> *Sister Mary Frances, nee Miss Elizabeth MacAdam, daughter of Allan MacAdam, and Margaret MacGillvary, was born in Eskasoni, East Bay, C.B. on Jan. 9th, 1869 A.D., entered the con. of St. Martha on October 4th 1894 A.D., received into the novitiate April 4th 1895 A.D., made her profession on June 26th, 1897 A.D. at Mount Saint Vincent, Halifax, N.S., and pronounced her perpetual vows on July 22nd, 1905 A.D. at Antigonish, N.S. Died at Bethany, Dec. 23, 1942.*[12]

The first postulants to enter the novitiate established at St. Marthas' Convent in Antigonish were Sister Mary Joseph Agatha Hynes of Ingonish, Cape Breton, Sister John Berchmans (Maria Margaret) MacNeil of Arichat, and Sister M. Stanislaus (Mary

Ann) MacDonald of South Side Harbour, Antigonish. Sister M. Stanislaus would prove a most capable young woman of firm will and conviction who would later succeed Mother Faustina as superior general (1910-1916 and 1922-1925) and make important contributions to the congregation. She would also be a central figure in establishing another congregation of Marthas on Prince Edward Island.

Another postulant from Antigonish County, who was also the grand niece of Bishop Cameron, entered in 1901. Twenty-three-year-old Sister John Baptist (Margaret Ann) Cameron would play a prominent role in the congregation for more than sixty years as a pioneer, secretary general (1907-1948), publicist, Scottish wit, historian (she wrote the congregation's first manuscript history), and playwright.[13] In her view, vocations to her congregation through the early years were slow, and she later offered this explanation: "The nature of the work did not appeal to many young women in an age that was becoming addicted to the love of ease and self-indulgence. Only those with a genuine love for God and a desire for self-sacrifice and self-immolation sought admission or remained within the Convent walls."[14]

These young novices were introduced to a way of life and an ideal that the pioneer Marthas constructed during their founding years. As with any religious community, this ideal required renunciation of secular life for detachment from the world and a life devoted to Christ, religion, and service. This radical step was symbolized by a young woman exchanging her secular clothes for the prescribed religious garb, surrendering her baptismal name for a religious name, and celebrating her patron saint's feast day in place of her own birthday at entry into the semi-cloistered congregation. There, as a sister, she would strive to become a true "spouse of Christ" and secure her eternal salvation and happiness. Her carefully regulated environment, with all its rules, customs, practices, and bells was designed to help the young religious along the path to perfection and paradise.

On her pilgrim way she would be moulded into not just any religious, but a Martha religious. All education or re-education was directed toward an ideal. For the community, the Biblical St. Martha, who was their patroness, embodied the ideal human qualities of hospitality, generosity, devotion to Christ, and service to others. As one sister put it, the novice came as "raw material from which religious are to be progressively formed in the true spirit of the Sisters of St. Martha. This distinctive character is 'a generous love for God and forgetfulness of self which prompts them to spend and immolate themselves for work dear to the heart of God.'"[15] The Marthas also cultivated among themselves a deep, prayerful trust in God's providential care over them. God had brought the congregation into being when the young sisters had decided for Antigonish by rising to their feet at the fateful retreat in Halifax, and the Holy Spirit was guiding them and would certainly lead them into the future. Concerning future trials, one sister mused, "Why worry about anything as long as there is a God in heaven to watch over the destiny of our little Communit?"[16] This conviction was a wonderful support in times of trouble and distress, and it also allowed the community to be somewhat carefree. Times of recreation and celebration were joyful, filled with good conversation, camaraderie, humour, dance, music, and good food. Sister John Baptist Cameron remembered evening recreation when "the walls of the Convent re-echoed with gales of laughter, as Sisters related the funny episodes of the day, or recalled amusing experiences of the past."[17] The Marthas learned to embrace both work and play, but work took priority and it came calling in 1902.

Call from Cape Breton

Less than two years into their life as a new congregation, the Sisters of St. Martha received a request to be involved in hospital work in Glace Bay, Cape Breton. This ethnically diverse mining town of about 7,000, situated on the Atlantic coast of Cape Breton, was rapidly growing and, along with the entire island, lacked a public hospital. For many years the need for hospital accommodation "was keenly felt. In the numerous mines operated in the vicinity accidents were frequent, and the difficulty of treating badly injured men at home was apparent to all."[18] The Dominion Coal Company had set aside two company houses for hospital work, but their bed capacity was grossly inadequate to meet the population's health needs.

Since Roman Catholics composed more than 50 percent of the population, two local priests–Fathers Ronald MacDonald of St. Anne's Parish, Glace Bay, and Charles W. MacDonald,

Immaculate Conception Parish, Bridgeport associated themselves "with men of weight and influence in the community, and after much discussion it was decided that the time to build a real hospital had come."[19] The priests visited the Roman Catholic Carney Hospital in Boston to examine its organization. The Henry MacDonald family freely deeded land on Chapel Hill, Glace Bay, to the diocese for hospital purposes, and then the founders secured funding from both Catholics and Protestants through a combination of mortgage, financial campaign, and loans.[20] The new fifty-bed hospital and school of nursing, named St. Joseph's, officially opened on Dominion Day, 1 July 1902, a year after Glace Bay's incorporation. The Dominion Coal Company and its employees, along with the Ladies' Aid societies of Glace Bay and Bridgeport, had donated substantially to its cost of $42,000.

The new St. Joseph's Hospital was governed by an incorporated board of trustees formed in 1902 and composed of thirteen men representing the mining municipalities of Glace Bay, Bridgeport, Reserve, and Dominion. Among them were three priests–Fathers Ronald MacDonald, president; Roderick MacInnis, vice-president; and Charles W. MacDonald, secretary–and Henry MacDonald, donator of the property; D.M. Burchell, mayor of Glace Bay; Norman MacKenzie, manager of Dominion No. 1; and John Cadegan, manager of International Mines. These "men of weight and influence" secured operating revenues for the new hospital from municipal and government grants, a weekly check-off system for the district's miners,[21] and donations from several Ladies' Aid societies. The trustees also hired a hospital superintendent, Janet E. Cameron, a native of Mabou and graduate of the Massachusetts General Hospital Nursing School, who would serve as superintendent from 1902 to 1910 and from 1912 to 1914, responsible for nursing services, the nursing school, hospital personnel, public relations, purchasing, and enforcing hospital regulations.[22] One doctor later reminisced, "She literally carried the organization on her shoulders."[23] The appointment of doctors to the hospital medical staff was also a board responsibility.

Since St. Joseph's Hospital served a Cape Breton region experiencing rapid industrialization, it grew rapidly. During 1912 the nursing staff alone was composed of three graduate and twenty-eight student nurses who treated 1,236 patients. Until the

The original St. Joseph's Hospital, Glace Bay, Nova Scotia.

construction of the Glace Bay General Hospital in 1915, both Catholics and Protestants used St. Joseph's. A nurses' residence was erected in 1905 and the hospital's bed capacity increased to seventy-five. Most patients were natives of Cape Breton, but some had roots in distant places such as Newfoundland, Austria, Bohemia, England, Germany, Poland, and Italy. They had recently migrated to find work in the region's rapidly expanding coal and steel industries. By far the largest number of patients were housewives and miners. Treatments were often given for lacerations, crushings, and bone fractures caused by mining accidents.[24]

The founding board of trustees recognized the crucial need to supply the new hospital with efficient household management. Before the opening, they decided that the Sisters of St. Martha, Antigonish, should "be appointed to look after the housekeeping and culinary departments."[25] The three priest-trustees, all graduates of St.F.X., knew of the sisters' recent founding and salutary work at the college. Apparently, they hoped that once the sisters had the necessary training, they would assume complete control of the hospital.[26] St.F.X. agreed to the release, for $6 a month each plus board, of five young sisters for this work: Sister M. Theodore Sampson, superior; Sister M. Benjamina Beaton, kitchen; Sister M. Potens Landry, laundry; Sister M. Jovita MacArthur and Sister John Berchmans MacNeil, general housework. Two other sisters (Sister M. Remegius MacArthur and Sister M.

Anne MacAdam) were to attend the school of nursing.[27] These two would become the congregation's first trained nurses and their assignment to the nursing school reveals the new congregation's early plans to enter the health care apostolate. The sisters' accommodation was on the second floor and included bedrooms, a community room, and a chapel. The superior, Sister M. Theodore, was to supervise housekeeping and laundry, order supplies, manage the domestic servants, and enforce "personal cleanliness, neatness and obedience to orders."[28] Household management at St. Joseph's Hospital was the Marthas' first mission beyond the St.F.X. campus; the superior general herself, Mother Faustina, supervised its opening.

The circumstances of the sisters at St. Joseph's were not completely satisfactory. They suffered from overcrowding and staff shortages. Relations with certain lay employees deteriorated and, in 1906, some sisters complained that the nurses showed them no respect, acted rudely, criticized their work, and treated them as inferior assistants.[29] In March of that year Mother Faustina even threatened to withdraw all her sisters if the situation was not remedied.[30] She believed that resistance to the sisters being trained as nurses was at the root of the conflict and claimed that the nursing sisters were never welcomed in the training school.[31] An investigation by the board of trustees discovered that fault lay on both sides. By September, Mother Faustina was asking college authorities to withdraw the sisters; remaining there, she concluded, would undermine their chances of gaining full control later and would damage vocations to her congregation.[32]

A typhoid epidemic raged through the hospital in the fall, laying low six lay nurses and some patients. Because of the crisis, Mother Faustina asked the college to temporarily delay withdrawing her sisters. Certain people charged that the nursing or housekeeping departments, or perhaps both, were responsible for the epidemic through lack of cleanliness. But a doctors' investigating committee exonerated both, to the relief of the sisters.[33] Nonetheless, the Marthas were finally withdrawn in 1908, probably to help staff a new hospital in Antigonish, but this was not the last word on the sisters and St. Joseph's Hospital.

The sisters' mission at St. Joseph's Hospital, Glace Bay (1902–1908), was a significant one in the congregation's history. As the first mission beyond the St.F.X. campus, it signalled their willingness to go where they were needed. A later commentator claimed that there the pioneer sisters "'blazed the trail' which future Sisters, assigned to the apostolate of care of the sick would follow".[34] Another mused philosophically: "As was natural, there were times when the secular and religious administration clashed, but not with a great deal of noise. It was not an ideal situation for the Sisters, but this was the Lord's way of introducing the Sisters to the field of nursing, and also of bringing them to Glace Bay, which has been the source of many blessings to them."[35] As important contributors to the founding of St. Joseph's Hospital, the Marthas began participating in the long tradition of Roman Catholic-sponsored hospital care. By 1900 the modern hospital, based on scientific advances of the 19th century, such as the discovery of anaesthesia (1842), steam sterilization (1886), and the development of x-ray (1895), was struggling to overcome its menacing public image as a "death house," or institution of last resort. St. Joseph's was the first modern Roman Catholic hospital in Cape Breton, but it would shortly be followed by others in the growing urban communities of North Sydney, Sydney, and Inverness.[36] The Sisters of St. Martha were important players from the start of this development of Catholic hospital services in Cape Breton.

Health Care Needs at Home

Back at home in Antigonish, the health care needs of the local community came beckoning at the door of St. Martha's Convent in 1905. At least 102 Antigonish citizens, both Protestant and Catholic, petitioned the town council in November 1905 for a "cottage hospital" under the management of the Sisters of St. Martha to reduce suffering through "expert medical attendance and patient, careful and intelligent nursing."[37] The only local facility for nursing the sick was the college infirmary, and there existed no hospital between New Glasgow in neighbouring Pictou County, and Sydney, Cape Breton, a distance of about 260 kilometres. Five local physicians–W. MacDonald, J.J. Cameron, W.H. MacDonald, J.C. Gillis, and C.S. Agnew–who daily ranged far and wide through Antigonish and neighbouring counties on house calls, strongly supported the proposal in their own joint statement:

Believing that the establishment of a properly conducted hospital would be attended with good results in the treatment of cases requiring urgent and special attention as well as expert nursing, we would welcome the opening of an institution which would provide proper accommodation for such local patients as cannot be properly treated at their homes.[38]

Bishop Cameron and the college authorities were receptive. The rector, Rev. Dr. A.M. Thompson, hosted a meeting on 6 November, of male citizens who decided to lay the proposal before the sisters. In contrast to the arrangement at St. Joseph's Hospital in Glace Bay, the sisters were asked to manage entirely the proposed hospital and also to raise the required start-up funds by collecting donations from door to door.[39] Fortunately for Antigonish, the sisters were receptive to the idea and almost immediately began fundraising.[40] Within eight months they had secured the rental of a private home, the "Campbell House," located almost immediately across from the motherhouse on St. Ninian Street and with the help of a board of trustees and small medical staff, they opened it to the public on 10 June 1906. Its bed capacity? Six. Statistics for the hospital's first year of operation demonstrated its usefulness: 117 patients treated and 18 (one source claims 38) operations performed. An eight-year-old had an appendectomy and an eighty-six-year-old a leg amputated.[41] Any local opposition to the tiny health care institution apparently melted away after the hospital, with its staff of two sister nurses–Sister M. Remegius MacArthur (superior, 1906-1911) and Sister M. Anne MacAdam, recent graduates of St. Joseph's nursing school–successfully treated a typhoid epidemic in the district. The epidemic had

1907 cottage hospital, Antigonish (the Campbell House).

required the hospitalization of several people who had previously been opponents of the new hospital.[42]

From the opening, the sisters considered the Campbell House a temporary, makeshift accommodation; it was entirely too small and the design too inconvenient for hospital purposes. However, it became more temporary than anticipated when the owner unexpectedly asked them to vacate the premises in June 1907 after occupying it for less than one year. Fortunately, the college gave patients and staff temporary shelter, in the summer of 1907, at its recently purchased farm (Mount Cameron), until new hospital accommodations were secured. Meanwhile, the congregation purchased for $6,500 the C.E. Harris property with its large family residence–"one of the finest in Antigonish"–most desirably located at the eastern extremity of the town on a hill overlooking it.[43] After the requisite renovations, the sisters moved in and opened the new twenty-bed, three-storey hospital in the fall.

The Harris House was the first property owned by the young congregation of sisters. Hence, it required that they be incorporated. Mother Faustina accomplished this with the aid of the new president of St.F.X., Rev. Dr. H.P. MacPherson (1906–1936), and the Liberal MLA for Antigonish (1891–1911), C.P. Chisholm.[44] On 28 March 1907 the Nova Scotia legislature passed a bill making the congregation "a body corporate under the name of The Sisters of Saint Martha, for the educational, philanthropical and charitable purposes declared in the rules and by-laws." The immediate object of incorporation was to permit ownership of the Harris House and thus the operation of a general hospital and nurses' training school, which would later be established in 1911. The bill also formally established a "St. Martha's Hospital Board" composed of seven sisters and representatives from town, county, and province.[45] Members of the first board, appointed 27 July 1907, were Bishop Cameron, honorary president; Msgr. D.J. MacIntosh, president; D.G. Kirk, vice-president; Mother Faustina secretary-treasurer; James Kenna, town representative; Angus MacGillivray, county representative; and five other sisters.[46] The hospital funded itself, always on a shoestring, through patient fees, donations, and government grants. The growth of the sisters' first hospital during the next two decades was rapid. They opened a new $16,000 three-storey wing on 15 December 1912 that increased bed capacity to fifty. The top floor was for paediatrics, the second floor was for women, and the first floor accommodated men. Not until 1918 did the nurses have a separate residence, which was built to the rear of the hospital.

In 1911 the Marthas had opened their first school of nursing at St. Martha's Hospital. To be admitted to the new program, applicants had to provide acceptable character and health certification, to have completed at least two years of high school, to be between nineteen and thirty years old, and to successfully complete an entrance exam.[47] Students learned the theory and practice of medical, surgical, and obstetrical nursing. Like other hospitals in North America, St. Martha's, following the apprenticeship system of nursing education, used student nurses as a source of free labour in exchange for room and board. Much of the learning was done as an apprentice to the director of nurses, Sister Mary Anthony (Catherine) MacPhee (1911–1919). However, doctors and the school director occasionally lectured on relevant subjects. The sisters trained their nursing students to be competent, charitable, and sensitive to both the physical and the spiritual needs of patients. The sick of all classes, all religions, and all races were to be treated equally.[48] Although the St. Martha's Hospital School of Nursing was not the first nursing school in the province, for others had already been established in Halifax and New Glasgow, it was a first for the sisters. Over time, they would establish more nursing schools in the region and beyond.

In 1914, the first year of the Great War (1914–1918), the sisters purchased a large house in Antigonish–the Hawthorne Street Bernasconi residence–to be used as a home for aged and infirm women.[49] The House of Providence, as they called it, was closely associated with their hospital and under the superiorship of Sister M. Francis MacAdam. Sisters collected money in the town to supplement their income from boarders. As well, local people donated furnishings, animals, and coal.[50] From 1916 to 1917, the aged women occupants shared the house with convalescent soldiers; then, for one year, the Marthas moved their novitiate program there from the motherhouse at the college; and finally, overcrowding at St. Martha's Hospital required the sisters to transfer its maternity unit there from 1918 to 1923. The property, valued at about $6,000, was sold in 1924, a time when the St. Martha's Hospital trustees were convinced of the "absolute necessity" for a completely new hospital building.[51]

By then it truly was a necessity, for the fifty-bed facility commonly treated seventy to seventy-five patients using "every conceivable inch of space," and still "patients had to be refused admission."[52] Back in 1907, 108 patients had been admitted and 38 operations performed; 1922 had witnessed the admittance of 1,021 patients and 555 operations.[53] Therefore, the trustees had determined to build a modern facility, enlisted for fund-raising the dynamic Dr. Moses Coady and Dr. Thomas O'Reilly Boyle from the college, and published the *Hospital Bulletin* to inform their constituency of hospital affairs and the financial campaign.[54] The summer campaign of 1925 realized $110,000 of its target of $150,000; but the "blighting strike of the Nova Scotia coal fields" and outmigration of "the flower of [thc] population" hampered its full success.[55] Actually, the relative success of the campaign was astonishing given the tough economic times faced by eastern Nova Scotians in the 1920s. Coady, Boyle, and the sisters' rapid organization and stimulation of Ladies' Aid societies throughout the district to a feverish level of activity, with teas, musicals, bazaars, card parties, box socials, dances, plays, debates, and sewing committees, were features of the vigorous campaign.[56]

The new four-storey brick, 125-bed St. Martha's Hospital formally opened on 11 May 1926. The final cost was over $400,000. The *Hospital Bulletin* rhapsodized: "At last–and it seemed so impossible only a few years ago–the constituency enjoys the realization of its fondest hopes in having an institution which will bring to the people the whole of the consoling message of the science of modern medicine."[57] In spite of its many benefactors[58] and annual government grants, St. Martha's Hospital, like other hospitals of the time, experienced regular financial shortfalls. The number of poor patients, and others who defaulted on their hospital fees, was a serious problem.[59]

Nonetheless, the sisters' new facility improved both district health care services and nurses' training. For example, in 1926 the congregation negotiated an affiliation between the hospital's nursing school and St.F.X. The college announced, "Beginning in September 1926, a Department of Nursing and Health will be opened which will give courses leading to the degree of B.Sc. in

St. Martha's Hospital, Antigonish, 1925. Harris House residence is to the left.

Nursing. The aim of this course is to afford a broader education than is given by the School of Nursing alone and to equip nurses who desire to fit themselves for teaching and supervision in schools of nursing and for public health nursing service."[60] The new department offered a five-year degree course in arts and nursing that required two years of college studies followed by three years training at the hospital.[61] Promotional materials claimed the new program would enable "young ladies" to rise "to the highest positions of their professions." Moreover, it would "ensure the highest standards of nursing and will provide Public Health nurses and Social Workers that are so badly needed in many communities."[62] A commentator ten years later claimed that the new hospital and college affiliation brought decided improvements to St. Martha's School of Nursing: "The entrance educational standards were raised; a new library of 500 volumes was opened; new models, maps and equipment were provided; recreational grounds were developed, and the social life of the nurses was given more attention."[63] The first graduate, Georgina Gerrior, finished the program in 1933, and by 1966, sixty-eight nurses (all but one female) had completed the program.[64] The affiliation brought into being one of the earliest Canadian degree programs in nursing, and the first in Nova Scotia. The Marthas were establishing themselves as regional leaders in nursing education.

The St. Martha's Hospital annals revealed the busy and rich life of the sisters missioned there. Day by day the annalist dutifully recorded reappointments of sisters, monthly hospital receipts, the admittance or discharge of noteworthy patients, the visits of important people, the appointment of new doctors, nurses' graduations, special dinners, holy days, and memorable recreations and celebrations. The annalist reported on 9 June 1927: "Dr. Hunt of England paid us a visit.... He complimented some of the staff very flatteringly, particularly the Physiotherapy technician and Lab and x-ray technicians. He also said, 'This hospital would be a credit to London.'" Other sample entries show what Martha life was like at the hospital: "Balance of Chevrolet car was paid out of current a/c $306.56" (August 1927); "John McNeil died on the nineteenth of the month. He was waked in the hospital parlour until Monday morning when his remains were escorted to the Cathedral by the College priests and students in procession" (November 1927); "Mrs. McDonald was received into the Church by Rev. Fr. Robataille. She received her first Holy Communion while a patient here" (October 1927).[65]

A young sister, Sister John de la Salle (Anne) Fougere, remembered a daring little episode during her time at St. Martha's Hospital in the 1920s. She was sent to the town post office with another sister. Their route was blocked by a train that had stopped where the railway tracks crossed the road. Sister John de la Salle recalled, "Sister Bernadine jumped up the steps and as the train was not moving she jumped through. My legs were short, I could not jump up. I was scared to. What did I do but go underneath the train! Anyway we were just young ... God saved me many times, I think, in lots of ways. I felt someone was praying for me. My mother said, 'Your father doubled his prayers for you after you left Antigonish for Western Canada.'"[66]

The Sisters of St. Martha had first arrived in Antigonish to manage and meet the household needs of St.F.X. College. By 1906 they had greatly augmented this first work by establishing St. Martha's Hospital. At considerable sacrifice and with great effort, they administered and financed an expanding hospital facility that became an important and permanent institution in the region. With a growing staff of doctors, and lay and religious nurses, it treated patients–infants, school children, farmers, housewives, domestics, labourers, and so forth–from Antigonish, Richmond, southern Inverness, Guysborough, and eastern Pictou counties, who were afflicted by a range of illness from mild to severe. By 1925 the hospital had served about 12,000 patients, both Catholic and Protestant, for no other hospital existed in the area. The annalist commented in 1927: "The hospital has always been a means of breaking down religious prejudice and bigotry."[67] The sisters consecrated their efforts in health care to God, as they worked and prayed for the full physical and spiritual recovery of their patients. St. Martha's Hospital would be the first among many health care institutions owned and operated by the congregation.

Experiment in Retirement Care, 1907-1927

One year after the Sisters of St. Martha established a hospital in Antigonish, they were called on to attend to the retirement needs of the diocesan clergy. It happened this way: In June 1907 the college had purchased from C. Ernest Gregory, a local barrister and St.F.X. lecturer, his 280-acre farm called "Fernwood," located on the northeast border of the town. The farm included a palatial home, which had been built in 1879, and farm buildings perched on the crest of a steep-sloped hill which overlooked Antigonish and its harbour; behind it to the north loomed Sugar Loaf Mountain, and a little to the west stood the Harris House, which was to become St. Martha's Hospital within the next few months. College officials hoped the farm would supply their institution with basic foodstuffs and a surplus income.

At the diocesan clergy retreat in early August, Bishop Cameron suggested an additional use for Fernwood: the farm home could serve as a refuge for aged and infirm priests. The clergy agreed, proposed that the retirement home be managed by the Marthas, recommended the farm be renamed "Mount Cameron" in the bishop's honour, and subscribed $40,000 to the new project.[68] St.F.X. took possession of the farm, assigned Rev. Moses Doyle to manage it, and in November 1907 signed an agreement with the diocese to provide a rest home and hostelry there for clerics. After the Marthas' little hospital had used Mount Cameron as a temporary home during the summer while the Harris House was being renovated, the congregation kept sisters at Mount Cameron to do the housework and to care for retired and ailing priests.

Rev. Dr. Angus Cameron (former rector of St.F.X. 1880-1884) who came in 30 December 1907 was the first guest, but he died from cancer the following July.[69] It turned out that Mount Cameron was unattractive to priests; most did not retire from their parishes until they were forced by illness into a hos-pital.[70] In addition, the farm was somewhat isolated from the town and college. The sisters' situation at Mount Cameron was likewise unattractive. In 1923 the mother general, M. Stanislaus (Mary Ann) MacDonald, baldly stated her objections to it: "the lack of a religious atmosphere, the absence of the stamp of any religious character on the work [the sisters] are doing, [and] the impossibility of keeping their rule, when they are surrounded by labouring men who are allowed to walk in on them anywhere and everywhere."[71] She kept sisters there only because the bishop insisted the congregation fulfil its commitment to the university.

The hoped-for relief from that part of college work probably came in 1928. In February a sister hinted at impending change: "A movement is on foot to free the Sisters from the domestic work at Mount Cameron once more .... May God grant it may be definitely settled."[72] By this time, the Marthas had established a tradition of providing respite and care for convalescent or overworked priests, an honourable tradition that they would continue to the present.[73]

By the end of their first decade as a separate congregation, and with little direct help from the aging Bishop Cameron, the Sisters of St. Martha had established the foundation of their new sisterhood. Their revised constitutions and customs had provided a clear framework for community life. Leaders had emerged, like Mother Faustina and Mother Stanislaus, who became pillars among their sisters. The congregation had grown in numbers and found itself called on to move beyond the college campus to assist in health and retirement care, and to establish a new institution, St. Martha's Hospital. Their willingness to be versatile to meet diverse human needs showed from the start that the Marthas would closely identify with people and would emphasize service in imitation of their biblical patroness. The needs in Canadian society were manifold during this period of industrialization and rapid expansion. The prevalent spirit of progressive reformism stimulated many people, especially middle class leaders, to address these needs. Hence, the sisters were soon beckoned to move beyond their home Diocese of Antigonish to found missions and meet urgent needs elsewhere.

Notes

1 Quoted in Sister May Mulvihill, "History of the Sisters of St. Martha," I:3:5.
2 Appendix VII presents congregational statistical charts and tables.
3 Quoted in CSM, *Sixty Years*, (Antigonish: CSM, 1960) p. 90.
4 Rules of the Sisters of St. Martha, 1901, F5,S2,SS2,f1,b254.
5 Notes on the early history of the congregation, found in the effects of M. Faustina MacArthur in 1954, F1,S2,SS1,f2,b1.
6 Quoted in "The Heritage of the Sisters of St. Martha," by Sister Irene Doyle, May 1967, p. 10.
7 The following several paragraphs are based on the 1901 Constitutions and the "Praiseworthy Customs" appended to the 1900 handwritten constitutions, F5,S2,SS1,f2,b254.
8 Certificate of Character, 30 April 1912, F5,S3,SS1,f3,b75.
9 Register of Money Brought by Postulants, 1912-1947, F5,S33,SS1,f5,b75.
10 Helen Fuchs Ebaugh, *Out of the Cloister* (Austin, Texas: The University of Texas Press, 1977), p. 12.
11 Bethany Annals, 3 August 1928, F6,S1,SS1,f1,b106.
12 First Register of the Sisters of St. Martha, 4 October 1894–16 June 1927, F5,S33,SS1,f1b75.
13 Her two major historical projects were "Brief Sketch of Life of Most Reverend John Cameron," 1951 and "History of the Sisters of St. Martha, 1894-1948," c. 1950. See fonds 2, for a collection of her writings.
14 Sister John Baptist Cameron, "History of the Sisters of St. Martha, 1894-1948," p. 17.
15 Sister John Baptist Cameron, "The Sisters of Saint Martha," n.d., 3, F2,S2,SS1,f3,b4.
16 Bethany Annals, 20 July 1927, F6,S1,SS1,f1,b106.
17 CSM, *Sixty Years*, p. 32.
18 St. Joseph's Hospital Silver Jubilee booklet, 1902-1927, F7,S2,SS1,f1,b119.
19 Ibid., p. 5.
20 Father Charles W. MacDonald to Bishop James Morrison, 11 June 1930, F7,S2,SS1,f1,b119.
21 Kathleen M. MacKenzie notes, "The check-off system ... might have been the first hospitalization prepayment plan in North America." See her "The Development of a Permanent Public Health Care System in Industrial Cape Breton, 1880-1930," MA thesis, St. Mary's University, 1991, p. 91.
22 Ibid., pp. 103-4.

23 Silver Jubilee booklet, 1902-1927, p. 16, F7,S2,SS1,f1,b119.
24 General Reports of St. Joseph's Hospital, 1 August 1902-31 December 1903, ibid.
25 St. Joseph Hospital Board Minutes, 1 May 1902, F7,S4,SS5,f1,b124.
26 Mother Faustina to Bishop James Morrison, 1917, F1,S1,SS4,f1,b1.
27 Minutes of St.F.X. Faculty Meeting, 17 October 1901, STFXUA.
28 General Reports of St. Joseph's Hospital, 1 August 1902-31 December 1903, p. 41, F7.S2,SS1,f1,b119.
29 Sister Anthony to Mother Faustina, 30 March 1906, F3,S1,SS3,f1,b5.
30 Mother Faustina to Rev. Ronald MacDonald, 29 March 1906, ibid.
31 Mother Faustina to Rev. Ronald MacDonald, 9 April 1906, ibid.
32 Mother Faustina to President H.P. MacPherson, 18 September 1907, ibid.
33 Rev. Ronald MacDonald to President H.P. MacPherson, 25 October 1907, ibid.
34 CSM, *Sixty Years*, p. 39.
35 Bethany Annals, 21 June 1927, F6,S1,SS1,f1,b106.
36 Kathleen MacKenzie, "Development of a Permanent Public Health Care System in Industrial Cape Breton," pp. 87-112.
37 Citizens' Petition, 2 November 1905, F1,S3,SS1,f1,b1.
38 Physicians' Statement, 2 November 1905, ibid.
39 Minutes of Meeting for Hospital, 6 November 1905, F10,S1,SS1,f14,b152.
40 *The Casket*, 9 November 1905.
41 Historical Notes, F10,S1,SS2,f7,b152.
42 CSM, *Sixty Years*, p. 40.
43 *The Casket*, 18 July 1907.
44 C.P. Chisholm to President H.P. MacPherson, 11 April 1907, RG 5/9/1631, President MacPherson Papers, STFXUA.
45 An Act to Incorporate the Sisters of Saint Martha, *Statutes of Nova Scotia* 1907, chapter 183, pp. 399-400.
46 St. Martha Hospital Board of Trustee Minutes, F10,S5,SS1,f1,b156.
47 At least these were the requirements by 1924. See St. Martha's Hospital Biennial Report, 1924, F10,S3,SS1,f13,b153.
48 "Hospitals and Nurses of the Sick," pamphlet, n.d., F5,S22,SS11,f1,b57.
49 Sources don't indicate much about the decision to establish this house, its residents, or the decision to sell it.
50 Financial Report of the House of Providence, 1914, in Incoming Mail #1948, Bishop Morrison's Papers (BMP), Antigonish Diocesan Archives (ADA).
51 Correspondence and notes, F10,S1,SS1,f2,b152.

52 St. Martha's Hospital Biennial Report, 1924, F10,S3,SS1,f13,b153.
53 Historical Notes, F10,S1,SS1,f14,b152.
54 See *Hospital Bulletin*, December 1925, F10,S1,SS1,f6,b152.
55 Executive Committee to Dear Friend, 23 May 1925, F10,S3,SS2,f2,b154.
56 Sixty Ladies' Aids were organized in 1926 alone. By 1930 they had raised about $30,000 plus supplies for St. Martha's Hospital. The Ladies' Aid Society of St. Martha's Hospital, Antigonish, n.d., F10,S3,SS2,f9,b154.
57 *Hospital Bulletin*, 1926, F10,S1,SS1,f6,b152.
58 See List of Benefactors, St. Martha's Hospital, 1912-1959, F10,S1,SS1,f12,b152.
59 Bethany Annals, 13 November 1929, F6,S1,SS1,f1,b106.
60 *St.F.X. Calendar* 1927-28, pp. 38-9.
61 *The Casket*, 29 April 1926, p. 12.
62 *Xaverian*, April 1926, p. 2.
63 *The Bethanite*, II, May 1935, p. 10, F5,S35,SS2,f2,b96.
64 J.J. MacDonald, "A Proposal to Establish the Department of Nursing at St. Francis Xavier University," p. 3, 2 March 1966, in the personal files of Sister Simone Roach.
65 St. Martha Hospital annals, F10,S1,SS1,f9,b152.
66 Recollections of Sister Anne Fougere, CSM Oral History Project.
67 St. Martha Hospital annals, F10,S1,SS1,f9,b152.
68 Minutes of Meeting, August 1907, RG5/9/12288a, PMP, STFXUA, and *The Casket*, 15 August 1907, p. 1.
69 Rev. A.A. Johnston, *Antigonish Diocese Priests and Bishops, 1786-1925*, ed. Kathleen M. MacKenzie (Antigonish: The Casket Printing and Publishing Co., 1994), p. 19.
70 Bethany Annals, 1 November 1927, F6,S1,SS1,f1,b106.
71 Mother Stanislaus to Bishop James Morrison, 16 April 1923, F5,S34,SS3,f1,b86.
72 Bethany Annals, 1 February 1928, F6,S1,SS1,f1,b106.
73 Bishop P.A. Bray to Mother Immaculata, 25 March 1941, F5,S34,SS17,f2,b91.

Chapter Three

Moving Beyond the Diocese of Antigonish

As word spread about the new congregation of young sisters in Antigonish, certain Canadian Roman Catholic ecclesiastics, such as the Archbishop of Toronto and the Bishop of Charlottetown, discovered needs in their own spiritual vineyards for which they believed the Marthas were ideally suited. These church leaders had connections through the Catholic network with the college or bishop in Antigonish. So, within thirteen years of their founding, the Sisters of St. Martha, Antigonish, received calls for help from beyond their diocese. During their second decade–the one that witnessed the horrific First World War in Europe–the Marthas accepted two requests "from away" that would have important repercussions for them. As well, they returned to a former mission, but with wider responsibilities than before.

Their mounting responsibilities occurred against a backdrop of intensifying British imperialism and Canadian nationalism among anglophones that was especially evident during the grim war effort. Unlike their Catholic counterparts in Quebec, the English-speaking Catholic commitment to Canada's participation in the war was strong; an historian comments, "Eager for acceptance as full-fledged Canadians, they were determined to demonstrate that they were no less British than the Protestants, and no less dedicated to the high ideals of sacrifice and service for the Christian cause."[1] In the sisters' home territory of the Maritimes, "progressive zeal" remained evident everywhere as reformers sought, through town planning, public health measures, female suffrage, and prohibition, to temper the worst affects of industrial capitalism. The Great War intensified both reform optimism and economic activity.

St. Augustine's Seminary, Toronto

Less than two years before the First World War convulsed Europe in deadly combat, the Archbishop of Toronto petitioned the Marthas to come and manage the domestic affairs of his new seminary.[2] St. Augustine's was to open in 1913 on the Scarborough Bluffs in the sprawling, growing Archdiocese of Toronto as a major seminary for the archdiocese and to train priests for the English-speaking Catholic dioceses of Canada. Toronto then had a population of nearly 400,000.[3] Its archbishop, Fergus McEvay (1908-1911), initiated the project and had the cornerstone laid on 23 October 1910, but died the following year on 10 May. His successor, Archbishop Neil McNeil (installed 22 December 1912), a native of Cape Breton and former rector of St. Francis Xavier University (1884-1891) with strong Antigonish connections, supervised the completion of the seminary.

Archbishop McNeil's request–the first from outside the Diocese of Antigonish–came shortly after two administrative changes important to the sisters. Mother Faustina had been replaced in 1910 by Mother Stanislaus, formerly Mary Ann MacDonald of South Side Harbour, Antigonish County. Mother Stanislaus MacDonald was only twenty-eight years old and had entered the congregation on 8 November 1900, four months after the Antigonish Marthas had severed their connection with the Sisters of Charity of Halifax. A sister described her as "young in years, physically strong, and a very capable worker [who] gave unstintingly of her strength and energy to the various works of the Congregation."[4] After serving at St.F.X., she had gained some administrative experience as superior of the sisters at St. Joseph's Hospital, Glace Bay, during their

Mother Stanislaus (Mary Ann) MacDonald, superior general, 1910-1916, 1922-1925.

final year there (1907-1908) before being recalled to Antigonish. Mother Stanislaus would serve as superior general from 1910 to 1916 and from 1922 to 1925. Her firm advocacy of the rights and interests of the sisters would, at times, earn her the enmity of certain priests at the university. Her approach to clerical authority was less diplomatic than Mother Faustina's style but revealed her deep concern for the best interests of her young congregation.

The second administrative change of consequence for the Marthas was the death of Bishop Cameron and the appointment of his successor, Bishop James Morrison. Bishop Cameron had been important to the sisters as a contributor to their original foundation. He had made the original agreement with the Sisters of Charity for training Marthas for his college, subsequently decided to withdraw them from the control of the Charities and established them as an independent diocesan congregation. However, through the first ten years of their existence until his death on 6 April 1910, Bishop Cameron was advanced in years, plagued by "increasing infirmities" and distracted by "diocesan disputes" with parishes and priests.[5] Therefore, the young congregation of Marthas had little direct ecclesiastical supervision from him and he made few, if any, formal visitations to the community.

Things changed in September 1912 with the arrival of Bishop James Morrison, a physically impressive fifty-one-year-old native of Prince Edward Island, former rector of St. Dunstan's College in Charlottetown (1892–1895), and administrator of the Diocese of Charlottetown. His episcopate would be the longest in the history of the Diocese of Antigonish–nearly thirty-eight years. The Marthas treated their cautious and conservative new bishop with great deference and respect. Toward the end of his career a sister-historian would reflect, "In His Excellency, Bishop Morrison, the Sisters of St. Martha always found a kind father, a wise counsellor, a faithful spiritual guide and a great benefactor."[6] When Bishop Morrison arrived, the congregation was twelve years old and had forty-one professed sisters and twelve novitiates. At his first official visit to Mother Stanislaus and her congregation at St. Martha's Convent, he presided at a profession ceremony where Sister M. Ignatius (Mary Catherine) Floyd pronounced her first vows. Bishop Morrison and Sister Ignatius (later the superior general) would have a stronger influence than all others on the congregation's direction during the 1920s, 1930s, and 1940s.

Bishop Morrison's correspondence with the congregation reveals the scrupulous concern he had for its affairs. Since the Marthas were a diocesan institute, they sent him statistical and financial reports, asked him to make formal and social visits, sent him gifts, had him examine new candidates and consulted him about major issues and decisions. He gave the Marthas space to make their own choices but showed no reluctance to offer advice. His regular visitation reports of private meetings with each sister reveal how intimately he came to know the internal life of the congregation. While sisters commonly professed contentment with the religious life and praised its many rewards, he often heard a litany of complaints about lack of charity among the sisters, violations of silence, loneliness among the postulants, bossiness, and insubordination. Complaints among sisters at Mount Cameron Farm were common. One sister told the bishop: "Father Miles Tompkins swears when angry. No attention paid to the rule."[7] A housekeeping sister at St.F.X. once claimed: "Boys partly naked in rooms when Sisters are making beds."[8] Another lamented, "Sister Superior too snappy and cross, so that some sisters don't want to go to her for interviews … too domin-eering … not considerate for sick sisters."[9] One persistent complaint was: "hard work, short help." These complaints and difficulties reveal the challenges faced by the sisters in both their work and community lives.

Anyway, in 1913 Bishop Morrison had to respond to Archbishop McNeil's request for sisters. He confirmed the arrangements for St. Augustine's Seminary agreed to between Archbishop McNeil, Mother Stanislaus, and the St.F.X. College council. Several sisters, at salaries of $20 per month each, would be appointed to St. Augustine's Seminary in July for a one-year trial period.[10] Two of these would go a few months before to help organize the new seminary's domestic affairs by purchasing kitchen, infirmary, and garden supplies and furnishings. The seminary provided accommodations for the sisters–bedrooms, a community room, and a chapel. The archbishop promised they would be provided for generously, and that recruits in Ontario would be forthcoming, a promise the Marthas would hear repeatedly from petitioners in future decades.[11]

Mother Stanislaus sent Mother Faustina MacArthur, former superior general (1901–1910), and Sister Francis de Sales (Annie)

MacLellan, former mistress of novices, to prepare the way for the seminary work of the Marthas. Mother Faustina would become a trailblazer for the congregation, establishing over the next three decades many new missions for the sisters. She found the archbishop somewhat uncommunicative about his future plans for them, but she happily informed President MacPherson in July: "We have a fine Jersey cow and our own fresh butter and eggs, and the air is grand out here."[12] For two years she remained the superior over the first sisters at St. Augustine's: Sister Francis de Sales MacLellan (assistant), Sister M. Dorothy Beaton, Sister M. Theodore Sampson, Sister M. Remegius MacArthur, Sister Mary Andrew MacDonald, Sister M. Jovita MacArthur, Sister Mary Theresa (Mary A.) Landry, and Sister Mary Alphonsus (Katie Flora) MacLellan.[13] These sisters discharged the same duties required of them at St.F.X.–cooking, baking, serving, housekeeping, laundering, sewing, and nursing.

As elsewhere, community life was central to the work of the Marthas at St. Augustine's. The sisters' experiences are revealed

FIRST STAFF OF THE CONVENT, ST. AUGUSTINE'S SEMINARY, TORONTO, 1913
SEATED (L-R): Sr. M. Theodore (Julia) Sampson, Sr. M. Dorothy (Isabel) Beaton, Mother M. Faustina (Mary) MacArthur, superior; Sr. Francis De Sales (Annie) MacLellan, Sr. M. Andrew (Margaret) MacDonald.
STANDING: Sr. M. Theresa (May A.) Landry, Sr. M. Alphonsus (Katie Flora) MacLellan, Sr. M. Jovita (Margaret) MacArthur, Sr. M. Remegius (Laura) MacArthur.

in the house annals and motherhouse correspondence. The annals describe visits of church dignitaries and special guests, the opening and closing of academic terms, the departure and arrival of sisters, retreats, feast days, entertainments staged by the seminarians, trips into Toronto for special religious events, deaths, and faculty changes.[14] Marthas at the seminary were semi-cloistered.[15] Their profile was very low, as they served quietly and unobtrusively behind the main seminary scenes. St. Augustine's paid their salaries to the college and the sisters received a small allowance from the motherhouse for clothing, books, travel, retreat masters, donations to charities, postage, and medicine.[16] After their periodic canonical visitations, successive superior generals issued recommendations, usually directing more strict observation of the Martha rule. For example, in 1927 the mother general vigorously and unrealistically called for no conversation between sisters and "externs" (for example, priests, students, and lay workers) and the observance of silence whenever possible.[17]

The longevity of the relation between the Sisters of St. Martha and St. Augustine's Seminary (1913 to the present) reveals their valued contribution through the decades. As at St.F.X., the resident domestic sisterhood helped keep institutional costs to a minimum. They offered efficient household management, created a homelike atmosphere and provided an edifying religious example for the young Canadian seminarians training in Toronto. The first rector, John T. Kidd (1913-1925), wrote Mother Stanislaus in 1922: "St. Augustine's Seminary and the priesthood is under a great debt of gratitude to your community for their labors here and I know the Divine Master will bless all richly for the sacrifices made."[18] Mother Faustina, the first superior at the seminary, saw the strategic value for the congregation's future of being at Canada's major English-speaking seminary. In 1914 she wrote President MacPherson, "All the priests of the Archdiocese, as well as the future ones, see and know our Community through the Seminary only, and as there is a great demand for Sisters, especially English-speaking, we have the very best kind of a chance to lay a foundation for work here in years to come."[19] Even the friendship established with Rector Kidd was crucial; it would eventually draw the Sisters of St. Martha even further west from Antigonish than Toronto.

Helping to Found Another Congregation

Another call from outside the Diocese of Antigonish followed closely on the heels of the one from Toronto. Again the request came from a Catholic educational institution, this one in Charlottetown, Prince Edward Island, the "cradle" of Canadian confederation and the seat of the provincial government. The city's population in 1915 was close to 11,000.[20] St. Dunstan's College had been established in 1855 to serve the Catholics of the Island, both in the capital and on the countless family farms from North Cape in the west to East Point.[21] As at St.F.X. before the Marthas, obtaining efficient and dependable domestic workers was a perennial problem because of low wages, backbreaking labour, poor working conditions, and high staff turnover. Moreover, the Diocese of Charlottetown harboured no indigenous congregation that could undertake the work. The Little Sisters of the Holy Family, a congregation of French-speaking sisters from Quebec, at some point after 1909 cared for the domestic needs of the institution, but they were rather unhappy there.[22] Bishop Henry J. O'Leary (1913-1920) believed an English-speaking congregation would better serve his diocese, and hence he made repeated requests to several congregations, including the Marthas of Antigonish, for sisters to come to St. Dunstan's. However, limited numbers restrained Mother Stanislaus of the Marthas in Antigonish from obliging him. Meeting the housekeeping needs of St. Augustine's Seminary, along with those of St.F.X. and St. Martha's Hospital, had overextended their resources.

Bishop O'Leary then decided on an action plan that paralleled the one pursued by Bishop Cameron in 1894 to gain sisters for St.F.X. Through the intervention of the provincial superior of the Sisters of the Congregation of Notre Dame, who approached Mother Stanislaus on his behalf, he arranged for recruits from the Charlottetown diocese to be trained by the Marthas in Antigonish. Afterwards, they would return and establish a new and fully independent congregation to do the domestic work at St. Dunstan's, and he also hoped to use them at the bishop's residence, the cathedral, and the Charlottetown hospital.[23] In 1914, Bishop O'Leary made satisfactory arrangements with Mother Stanislaus and Bishop Morrison, who, by the way, had tried to participate in, and benefit from St.F.X.'s plan for a new sisterhood back in 1894 when he was rector of St. Dunstan's College.[24]

The exact terms of the agreement reveal Bishop O'Leary's plans and the role of the Antigonish Marthas:

1. It is the expressed and understood intention that the Bishop of Charlottetown has in view the establishing of an independent branch of the Sisters of St. Martha, said branch to be entirely independent of the Sisters of the St. Martha, Antigonish.

2. The Sisters of St. Martha Antigonish agree to send a sufficient number of professed Sisters to take charge of St. Dunstan's College, namely ___. The Bishop of Charlottetown agrees to send to Antigonish a subject for every professed sister whom the Sisters of St. Martha send to Charlottetown.

3. When the subjects sent by the Bishop of Charlottetown to Antigonish shall be considered sufficiently formed and experienced and in sufficient number to begin a diocesan branch of the community, they shall all return to the Diocese of Charlottetown, and all the Antigonish Sisters shall return to Antigonish. The Superioress shall, however, remain in Charlottetown until another competent Superioress shall be found to take her place and at least one Sister from Charlottetown shall remain to replace her in Antigonish until she returns.

4. All expenses connected with the sending of subjects to Antigonish and the bringing the Sisters from Antigonish shall be borne by the Bishop of Charlottetown.[25]

Even though Bishop Morrison had some misgivings about this arrangement and believed that "Antigonish has the heaviest side of the burden," he and Mother Stanislaus agreed to it. In 1915, while the war waged overseas, four recruits–Mary Clare Murray, Mary Bernardine McQuaid, Mary St. John Farrell, and Mary Bonaventure Cahill–travelled from the Island to Antigonish. They entered the novitiate at St. Martha's Convent to begin their training so ultimately to establish a new sisterhood of Marthas on Prince Edward Island.

The following spring, Bishop O'Leary wrote from Charlottetown: "I may say that we are very anxious to have a beginning made by the Sisters, as there is a splendid future before them here, and the sooner they commence the better." The Little Sisters of the Holy Family were leaving St. Dunstan's in July, so Bishop O'Leary arranged with Mother Stanislaus and Bishop Morrison that the four Island sisters then at the St.F.X. convent, accompanied by three professed Antigonish Marthas, would proceed to Charlottetown in the same month. The three Antigonish sisters were to be paid $6 monthly and replaced at the convent by three postulants from the Island. The Antigonish Marthas were to remain at St. Dunstan's College until the Island sisters were properly trained; then they would form an entirely independent congregation of Island Marthas, and the Antigonish sisters would return home.[26] Immediately after Mother Stanislaus completed her superiorship in 1916, Mother Faustina, her successor, appointed her superior of the new Charlottetown community, which included the Island novices and her own sisters: Sister Mary St. Hugh (Jessie) MacDonald and Sister Joseph Agatha (Mary Josephine)Hines. From the standpoint of St. Dunstan's, the timing could not have been better, for their first superior, Mother Stanislaus, was a competent and experienced administrator who had just completed two terms as superior general of the Antigonish Marthas. Sister Mary St. Hugh became the novice mistress for the newly established novitiate at St. Dunstan's College.

The small group of novices and professed sisters arrived at St. Dunstan's on 17 July 1916 after the departure of the Little Sisters of the Holy Family. An annex attached to the Main Building served as their first home. The college then had about ninety students and six priest professors. On 15 August 1916, Bishop O'Leary sent a circular letter to his diocesan clergy informing them of his intention to establish a congregation of women religious on the Island and asking for their help to recruit members. As a result, six postulants joined the community that September. All the sisters found conditions at St. Dunstan's rudimentary indeed. And within two years, the Great War finally ended, bringing an influx of students that strained both the resources of the college and the endurance of its young sister housekeepers.[27]

The ranks of the St. Dunstan's Marthas gradually swelled. By 1921 they had nineteen professed sisters and their own motherhouse. Their bishop, Henry J. O'Leary, had been replaced by his brother Louis J. O'Leary, who also drafted constitutions for the Island Marthas. To his chagrin and the keen disappointment of the Island sisters, Mother Stanislaus, who had successfully shepherded the fledgling community through its founding years, was recalled to Antigonish in 1921 and assigned other work; shortly thereafter, the Antigonish Marthas re-elected her as their superior general (1922-1925). Bishop Louis O'Leary urged Bishop Morrison to "use your influence with the Reverend Sisters of St. Martha to permit Rev. Mother Stanislaus to remain here in charge of the Sisters for some time longer."[28] He believed the Charlottetown Marthas needed more training and felt that the Antigonish Marthas were abandoning them at a most inopportune time. Unfortunately for Bishop O'Leary, both Bishop Morrison and Mother Faustina believed that Antigonish had more than fulfilled its side of the bargain struck earlier with St. Dunstan's and its bishop. Mother Stanislaus would remain at home. Bishop O'Leary reluctantly accepted this loss and thanked Bishop Morrison and the "mother" community in Antigonish for all they had done.[29]

The Charlottetown sisters now had to make it on their own and were somewhat dismayed. Mother Faustina wrote from Antigonish to encourage them. She described how her own young congregation had struggled yet survived through its first years, and she confidently predicted, "your community too will succeed with the work you have undertaken if only you acquire a little more confidence in God and in yourselves, and keep up the constant spirit of humility and obedience."[30] They regretfully accepted their new situation and replied to Mother Faustina: "We fully realize the great sacrifice you made during the past five years and the debt of filial gratitude we owe to your Community …. We wish to assure you, dear Mother, that in our poor prayers, we shall never forget you, your community, nor Mother Stanislaus."[31] The special relationship of Mother Stanislaus to the Island Marthas, and their high regard for her, were demonstrated in 1970 after her death on 19 January at age 87; at their request, her body was transferred to the Island and interred at Mount St. Mary's Cemetery, the sisters' burial ground. A spokesperson for the Antigonish congregation commented: "The Sisters of Prince Edward Island claim her as their foundress and her heart was always with them. We thought it fitting that we should give them the privilege of having her buried among their pioneers."[32] For their part, the Island Marthas had maintained a close friendship with Mother Stanislaus over the decades. One wrote, "She ever gave her Sisters the example of devoted generosity and sublime self-sacrifice in God's service along with courage and steadfastness in meeting pioneer difficulties. Her Christ-like kindness remains a cherished tradition with the Island Sisters."[33]

Just as the Sisters of Charity, Halifax, had helped found the Antigonish Marthas, so the latter, two decades afterwards, contributed to the founding of the Sisters of St. Martha in Charlottetown. The Marthas of Antigonish trained the first Charlottetown sisters,[34] supplied them with an experienced superior, Mother Stanislaus (1916–1921), helped reorganize and improve the domestic affairs of St. Dunstan's College and even contributed to the establishment of a new Catholic hospital in 1925. For their part, the Island Marthas, after acquiring written constitutions and electing a superior–became an integral part of the Catholic establishment on Prince Edward Island. They grew rapidly, became "woven into the fabric" of St. Dunstan's College,[35] administered the household affairs of the bishop's residence, taught school in Catholic communities and worked with orphans, the elderly, and the sick.[36]

Recall to St. Joseph's Hospital, Glace Bay

The Sisters of St. Martha had managed the household affairs of St. Joseph's Hospital, Glace Bay, from 1902 to 1908 but had then withdrawn and returned to Antigonish. However, in 1914, the board of trustees unanimously decided to invite the sisters to return, this time to assume full administrative responsibility for the debt-free hospital and school of nursing. They did so on 1 January 1915 with the blessing of their bishop, who retained title, along with the trustees, to the hospital.[37] Their decision was difficult, for St.F.X. was unenthused about the assignment and some people in the Glace Bay community and the hospital opposed the sisters' takeover. Mother Faustina was appointed superintendent and Sister Maris Stella MacDonald became director of the nursing school. Six other sisters accompanied them. Now the Marthas ran two hospitals and two schools of nursing. It was a stressful time for a hospital takeover. Many miners, who subscribed to St. Joseph's for hospital services, had enlisted in the war effort, a war that was also causing inflation. Second, a general hospital opened in Glace Bay that year, resulting in some loss of local support for St. Joseph's. In spite of these hardships, the new Martha administration did well. The hospital trustees who appointed the superintendent, Mother Faustina, as the first female member of their board in 1917 highly approved of the sisters' work.

St. Joseph's was in serious need of improvements. When the Marthas returned in 1915, it had no x-ray, no laboratory, and no medical records system. Its Glace Bay constituency had grown to over 16,000–about 50 percent Roman Catholic–and so had its health care needs.[38] Gradually the sisters upgraded the hospital by purchasing modern equipment, keeping proper records, establishing new departments and repairing and expanding the buildings. During Sister M. Ignatius's superintendency (1919–1925), St. Joseph's achieved accreditation from the American College of Surgeons (1921), which had established widely accepted and demanding hospital standards in hospital organization, medical records, laboratory and x-ray facilities, and so forth. Sister M. Ignatius was an energetic, capable, and inspiring administrator with high standards of duty; the hospital's rising prestige was due to her leadership and support from staff, doctors, and trus-tees. Of course, the sisters' efforts would have been impossible without adequate funding, which came from government grants, patient fees, miners' subscriptions, and the district Ladies' Aid societies.[39] The miners' contributions for services accounted for more than 50 percent of the hospital's income, so a serious labour disruption in the coalfields in 1924 and 1925 temporarily sabotaged its finances.[40]

At St. Joseph's Hospital silver jubilee in 1927, Sister Francis Teresa (Mary) Herrgott was the superintendent and superior. Her twelve sisters managed the nurses, the laboratory, x-ray, bookkeeping, medical records, food services, social services, sewing, laundering, and chapel sacristy.[41] By 1929, sisters also ran the pharmacy and physiotherapy departments. Their hospital had maintained its accreditation and the medical and surgical staff numbered thirteen doctors. That year the sisters admitted 2,866 patients.

In 1930 the Marthas were given title to St. Joseph's Hospital. Originally, the hospital site had been donated and title transferred to the Diocese of Antigonish in order to secure a mortgage. Through time, the hospital trustees also gained title to adjacent properties acquired for hospital purposes. By 1930 the bishop and some trustees, but certainly not all, urged that title to the entire hospital complex be consolidated and then transferred to the Sisters of St. Martha. This step would eliminate dual ownership and promote efficiency, they argued. The congregation agreed to the transfer, along with all the obligations, debts and contracts with it; as well, they consented to make much-needed improvements to the hospital.[42] The Board's action was taken without discussion with hospital subscribers in the district; this was regrettable, as it rankled for decades among those who believed that St. Joseph's Hospital had been wrongfully transferred from its perceived rightful owners to the Sisters of St. Martha.

The hospital annals reveal the bustle and concerns of the sisters: transfers, sicknesses, professional upgrading, retreats, visitations, social calls on neighbouring missions, special clinics, and their patients' physical and spiritual conditions. Here are three sample entries: "[J.V.], after an illness of some months and after neglecting the sacraments for over 25 years, made his peace with God and died a very happy death" (6 September 1927); "The Ladies Aid of Bridgeport conducted a 'barn dance' in our new barn. About 600 people attended and $417 were the proceeds" (1 August 1928); "Dr. Tompkins did blood transfusion today. This new method he learned during his last course in Toronto" (3 May 1929).[43]

As war clouds gathered and broke in Europe, and imperial loyalty, economic bustle, and crusading reformism abounded in Nova Scotia, the work of the Marthas expanded in the province and beyond. Founding a new housekeeping mission in Toronto, helping to bring a new congregation of Marthas into being in Charlottetown and assuming full administrative responsibility for St. Joseph's Hospital in Glace Bay were major undertakings. Each of them would deeply affect the future of the congregation. And, of course, the sisters' limited human resources had forced them to refuse other appeals for help. By 1917, their diverse missions and devoted services brought respect and growing admiration, along with inevitable strains, stresses, and conflicts, including increased tension with the college that had brought the congregation into existence.

NOTES

1 Terrence Murphy and Roberto Perin, eds., *A Concise History of Christianity in Canada* (Toronto: Oxford University Press, 1990), p. 337.
2 Archbishop Neil McNeil to President Hugh MacPherson, 28 December 1912, uncatalogued file, STFXUA.
3 *Census of Canada*, 1911, I:554.
4 Biographical Notes, F5,S33,SS5,f2,b78.
5 R.A. MacLean, *Bishop John Cameron: Piety and Politics* (Antigonish: The Casket Printing and Publishing Co., 1991), pp. 161-89, and Rev. Dr. R.B. MacDonald, "Diocesan Disputes" in *The Casket*, 2, 9, and 16 September 1992.
6 Sister John Baptist Cameron, "History of the Sisters of St. Martha, 1894-1948," p. 56.
7 Bishop Morrison Visitation Report, 15 August 1921, Incoming Mail, #8392, BMP, ADA.
8 Visitation Report, 24 July 1922, # 9255a, ibid.
9 Visitation Report, 27 June 1924, #11524, ibid.
10 President MacPherson to Archbishop McNeil, 29 February 1913, b244.
11 Archbishop McNeil to President MacPherson, 6 and 31 March 1913, uncatalogued, STFXUA.
12 Mother Faustina to President H.P. MacPherson, 19 July 1913, F3,S1,SS2,f2,b5.
13 St. Augustine's Seminary Staff List, b244.
14 House Annals, b244.
15 Also, seminary discipline was rigid for the first fifty years; faculty were discouraged from fraternizing with the Marthas. See Karen Marshall Booth, ed., *The People Cry–"Send Us Priests": The First Seventy-Five Years of St. Augustine's Seminary of Toronto, 1913-1988* (Toronto: St. Augustine's Seminary Alumni Association, 1988), p. 15.
16 Financial Statements, b244.
17 Mother Ignatius Visitation Report, 30 November 1927, b244.
18 Rector John T. Kidd to Mother Stanislaus, 29 July 1922, F5,S34,SS17,f8,b92.
19 Mother Faustina to President MacPherson, 30 October 1914, F3,S1,SS2,f2,b5.

20 *Census of Canada*, 1921, I:235.
21 G. Edward MacDonald, *The History of St. Dunstan's University, 1855-1956* (Charlottetown: Board of Governor's of St. Dunstan's University and Prince Edward Island Museum and Heritage Foundation, 1989).
22 MacDonald, *The History*, 264.
23 MacDonald, *The History*, 265.
24 In the fall of 1894, when Father James Morrison had heard of Dr. Daniel Chisholm's plan to establish a congregation, he wrote: "[Our] Bishop is of opinion that some recruits could be obtained in this diocese, who would go to swell the number and perhaps make it sufficient to supply the requirements of our provincial college. On his advice I write to you on this matter, hoping it may be brought to some practical issue." Rev. Dr. James Morrison to Rev. Dr. D.A. Chisholm, 6 November 1894, F5,S34,SS3,f1,b86. Chisholm's papers do not indicate why the matter was not then "brought to some practical issue."
25 Quoted in Sister May Mulvihill, "History of the Sisters of St. Martha," I:3:44a.
26 Bishop O'Leary-Mother Stanislaus correspondence, F5,S34,SS13,f1,b91.
27 Transcript of interview with Mother Frances Loyola Cullen, 11 November 1979, F5,S34,SS13,f27,b91.
28 Sister May Mulvihill, "History of the Sisters of St. Martha," I:3:51.
29 Bishop Louis J. O'Leary to Bishop Morrison, 8 August 1921, Incoming Mail, #8375, BMP, ADA.
30 Sister May Mulvihill, "History of the Sisters of St. Martha," I:3:56.
31 Sisters of St. Martha, Charlottetown, to Mother Faustina, 14 August 1921, F5,S34,SS13,f2,b91.
32 *The Casket*, 30 April 1970.
33 Tribute by Sister Ellen Mary Cullen for *The Casket* in "In Memoriam," Sister Irene Doyle's files.
34 Sister May Mulvihill, "History of the Sisters of St. Martha," I:3:Appendix B.
35 MacDonald, *The History*, p. 265.
36 For an overview of the Charlottetown Martha experience and contribution, see *The Story of the Sisters of St. Martha, 1916-1991* by the 75th Anniversary Committee, Charlottetown, 1991.
37 Bishop Morrison to President H.P. MacPherson, 1 December 1914, F5,S34,SS3,f1,b86.
38 *Census of Canada 1911*, I:29 and 554.
39 St. Joseph Hospital Board of Trustee Minutes, 8 October 1929, F7,S4,SS5,f1,b124.

40 St. Joseph's Hospital Historical Highlights, pp. 1-3, F7,S1,SS1,f1,b118.
41 St. Joseph's Hospital Annals, 27-29 June 1927, ibid.
42 Minutes of Special Meeting of the St. Joseph's Hospital Directors, 26 May 1930, Incoming Mail, #16781, BMP, ADA.
43 St. Joseph's Hospital Annals, F7,S1,SS2,f1,b118.

Chapter Four

Home Rule and Diversification

The year 1917, close to the end of World War One, was a pivotal one for Canada. A war-weary country was deeply divided along linguistic lines by the issue of conscription for overseas military service. It was also a crucial year for the Sisters of St. Martha. Like other Canadian congregations founded by institutions that had urgently needed more adequate household management, the Marthas experienced a separation crisis and gained their independence from St. Francis Xavier University. This watershed event naturally heightened the sisters' desire for a new motherhouse located on their own property away from the college campus. During the post-war years, the Sisters of St. Martha also diversified their works and expanded their existing missions. They began caring for orphans and unwed mothers and, in spite of the economic stringency of the 1920s, established two new hospitals in Cape Breton, Nova Scotia.

Struggle for Autonomy

Since 1902 the sisters had strained their limited resources to meet the new demands made of them for domestic and hospital services. However, their motherhouse remained at St.F.X. and the sisters continued to be responsible for the domestic needs of this "cradle of their congregation." In spite of the distraction of war, the university's household needs had expanded between 1910 and 1920, as five new buildings were erected–a science hall, a chapel, a residence hall, a gymnasium, and a library–and enrolments increased from 251 to 315.[1] The sisters worked hard to meet their multiplying duties. Because money was scarce, farming families sometimes paid their sons' college tuition fees with potatoes, turnips, or meat. In the winter, the sisters had to cut frozen carcasses with a small handsaw to fit them into the roasting pans. Stoves, machinery, and storage facilities were rudimentary, and rats and mice plentiful. The "great odor [or excitement] of hockey" on campus regularly filtered into the convent and the sisters commonly prayed that their St.F.X. boys would prevail over all competitors.[2] The Marthas witnessed and experienced the varied rhythms and rituals of student life–lectures, examinations, recreations, chapel services, retreats, holidays, pranks, sicknesses, concerts, and graduations. The Sisters of St. Martha were becoming part of "the warp and woof of Xaverianism," as a faculty member later put it.[3] However, a crisis began to develop in the relationship between college and congregation.

Actually, the congregation was outgrowing St.F.X.'s paternalistic relationship with it; the Marthas needed freedom to strike out on their own. In 1900, after their break with the Sisters of Charity, Halifax, the Marthas had been made subject to a college council that approved new missions and new candidates for the congregation and controlled the sisters' finances. Sharp disagreements between Mother Stanislaus and the college around 1913, over the names, quality, and numbers of sisters assigned to St. Augustine's Seminary and St. Joseph's Hospital, fostered discontent; so did the undesirable circumstances of the Marthas assigned to St.F.X.'s Mount Cameron Farm. Mother Stanislaus and the sisters believed St.F.X. was retaining the most robust sisters for its own work while sending less healthy and less competent ones out on the missions; in certain cases, this was proving to be an embarrassment to the congregation. In order to gain control over their own affairs, some Marthas advocated "home rule" and a motherhouse located away from the campus. Mother Faustina, then superior at St. Augustine's, played a mediating role in the intensifying dispute, since Mother Stanislaus and President MacPherson seemed at loggerheads.[4] She was little intimidated by male authority and, when required, gave her opinion, as she put it, "without much varnish."[5] In 1914 she warned President MacPherson, "The College will lose nothing by consenting to some kind of a new arrangement if they don't wait till the Sisters are all so much against them that little or nothing can be counted on."[6]

College authorities had their own reasons for retaining a close rein over the congregation. Naturally, they wanted their own institutional needs given first priority, and unsuccessful financial campaigns (1907 and 1913), along with the outbreak of war in 1914, created serious financial concerns, including worries about the numbers of sisters St.F.X. had to support on campus and the income of those out on the missions. In 1914 some sisters did not think the congregation was ready for full independence. Mother Faustina was one: "The time may come when I too may think that it would be for the best interest of both institutions to be independent of each other, but it has not yet arrived. I believe each needs the other's assistance for at least some years to come."[7] However, following the proverb that safety lies in the multitude of counsellors, she, Bishop Morrison, and Mother Stanislaus believed a small general council of advisors—sympathetic with the St.F.X. mission to assist the mother general—would heal relations with the college authorities. Hence, the first general council was elected in 1915, with four members and Mother Faustina as the first councillor.

By 1917, Mother Faustina (re-elected superior general in 1916) and her council concluded that the time for independence from St.F.X. had arrived. With the help of several priests, especially Rev. Dr. Moses Coady, a young professor at St.F.X. and a firm friend of the sisters, the Marthas succeeded in revising their relationship with college authorities.[8] Mother Faustina and Dr. Coady convinced the bishop, the college president, and the other opponents of independence that "home rule" was in the best interests of both college and congregation, and that "the only way to hold the Sisters was to let them go."[9]

The revised formal agreement was surely weighted in favour of St.F.X. It stipulated that "[the sisters and] their successors ... efficiently serve [St.F.X., including Mount Cameron Farm] in all domestic duties attached thereto and usually performed by women and as long as [it] may require the services of the [sisters]." In addition, the Marthas agreed to continue domestic work in all the college buildings, including any erected in the future. They even agreed to withdraw sisters from and close missions, if necessary, "to supply a sufficient number of efficient sisters for the satisfactory performance of the said domestic work in the said University buildings." Evidently, St.F.X. authorities held firm that service to their college remain the congregation's first priority. Sisters on staff would receive only $6 monthly. Nevertheless, the new arrangement did have a credit side: the congregation was now "empowered to direct its own organization subject to the bishop of the diocese of Antigonish" and to control its entire income.[10] St.F.X. also agreed to make certain improvements in the sisters' working conditions on campus, for example, male help for all heavy lifting and carrying, such as moving coal to the laundry, kitchen, and bake-rooms.[11] Relations between college and congregation remained positive.

The congregation was wise to press for independence in 1917 and the college was prudent to grant it. The community's growing membership, expanding missions, and increasing experience had equipped the sisters to control their own affairs. Because the founding sisters' early training in Halifax had not prepared them for leadership positions, dependence on the college "had undoubtedly been a source of strength and support" through the early years.[12] But there is a time for everything; by 1917 the season for paternalistic control by college authorities had passed. At last the congregation was fully self-governing, subject only to the bishop of the Diocese of Antigonish. This all happened in the same year that Canadian women gained the right to vote in federal elections.

A New Motherhouse

The achievement of autonomy in 1917 no doubt strengthened the sisters' resolve to obtain a new, larger motherhouse situated off the college campus. Overcrowding at St. Martha's Convent, the need for adequate novitiate facilities, and the need for a shelter for sick and exhausted sisters created some urgency.[13] Bishop Morrison was very sympathetic and considered the motherhouse at St.F.X. an anomalous situation that had retarded the normal development of the congregation.[14] In 1918 he placed the sisters' needs before the clergy on annual retreat. Together with the parishes, they subscribed nearly $40,000 to a new motherhouse building fund; this sum boldly demonstrated the good will the sisters had already inspired during their short working history in the Diocese of Antigonish.[15]

In 1919, Mother Faustina set forth a plan for the new motherhouse:

> *It is necessary for us to erect a building sufficiently large to accommodate seventy or eighty sisters. This building will be the training-house for our Novices and Postulants, the home for our sick and infirm sisters, as well as the place where our annual retreats will be held. It is here, too, that the vestments, Altar breads, etc. will be made for the parishes of the Diocese, to help support our Community.*[16]

Her building fund campaign, chaired by Bishop Morrison, along with loans of about $79,000 that saddled the congregation with a burdensome debt (much of it guaranteed by the diocese), made this plan a reality when the sisters officially opened a new motherhouse on 21 September 1921. Costing about $145,000, the impressive four-storey brick structure, with a basement for furnace and storage, was located on the former D.G. Kirk property just above St. Martha's Hospital on the east side of Antigonish. From many angles it was an ideal and idyllic setting with a panoramic view of the town and considerable space for expansion. Appropriately, the sisters named it Bethany, after the home of St. Martha, their biblical patroness. Sister John Baptist reported how the naming occurred:

Original Bethany Motherhouse, 1921.

> *One evening during recreation, while Mother M. Faustina was showing the plans of the new building to the sisters in the community room, she suddenly asked: "What shall we call our new Motherhouse?" A voice seldom heard down the ranks, said a little above a whisper: "Bethany." It was Sister M. Columba Bryden who spoke and many of us heard no more about it till we heard it from Monsignor MacIntosh on the day of the formal opening.*[17]

After the somewhat emotional transfer of many sisters from the original motherhouse at St.F.X. to Bethany–St. Martha's Convent now became a mission with a local superior–the new motherhouse came to be the important congregational place Mother Faustina had anticipated: administrative and hospitality centre; novitiate; retreat facility; house of prayer and devotion; renewal and educational centre; producer of church vestments, altar breads, bookbinding, printing and other varied crafts; congregational home; and place of convalescence, retirement, and final rest. The sisters opened a cemetery on the property in November 1920 at the death of Sister Anselm (Mary A.) Doyle. In the spring of 1922, three men were hired to start a farm. Bethany became a true motherhouse to the expanding missions of the congregation.

Not until June 1927, six years after the opening, did a house annalist begin the work of charting life at the busy motherhouse. Her first entry opened: "Trinity Sunday. In the name of the Father and the Son and the Holy Ghost, we begin to take notes of our doings in the Community. May this book contain an account of deeds and acts of Saints, no matter how little and trivial they may appear in themselves." The Bethany community then numbered forty-three, composed of six postulants, eighteen novices, and nineteen professed sisters. Among the professed were the superior general (Mother Ignatius Floyd), the local superior (Sister M. Thecla [Henrietta] Price), the mistress of novices (Sister Mary James [Stella] Campbell), a printer and artist (Sister Mary Columba [Mary Elizabeth] Bryden), a seamstress (Sister Mary Theresa Landry), a fourteen-year invalid (Sister Joseph Agnes MacDonald), a musician studying at Mount St. Bernard (Sister Mary Paula [Marguerite Josephine] LeBlanc), a gardener (Sister M. Francis MacAdam), a person in charge of poultry, a seamstress, a kitchen supervisor, and an altar-bread baker. The chaplain was Rev. Dugald C. Gillis, a retired St.F.X. professor of philosophy. The annalist regularly and religiously reported on the following: the weather, the sisters' comings and goings, visitors, feast days and religious ceremonies, the entry of candidates, profession ceremonies, memorable celebrations and recreations, deaths, startling events, fires, earthquakes, storms, humorous anecdotes, retreats, financial problems, and special accomplishments of the congregation.[18]

Even though Bethany was removed from the college, the sisters could still draw on the rich intellectual and cultural resources of that institution. The annalist reported on 25 September 1928: "Father Hugh Somers opened his class of History at 5 P.M. today. It was most interesting. Father Bannon also had class at 7:30. We are so fortunate to have these priests take such an interest in the Community. Father Bannon is a wonderful professor of English Literature."[19] The year before, Dr. Coady had given a series of fascinating psychology lectures to the sisters.

As everywhere in the Roman Catholic tradition, the visits of church dignitaries were gala affairs. The Marthas, along with the entire local Antigonish Catholic community, made a great fuss over the visit of the Papal Delegate who arrived by train in a private coach on 30 June 1928; he was welcomed at the station by residents in hundreds of autos.

Christmas was also a special occasion. In 1927 the Bethany annalist reported:

> *For us in God's acre here at Bethany–we were warm, comfortable, peaceful, and happy. Our chaplain–Rev. D.C. Gillis–sang High Mass at midnight, and the choir was in excellent form. The chapel looked lovely. Everything was so dainty and tasty. The crib was sweet. Everything made one feel that it was really Christmas and that the Christ-Child smiled on Bethany.*[20]

Santa Claus visited and one special gift was a Victrola. A make-believe fireplace was set up, and rocking chairs were positioned on either side for the superior general and the oldest sister. Mother Ignatius allowed all the sisters to sleep in until 6 A.M. that week.

Working with Orphans and the "Disgraced"

In 1916, one year before the Marthas achieved "home rule," Bishop Morrison and his clergy set in motion events which quickly drew the sisters into a new kind of challenging work. As an expression of the reformist progressivism of the time, they called for the creation of a diocesan orphanage.[21] A Protestant orphanage already existed in Sydney, one among several that had been opened in urban centres around the province. In 1912 the parish priest in Glace Bay had urged the Marthas to open an alternative Catholic home for orphans and unwed mothers. He had lamented, "There is a Protestant institution in Sydney called the Door of Hope. Catholic girls from all over the diocese come there to hide their disgrace, and their children only too often fall into Protestant hands."[22]

The problems of orphans, "half-orphans," children born out of wedlock, and neglected or deserted children were urgent issues by 1916. The existing St. Anthony's Home in Sydney, established by the diocese in 1903 and administered by the Daughters of Jesus, was grossly inadequate; it tried to provide shelter under one roof for the aged, orphans, and unwed mothers. The industrial area of Cape Breton was growing rapidly because of its steel and coal industries, and its social problems were multiplying. The Great War and the Spanish influenza epidemic of 1918 added to the problems of neglect, abandonment, and single parent families.[23] So the diocese, enjoying the economic fruits of wartime industry and full employment, decided on a fresh start for work with orphans and unwed mothers: it purchased for $16,000 the "Moseley property" on King's Road, Sydney, with its large, three-storey private residence. Bishop Morrison issued a diocesan circular that laid out the orphanage plan and exposited for two pages on Christian charity. He declared, "It would be an error bordering on neglect if such a pressing need were left to another year without doing all that can be done for its promotion." He concluded by urging the faithful to contribute to an orphanage fund. [24]

Neither the Daughters of Jesus, who continued for many years to care for the aged at St. Anthony's Home, nor the Sisters of Charity of Halifax could staff the planned orphanage. However, in 1917, the Marthas, with the college's grudging approval, agreed to undertake the daunting project and opened St. Mary's Home in July.[25] The orphans at St. Anthony's were transferred to the new institution. The first staff of six–Mother Faustina, Sister M. Remegius MacArthur, Sister M. Benjamina Beaton, Sister Marie of Perpetual Help (Agnes) Dwyer, Sister Mary Elizabeth (Mary) Ross, and Sister Mary Colina (Jessie) MacDougall–had no experience in caring for orphans or helping unwed mothers, so it was a daring plunge. Moreover, public attitudes toward unwed mothers complicated the difficulties of helping them. Father Peter A. Nearing comments,

> *Helping them and their children was, to some, like subsidizing sin and perpetuating promiscuity.... The children of these unmarried mothers bore their parents' stigma. Few wanted to adopt them. Hence the continuing struggle to meet the needs of both.*[26]

A dearth of sources makes it nearly impossible to glimpse inside the institution during the early years, but anxiety and stress there must have been. Insufficient funds collected from parent or guardian receipts, government grants, and Children's Aid support created regular financial shortfalls;[27] the sisters' meagre income was supplemented with parish collections and donations from the Catholic Women's League and other benefactors. From 1917 to 1925, St. Mary's admitted 601 children; the daily average in residence was 60, even though the official capacity was 45.[28]

Almost from the beginning, the sisters at St. Mary's faced overcrowding. After a visit there in April 1918, a parish priest informed Bishop Morrison: "They have there now sixty children and four unfortunates soon to become mothers. Two of the sisters are sick at present and one confined to bed. How can the other three attend to such an enormous amount of work?" The serious problems–shortages of staff, rooms, and supplies–required the sisters to turn away little ones almost every day.[29] So in 1919 the diocese planned a new building, but the government rejected the plans, much to the bishop's annoyance.[30] The following year, when slightly amended plans were finally approved, Bishop Morrison himself delayed building so the diocese would not be burdened with a new, heavily indebted orphanage. However, he kept increasing his orphanage building fund. Meanwhile the problem of overcrowding remained as serious as ever, and the sisters became evermore restless for improved facilities.[31]

In 1925 the Catholic Women's League locals in the Sydney-Glace Bay region led a new orphanage campaign on behalf of the Marthas and children at St. Mary's Home. Despite economic hardships created by labour strife in the coalfields, they invited the bishop, along with parish delegates from Sydney, North Sydney, and the smaller colliery towns, to an orphanage meeting in November. All speakers professed their undivided support for a new orphanage to replace the obsolete St. Mary's Home.[32]

The following year, the bishop and Cape Breton County clergy purchased a twelve-acre property at Bras d'Or, a short distance north of the industrial district; it cost $8,000 and the new orphanage building $45,000.[33] Christened the "Little Flower Institute," it formally opened on 27 August 1927. The first superior, Sister Maris Stella MacDonald, and her sister staff were accommodated at nearby Sacred Heart Convent. Operating funds for the new institute came from government grants, the Catholic Women's League, the Children's Aid, parish collections, and benefactors. St. Mary's Home in Sydney continued in use as a shelter, now exclusively for unwed mothers, while the sisters devoted the Little Flower Institute strictly to work with orphaned, neglected, or abandoned children. Surviving records reveal little of the institute's internal life through its founding years. E.H. Blois, Director of Child Welfare for the province, referred to it as "a temporary shelter … where neglected and destitute children are kept and trained by thoroughly competent persons under wholesome, home-like conditions…." One priest claimed, "There is none of the heavy atmosphere of repression here that characterizes the old type of institution… . Here there is spontaneity, laughter, freedom from restraint, and at the same time there is the orderliness and good manners that come from training." Such were the impressions of two observers of the new orphanage.[34]

Sister Loretta Marie (Marianne) Exner with children at Little Flower Institute, Bras d'Or, Cape Breton.

Origins of Catholic Hospital Work in Sydney

Soon after the congregation had won its independence from the college and opened St. Mary's Home, Catholics called on the Marthas to open a hospital in Sydney.[35] Their involvement began, notwithstanding the financial misgivings of Bishop Morrison, even while they campaigned and planned for a costly new motherhouse in Antigonish. The "steel town" had already opened a fifty-bed general hospital in 1915. And during the war, Commander J.K.L. Ross of the local steel company had placed his spacious residence on King's Road at the disposal of the military, which had used it for nursing convalescent soldiers. After the war, the soldiers were removed from the hospital, and the Ross property, located opposite the recently opened St. Mary's Home, was sold to the Sisters of St. Martha for the nominal sum of $15,000. Commander Ross loaned them $10,000 of this amount.

Sydney, the principal city on Cape Breton Island, had incorporated and expanded rapidly after the Dominion Iron and Steel Company opened there in 1900. Its population had more than doubled to 22,545 by 1921.[36] Roman Catholics of diverse ethnic backgrounds accounted for 46 percent of its people. Sacred Heart Parish (est. 1825) was subdivided into Holy Redeemer (est. 1902), St. Mary's (est. 1913), St. Nicholas (est. 1908), and St. Patrick's (est. 1912) parishes in order to more adequately meet their spiritual needs. Bishop Morrison and other leading Catholics had long hoped for a Catholic hospital in this expanding urban centre.[37] When the news broke that the Sisters of St. Martha would open one, some Protestants condemned the plan.[38] However, Doctor J.G.B. Lynch, a well-known Sydney physician, advocated the idea and the Catholic population largely supported it. The Knights of Columbus, Sydney Council, even loaned $5,000 toward it.

Despite their mixed reception, the sisters opened "Ross Memorial Hospital" on 1 May 1920. Although renovated as a maternity hospital, within two years it admitted women and children. Shortly thereafter it became a general hospital open to all "with no distinction of color, class, or creed," with twenty-five beds and a staff of four sisters and three graduate nurses. The pioneer staff in 1920 was Sister M. Jovita MacArthur (superintendent), Sister Mary Georgina (Mary Martha) Campbell (floor supervisor), Sister Mary Andrew MacDonald (laundress), and Sister Mary Aloysius (Sophia) Fougere (kitchen supervisor).[39] Three lay nurses were also hired. Some hospital equipment was obtained from Commander Ross, the former owner, and more was purchased from the federal Department of Soldiers' Civil Re-Establishment. Neil R. MacArthur, a local lawyer and brother to Mother Faustina, convinced government officials to leave hospital equipment in the residence when they withdrew.

Even though some Sydney doctors of vigorous Protestant persuasion convinced their patients not to use the hospital, it was taxed to the limit and beyond by 1923.[40] Therefore, Sister Mary of the Sacred Heart (Mary Bell) MacKinnon, the supervisor/superior, conceived ambitious plans to expand the hospital, achieve accreditation and open a one-year school of nursing. That year, Commander Ross, the original owner, permitted the sisters to use an adjoining cottage for hospital purposes that allowed them to "carry on their work for God and suffering humanity."[41] This was the Marthas' third nursing school, since they already had schools at St. Joseph's and St. Martha's hospitals. Sisters and representatives of the local Catholic elite formed a board of trustees in 1924 to help with hospital planning and financing, and they soon acquired limited municipal and provincial support. Patients who came from within the hospital's far-flung constituency–Sydney, East Bay, Mira, Westmount, Whitney Pier, Red Islands, and Louisbourg–often lacked cash. One sister recalled, "Many of the patients came from Richmond County and they usually paid their bills with meat, vegetables, and butter, commodities that were useful but did very little to pay the bills."[42]

The trustees first discussed the need for expansion in 1926 and two years later they began serious planning and fundraising for a new wing and required renovations. Meanwhile, they had purchased a large barn close by and renovated it as a nurses' training school and residence. Rev. Dr. T. O'Reilly Boyle, the professor of philosophy at St.F.X. who had helped Dr. Coady in 1925 to lead a successful campaign for St. Martha's Hospital, Antigonish, organized the financial drive in July and August 1928. For the sisters and their co-workers, it was a period of great excitement.[43] The new $74,000 extension finally opened on 12 September 1929. Now the hospital had forty beds and a laboratory, x-ray, operating room, and kitchen and dining room facilities. At the insistence of Rev. John Hugh MacDonald, pastor of Sacred Heart Parish and hospital board president (who was angered in 1927 by Commander Ross's insistence that the Marthas immediately repay their loan of $10,000), the renovated and expanded facility was renamed St. Rita Hospital.[44]

The Marthas at Ross Memorial/St. Rita Hospital found life challenging and endlessly varied. Lacking a chapel, they had to trek daily across the street to join their sisters at St. Mary's Home for mass and other devotions. Their house annals report a steady stream of happenings–reappointments of sisters, spiritual conversions, festivities and recreations, lectures, visitors, and donations from benefactors. Sample entries from the late 1920s open a window on the sisters' experiences: "The year of 1926 began with great crosses. Two of our Maternity cases died, this meant a great deal of criticism and blame for the Hospital" (1926); "Father MacLean brought us over a Radio and we learned to operate it, getting the stations O.K., and hearing some music and some useful and useless talks and speeches" (January 1928); "Sister Marie Carmel ... succeeded in the attempt of making solutions for developing X-Ray films and is becoming quite an expert technician" (2 March 1928); "Doctor Nutter, a famous orthopedic surgeon from Montreal, performed an operation here today" (28 August 1928); and, "During the night a speed cop had to be sent to the Hospital to take care of a sick patient who was speeding around through wards and corridors" (20 September 1928).

The original Ross Memorial Hospital (on right) with wing added on left in 1929.

In 1927 the sister annalist recounted the incident of an alcoholic male patient and nominal Catholic who, in an irrational delirium, terrorized the hospital, escaped along the road, and made a public spectacle of himself. Eventually he was apprehended by the police, imprisoned and finally returned to the hospital under police guard. She wrote,

> *Father MacLean came to see him that night, he mocked the priest by making the Sign of the Cross over a glass of water which was offered him and appeared as one possessed. The priest said it would be a miracle if he ever came back to the faith. Intercession was made to St. Theresa of the Child Jesus and within twenty-four hours he asked for a priest, went to confession and received Holy Communion the next morning with the greatest fervour. These ... cases seemed to give us courage and buoyancy amid the trials of hospital difficulties, and made us think that after all the Lord was pleased with our little mission, even though not the most successful, when He permitted souls to return to Him under the roof of our little Hospital."*[45]

A Hospital for Inverness, Cape Breton

In early April 1925, Mother Stanislaus, who had been re-elected in 1922 after her return from Charlottetown where she had helped to found the Island Marthas, received a letter at Bethany from Father J.B. Kyte, curate at Stella Maris Parish. She read, "The new Hospital, the erection of which was begun almost one year ago by the Catholics of the County of Inverness, is now about completed and ready for occupation." Father Kyte described it for her as a three-storey facility "built according to the latest ideas in hospital construction." It would accommodate about forty beds. His enthusiasm unchecked, he effused: "According to the testimony of persons in a position to judge, [it] is one of the finest buildings of its size in eastern Canada."[46]

Father Kyte's parish was located in the town of Inverness on the west coast of Cape Breton Island. Inverness, a mining town of about 3,000 people of predominantly Scottish lineage, was over 70 percent Roman Catholic.[47] Stella Maris Parish had acquired its first pastor in 1904, just four years after the Marthas had been established as an independent congregation. That year the town incorporated while experiencing an economic boom. Mother Stanislaus read in Father Kyte's letter: "This vast County

–one of the largest in the Province [population c. 23,000], is practically without Hospital accommodation. We think we may predict therefore, for our Hospital, a career of great usefulness in the large territory which it is called upon to serve."[48] Actually, the Marthas had known for some time about the urgent need for a hospital in Inverness. Dr. Coady, a native of the county, had informed them in 1923: "The good people of Northern Inverness have long suffered the need of an institution to serve their seriously sick. Owing to the lack of proper railway accom-

St. Mary's Hospital, Inverness, Cape Breton, opened 1925.

modation, the removal of the sick to the nearest Hospital is attended by much suffering and risks."[49] Thus, in 1924 the Inverness Catholics, led by their parish priest, Rev. Alexander L. MacDonald, and his assistant, Father Kyte, constructed a Catholic hospital. The miners contributed generously, even though a mine closure threatened in 1925. The local MLA stated at the hospital opening: "The hospital showed what was generally conceded–that no class of workingmen can equal the miners for kindness and generosity; for the building of the hospital was practically financed by them."[50] However, Father Kyte's crafty compliment actually slighted the role of the county's women, such as Mrs. Christie MacLennan of Broad Cove and Maggie Bell MacIsaac of Inverness. They held countless teas and suppers, and organized other fundraising projects whose proceeds they contributed to the hospital building fund. The pastor also gave generously. The final cost for the land and new building was about $50,000.

That day in early April 1925, when Mother Stanislaus opened Father Kyte's letter informing her of the new hospital, she also read: "It is the unanimous and heartfelt desire of our people to have our Hospital in charge of your good Sisters, whose efforts at Hospital Management have been crowned with success in this Diocese. We therefore make application for as many of your Sisters as you may think necessary, to come and take charge of our Hospital."[53] Mother Stanislaus, her council, and Bishop Morrison unanimously approved this request. The superior general had the "Inverness Brigade" ready by the spring; it included Sister Mary of the Sacred Heart MacKinnon (superintendent), Sister Bernardine (Viola) Livingstone, Sister M. Chrisostom (Philomena Loretta) Bates, and Sister M. Veronica (Caroline) Campbell.

The sister "brigade" formally opened St. Mary's Hospital on 24 May 1925, five years after the opening of their Ross Memorial Hospital in Sydney. Ross Memorial was owned by the sisters, but St. Mary's, Inverness, was owned by a board of trustees that incorporated in 1926. That first board, composed of sisters, local citizens, and government representatives, vested management and authority for hiring and firing in the hospital's sister superintendent. It also appointed a medical staff and made St. Mary's subject to the American Medical Association and American College of Surgeons' code of ethics, as well as the surgical code of the Catholic Hospital Association of the United States and Canada.[52]

By 1926 the Sisters of St. Martha had full administrative responsibility for four hospitals in Nova Scotia: St. Martha's (est. Antigonish, 1906), St. Joseph's (est. Glace Bay, 1902), Ross Memorial (est. Sydney, 1920), and St. Mary's (est. Inverness, 1925). Health care was an apostolate they would remain deeply involved in and firmly committed to for most of the twentieth century. By 1926 they had also achieved full autonomy from the college that had given them birth, and had built an impressive new motherhouse called Bethany. Institutional social work with orphans and unwed mothers, first at St. Mary's Home, Sydney, and then also at the Little Flower Institute, Bras d'Or, had been added to their work as well. And just around the corner lay a further challenge in a new type of work.

Notes

1. James D. Cameron, *For the People: A History of St. Francis Xavier University* (Montreal and Kingston: McGill-Queen's University Press, 1996), pp. 144–48, 157–59, and 393.
2. Sister John Baptist Cameron, Retreat Booklet Notes, 1934, F2,S4,SS1,f1,b4, transcript of interview with Sister M. Romuald MacNeil, 19 December 1977, F1,S2,SS1,f2,b1, St. Martha's Convent Annals, 20 January 1928. F21,S1,SS1,f14,b191.
3. Phrase used by Rev. Dr. Daniel MacCormack, Notes, F21,S2,SS1,f1,b191.
4. Mother Faustina commented on her own role in the dispute, "I happen to be between the 'two fires' at present, being called upon by both sides for support for their respective cases." Mother Faustina to Bishop James Morrison, 11 December 1914, F3,S1,SS2,f2,b5.
5. Quoted in Sister Yvonne Vigneault, "Grace and an Unvarnished Woman," 1991, p. 19.
6. Mother Faustina to President H.P. MacPherson, 7 December 1914, F3,S1,SS2,f2,b5.
7. Mother Faustina to President H.P. MacPherson, 27 April 1914, ibid.
8. Sister John Baptist Cameron to Bishop James Morrison, 11 July 1917, F1,S1,SS4,f1,b1.
9. Sister Irene Doyle, "The Heritage of the Sisters of St. Martha," 1967, p. 12.
10. Articles of Agreement, 7 August 1917, F1,S1,SS4,f1,b1.
11. Bishop James Morrison statement, 4 August 1917, F1,S1,SS4,f1,b1.
12. Sister May Mulvihill, "History of the Sisters of St. Martha," I:3:30-1.
13. Sister John Baptist Cameron to Bishop James Morrison, 23 November 1917, F5,S34,SS3,f1,b86.
14. Bishop Morrison to Rev. D.M. MacAdam, 12 March 1918, Outgoing Mail #5021, BMP, ADA.
15. Bishop James Morrison to Mother Faustina, 23 June 1919, F5,S34,SS3,f1,b86.
16. Mother Faustina to Rev. R.H. MacDougall, 7 February 1919, F6,S2,SS1,f4,b110.
17. Sister John Baptist Cameron, "History of the Sisters of St. Martha," p. 80.
18. Bethany Annals, F6,S1,SS1,f1,b106.
19. Ibid.
20. Ibid.

21 Bishop Morrison to President MacPherson, 30 September 1916, F5,S34,SS3,f1,b86.
22 Quoted in Sister May Mulvihill, "History of the Sisters of St. Martha," I:3:60.
23 Handwritten note by Mother Faustina, 1917, F19,S1,SS1,f2,b181.
24 Bishop Morrison to Rev. Clergy and Laity, 13 December 1916, Outgoing Mail, #3700, BMP, ADA.
25 Committee Meeting Minutes, 26 September 1916 and 27 February 1917, F19,S3,SS1,f1,b181.
26 Peter A. Nearing, *He Loved the Church* (Antigonish: The Casket Printing and Publishing, 1975), p. 66.
27 Mother Stanislaus to Bishop James Morrison, 19 April 1922, F19,S2,SS1,f1,b181.
28 Orphanage Meeting Minutes, 11 November 1925, F19,S3,SS1,f1,b181.
29 Father J.J. MacNeil to Bishop James Morrison, 30 April 1918, F19,S2,SS1,f1,b181.
30 Bishop Morrison to E.H. Blois, Superintendent of Neglected and Dependent Children, 8 April 1919. ibid.
31 Mother Stanislaus to Bishop Morrison, 19 April 1922, Orphanage Meeting Minutes, 11 November 1925, F19,S3,SS1,f1,b181.
32 Orphanage Meeting Minutes, 11 November 1925, ibid.
33 Clergy Meeting Minutes, 14 April and 22 July 1926, F19,S3,SS1,f1,b181.
34 See *Little Flower Messenger*, 1928, pp. 8 and 13.
35 For a more detailed account of Martha hospital work in Sydney, see Sister Sarah Janet MacPherson, "The Struggle Gives the Meaning: The Contribution of the Sisters of St. Martha to Health Care in Sydney, N.S., 1920–1980," n.d.
36 *Census of Canada 1921*, I:235 and 758.
37 Bishop Morrison to Mother Faustina, 4 October 1919, F8,S2,SS1,f8,b132.
38 Sister Mary Sacred Heart to J.K.L. Ross, 19 July 1923, ibid.
39 Sister May Mulvihill, "History of the Sisters of St. Martha," I:4:35, lists somewhat different names.
40 Sister Mary Sacred Heart to J.K.L. Ross, 19 July 1923, F8,S2,SS1,f1,b132.
41 St. Rita Hospital Annals, F8,S1,SS1,f5,b129.
42 Interview transcripts, F8,S1,SS2,f2,b130.
43 St. Rita Hospital Annals, 17 and 23 July, and 14 August 1928, F8,S1,SS1,f5,b129.
44 St. Rita Hospital Annals, 11 December 1928, F8,S1,SS1,f5,b129. At considerable hardship to themselves, the sisters had to pay $10,000 to Ross in July 1927.

45 St. Rita Hospital Annals, July 1927, ibid.
46 Rev. J.B. Kyte to Mother Stanislaus, 30 March 1925, F16, S2,SS1,f1,b176.
47 *Census of Canada 1921*, I:615.
48 Rev. J.B. Kyte to Mother Stanislaus, 30 March 1925, F16, S2,SS1,f1,b176.
49 Dr. Coady to Mother Stanislaus, 4 August 1923, F30,S1,SS1,f4,b226.
50 Newspaper clipping, 25 May 1925, F16,S3,SS1,f5,b176.
51 Rev. J.B. Kyte to Mother Stanislaus, 30 March 1925, F16, S2,SS1,f1,b176.
53 St. Mary's Hospital Act of Incorporation and Bylaws, F16,S1,SS1,f2,b176.

Dr. Moses Coady, great friend and admirer of the Marthas and first director of St.F.X. Extension Department, 1928–1952.

Chapter Five

Rural Education, Deepening Maturity, and Papal Approval

Dr. Coady had loomed large in the life of the congregation in 1917, during its struggle for home rule, and he did so again during the 1920s when he, along with other diocesan Catholic leaders, became evermore distressed by the decline of fishing and farming communities in eastern Nova Scotia. These leaders would enlist the aid of the Marthas in the battle to revitalize rural life. Again, this would require the sisters to take a risk by striking out in new directions and assuming broader responsibilities. Then, by the end of the 1920s, the congregation would reach a new level of institutional maturity, one that moved them to apply for approval as a papal institute. This historic step would reveal the Marthas' growing confidence and sense of having become much more than merely a small, parochial, diocesan institute.

The 1920s brought important changes for Maritimers, changes that would touch the Marthas in diverse ways. It was a bleak decade economically and outmigration reached disturbing levels. For many people, incomes fell and unemployment became evermore common. The Cape Breton coal fields and steel industry were plagued by bitter strikes. Labour candidates appeared in provincial elections and the Maritime Rights movement pressed the federal government to address the region's problems.

Catholics witnessed a union of Protestants into the new United Church of Canada in 1925 and faced the question of university federation. Automobiles and radios helped to reduce isolation.

THE CALL FROM RURAL SCHOOLS

While Mother Stanislaus and her Marthas strained to fulfil their expanding missions in the mid-1920s, several rural districts urged them to supply sister teachers. The first summons came from Dr. Moses Coady, the St.F.X. priest professor who had been the sisters' advocate in 1917. Coady (b. 3 January 1882) flourished as a youth in the Southwest Margaree Valley of Cape Breton. He attended Margaree Forks High School (1897 to 1900) and after studying education at the Normal School in Truro, became his high school's principal from 1901 to 1903. Thus he was intimate with the people of his home district and dedicated to their welfare. After graduating from St.F.X. (1905), and the Urban College in Rome, where he was ordained in 1910, Coady returned to his alma mater and served as teacher and principal at the St.F.X. High School (1916–1925), and then as professor of education (1916–1928). In 1921, he helped to reorganize the moribund Nova Scotia Teachers' Union, became its secretary for four years and edited the Nova Scotia *Teachers' Bulletin.*[1] Dr. Coady was a tall, rugged, optimistic individual with an immense capacity for work, a lively imagination, and a healthy sense of humour. He was also a keen admirer of the Marthas.

Along with other lay and clerical leaders of eastern Nova Scotia, Dr. Coady was deeply concerned about the exodus of youth and the deterioration of the region's rural communities. His own rural community of Southwest Margaree, with its long-time resident pastor (Father Finlay J. Chisholm, who had served from 1880 to 1937), had suffered from decline. Over 1,000 citizens in 1901 had become little more than 800 by 1921.[2] Coady concluded that competent teachers and good schools were the way to revitalize rural districts. By 1923, he had big plans for his home territory, and he expected the Marthas to play a major role in them. He wanted the sisters to take over the two-department public school at Margaree Forks, establish a domestic science boarding institute, and staff a small hospital. Thus, in August 1923, he sent to Mother Stanislaus at Bethany a petition signed by leading Protestants and Catholics from Cheticamp, Margaree Habour, East Margaree, Belle Cote, and Margaree Forks that asked for assurance from the sisters that they would undertake this work in two to three years and concluded: "We feel that the Sisters of St. Martha would be able to do this combined educational and health work in a manner most satisfactory to all concerned."[3]

For Coady, a "no" from the congregation was unthinkable. However, the Sisters of St. Martha at that time had no intention of entering the teaching field. Any sisters who had entered the congregation with teaching qualifications had been generally absorbed into hospital work; and in 1923 none were being prepared for the teaching profession. Some sisters argued that the congregation should not enter the teaching field, as it had been founded, they claimed, for other purposes that required physical labour and service to the needy. In addition, the community's missions had stretched its human resources to the limit. Nonetheless, Sister John Baptist Cameron, then one of the general councillors, reported: "Doctor Coady had an answer for every objection. He saw many possibilities in the teaching field, and had the faculty of presenting them very forcibly."[4] The potential for fundraising and for new vocations to the congregation, he argued, was endless. With such a convincing and forceful friend, and with Bishop Morrison warmly supporting him, the Marthas could do little but acquiesce.

Coady was both talk and action. One sister reported, "He organized picnics, worked like a Trojan himself in overalls and shirt sleeves until the perspiration rolled off him. One of the finest schools in the Province was ready for the Sisters in the Autumn of 1925."[5] He also purchased at his own expense a nearby residence for a convent and supplied it with fuel for the first seven years. The 1923 petition to the Marthas, generous subscriptions to the building fund, and willing volunteer labour showed he had the active support of the people of Margaree.

In January 1925 the Margaree Forks School section formally requested teachers from the Sisters of St. Martha to staff their new two-department school (grades one to eleven).[6] The plan for a hospital had been shelved (St. Mary's was nearing completion in Inverness), and work in domestic science was delayed for several years. Mother Stanislaus accepted the request and sent three sisters–Sister Mary Hugh (Tena) Cameron (principal and grades 9–11), Sister Rita Marie (Bertha) Gillis (grades 1–8), and Sister Mary Austin (Harriet) MacDonald (domestic); the former two had some teaching experience before entering and had upgraded in preparation for their new assignment. Mother Stanislaus herself supervised the mission's opening, for her term as superior general had concluded in July 1925.

The school at Margaree Forks, Cape Breton, was opened in 1925; the Marthas' first teaching assignment in 1925.

The convent was dedicated to the recently canonized St. Therese of the Child Jesus. The hundred-year–old house would have no wiring until the 1930s; kerosene lamps and a hand pump were among its rudimentary fixtures. To help with financing, boarders were taken in over the years–an old and rheumatic Mrs. Campbell, a Mrs. Downey, and Fathers Jimmy Tompkins, D.J. Rankin, and A. Briand. On some occasions, the sisters gave youths free lodging so they could continue their high school education. The irregular payment of local taxes meant irregular salaries for the sisters; however, residents were generous with donations of vegetables and other produce.[7] The first commencement exercises in the spring of 1926 showcased speeches by Father Jimmy Tompkins, a pioneer in adult education, and Dr. H.F. Munroe, Nova Scotia's Superintendent of Education.

In quick succession, the Sisters of St. Martha received requests from two other rural school districts. Meanwhile, Mother Ignatius Floyd, a thirty-four-year-old native of Springfield, Antigonish County, was elected superior general of the congregation at the conclusion of Mother Stanislaus's term. Mother Ignatius, whose ethnic lineage was both Irish and Scottish, had entered in 1910 after completing a high school and commercial course at Mount St. Bernard College, Antigonish. She had graduated from the St. Martha's Hospital School of Nursing in 1916 and had then served as superintendent of St. Joseph's Hospital,

Glace Bay, from 1919. Observers remarked on her rapid development as a faithful daughter of the Church and as a successful hospital worker and administrator. Glace Bay Catholics were distressed to lose their efficient hospital administrator, and Mother Ignatius herself "seemed very much crushed under the burden of her [new] office" and the authority it required her to exercise.[8] However, she was to become the longest-serving general superior of the Marthas and strongly influenced their growth and development.

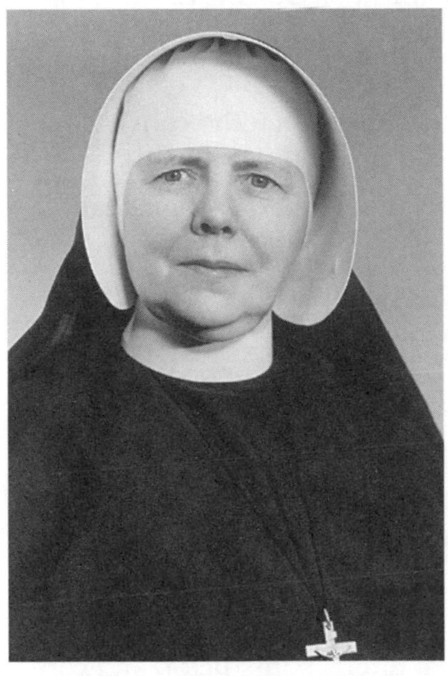

Mother M. Ignatius (Mary Catherine) Floyd, superior general, 1925–1937, 1943–1961

Mother Ignatius received a letter containing the following uncompromising demand in October 1925: "Next year we propose to build a new up-to-date school and shall need four teachers. You must supply them at all costs."[9] The bold writer, Father H.D. Barry, pastor of Bras d'Or, Cape Breton (population c. 3,000), was a St.F.X. alumnus (1897) who had served as headmaster of the St.F.X. high school from 1900 to 1906. He had witnessed the Marthas' founding at the college and had observed their wonderful reformation of its domestic affairs. Somehow, Mother Ignatius, experiencing a rapid baptism as congregation leader, found sisters to staff the pastor's four-room school in September 1926. She appointed Mother Faustina as superior and sent along teaching sisters–Sister Mary Colina (Jessie) MacDougall, Sister Rita Marie (Bertha) Gillis, Sister Mary of Good Counsel (Catherine) MacDonald, Sister M. Martin (Margaret) MacDonald, Sister Mary Raphael (Eileen) Watt–and a housekeeper, Sister Mary Rose (Rose J.) Landry. The sisters' residence was called Sacred Heart Convent; and, in 1927, when the nearby Little Flower Institute opened, its sister staff merged with those at Sacred Heart Convent to form one community. School-age children from the institute attended the Bras d'Or school until overcrowding required classes to be held at the orphanage itself.[10] The novice teaching sisters at Bras d'Or experienced the same financial stringency faced by their sisters at Margaree Forks School.

On 27 August 1928 the motherhouse annalist recorded the recent departure of Sister Mary Colina MacDougall, Sister Mary Helen (Mary Elizabeth) Cathcart, and Sister Mary Celestia (Mary A.) MacNeil for St. Andrews, a nearby rural Scottish Catholic farming community.[11] Their mission? To assume responsibility for the district school. Father Donald L. MacDonald, the parish priest until his untimely death in early September 1928, had orchestrated their entry. The three pioneer sisters stayed in a little "shanty" until November when the convent was ready. A sister reported poetically on the shanty experience: "The wind, finding its way through the numerous chinks and crevices, sang us to sleep about 8:45 p.m.; an hour or so later, myriads of spiders danced on our faces and hands, to the music of the wind, and for the rest of the night our sleep was interrupted–more or less."[12] Marthas on mission were becoming evermore familiar with rustic living conditions.

School began that fall with fifty-two students. Living conditions vastly improved for the sisters when they moved into a new convent. Another pleasing development was the parish appointment in October of Father John R. MacDonald (future bishop of the Diocese of Antigonish, 1950–1959), a good friend of the Marthas and their novitiate spiritual director, instructor, and confessor since August 1927.[13] The motherhouse at Bethany and the people of the district supported the sisters in diverse ways. An annalist reported in 1929: "The people of the parish, together with the pastor are very, very good to us.... In May 1929, two young ladies of the parish, Miss Mary F. MacGillivray and Miss Helen MacDonnell, left to join our community. May they persevere–our first fruits!"[14] The sisters' work was also fruitful academically. In 1931 the school was awarded "the Dent Citizenship Cup for the most progressive school in the Province."[15] The sisters, of course, found the work challenging. Teaching, like other tasks, had its rhythms and repetitions, but the Martha teachers saw it as work for God. One sister later reflected: "Each day is just a repetition of the day before, and the day before that, but be it ever so routine it is God's work, and we hope to get God's pay."[16]

The congregation's decision in 1925 to heed Dr. Coady's persuasive summons on behalf of rural schools for teaching sisters had many repercussions. It strained the sisters' resources and initially yielded little financial reward. Moreover, it aroused some internal controversy; certain Marthas insisted that they should stay out of teaching and that other congregations in the diocese were already doing a good job of it. On the positive side, it opened up for them a challenging new field of endeavour. The congregation began preparing sisters for teaching by sending them to St.F.X., the Normal School, Truro, or other universities

Sister M. Donalda (Anne Cecilia) MacDonald with students at St. Andrews, Antigonish County.

in Canada and the United States. Sister Mary Hugh Cameron at Margaree Forks held the first teaching appointment in the congregation; she had a first-class license with grade eleven, Normal School Training, and courses at St.F.X.; Sister M. Sylvester (Nora) Sullivan earned a grade twelve certificate in 1927, also a first in the community; and Sister Mary Beatrice (Mary) McMahon was the first sister college graduate, earning a bachelor degree from St.F.X. in 1929. Along with preparation for hospital work, the preparation for teaching in rural schools increased the young congregation's formal academic credentials. Schoolwork likewise placed the sisters in closer touch with the grassroots of the Diocese of Antigonish; their dedicated service in local rural communities expanded the growing fund of goodwill toward them and revealed their determination to be of service as a people's congregation. Finally, the teaching Marthas modelled a future lifestyle option for young Catholic women in the diocese; some chose it, made their way into the novitiate at Bethany and became valued members of the congregation.

College and Congregation

Dr. Coady and St. Francis Xavier University helped the Sisters of St. Martha develop teaching expertise. For example, in September 1929, they sponsored at Bethany a "Short Course of Lectures and Conference for Teaching Sisters." Rev. Dr. Hugh MacPherson of Mount Cameron Farm spoke on "The Present Status of Rural Life in Eastern Nova Scotia"; then the agricultural representative for the county, R.J. MacSween, discussed "Agencies Engaged in Bettering Conditions and Remedies Being Applied"; A.B. MacDonald, the county school inspector, examined "The Objective of the Rural Life Movement"; Dr. Coady himself lectured on "The Development of Citizenship and the Co-operative Spirit"; and finally, Rev. Michael Gillis talked on "Household Science in Rural Schools."[17] These lecture themes represented the preoccupations of diocesan clergy who had been witnessing the rapid depopulation of rural parishes and the economic hardships and demoralization of their people.

Through the 1920s, people employed in the fisheries, forestry, mining, agriculture, and manufacturing sectors faced crisis conditions. The number of occupied farms in the region declined precipitously, and grave labour-management conflicts developed in steel and mining communities such as Sydney and Glace Bay. About fifty-eight strikes erupted in the Sydney coal field between 1920 and 1925, some of them violent and all of them bitter. The region's general economic difficulties and the promise of finding prosperity elsewhere stimulated a rapid exodus. Apparently, about 147,000 people moved from the Maritimes between 1921 and 1931, and among the emigrants was "a high proportion of the more productive elements in society."[18] In Antigonish County, Bethany's home district, where the population decrease had been especially pronounced (dropping from 16,114 in 1891 to 10,073 by 1931),[19] people had a keen sense of economic and social decline. President H.P. MacPherson at St.F.X. reported dejectedly in 1926: "Business is slack and the people are leaving one by one for the United States. A spirit of pessimism [exists] among the people, and really the outlook is not at all bright."[20] Many people were plagued by "near destitution"; there were then no general government aid programs such as unemployment insurance, old-age pension, and social assistance.

In response to these conditions, and encouraged by the call for social justice found in the papal encyclical *Rerum Novarum* (1891), diocesan clerical and lay leaders began holding annual rural conferences at St.F.X.[21] From 1923, participants presented, debated and discussed papers on vital topics such as rural schools, rural depopulation, agricultural methods, housing, collective bargaining, unemployment, and cooperation. Certain clerical leaders, for example, Revs. Moses Coady, Michael Gillis, John R. MacDonald, James Boyle, Thomas O'Reilly Boyle, and Jimmy Tompkins, who shared similar convictions about social problems and reform, used the conferences to develop and promote a reformist agenda in the diocese.[22] As a congregation closely associated with St.F.X. and committed to serving the people of the diocese, the Marthas would inevitably be caught up in these concerns.

In November 1926 the Fourth Annual Rural Conference unanimously favoured a plan for a School of Rural Education and Home Economics run by the Marthas at Bethany and under the sponsorship of the St.F.X. Department of Education. After careful consideration, Bishop Morrison rejected this petition for such a school. Instead, he approved a new four-year program in home economics then being planned by the Sisters of the Congregation of Notre Dame at Mount St. Bernard College, the women's institution affiliated with St.F.X.,[23] who already had an established tradition of education in home economics.[24] The conference participants were disappointed; they favoured the Marthas for work in home economics because the Marthas had more direct contact with people in the rural districts and their motherhouse had its own farm. The conference in 1927 passed another resolution, "that this Rural Conference should encourage and help the Sisters of St. Martha to have prepared without delay at least nine sisters for extension work in home economics, and also give all reasonable assistance to enable them to give short courses throughout the Diocese."[25] However, as the bishop directed, Mount Saint Bernard would continue to offer formal courses in home economics, and the Marthas would be limited to offering courses in the field. It was a division of labour imposed by the bishop, and poorly received in certain quarters. However, the Marthas themselves seemed little disappointed.[26]

In 1926 the congregation had sent sisters to Guelph, Ontario, and two prospective postulants to the MacDonald College, Quebec, for training in home economics. The congregation's first fieldwork in this area began in the summer of 1927 when it offered two or three-week courses to miners' wives in Westville, Pictou County. The Bethany annalist reported, "The home economics fever is ... very high these days. The Sisters going to Westville to give a short course in this subject has awakened some dormant minds. May God bless and prosper this work for His greater honour and glory."[27] In August, sisters gave courses in the Antigonish County districts of Maryvale and Georgeville, and the following summer "along the coast of Guysborough" County and in New Glasgow, Pictou County.[28] A few years hence, several Marthas would participate in a more formal outreach to the region's economically distressed through St.F.X.'s newly established extension department.

Congregational Profile

By 1928 the Sisters of St. Martha, Antigonish, had grown substantially in numbers and experience. The original fifteen volunteers in 1900 had become 151 women. The sisters' ethnic origins reflected that of the diocesan population: nearly 60 percent were of Scottish background and others were of Irish (14 percent), English (12 percent), and Acadian (11 percent) lineage. Most came from within the diocese–Antigonish County (24 percent), Inverness (19 percent), Cape Breton (19 percent), Richmond (6 percent), and Pictou (6 percent). But more than fifteen had travelled from Newfoundland, still a British colony, and a smaller number from Ontario.[29] Forty-two candidates had entered from 1900 to 1910, 65 between 1911 and 1920, and 163 between 1921 and 1930.[30] Almost all the sisters came from devout Catholic homes of modest economic standing. More than twenty sisters had died by 1928, and their average age at death had been less than forty. Tuberculosis, a frightfully common illness of the time, was a leading cause of death. After 1921 the dead had found their final resting place in the little cemetery on the grounds of the new motherhouse at Bethany, Antigonish.

The sisters ran eleven missions in 1928 and, of course, staffed their own motherhouse at Bethany. Two missions were domestic (St.F.X., and St. Augustine's Seminary, Toronto); four were hospitals–St. Joseph's (Glace Bay), St. Martha's (Antigonish), St. Rita (Sydney), and St. Mary's (Inverness); one was an orphanage (Little Flower Institute, Bras d'Or), one a home for unwed mothers (St. Mary's, Sydney); and three were rural schools–Margaree Forks, Little Bras d'Or, (both in Cape Breton), and St. Andrews, Antigonish County. The largest communities of sisters were at the motherhouse, the university, and St. Joseph's and St. Martha's hospitals. In 1900 the newly established congregation had owned not a single piece of property; by 1928 their real estate holdings were substantial–a motherhouse and two hospitals. Their sources of income included salaries of sisters on the diverse missions, fundraising campaigns for special projects, donations, and bequests. Clerical friends, all with meagre incomes, often gave generously to the sisters. For example, Father James M. Kiely, St.F.X. bursar from 1908 to 1918, gave a valuable gift to the sisters after each annual clergy retreat. Jack MacIsaac and William Chisholm, a local Antigonish undertaker and a lawyer, respectively, kindly provided free services to the sisters for many years. Those of other faiths also numbered among the congregation's many benefactors.[31]

While the Sisters of St. Martha had expanded in membership and external works, their internal community and spiritual life had also matured. Individual and communal prayer was an especially important part of their life. In 1913 they replaced the Sisters of Charity prayer book, used by them from the start, with their own printed prayer manual bearing the bishop's imprimatur. It contained morning, afternoon, and evening prayers and those to be used at Holy Communion, before the Blessed Sacrament, and on particular occasions, for example, when the clock strikes, before recreations, when walking, and at the sight of a crucifix. The prayers aimed to foster the religious virtues of thankfulness, adoration, reverence, humility, repentance, forgiveness, obedience, faith, hope, and charity. The 1913 prayer book also outlined the two forms of examination of conscience practised by the Marthas. Each sister made the general examen twice daily by reviewing all her actions and thoughts, and asking pardon for those that were sinful; she made the particular examen once daily by concentrating on one facet of her life, for example, the vow of obedience.[32]

Prayer was central to Martha spirituality, and so was "going on retreat." Each sister was required to make an annual eight-day retreat, a three-day retreat before her annual renewal of vows, and a monthly Sunday retreat. Retreat masters, usually Jesuits or Redemptorists, inevitably covered themes such as these: how to make a good retreat, the purpose of life, the purpose of the religious life, the vows, sin, confession, penance, the inevitability of death, judgement, hell, works of salvation, the importance of following the rule, the mass, and prayer. Retreats were times of intensely concentrated spirituality, respite, spiritual joy, challenge, and consolation. At the conclusion of an especially successful Jesuit-led retreat at Bethany in 1927, a sister commented: "Every Sister is delighted with the matter they received during the Exercises. They all claim with all due regard and gratitude for lights received during past retreats that this one has excelled them all from every angle. May God grant the fruits may be multiplied and permanent." She added wryly, "The Sisters did not certainly lose the gift of speech during the retreat, judging by the sounds in the air today."[33]

In 1926 the Sisters of St. Martha published in two editions their first *Directory and Book of Customs*, one edition for the professed and one for the novices. The professed sisters' edition included an introduction by Bishop Morrison containing sober and serious advice on the manifold duties and obligations of the religious life.[34] The *Directory* reveals how extensively the sisters' lives were regulated. Part One provided each sister with general directions on her vocation, with the need for regular observance, and with maxims from spiritual masters. Part Two on the "Order of the Day" gave her detailed directives about daily spiritual exercises–morning devotions, visits to the Blessed Sacrament, Holy Communion, the examen of conscience, and so forth. Her prescription for entering the chapel read: "Proceed through the main aisle in double file and order of priority. Have your hands reverently joined, the fingers together but slightly inclined from the vertical" (p. 15). Another section of the *Directory* outlined more general spiritual exercises. It discussed confession, benediction, retreats, the vows, and devotions, such as those to the Sacred Heart, to the Holy Ghost, to the Blessed Virgin, and to

St. Martha. Each sister was counselled to practice modesty in looks, walk, dress, and conversation: "The eyes should be modestly lowered, particularly when on the street, in church, in company of lay-people, when conversing with persons of the opposite sex, during time of prayer, of conference, of silence and at meals" (p. 51). Other sections dealt with cordiality and prudence, sisterly love, sickness, good use of time, order and cleanliness, and the chapter of faults where sisters monthly examined one another's lives against the standards of the Martha constitutions and customs. The sisters seemed to view the chapter of faults as a necessary evil; it was never popular but remained part of their constitutions until the 1960s.

The 1926 *Directory* also prescribed the governance of the institute. The mother general was asked to "render yourself to all like a true mother" and to "exact the strict observance of the constitution" (p. 71). There were also dictums for councillors, the general secretary, the general treasurer, superiors, and the novice mistress. The detailed regulations of the 190-page directory are overwhelming. The first aim of all secular duties was "to acquire purity of intention, by which you perform your duties for the love of God only" (p. 89). The proper methods of sweeping, cleaning, and bed making were all carefully described. Over five pages cover the refectory or dining hall–where, when, and how to sit, hand signs for requesting things during silence, and table etiquette. The sister was told: "You are exhorted to show every mark of good breeding and refinement which is so becoming in a soul consecrated to God" (p. 100). Other parts prescribe acceptable recreation activities, when and how to make trips away from the convent, how to receive visitors, costume regulations, holidays (two weeks yearly), feast days, and the three annual grand holidays–the feast of St. Martha on July 29, which marked the foundation of the congregation; the patronal feast of the current mother general; and the day commemorating the opening of the motherhouse on 21 September 1921. The final part of the *Directory* outlined rules for sisters in charge of duties, for example, the sacristan, infirmarian, kitchen supervisor, clothes room supervisor, pharmacist, portress, baker, orphanage supervisor, and superintendents of nurses and teachers.

The *Directory and Book of Customs* for the novices had special sections on the purpose of the novitiate, on vocation, and on the "picture of a good novice."[35] The aim of the text was "to help the Novices to acquire the true spirit and character of the Institute" (p. 8). It described a good novice with key phrases, such as, "she conceals nothing from her spiritual guides," "she steadily combats self-love," "she avoids the smallest violation of the rules," and "she is always satisfied and cheerful" (pp. 11–12). The novice was directed to meet with her mistress of novices monthly and to develop the qualities of humility, docility, submission, and teachability. The novice aspiring to make her first or temporary vows had to petition the superior general for the right, and then undergo an intimidating canonical examination for profession conducted by Bishop Morrison. Many of the other *Directory* prescriptions were the same as those contained in the edition for the professed sisters. The novitiate also used from 1926 to 1945 a fifty-page booklet entitled "Directions for the Novitiate."[36] Its contents were similar to the novitiate *Directory*. The Marthas evidently embraced zealously the highest standards of Roman Catholic religious life. Their program aimed to produce spiritual Olympians who would give no quarter whatsoever to the world, the flesh, or the devil, as each sister single-mindedly strove for the prize of eternal life.

From 1925 the Marthas used printed vocation literature to attract young women into their novitiate.[37] Diocesan priests played an important role in recruitment. One pastor wrote a Martha vocation pamphlet in 1927, and the year afterwards two great friends and promoters of the sisters–Fathers Michael Gillis of Boisdale, Cape Breton, and John R. MacDonald of St. Andrews (also the confessor and novitiate instructor)–made a recruitment trip to the Boston area where the greatest concentration of Nova Scotia expatriates lived.[38] Several priests also discussed with Mother Ignatius other ways and means "of getting recruits for the Congregation"; shortly thereafter, the congregation sent vocation literature to all the diocesan priests "to help them get subjects for the Community."[39]

Women who entered the Martha novitiate at Bethany submitted to a highly regulated daily life that began at 5 A.M. each morning. The mistress of novices–Sister Mary Anthony MacPhee (1919–1922) and, later, Sister Mary James Campbell (1922–1929)–supervised their training, and a priest acted as spiritual director and instructor. The postulants and novices lived separately from the professed sisters and were permitted little contact with them. Senior postulants became novices at a reception ceremony in the Bethany chapel where they were clothed in their "holy habits" and received a religious name. For example, Amelia Reashor became Sister Mary David in religion.[40] They wore white bridal attire and became "true spouses of Christ."

Postulants at clothing ceremony in the Bethany chapel.

The patron of the Martha novitiate was St. John Berchmans. Novice diaries (always anonymous) from this era record the entry of postulants, the difficulties of adjusting to religious life, reception ceremonies, retreats, profession ceremonies, visits of the bishop and priests, celebrations, and daily duties. The novices' assigned duties included kitchen work, making beds, cleaning, weeding the garden, and setting tables. However, their lives were not all duty-ridden and burdened with an unremitting round of work and devotions. One novice reported, "After Benediction at the Grotto we had permission to dance, and the Feast of St. Ignatius ended merrily" (31 July 1927).[41] And there were frequent joyful forays into the woods for walks, talks, and picnics. Neither did the novitiate experience stifle humour. An entry in 1930 stated, "A Murder in the Refectory Today. Sr. M. Ambrose with the aid of Sr. Regina ends the happy life of a rat. Both of these Srs are to receive the Victoria Cross (medal). The presentation to be made by Sr. M. Redempta who is supposed to be the 'Bethany Brave.'"[42] Novitiate sisters usually developed a strong sense of community, and there was much good-natured repartee and practical joking.

The Martha community experience was somewhat isolated from general cultural trends in Canada. American mass culture was exerting a hefty impact through radio, films, and magazines. More Canadians were going places using the "horseless carriage," or automobile. Many dismayed clergy censored the "free-spending," free-wheeling, self-indulgent ethos of consumerism and concluded that the nation was "adrift from its moral and reli-

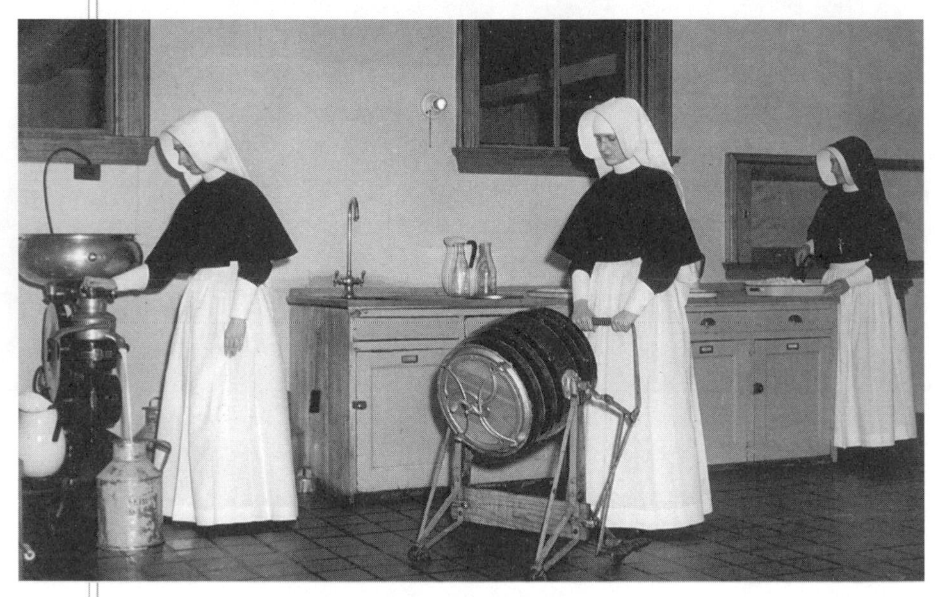

Novices in Bethany kitchen on milk and butter duty.

gious moorings."[43] Among Protestants, inter-church cooperation was on the rise, and Catholics found themselves sharing the religious landscape with a new national denomination, the United Church of Canada, which was formed on 25 June 1925. Protestants were also continuing to grapple with new intellectual developments, such as the theory of evolution and biblical criticism. However, little of this ferment and change seemed to penetrate the convent walls of the Sisters of St. Martha, Antigonish.

A mark of the congregation's growing maturity by the end of the 1920s was the sisters' developing sense of tradition and emulation for the pioneer Marthas. The pioneers were becoming a touchstone or model of what the sisterhood should stand for. Mother Ignatius declared in a circular letter: "We should practice great generosity at all times. Our older sisters are an example of this virtue, and we must leave their tradition bright and untarnished. The young sisters can do this by imitating their devotion, their unselfishness, and the absolute simplicity of heart with which they upheld authority, and lived for the common good."[44] Some years later, a statement by Mother M. Immaculata (Jennie) Fraser revealed this same reverence for the lives of the pioneers. She counselled, "We should never push ourselves forward at any function where so many other sisterhoods are older and more experienced. We should and must show that lovely, simple, humble, and generous spirit of our pioneers."[45]

Application for Papal Approval

In 1928 the Congregation of the Sisters of St. Martha had been in existence nearly thirty years. Given their rapid growth in missions and deepening maturity in community life, it was no surprise that the administration decided to apply to the Vatican for approval as a Papal Institute. Such commendation would bring recognition and status. As well, the congregation could open and conduct missions in other dioceses without reference to the Bishop of Antigonish, and neither could he interfere in the internal affairs of the congregation. Constitutional amendments would henceforth require the approval of Rome. In other words, papal approval would bring the Marthas more independence from the local bishop and direct accountability to the Vatican. However, the sisters had not even been assured of official diocesan status until 1923 because Bishop Cameron had not prepared a decree of erection at their founding in 1900, or the original had been lost. In 1922, the Vatican decree *Quod iam per Constitutionem,* which required religious congregations to revise their constitutions according to the 1917 Code of Canon Law, alerted the sisters to their lack of formal status. Thus, they revised their constitutions and Bishop Morrison formally "erect[ed] and establish[ed] the Congregation of the Sisters of St. Martha of the Diocese of Antigonish as a diocesan congregation."[46] Two years later, on 19 July 1925 at Bethany, the community held its first general chapter composed of nineteen sister delegates who approved the recently revised constitutions and elected Mother Ignatius and six other officers–Mother Stanislaus (assistant general), Mother Faustina (second assistant), Sister Maris Stella MacDonald (third assistant), Sister Mary Anthony MacPhee (fourth assistant), Sister

John Baptist Cameron (secretary general), and Sister Mary Colina MacDougall (treasurer general).[47]

In 1927, one year after the publication of the Marthas' first *Directory and Book of Customs*, Mother Ignatius had the constitutional revision of 1923 edited and printed.[48] It included a pleasing rationale for the congregation's name: "that the members who compose it may serve their neighbour with the same care, diligence and love with which their holy patroness St. Martha served our Lord at Bethany" (p. 6). It also reiterated that the sisters' true spirit was "a generous love for God" (p. 6). Optimism about future congregational growth was reflected in the provision allowing for provincial superiors and councils to be appointed (p. 46). The new constitutions required the Marthas to convene a general chapter every six years and described the criteria for selecting delegates and officer nominees.

Finally, in 1929, Mother Ignatius applied to Rome for approval of their constitutions in the form of a Decree of Approval. Bishop Morrison and other Canadian churchmen who knew the Marthas well, for example, Archbishop Neil McNeil of Toronto and Bishop John T. Kidd of Calgary, warmly endorsed the sisters' application to Rome.[49] Mother Ignatius had written to the archbishop "for a line of recommendation and anything else you might consider helpful to this cause ....We are anxious to succeed with this project and we are fully aware that your word would go far towards this end."[50] On 22 December 1931, the Vatican issued a Decree of Approval which stated that, at the request of the Superior General and with the advice of her Councillors, Pope Pius XI had approved the institute and its constitutions for seven years.[51] The Marthas were gratified with the happy, though temporary, result; they were now a Papal Institute. A sister described the reception of the documents on 28 March 1932:

> *His Excellency [Bishop Morrison] presented Mother [Ignatius] with a copy of the new constitution compiled, completed and fully approved of for seven years, with the Decree published at the end. Anyone can imagine with what a light heart and a light step Mother carried the precious burden home, and we feasted our eyes on the precious piece of literature, the observance of which will gain for us a High Place in Heaven.*[52]

All the houses of the congregation were immediately notified of the happy news and offered thanksgiving to God.

For the Sisters of St. Martha, the era from 1917 to 1931 opened with a struggle for independence from St. Francis Xavier University, and concluded with a successful application to Roman authorities for approval as a Papal Institute. The sisters had experienced rapid growth in numbers and missions. Their new works included a diocesan orphanage, a home for unwed mothers, two new hospitals, teaching in rural schools, and experiments in adult education, all against a backdrop of regional economic distress and outmigration. In spite of this reality, the sisters had built a new motherhouse and even purchased a hospital. And finally, their community life had matured: some sisters had gained administrative and educational expertise, they had revised their constitutions, developed a *Directory and Book of Customs*, gained status as a diocesan institute, and finally, achieved recognition as a Papal Institute. The future looked bright, and voices calling for their help would soon come beckoning from afar.

Notes

1 Rev. A.A. Johnston, *Antigonish Diocese Priests and Bishops 1786–1925,* ed. Kathleen M. MacKenzie (Antigonish: Casket Printing and Publishing Co., 1994), p. 30.
2 *Census of Canada 1921*, I:17.
3 Petition to the Sisters of St. Martha, 15 August 1923, F30,S1,SS1,f1,b226.
4 Historical Highlights, F30,S1,SS1,f4,b226.
5 Ibid.
6 School Trustees to Sisters of St. Martha, 14 January 1925, F30,S1,SS1,f1,b226.
7 Notes on St. Theresa's Convent Margaree Forks School, n.d., F30,S2,SS1,f1,b226.
8 Quoted in Sister May Mulvihill, "History of the Sisters of St. Martha," I:5:3.
9 Father H.D. Barry to Mother Ignatius, 30 October 1925, F20,S1,SS2,f1,b190.

10 Historical Notes, F20,S1,SS1,f1,b190.
11 Bethany Annals, 27 August 1928, F6,S1,SS1,f1,b106.
12 St. Andrews Convent, supplementary account, b243.
13 Bethany Annals, 5 August 1927, F6,S1,SS1,f1,b106.
14 St. Andrews Convent, supplementary account, b243.
15 CSM, *Sixty Years*, p. 56.
16 *The Bethanite*, September 1944.
17 Bethany Annals, 3-4 September 1929, F6,S1,SS1,f1,b106.
18 Ernest R. Forbes, *Maritime Rights Movement, 1919 1927: A Study in Canadian Regionalism* (Kingston and Montreal: McGill-Queen's University Press, 1979), p. 65.
19 *Census of Canada 1931*, 1:348.
20 President H.P. MacPherson to Eric F. MacNeill, 23 September 1926, RG5/9/14592, PMP, STFXUA. For a good first-hand grass roots account of the problems many people in eastern Nova Scotia faced keeping body and soul together during the twenties, see Ida Delaney, *By Their Own Hands: A Field Worker's Account of the Antigonish Movement* (Hantsport, N.S.: Lancelot Press, 1985), chapter one.
21 See John Francis Glasgow, "The Role of Educational and Rural Conferences in the Development of the Extension Department of Saint Francis Xavier University," BA thesis, St.F.X., 1947.
22 Dr. Moses Coady to Rev. Michael Gillis, 31 August 1951, MG20/1/954-55, Coady Personal Papers (CPP), STFXUA.
23 *Mount Saint Bernard Centennial 1883–1983*, p. 36.
24 Sister Margaret MacDonell, CND, *Mount Saint Bernard College, Antigonish, Nova Scotia, 1897–1947* (Montreal: Sisters of the Congregation of Notre Dame, 1998), pp. 36–39.
25 Quoted in Peter A. Nearing, *He Loved the Church* (Antigonish: Casket Printing and Publishing Co., 1975), p. 30.
26 Sister John Baptist Cameron, "History of the Sisters of St. Martha," p. 99, and Bethany Annals, 26 July 1927, F6,S1,SS1,f1,b106.
27 Bethany Annals, 9 July 1927, ibid.
28 Bethany Annals, 18 August and 1 September 1928, ibid.
29 Based on First Register of the Sisters of St. Martha, 1894–1927, F5,S33,SS1,f1,b75.
30 Statistics of Numbers Entering, Making Profession, Leaving and Deceased, F5,S33,SS2,f1,b77.
31 List of Benefactors, F6,S2,SS1,f8,b110.
32 *Manual of the Sisters of St. Martha, Antigonish, Nova Scotia*, 1913, F25,S1,SS1,f1,b200.
33 Bethany Annals, 31 December 1927, F6,S1,SS1,f1,b106.
34 *Directory and Book of Customs for the Professed Sisters of St. Martha*, 1926, 190 pages, F5,S6,SS1,f1,b257.

35 Directory and Book of Customs for the Novitiate Sisters of St. Martha, 1926, F5,S6,SS1,b257,f1.
36 "Directions for the Novitiate," F5,S6,SS4,f1,b257.
37 See pamphlets in F25,S2,SS1,f1,b206.
38 Bethany Annals, 13–17 March and 1 April 1928, F6,S1,SS1,f1,b106.
39 Bethany Annals, 17 May and 25 June 1928, ibid.
40 The sisters' religious names were often those of male saints.
41 Novitiate Diary, 31 July 1927, F6,S5,SS1,f1,b116.
42 Novitiate Diary, 1930, F6,S5,SS1,f1,b116.
43 Murphy and Perin, eds., *A Concise History of Christianity in Canada*, p. 340.
44 Mother Ignatius, Circular Letter, 18 February 1931.
45 Mother Immaculata, Circular Letter, 1941.
46 Bishop Morrison to Your Eminence, 18 September 1923, F5,S1,SS1,f2,b254.
47 General Chapter Proceedings, 1925, F5,S8,SS1,f1,b6.
48 "Constitution of the Sisters of St. Martha, Antigonish," 1927, F5,S2,SS3,f1,b254.
49 Bishop Morrison to Alexius M. Cardinal Lepicier, 8 April 1929, F5,S5,SS1,f1,b256.
50 Mother Ignatius to Archbishop Neil McNeil, 23 January 1929, b244.
51 See Constitution of the Sisters of St. Martha, 1931, F5,S2,SS4,f1,b254.
52 Bethany Annals, 28 March 1932, F6,S1,SS1,f1,b106. For the complete text of the 1931 Decree of Approval, see Appendix III.

Two Marthas–Sister John de la Salle (Marie) Fougere and Sister Catherine Hugh (Annie Catherine) Peck–with first communicants at Canmore, Alberta, 1941.

Chapter Six

Going West, 1930-1940

Two lonesome Marthas–Sister Francis Teresa Herrgott and Sister Mary Daniel MacLellan–boarded a westbound train in Antigonish at 2 A.M. on 1 May 1929, and ten days later they wearily stepped off nearly 3,500 kilometres away in Lethbridge, Alberta. An old friend of the congregation, Bishop John T. Kidd, then Bishop of Calgary, mingled with those who welcomed them. Sister Francis Teresa and Sister Mary Daniel had arrived in the west to take over a small hospital called the Van Haarlem. This new Lethbridge mission was a landmark in the congregation's history as its first western Canadian mission, and it would be followed in quick succession by further missions in Alberta at Banff, Canmore, and Blairmore, and several in Saskatchewan at Regina, Broadview, and Melville. Often underpaid, overworked, and ill-prepared, sisters assigned to these missions would be involved in the full range of congregational work: hospital administration, nursing, parish visiting, catechetical instruction, housekeeping, education, and social work. Thus the 1930s witnessed the congregation's extension from the Atlantic to the Rockies and its evolution into a national religious order.

The Sisters of St. Martha entered a west experiencing rapid immigration, ethnic diversification, rural and urban development, and political ferment. Cities such as Winnipeg, Regina, Saskatoon, Calgary, and Edmonton bustled with newcomers.

However, the farm remained "the paramount institution" on the prairies, where wheat was king.[1] Tragically, the Great Depression of the 1930s would strike the prairies a staggering blow. Drought and dust storms would ravage farms and visit intense suffering on many people. And the hardships would stimulate the growth of new political parties. While Richard B. Bennett's federal Conservatives came to power in 1930, the Communist Party gained ground, and the Co-operative Commonwealth Federation (CCF) was formed in 1932. William "Bible Bill" Aberhart led Social Credit to power in Alberta in 1935. Political ferment and economic suffering were the prairies' stock-in-trade during the "Dirty Thirties" when the Marthas appeared on the scene.

Alberta's Diocese of Calgary, which would become an important theatre of work for the Marthas, had been established in 1912. Its boundaries were formed by British Columbia to the west, Montana to the south, and Saskatchewan to the east, and it included the striking geography of bald, dry prairie, open grassland, rolling foothills, and rugged mountain ranges. Pioneer religious work had been undertaken by religious congregations of men and women such as the Oblates of Mary Immaculate, the Faithful Companions of Jesus, the Sisters of Service, and the Sisters of Charity, Montreal. English-speaking Catholics faced the challenges of assimilating new Catholic immigrants from eastern Europe and developing and maintaining their Catholic institutions during the hardships of the Depression.

Lethbridge, a town about 170 kilometres south of Calgary, had grown rapidly since the Galt family organized their North West Coal and Navigation Company to mine local coal deposits in the 1880s. Shortly thereafter, Roman Catholics built their first church called St. Patrick's. The city incorporated itself in 1906 and became a marketing and distribution area for the region. By 1931, its citizens numbered 13,489 and about 20 percent were Roman Catholic. Nearly four thousand were recent immigrants of European background, and a little over two hundred had Asian roots.

St. Michael's Hospital, Lethbridge

While not the first or only voice calling from the west, Bishop John T. Kidd was the first to succeed in luring the Marthas to the prairies. During his years as rector of St. Augustine's Seminary in Toronto (1913-1925), where the congregation had managed household affairs, Bishop Kidd had developed a high regard for the sisters and became a warm personal friend. Now he was most anxious to have them in his Alberta diocese. In 1928, when Mother Ignatius showed interest in his several propositions, he stated: "Knowing your Community so well, I would naturally be more pleased to have the Sisters of St. Martha than others, as you are doing various kinds of work and that is what is really needed in the West."[2] Recognizing the Martha's versatility, the bishop convinced Mother Ignatius and Mother Faustina in 1928 to travel to the west on an investigative trip. On their return, they regaled their sisters with "glowing tales of their travels and of all that can be done for God and souls in the West."[3]

The general council accepted Bishop Kidd's proposition to assume control of a twenty-seven-bed private hospital in St. Patrick's Parish, Lethbridge, that had belonged to Marie E. Van Haarlem for over twenty years. It was one of the countless small hospitals built in prairie frontier communities by private individuals, Canadian churches, the Red Cross, or the Victorian Order of Nurses. After arriving in Lethbridge, Sister Francis Teresa (superintendent/superior) and Sister M. Daniel (nursing director) on behalf of the congregation, purchased the hospital for $35,000, and Bishop Kidd renamed it St. Michael's. The existing staff–nurses, maids, cook, and janitor–were retained. The sisters soon had St. Michael's Hospital accredited by the American College of Physicians and Surgeons.

The sisters' hospital was not the only one in Lethbridge. A sixty-five-bed municipal hospital called the Galt also existed. But the growing city needed more hospital beds, so plans existed to expand the Galt. Some Lethbridge Protestants hoped that enlarging the Galt would forestall the entry of Roman Catholic sisters, whom they considered an arm of the Pope. However, when the Marthas publicly announced their intention to buy the Van Haarlem and then later build a new one hundred-bed hospital, civic plans to further develop the Galt were shelved. Relations between the two hospitals would sometimes be strained. But unfortunately for the sisters, the great economic collapse intervened between their announced intention to build and the beginning of new construction. Financing a new hospital became a nightmare. However, the congregation was caught, for neither it, nor the bishop, nor the new hospital advisory board, nor the parish priest wanted to disappoint public expectations. Therefore, the Marthas forged ahead to fulfil their public commitment to construct a modern hospital in Lethbridge, depite the fact that economically, the timing could not have been worse.

The new hospital was built on six acres of land at the edge of the city. A glowing media report described in detail the "city's new $300,000 institution" that "embodies [the] very latest fea-

St. Michael's Hospital, Lethbridge, Alberta, opened in 1931.

tures in modern hospital construction."[4] Such boosterism was gratifying to the citizenry, but for the Marthas, during the early 1930s, the completed project was a dream turned into a nightmare. They had mortgaged the building at $360,000, a staggering burden of debt at the outset of a major worldwide economic depression. Ultimately, they borrowed $450,000 for St. Michael's Hospital and incurred annual payments of nearly $25,000. A sister reflected on the hospital opening of 9 September 1931: "It was a lovely celebration for the opening, but we had only eleven patients. It was very discouraging. Mother Ignatius was seen in the chapel before the Blessed Sacrament with outstretched arms, weeping. We kept pushing and praying and had to get along with as little staff as possible. At one point a firm refused to give supplies on more credit."[5] The sisters struggled valiantly to keep the creditors at bay. Bishop Monahan castigated a Toronto firm for pressuring the sisters and not appreciating their dire situation. He wrote, "The willing horse can do so much and applying the lash after that is cruelty, and that is what I feel you have been doing for some time past, and we resent it very keenly."[6] Sisters in the east made many sacrifices to sustain the new hospital, and friends of the Marthas helped out when they could. Later, Bishop Kidd, who could neither foot the bills nor secure the loan–although earlier he had suggested he would–because of his own financial difficulties, admitted to Mother Ignatius: "I was afraid the expenditure would be too burdensome for some years when the unforeseen depression came like a western wind storm."[7]

The sisters tried to finance St. Michael's through government grants, patient fees, and donations. During the worst of the Depression, people avoided hospitals except in emergencies, and when they could not avoid them, they frequently left their bills unpaid. In 1932 the hospital had about forty employees, annual operating expenses of over $28,000, plus debt servicing. The financial crisis continued through 1933. Sister John Baptist Cameron reflected that year: "We ... hope that this terrific worry that is breaking down our Superior General's health and worrying the life out of many of us, will be a lesson to future Sisters of St. Martha not to tamper lightly with contracting debts and making loans."[8] The Marthas frequently found themselves in the ironic position of praying for more patients. However, by 1935 the financial stress had eased, the worst of the Depression was over, and admissions increased, sometimes even to unmanageable levels. And by the late 1930s, St. Michael's Hospital had concluded hospitalization contracts with district mining companies which further stabilized its revenues.

The sisters at St. Michael's encouraged the formation, in September 1929, of a hospital board composed of laymen, sisters, and the local parish priest, Rev. Dean Michael Murphy. Although unincorporated, the board formulated institutional policies and was a useful liaison with the community. Board members were preoccupied with the physical plant, fee rates, salaries, and the approval of medical staff membership. The hospital's doctors generally enjoyed a congenial and mutually respectful relation with the sisters. A Ladies' Aid Society was formed and greatly assisted the sisters' health care work.

In addition to financial anguish, the pioneer sisters in Lethbridge experienced loneliness and isolation. Thus, Sister Francis Teresa, former superintendent of St. Joseph's Hospital, and Sister Mary Daniel, former director of nurses at St. Rita Hospital, Sydney, welcomed with joy the other sisters when they arrived later in 1929–Sister John de la Salle (Anne) Fougere (laboratory and x-ray); Sister Mary Bernardine Livingstone (dietary); Sister Mary Mercedes (Margaret) Garvin, RN; and Sister M. Dionysius (Margaret Ann) Chisholm (bookkeeping and admissions).

The small community was badly shaken in November 1930 when twenty-seven-year old Sister Dionysius, a native of Malignant Cove, Antigonish County, suddenly died after spinal surgery. The hospital annals give an account of the tragic development: "She was taken to the operating room for surgery, and said courageously and cheerfully: 'I am in God's hands, and if He wills it, I sacrifice my life for the work in the West and for the Holy Souls.' Her condition was good during the operation and everything seemed normal, when suddenly she collapsed and died in the operating room."[9] She was the first Martha buried in western Canada.

The responsibilities of these western pioneer sisters were manifold: pharmacy and hospital supplies, operating room, sewing room, floor supervision, housekeeping, laundry, x-ray, medical records, laboratory, finances, and nursing. On the cultural side, the sisters met patients from interesting groups unknown in eastern Canada, for example, Mormons, Hutterites, and Mennonites. And local rodeos rendered a yearly quota of cowboys suffering from crushes, sprains, and fractures. The sisters also visited in the Lethbridge district, contributed to parish work, entertained visitors, and fulfilled their daily devotions as faithful religious. The spiritual state of their patients was of great concern to them too. And their strong religious convictions occasionally led to conflict with certain doctors. For example, in 1937 the St. Michael's sisters opposed a doctor's decision to induce an abortion in a mother who had heart and kidney problems.[10]

Their new hospital would be the largest Martha mission in western Canada, requiring nineteen sisters by 1941 who supervised a staff of about sixty; together they served the health care needs that year of 3,553 patients.[11] One Lethbridge citizen was impressed by both the work of the sisters and the hospital's striking physical presence:

Those who went to work in the semi-darkness of early morning today from the south-east section of the city may have noticed–surely they must have been inspired–by the cross on St. Michael's General Hospital. The illuminated cross, shining forth against the shadows, seemed to be a symbol of the enduring qualities of our Christian life and culture. What a heartening start for the day that shining symbol was.[12]

Teaching in Lethbridge

Public knowledge about the Marthas in Lethbridge spread. Soon the local Catholic school board, perhaps at the behest of Bishop Peter Monahan, the new bishop of the diocese from 1931, requested sister teachers for St. Basil's School. One Catholic school existed in each of the two Latin rite parishes in the city: St. Patrick's School was run by the Faithful Companions of Jesus, and St. Basil's had been established in 1914 on the north side of the city, where many people were of European background and Communists were active. In 1933 the congregation agreed to appoint two academic teachers and one music teacher to St. Basil's. Sister Mary Beatrice McMahon was the congregation's first arts graduate (St.F.X.) and had three years experience in the schools of Nova Scotia. Sister M. Petronilla (Susanne) LeBlanc had a grade 11 diploma and a Nova Scotia teacher's license, class B. The sisters were assigned to live at St. Michael's Hospital convent with the music instructor, Sister Mary Raphael Watt, and the other hospital sisters.

The prospective teaching sisters found trouble awaiting them in Alberta. First, the provincial government refused to certify Sister Mary Beatrice to teach in Alberta until she had completed one year of study at the Calgary Normal School. Hence, Mother Ignatius transferred Sister Mary Margaret (Elizabeth) MacIsaac from Margaree Forks, Cape Breton, to St. Basil's, where she discovered that the school board had already hired a local replacement. So Sister Mary Margaret was restricted to substitute teaching. The second form of trouble came from separate school board members, St. Basil's school principal, the Alberta Teachers' Association (ATA), certain local citizens, and the provincial education authority. Because of a large surplus of teachers in the province, they all opposed licensing and hiring outsiders.[13] Sister Mary Anthony MacPhee thought that this was why a group of

Lethbridge citizens publicly criticized the teaching ability of certain sisters.[14] The sister annalist at St. Michael's Hospital reported a persisting agitation against the sisters teaching at St. Basil's: "Lethbridge ATA working strongly to upseat them, also many other anti-religionists writing Dept. of Education, one of the ringleaders being their principal."[15] However, enough support existed among Catholics, as well as from the bishop, that the sisters stayed. The Marthas themselves believed the children needed teaching sisters to help with their religious and character training. Added to the above difficulties were health problems that caused two sisters to withdraw from the Calgary Normal School in 1934.

In spite of the bumpy beginnings, two teaching sisters–Sister Mary Margaret MacIsaac and Sister M. Sylvester (Nora) Sullivan –would remain at St. Basil's for more than twenty years. When they were eventually transferred to a new school (Assumption Elementary) on the south side of Lethbridge in 1957, the parents and principal of St. Basil's made a valiant but unsuccessful bid to keep them. Time had worked a remarkable change in attitude. However endeared the sisters became to the local Catholics, the Lethbridge Separate School Board was slow to match their salaries with those of secular teachers. In 1954, sisters still received 75 percent of lay salaries, and only in 1969 did the board grant them equivalent pay.

Mineral Springs Hospital, Banff

To the northwest of Lethbridge about 270 kilometres, nestled in the magnificent Rocky Mountains and beside the Bow River, lay the town of Banff, Alberta. In 1883, the year the Canadian Pacific Railway (CPR) first snaked through the mountains, Dr. Robert G. Brett, a railroad physician, built a small cabin hospital there. Mineral hot springs with alleged curative properties had been discovered, and the Canadian government later declared the awe-inspiring region, promoted as "the Switzerland of Canada," a national park. Banff soon became widely known as a highly desirable tourist and health resort, and the CPR built a first-class hotel there in 1888 called the Banff Springs.

To meet the health needs of locals and tourists, Dr. Brett built a larger hospital early in the twentieth century on Spray

Avenue near the Bow River and named it the Brett Sanatorium. The government granted him the right to exploit the curative properties of the hot springs for those suffering from conditions such as arthritis and rheumatism by piping the mineral water into his sanatorium. Two wings of two stories each flanked the main three-storey section. His hospital provided patient accommodation (ninety-two beds), an operating room, an x-ray department with diathermy, hot mineral water baths and dressing rooms, hot pool and tub, a medical library, a large kitchen, and a dining room.

Banff resided in the western extremity of Bishop Kidd's Diocese of Calgary. This old friend of the Sisters of St. Martha, who had just brought them to Lethbridge, was not unaware of the needs of his Catholic flock, both resident and visiting, in the parish of St. Patrick's, Banff. Catholics probably represented about 10 percent of the town's population of nearly 3,000.[16] In a letter to Mother Ignatius in 1929, Bishop Kidd tagged on a Postscript: "I wish you were in a position to take charge of a Hospital and Sanatorium at Banff that will be for sale in the near future. The owner, Dr. Brett, former Lieutenant-Governor of Alberta, died a week ago. It will be sold for a very reasonable price, possibly sixty-five thousand. There are good opportunities there."[17]

To the bishop's delight, Mother Ignatius's general council accepted his challenge and at a cost of $58,000 assumed ownership in June 1930 when Mother Faustina and Mother Stanislaus arrived. Other sisters–Sister M. Augustine (Rebecca) Kennedy (administrator/superior, 1931-1937), Sister M. Annunciata (Philomena) Lawlor, Sister Mary Pauline (Mary Louise) MacNeil; Sister M. Boniface (Mary) MacDonald, and Sister Mary Anita (Jenette Gertrude) Chisholm–arrived shortly thereafter and began in earnest the cleaning and refurbishing, with some help from the Lethbridge sisters. The building had been closed for years, so after chasing out the packrats, and working with grit and determination for several weeks to rescue the building from its dilapidated state at a further expense of $23,000, the sisters had the hospital ready to open. They renamed it Mineral Springs Hospital and offered medical, surgical, and obstetrical services, and mineral baths. Bishop Kidd attended the opening on 14 July 1930 and reported to Mother Ignatius back in Nova

Scotia, "The residents were quite emphatic in expressing their pleasure in seeing the Sisters in charge."[18]

The sisters at Mineral Springs Hospital faced the same economic trials as those at St. Michael's Hospital, Lethbridge. Although their new institution enjoyed accreditation, some government funding, and the assistance of an unincorporated advisory board of representative town citizens, it opened as the worldwide depression shrivelled people's economic resources. Occupancy rates remained stubbornly low, charity cases unfortunately increased, and overhead expenses remained distressingly high. Support from public-spirited individuals and local businesses—donations of coal, food, and supplies—eased the hardship but in no way removed it. Sister May Mulvihill surmised: "For many months, particularly as the effects of the depression accelerated, the wisdom of having accepted the Banff hospital must have been seriously questioned by both Bishop Kidd and Mother M. Ignatius."[19]

Mineral Springs Hospital, Banff, Alberta. Administered by the Marthas from 1930.

The sisters fought to save their new mountain mission. They obtained cash donations and free international advertising from the CPR. Their promotional pamphlet trumpeted the breath-taking setting—"Fifty Switzerlands in One!"—and the marvellous curative properties of the hot mineral springs: "The Banff Mineral Springs Hospital has been opened by the Sisters of St. Martha to allow sufferers from all forms of rheumatic diseases, neuritis, painful and stiff joints and allied afflictions, to avail themselves of the curative treatments of the waters of this warm, health-giving spring throughout the year."[20] The national park supplied the mineral waters free, and the Department of the Interior, which had established relief camps nearby for unemployed men, paid the sisters to heal their sick and injured.

The sisters also urged the federal government to place convalescent soldiers in the Mineral Springs Hospital. Fortunately, the financial picture brightened in the mid-1930s as admissions increased. Then, in 1938 the sisters' monetary resources were substantially augmented by an arrangement clinched between Sister Superior, M. Anthony MacPhee and Dr. C.F. McGuffin of Calgary. Dr. McGuffin established and ran a physical therapy department at Mineral Springs that treated Alberta Workers' Compensation cases. The Second World War also contributed to the upswing in hospital finances, so that by 1942 the sisters were able to build a new three-storey staff residence and two years afterwards happily retire their original debt of $81,000.

Mineral Springs Hospital was a small but fascinating mission. About six sisters staffed it annually through the 1930s and 1940s. In 1947, over 750 patients were admitted, and that year the sisters and lay staff together numbered more than twenty. One staff member, Henry Covie, developed an especially close and long-lasting relationship with the sisters. Decades later in the 1970s, when admitted as a patient, he was asked for the name of his next of kin. He replied, "'The Sisters of St. Martha.'"[21] The advisory board had organized a medical staff in 1931, and it included a resident CPR physician, Dr. Dean Robinson, and several other doctors who were practising in the region. The Marthas in Banff served a fascinating succession of patients, including celebrities, who came from the four corners of the continent and beyond. Those from afar were lured to the resort by its majestic scenery, hot mineral springs, and healthy mountain air. Patients were commonly long-term convalescent cases or casualties of mountain climbing or skiing. In the late 1930s, two seriously wounded Doukhobor men, probably from the radical Sons of Freedom sect, were admitted in an emergency; they had killed several Mounties in a gunfight and died themselves later that day. One year an adventurous deer jumped through a window and smashed around in a doctor's office; and hungry bears occasionally nosed about the property. Sisters assigned to Banff found intriguing the dramatic setting, their hospital guests' diverse backgrounds, and the colourful wildlife of the Rocky Mountain region.

CANMORE, ALBERTA

Just as St. Michael's Hospital, Lethbridge, spawned a city teaching mission shortly after its founding, so Mineral Springs Hospital in Banff spawned a nearby mission in Canmore, a coal-mining town in the Bow Valley, twenty-three kilometres east of Banff. The CPR railway and the discovery of coal deposits had brought it into existence in the 1880s, and by 1891 it was flourishing. In 1930 the town's one thousand residents were racially diverse–Polish, Finnish, British, Ukranian, Russian, Italian, Czech, and Slovak. Their company housing was poor; some of the workers had become Communists or Communist sympathizers. Catholics composed about one-third of the town population, but most were "fallen away." The local parish priest, Father Francis J. Stefanski (1930-1937), found distressing the empty church pews and absence of religious observance. He wrote Mother Ignatius in 1933 and laid before her the lamentable religious state of Sacred Heart Parish–nominal Catholics, uncatechized children, mixed marriages, Protestant teachers in the local school, and the circulation of atheistic Communist propaganda. He knew the sisters in Banff and some had already intermittently helped him with parish work. So in 1933, Father Stefanski pleaded with Mother Ignatius to send sisters into his "God forsaken parish."[22] Being poor, he could only promise $12 monthly for ten months and the charity of his parishioners. However, he did offer the sisters his five-room rectory for use as a convent.[23]

At the urging of Bishop Kidd's episcopal successor, Bishop Peter Monahan, the congregation accepted Father Stefanski's offer. Sister Mary Anthony MacPhee and Sister Francis Teresa Herrgott received a warm parish welcome at their arrival on 3 March 1934. They undertook an ambitious range of activities–family visiting, the formation of youth and adult sodalities and sewing circles, the distribution of used clothing, as well as care of the church altar linens and helping with the choir. The sisters also worked once a week in Exshaw, a town with twelve Catholic families about fifteen miles east of Canmore and home to the Canada Cement Company. In 1942, five years after the Bishop of Calgary had bought the Canmore sisters a new convent, which the parish priest had appropriately named Mount Carmel,

Sister Leonard Marie (Frances) MacNeil opened a kindergarten in the dining room. The first Marthas in Canmore were especially concerned to salvage the Catholic faith of the children by fortifying them against Protestant influences.[24] Sister John de la Salle Fougere commented about the new teaching project: "This is going to mean a lot to us, perhaps not materially yet, but the people are very pleased."[25] Of course, where possible, they also encouraged lapsed adults back to the sacraments.

Over the years, the congregation usually assigned three Marthas to Canmore. At times, the general council threatened to close the mission because of personnel shortages, but the sisters remained, became close to the families and found aspects of the work rewarding. In 1941 a sister reported in the *Bethanite*: "When evening comes we are always glad to come back to our little convent, where the first ones home get the supper. It is a busy life, but we enjoy it, and even if the results are few and far between … we are content to know we are doing God's will and that others in the dim distant future may reap the harvest which we are trying to sow."[26] Although the Canmore sisters received good support from their sisters at Mineral Springs, the convent was isolated because the sisters did not drive, and their small numbers made community life difficult. They faced challenges in the local community too, for example, the influences of atheistic communism and anti-Catholic Protestantism, and ethnic tensions among Catholics themselves. The lack of dramatic religious results was also discouraging. The superior general's visitations frequently sought to lift up the heads that were drooping. Mother Ignatius wrote in 1945, "The majority of the people are very careless Catholics and no doubt you see little returns for your hard work."[27] However, the bishop, successive parish priests, and their parishioners in Canmore and Exshaw highly valued the sisters' work and presence.

St. Michael's Hospital, Broadview, Saskatchewan

In 1936 the Sisters of St. Martha expanded their small network of western missions into Saskatchewan. They opened several in the province, including a social work agency in Regina. In Broadview, an important meeting of town councillors and other folk convened in 1935. The prominent guests of the meeting–Archbishop Peter Monahan of Regina and Mother Ignatius–were addressed as follows: "We the representatives of the Broadview Town Council and the Broadview Hospital Association, together representing the entire body of citizens, cordially welcome you to the town of Broadview. We would respectfully urge you to consider the following reasons why we consider your proposed hospital should be located in Broadview."[28] The plea then outlined Broadview's many advantages: its population of nine hundred, its strategic location at a divisional point of the CPR's main line, its excellent train service, its good roads linking the town to surrounding districts, its good quality water supply, its sound financial condition in spite of the Depression, its promise for future development, its offer of a possible hospital building and site, and, finally, its citizens' singular enthusiasm for the congregation to locate there.

Broadview, created by the railway in 1882 and incorporated in 1907, sat on the flat prairies 154 kilometres east of Regina. Its satellite districts included Oakshela, Percival, Whitewood, Grayson, Kipling, and Grenfell, and its citizens were of varied ethnic and religious backgrounds. The town had incorporated in 1907, and only in 1934 had its Catholics established a parish. In its bid to obtain hospital services, the town formed a Hospital Association in 1935, and found itself competing with nearby Grenfell for the health services of the Sisters of St. Martha. However, Broadview won over its neighbouring competitor. Its Hospital Association offered the sisters a temporary rental property and money for renovations to help them get established in the town. The successful movers and shakers on behalf of Broadview were Archbishop Monahan, a native of Quebec who had come to admire the Marthas during his years (1932-1934) as bishop of Calgary, the local parish priest Rev. A.P. Ryan, and W.G. Wellbelove, a contractor who was also president of the Hospital Association. Each one contributed substantially to support the sisters' work through their early years in the prairie town.

The first sisters arrived in Broadview on 29 September 1936 to establish the much-anticipated hospital. Mother Faustina, the veteran "new-mission-pioneer," Sister M. Maurice (Hilda) Brocklehurst (superior), and Sister Mary Matthew (Mary Magdalena) Kurtz renovated the rental quarters to accommodate six patients and opened it on 22 October. Within five years, however, the sisters used three different facilities for their hospital. The first rental property was too small, failed to gain government approval and therefore did not qualify for support. Hence, in 1938, they purchased for $3,000 an eleven-acre property with a three-storey residence that did qualify for government assistance. Nonetheless, this building also soon proved inadequate. So, the congregation, at the urging of Sister M. Augustine Kennedy (superior, 1938-1941), borrowed $30,000 in 1940 and built a new and improved hospital on the property; the former hospital was converted into a staff and sisters' residence. The new single-storey brick facility had eighteen beds, a two-bed isolation department, an operating room, a case room, a laboratory, and an x-ray department.

Archbishop P.J. Monahan, 1933. He was responsible for drawing the Marthas to Saskatchewan in the 1930s.

Like their pioneering sisters in Lethbridge and Banff, the Broadview Marthas found their responsibilities varied and demanding. They worked with the advisory board of trustees (est. 1937) and medical staff to successfully run the institution and supervise its several departments. In the parish community, they visited Catholic families, directed the choir and taught catechism. Daily recreation and annual holidays and retreats were a wonderful release from the long hours and gruelling seven-day weeks working to fulfil both their hospital and religious duties. In 1940, five sisters worked at St. Michael's in Broadview, along with seven lay staff.[29] About one-half of their patients were native people from surrounding reservations, and their hospital bills were paid by the Department of Indian Affairs, a definite boon for hospital finances. The convent annals reveal the prairie flavour of the sisters' working environment: "A young man was brought in from the Kipling district who was badly mangled in a threshing machine. He died within five hours" (October 1943); "Thermometer registered 34 below" (March

1943). During one annual fall harvest, the annalist recorded: “Donations of vegetables, etc. have been coming in during the past week from the different country districts.”[30]

New Mission Assignment in Blairmore, Alberta

Back in 1928, when Bishop Kidd of the Diocese of Calgary had invited the Marthas to his spiritual vineyard, he wrote to Mother Ignatius about the Crow’s Nest Pass district in the Rocky Mountains of southwestern Alberta. The CPR mainline, southern section, passed through this area. He commented: “Blairmore [about 160 kilometres west of Lethbridge] is the centre of five towns, one strung after the other with a population altogether of between seven and eight thousand. Those are principally mining towns. Blairmore’s population is about two thousand, nearly one-half of whom is Catholic. They would be very pleased to help Sisters with a hospital.”[31] The string of towns in the Crow’s Nest included Frank, site of the famous 1903 Frank Slide, Coleman, Hillcrest, and Bellevue. Each community had suffered its share of mining disasters. Like Canmore, their peoples were of diverse nationalities. Bishop Kidd concluded his epistle: “You probably know some of the Catholic residents of Blairmore as a number are from Nova Scotia and students of St. Francis Xavier University. Some of them are prominent citizens down there.”[32] But the sisters just then had to decline his invitation to that area. Nevertheless, Catholic hopes for a hospital at Blairmore remained alive, and the congregation investigated, and even made a commitment in 1937 to operate one.[33] However, Mother Ignatius could not marshal the resources then; when the sisters did go to Blairmore two years later, they went as parish workers, not as nurses.

Actually, the first sisters to work in Blairmore had gone from Lethbridge in 1936 to help with religious vacation schools in the district parishes. But not until 1939, ten years after the initial request from Bishop Kidd, did the bishop and his parish priest, Michael Alphonsus Harrington, succeed in getting sisters to establish a convent there. Father Harrington, a graduate of St. Augustine’s Seminary, Toronto, knew the sisters who did housekeeping there, and he had also observed their impressive new hospital operation in Lethbridge. During his Blairmore years

(1926-1950), he established a long and happy relationship with the congregation that extended to his death in the 1970s in Kamloops, British Columbia. He was undoubtedly elated on 26 September 1939 when six Marthas arrived and opened a convent that they named St. Alphonsus in his honour.

The pioneers–Sister M. Thecla Price, Sister Joseph Helen (May Veronica) Mulvihill (superior), Sister Mary Anita Chisholm, Sister M. Gonzaga (Mary) Disano (known for her effective work with Italian parishioners), Sister Mary Regina (Margaret Ellen) MacDonnell, Sister M. Stephanie (Isabel) Cormier, Sister Mary Edward (Annie) Fraser, and Sister Mary Matthew Kurtz–really established a parish service centre in

Sister Edmund Marie (Theresa) Kurtz with kindergarten graduates, Blairmore, Alberta, 1948.

Blairmore. Their mission was more ambitious than the one in Canmore because it served a larger area and population. However, the sisters' aims and activities were similar: family visitations, youth work, choir direction, music lessons, a kindergarten (begun by Sister Mary Regina in December), cleaning of church linens and the rectory, and a daily meal for Father Harrington. One major goal they had was "to bring back to a forgotten God and the Church the poor, nominal Catholics."[34] In 1940 the Blairmore sisters reported to the congregation: "In general the reception of the Sisters in the various towns has been very good, although of course there have been embarrassing and unfortunate exceptions."[35] One stated the purpose of their family visiting: "To make the people feel that we are their friends. During these visits when we are trying to gain their friendship, religion is never mentioned unless they bring up the subject themselves. Perhaps it will be many years hence before we can hope to see the fruit of our present efforts."[36] The Blairmore Marthas found, just as their Canmore sisters did, that efforts to restore lapsed Catholics to active faith often proved disheartening. They remarked in 1942: "After two and a half years of almost constant visiting in the four towns which make up the Crow's Nest Pass, we wonder if our efforts are bearing any fruit or if we are simply wasting our time. However, the occasional ray of light shines through."[37] This "occasional ray of light" was enough to keep the congregation working in Blairmore and its neighbouring parishes for thirty years. The wonderful support of the local Catholic Women's League chapters, with their annual pantry showers for the sisters, and the thoughtful improvements in convent life arranged by Father Harrington, their "most generous benefactor," fortified the Martha commitment to the people of Crow's Nest.[38]

St. Peter's Hospital, Melville, Saskatchewan

In November 1940 the Sisters of St. Martha, now scattered across Canada on missions stretching from Sydney, Cape Breton, to Banff, Alberta, read the following announcement: "This is the voice of Saskatchewan, Station S-T. P-E-T-E-R'S, established June 29, 1940, with three horsepower, and very recently improved by the addition of one more horsepower."[39] The "horsepower" was, of course, provided by the sisters–Sister Daniel MacLellan (superintendent/superior); Sister Mary Claudia (Helen) Mason (kitchen); Sister Mary Annette (Isabel) MacDonald (nursing supervisor); and Sister John of Avila (Annie Basil) MacDonald (accountant). Their St. Peter's Hospital was the last hospital established by the congregation during its first important decade of going west. It was located in Melville, a town then recovering from years of severe drought and depression. The Grand Trunk Railway had given birth to the town in 1906, one year after Saskatchewan entered Confederation, and rapid growth brought town incorporation in 1909. In 1940, its citizens numbered about four thousand and, like in most prairie communities, they came from diverse ethnic backgrounds–English, Irish, Scottish, French, German, Polish, and Ukrainian. Melville was on the Canadian National Railway line, about 130 kilometres east of Regina, and functioned as an important service and marketing centre in the region.

Sister Daniel MacLellan and Sister M. Consolata (Catherine Rose) MacDonald arrived on 28 June 1940, the feast of St. Peter; thus the hospital name, to establish the hospital mission in Melville. The following day they assumed ownership of the fifteen-bed municipal hospital that had been erected in 1911. By 1940 the facility was in disrepair, supplies were scarce, and cockroaches and flies altogether too plentiful. Thus, the sisters were required to feverishly renovate and upgrade.[40] However, they

St. Peter's Hospital, Melville, Saskatchewan, opened by the Marthas in 1942. The convent is on the left, and on the right is the nurses' residence.

cherished plans to build a modern hospital. The motherhouse granted permission in 1941, and an advisory hospital board of leading male citizens provided assistance. Thus, a new $75,000, fifty-five-bed St. Peter's Hospital, funded through motherhouse contributions, a bond issue, and donations, opened on 28 May 1942. The impressive three-storey brick facility boasted all the departments required of a modern hospital. Local newspapers lavishly praised the sisters' new Melville institution. In 1945, it admitted 2,174 patients and had about five sisters on staff.

Unfortunately, it suffered serious short-term financial deficits in spite of provincial approval and government assistance.[41]

The sisters went to Melville, as they did to other western missions, on urgent invitation from local Catholics and their bishop. In some cases, and Melville was one of them, local citizens ignored religious differences in order to obtain basic institutional services, such as hospitals. In Melville and nearby Esterhazy, town residents had petitioned Bishop Monahan in 1938 to obtain the hospital services of the Marthas for them. Originally he hoped they would take on missions in both towns, but by 1940 he found another religious congregation to accept Esterhazy. As spokesman for the Melville residents, he forwarded their offer of the existing hospital and its equipment, as well as of free land for a new hospital, and stressed the broad citizens' consensus that the sisters should come. In urging the Marthas on, Archbishop Monahan in 1938 mustered all his diplomatic skills. Some of his urgings painted a rosy financial picture of the future; others bordered on ecclesiastical bullying. In 1940, he concluded an especially urgent letter to Mother Immaculata thus: "Why should we mistrust Divine Providence calling us to do the work assigned to us and for which your Sisters are well prepared?"[42] Mother Immaculata let Bishop Monahan know in her acceptance letter the sacrifice it required of her congregation to satisfy some of his demands: "We have many needs in the East which we are overlooking for the present in order to meet the needs of the West."[43]

Religious Vacation Schools on the Prairies

From 1933, Marthas in the west could be seen during summer months moving out from their missions and roving to and fro among neighbouring towns and rural parishes. They were generously responding to the Calgary Diocesan Council for Religious Instruction's request for help to run religious vacation schools on the prairies. Five sisters pioneered in the arduous adventure: Sister John de la Salle Fougere, Sister Mary Anita Chisholm, Sister M. Anthony MacPhee, Sister Mary Raphael Watt, and Sister Mary Colette (Sarah Margaret) Beaton. It worked like this. Parish priests would tender a request for sisters to the superior at St. Michael's Hospital, Lethbridge, who then scheduled and assigned the sister catechetical instructors. The sisters travelled and worked in pairs, using transportation and facilities–often makeshift and primitive–provided by grateful local parish priests. One sister remembered that they were welcomed into the parishes "with great kindness and true western hospitality."[44] Five sisters taught in three locations in 1933 Raymond, Taber, and Carstairs/Crossfield. By 1953, thirteen Marthas operated religious vacation schools in eleven parishes, attended by about 1,325 prairie children. Usually the schools lasted one or two weeks and enrolled anywhere from a mere handful to over one hundred students. From 1952 to 1955, several sisters accepted a challenging religious vacation school assignment each summer on a native reserve in Brown-ing, Montana.

Sister M. Gonzaga (Mary) Disano with vacation school students at Grassy Lake, Alberta, 1930s.

Through the years, the travelling Martha religion teachers developed considerable expertise and resource materials. At St. Michael's Hospital, Lethbridge, in 1938, the annalist recorded, "Preparation for Religious Vacation Schools. The old vegetable room has been changed into a room for the books, pictures, charts and other material needed in these schools. Bishop Carroll paid this room a visit and liked it. He thought our material was very well organized."[45] The sisters' western experience and developing expertise would benefit sisters in the east when they were asked to teach catechism in isolated parishes within the Diocese of Antigonish. An anonymous poem that appeared in *The Bethanite* in 1938 revealed features of the Martha experience and their perceptions of the prairie summer school circuit:

Drowsy, weary, I sit down
Musing in this little Western town
Where more wealth than faith abound
Where not much of God is found.

Eighteen children is our lot,
To whom the Word of God is taught ...
They know not much of God,
Who watches from His heavenly throne.
Some have never heard of Mary,
God's own mother, pure and fair,
Or of dear Saint Joseph
With his foster father care.

Dearest Jesus hear our prayer
In favour of this little Western town
That when next we come ateaching
May both faith and wealth abound
And may much of God be found.[46]

Evidently the sisters found the travel and daily classes draining, and the lack of religious knowledge and commitment among children and parents distressing. Back at their home missions, the temporary loss of sisters to the religious vacation schools exerted extra work pressure on those left behind. However, the sisters' schools were certainly an adventure, as well as a valued service, and they would conduct them for over thirty years in the Canadian west.

The Significance of Going West

With the vow of obedience, each Martha surrendered the right to control where she would serve God. Willingly or not, some found themselves assigned, in the 1930s, to the Canadian west. It was a huge cultural, geographical, and climatic leap for them. On the prairies and in the mountains they travelled vast distances, admired dramatic scenery and witnessed wild climatic changes–blizzards, hail and electric storms, torrential rains, parching droughts, chinooks, and arctic cold. One sister wryly remarked on a dust storm in Saskatchewan: "From a window in the Hostel we viewed every farm within forty miles go by at a rate of 90 miles an hour, and we ourselves felt that we had enough dust within us to make a good-sized ranch."[47] The Marthas often commented on the great ethnic and religious diversity of the prairie communities. They were likewise startled by the widespread indifference to religion among Catholics in the west and the hard drive for material success.[48] Hence, they viewed western Canada as a vast mission field. In 1931, a Lethbridge sister declared, "Our main object in coming here was to establish a centre of Catholic influence, with the hope of bringing back to our Holy Faith at least a few of the many unfortunate ones who have strayed away since coming to the West."[49] The western sisters, of course, experienced great isolation. However, as their network of missions expanded, they often exchanged visits and made retreats and vacations together. Sisters also made close friends with lay staff, parishioners, and others in their local prairie communities.

Group of "western" sisters enjoying the Rocky Mountains.

The western missions called forth *The Bethanite*, a journal that bore congregational news to each sister member. The first sign of its dilatory birth appeared in the motherhouse annals in December 1929: "We are getting out a type written make believe magazine to send Mother [Ignatius]. The name of it is *The Bethanite*, published free of charge. It is about the size of the Ave Maria with a very fine Christmas design on the cover. The artist designer is Sister Mary of Good Counsel; Editor-in-Chief Sister John Baptist."[50] The sister editor stated her purpose: "that of a happy Christmas messenger carrying its light burden of love and cheer to our Mothers and Sisters who are 'in fields a-far' beyond the Western Prairies."[51] Mother Ignatius enjoyed the "light burden of love and cheer"; in 1930 she directed Sister John Baptist Cameron, general secretary, to make the literary piece a periodical. Although the Depression appeared to frustrate Mother Ignatius's directive for about five years,[52] *The Bethanite* eventually became an important bearer of congregational news to its far-flung missions. With its characteristicly light, upbeat, optimistic, and pious mood, the "Official Organ of the Sisters of St. Martha" served to amuse, entertain, edify, and inform.[53] As the Marthas stretched across the country in the 1930s, *The Bethanite*, along with circulars, letters, official visitations, telegraph messages, and telephone calls, maintained and strengthened the bonds of sisterhood. Its regular fare included poems, lists of reappointments, news of sicknesses and deaths, mission reports, humorous anecdotes, and reports about celebrations, special visitors, and events at the motherhouse. And woe betide those missions that failed to make a regular contribution to the pages of *The Bethanite*. Sister John Baptist poetically chided the western sisters in 1943: "Wake up sleepy West, write notes sleepy West. Get off your little nest, do your very best. In type or in ink, iron out that little kink. Get your fingers going smart, or with me you will part."[54]

For the congregation overall, going west in the 1930s had created a financial crisis. Because the Great Depression set in shortly after they established, at great expense, the first mission in Lethbridge–St. Michael's Hospital–the congregation found itself tottering on the brink of insolvency. Great sacrifice and resourcefulness, along with patience from creditors and support from benefactors, sustained them, but barely. Hospitals, of course, were the congregation's most expensive type of mission, and they eventually owned five in the west. Fortunately, by 1937 the Marthas had regained a strong financial position.[55] Western missions, moreover, greatly increased the congregation's transportation costs, both in time and money, as well as its difficulties in communication. Before air travel, many sisters became intimate with the long, wearisome pilgrimage by rail that linked Antigonish, Truro, Montreal, Winnipeg, Calgary, and Banff. Miscommunication because of the distances caused Mother Faustina grief and cost the congregation about $3,000 in the 1930s when it agreed to open a mission in Kelowna, British Columbia. While Mother Faustina met and negotiated with authorities in Kelowna, the motherhouse assumed that financial arrangements were other than they were, and the proposed mission failed to materialize. Mother Faustina wrote to Mother Ignatius: "You can imagine how sick at heart a person can feel, when something like this comes up thousands of miles from headquarters, and no way of knowing what the different authorities, East and West, really wish or mean to do."[56]

Although going west brought headaches, the congregation did realize benefits over time. The western missions became much stronger financially during and after the Second World War. Moreover, some young prairie women (about thirty-four by 1960) came to admire the Marthas and joined the congregation. Bethany received the first applicant from the west in December 1930.[57] Then too, the Marthas were gratified by the obvious and appreciated contributions their western missions made to local health care, education, and parish life. As in the east, they provided important local services, and created a legacy of goodwill through their selflessness and willingness to sacrifice.

While the congregation's incursion into western Canada limited what it could do in the Maritimes, the sisters helped to strengthen the national English-speaking Catholic network that developed as the country matured. It also demonstrated the "conspicuous influence" of the Diocese of Antigonish on that network.[58] Western bishops and parish priests faced immense work in extending and invigorating Catholicism in the west, where they faced religious indifference, new immigrants of diverse background, and the growth of competing Protestant denominations. They were well aware that religious congregations and priests from central and eastern Canada could help them win their spiritual battles. The Sisters of St. Martha, a young, energetic Nova Scotian congregation,[59] were part of the Catholic army that went west in the 1930s. They believed that the needs were great and that they should devote a least some of their resources to the mission fields of western Canada. Their only regret? That limited resources forced them to refuse most of the requests they received from church leaders and parish priests in the region.

Notes

1 Gerald Friesen, *The Canadian Prairies: A History* (Toronto: University of Toronto Press, 1987), p. 301.

2 Bishop John T. Kidd to Mother Ignatius, 22 August 1928, F5,S34,SS17,f8,b92.
3 Bethany Annals, 22 August 1927, F6,S1,SS1,f1,b106.
4 Newspaper clipping, 9 September 1931, F9,S6,SS3,f6,b148.
5 Reminiscences of Sister Anne Fougere, F9,S1,SS2,f5,b143.
6 Bishop Monahan to F.J. Bell, 10 April 1933, Bishop Monahan Papers, Archives of the Diocese of Calgary, Catholic Pastoral Centre, Calgary, Alberta.
7 Bishop John T. Kidd to Mother Ignatius, 10 December 1936, F15,S2,SS1,f2,b175.
8 Bethany Annals, 8 October 1933, F6,S1,SS1,f2,b107.
9 Quoted in *Sixty Years*, pp. 28-9.
10 St. Michael's Hospital Annals, 22 July 1937, F9,S1,SS1,f2,b142.
11 St. Michael's Hospital Personnel List, 1929-1988, F9,S1,SS2,f7,b145.
12 *Lethbridge Herald*, 13 December 1941.
13 J.T. Ross, Deputy Minister of Education to Michael Flynn, Lethbridge Separate School District, 7 September 1933, F5,S25,SS6,f1,b162.
14 Sister M. Anthony to Mother Ignatius, 16 January 1934, ibid.
15 St. Michael's Hospital Annals, 14 September 1933, F9,S1,SS1,f1,b142.
16 *Census of Canada 1971,* 1.1:2-106.
17 Bishop Kidd to Mother Ignatius, 1 October 1929, F5,S34,SS17,f8,b92.
18 Bishop Kidd to Mother Ignatius, 15 July 1930, ibid.
19 Sister May Mulvihill, "History of the Sisters of St. Martha," I:5:85.
20 Promotional Pamphlet, n.d., F11,S1,SS2,f6,b159.
21 Mineral Springs Hospital Annals, 1979, F11,S1,SS1,f2,b159.
22 Bishop Carroll to Mother Ignatius, 29 August 1945, F5,S34,SS17,f3,b92.
23 Rev. Francis J. Stefanski to Mother Ignatius, 12 February 1933, F48,S1,SS1,f6,b241.
24 *The Bethanite*, February 1935.
25 Sister John de la Salle to Mother Immaculata, 21 October 1942, F48,S1,SS1,f6,b241.
26 *The Bethanite*, March 1941.
27 Visitation Report, Mount Carmel Convent, 11 November 1945, p. 1, F48,S1,SS1,f3,b241.
28 Speech to Archbishop Peter Monahan, Mother Ignatius and Sisters, 1935, F15,S2,SS1,f1,b175.
29 St. Michael's Hospital Statistics, Broadview, F15,S1,SS2,f2,b175.
30 St. Michael's Hospital Annals, F15,S1,SS2,b175.

31 Bishop Kidd to Mother Ignatius, 30 March 1928, F37,S1,SS1, f5,b234.
32 Ibid.
33 St. Michael's Hospital, Lethbridge, Annals, July 1937, F9,S1,SS1,f1,b142.
34 Mother Immaculata, Visitation Report, 23 October-2 November 1940, F37,S1,SS2,f3,b234.
35 *The Bethanite*, VII, March-April 1940, p. 21.
36 St. Alphonsus Convent Annals, Sept/Oct. 1939.
37 *The Bethanite*, March 1942, p. 10.
38 St. Alphonsus Convent List of Benefactors, F37,S1,SS1,f5,b234.
39 *The Bethanite*, VII, November 1940, pp. 9-10.
40 Bethany Annals, 27 May-12 October 1940, F6,S1,SS1,f7,b107.
41 St. Peter's Hospital, Statistics Data, F13,S1,SS2,f1,b169.
42 Archbishop Monahan to Mother Immaculata, 26 February 1940, F13,S2,SS1,f1,b170.
43 Mother Immaculata to Archbishop Monahan, 16 March 1940, F5,S34,SS17,f12,b93.
44 Sister Nora Sullivan, "Religious Vacation Schools in Western Canada," April 1984, p. 2, F5,S26,SS2,f1,b64.
45 St. Michael Hospital Annals, 15 June 1938, F9,S1,SS1,f2,b142.
46 *The Bethanite*, 1938.
47 St. Martha Hostel, Regina, Historical Note, F18,S1,SS2,f1,b177.
48 *The Bethanite*, III, June 1936, p. 3.
49 Sister Anthony MacPhee's Appeal, 1931, F9,S3,SS1,f1,b144.
50 Bethany Annals, 15 December 1929, F6,S1,SS1,f1,b106.
51 *The Bethanite*, I Christmas 1929.
52 *The Bethanite*, II February 1935.
53 Ibid.
54 *The Bethanite*, X September 1943, p. 1.
55 Bethany Annals, 28 July 1937, F6,S1,SS1,f5,b107.
56 Mother Faustina to Mother Ignatius, 30 November 1930, F9,S3,SS1,f1,b144.
57 Bethany Annals, 22 December 1930, F6,S1,SS1,f1,b106.
58 Mark G. McGowan, "Conspicuous Influence: The Diocese of Antigonish and the Development of the Canadian Catholic Church, 1844-1994," pp. 1 and 16-18. Presented to the Rev. A.A. Johnston Memorial Conference, 19-20 August 1994, St. Francis Xavier University, Antigonish, Nova Scotia.
59 The average age of the perpetually professed in 1931 was forty; their ages ranged from twenty-three to sixty-seven. List of Sisters under Perpetual Vows, 1931, F5,S8,SS1,f1,b6.

A Martha doing home visitation, 1940s.

Chapter Seven

A New Apostolate: Social Work

Going west was a major pioneering adventure for the Sisters of St. Martha during the 1930s, but it was not the only one. While they established a scattered network of new missions in western Canada, they also began new works in eastern Canada. In the mid-1930s when Angus L. MacDonald, a Roman Catholic and graduate of St.F.X., led Nova Scotia's Liberal government, the congregation moved into parish social work. And even before that, the Marthas became more deeply involved in a closely related apostolate during those harsh economic times–adult education that aimed at spurring local economic development. Beginning in the 1930s, the Marthas made substantial contributions in adult education and social work, and these new ventures would, in turn, shape and influence them.

Early Forays into Community Development

Many Maritime farming, fishing, and industrial communities suffered intense economic hardship during the 1920s. Often Maritimers decided to abandon their home communities and seek better times in the larger urban centres of New England and central Canada. In the Diocese of Antigonish, concerned clergy held annual conferences at St. Francis Xavier University to discuss ways of strengthening community life in their region. The motherhouse annalist recorded in October 1925: "The Rural Conference closed yesterday and it was a wonderful success–the best they ever had. They were all of one mind–and that a very progressive one."[1] Among the many progressive proposals considered by these rural and industrial conferences was a plan in 1926 for the Sisters of St. Martha to establish a school of home economics at their motherhouse. Although Bishop Morrison had vetoed this plan in favour of home economics training at Mount St. Bernard College, the Marthas did undertake home economics fieldwork with women in certain Pictou and Antigonish county communities in the late 1920s.

In 1930, St.F.X. established a department of extension.[2] The new, ambitious program was directed by Dr. Moses Coady, a great friend of the Marthas and the person who had orchestrated their first work in public rural education at Margaree Forks, Cape Breton, just five years earlier. Coady proposed to help the primary producers of the region–farmers, fishermen, miners, and lumbermen–achieve "the good and abundant life." He and his fledgling department staff inaugurated a program of adult education through economic cooperation. The study club, or small communal study/discussion group, became a central technique and many of them soon became the nucleus of purchasing, producer, and consumer cooperatives. Dr. Coady's adult education program struck while the iron was hot, for many Maritime communities were desperate for ways to upgrade their impoverished standard of living.

The Marthas at Bethany were privy to extension happenings at St.F.X., and Dr. Coady and others involved with the new undertaking were frequent visitors to Bethany. In February 1930 the annalist noted Coady's return from a fact-finding tour about adult education which took him across Canada and into the United States: "Dr. Coady arrived in Antigonish today, chock full of progressive ideas."[3] Another typical entry reported, "Dr. Coady gave us a wonderful lecture last night on cooperation. We were all so enthusiastic over it that we found it hard to go through [the] ordinary routine of going to bed after the lecture was over."[4] Revs. Michael Gillis, John R. MacDonald (by then the spiritual director and confessor of the congregation's novitiate), and Jimmy Tompkins also visited often at Bethany and talked progress; they were well-respected by the sisters and influential. The sisters imbibed the philosophy of extension through these talks and adopted some of the department's methods, such as the study club. In addition, Marthas, such as Sister John Baptist Cameron, occasionally helped Coady with writing and typing.[5] However, the relationship between the St.F.X. extension department and the congregation went beyond this, for in the mid-1930s, two sisters were assigned to work in Dr. Coady's extension office.

In 1931 the rural conference at St.F.X. had called for the organization of study clubs among women, and cooperation with women's agencies, for example, the local Catholic Women's League and Women's Institute chapters. A year later, Dr. Coady was consulting the sisters, such as Mother Faustina and Sister John Baptist Cameron, about books and suggestions for women's study clubs.[6] Then, in August 1933, Mother Ignatius appointed Sister Marie Michael (Sarah) MacKinnon to extension. The Bethany annalist recorded this development:

> *We had a meeting at the hospital today to discuss the forming of Women's Study Clubs in the Extension Department under the direction of Sister Marie Michael. Dr. Coady, A.B. MacDonald, Katherine Thompson (sec'y of Extension Dept.), Sister John Baptist and Sister Marie Michael attended the meeting. A program was outlined. Sister Marie Michael will take up her duties next week at a salary of $1000 per annum.*[7]

Sister Marie Michael was from Father Michael Gillis's parish of Boisdale, Cape Breton. She had studied home economics in Quebec, and then entered the congregation. In 1933, she graduated from St.F.X. and was awarded the Governor General's medal for the highest aggregate grade in her class. Her assignment at extension was to develop a women's program, but neither Coady nor his assistant director, A.B. MacDonald, gave her a detailed blueprint. She later recalled that Coady created an "environment of freedom and trust, and of support ... which gave us a confidence we should never otherwise have had."[8] Sister Marie Michael's duties were manifold: organizing women's study clubs, editing the woman's page in the department's bimonthly *Extension Bulletin*, writing and giving speeches, participating at conferences, and helping with the extension department library. Extension reported that "Within one year, about three hundred women's study clubs had examined problems in homemaking, health, rural recreation, handicrafts, and cooperative organizations."[9] Later, Sister Marie Michael would earn a library science degree and work as the extension librarian from 1947 to 1957. Patrons had warm recollections of her hospitality. One wrote, "[Sister Marie Michael's] library was always a joyous place. When borrowers came to town, they received not only books but also a traditional Scots welcome, a cup of tea, no matter how busy she was. The Extension Library was always a mecca for home-sick foreign students and for many of the university professors."[10]

Her sisters at Bethany sometimes had fun with her new role. They knew that Dr. Coady and his extension staff were sometimes accused of radicalism. During an evening of recreation at Bethany, the novices in 1934 amused the professed sisters by staging a mock trial of Sister Marie Michael. She was accused of "spreading seeds of communism throughout the country and trying to form a Soviet Government"; she was found guilty and sentenced to judge a subsequent debate.[11]

A second Martha was assigned to extension in 1935. Sister Anselm (Irene) Doyle, a twenty-two-year old native of Melford, Inverness County, Cape Breton, had joined the Marthas in 1930; in 1935 she completed a BSc in Home Economics at St.F.X. Like Sister Marie Michael, who remembered that her new colleague "could more than hold her own in any skirmish that might occur," Sister Anselm's duties were manifold; they included secretarial work, fieldwork, and countless other tasks that cropped up daily.[12] Both sisters would have long and fruitful associations with St.F.X.'s extension program as they worked with women in nutrition, handicrafts, and cooperation; their emphasis was on rejuvenating rural life. They found the extension office a stimulating, and exciting place to work. The office staff developed a strong spirit of family and cooperation. And Coady, who valued the opinions and contributions of all, male and female, regularly appeared in a state of excitement and exhilaration over promising new ideas and developments. His enthusiasm was infectious.[13] All these connections, both formal and informal, between the St.F.X. extension office and the congregation affected the sisters. No doubt it developed among them broad social concerns, new types of skills, and intimacy with Maritime people and their economic and social problems.

The Canso Welfare Bureau

The sisters' new adult education skills and concerns were demonstrated in another project they undertook in the early 1930s. The Bethany annals reported in November 1932: "Dr. Tompkins of Canso was here today negotiating for Sisters to take over some sort of social and welfare bureau in Canso. Mother Gen. spent a hectic day."[14] Since 1923, Father Jimmy Tompkins had been parish priest of Canso, an old fishing community in Chedabucto Bay on the easternmost tip of mainland Nova Scotia. Between 1881 and 1894, transatlantic cables made Canso a major communications link between North America and Europe. In 1901 it incorporated, and by 1931 its population numbered close to 1,600.[15] Tompkins was Dr. Coady's cousin and, like him, was deeply committed to the region's social and economic revitalization. The restless "Father Jimmy" deplored the poverty and hopelessness he discovered in Canso and its neighbouring communities–Fox Island, Queensport, and Little Dover. He became a voice for, in his words, "the forgotten men and the forgotten women of this part of the world." In 1927, on the sixtieth anniversary of the Canadian Confederation, Canso created, as he put it, "a vigorous howl" that brought its plight to the attention of politicians. Later he reflected, "I can flatter myself that I had very considerable to do with arranging the music of the howl."[16] He also had a great deal to do with goading the fisherfolk themselves into thought and action to improve their lot; by the early 1930s they had created several fishing cooperatives.[17]

In late 1932, when Tompkins visited Bethany, he was orchestrating another movement in favour of Canso, and one which he fervently hoped would involve the Sisters of St. Martha as major players. He used his considerable skills in fundraising, honed while serving as vice-president of St.F.X. (1907-1922), to convince a retired and childless couple in Canso (Mr. and Mrs. Albert Sampson) to donate $10,000 in bonds to the congregation so it could establish a welfare bureau there. The Marthas accepted the Tompkins proposal, along with the money, and purchased two double houses from the Western Union Telegraph Company. They rented one house and renovated the other as a convent and welfare centre to serve Canso and its surrounding missions.

It became known as the Canso Welfare Bureau. Thus, Father Jimmy had successfully coaxed the sisters into a new type of ministry, namely community social work.[18]

Mother Faustina, who had recently been employed establishing hospital missions at Lethbridge and Mineral Springs, was once again called on to blaze the trail, this time in isolated Canso. She left the motherhouse to arrange for the new opening, along with Sister Maria Concepta (Helen) Fougere, on 29 December 1932. Father Jimmy was anxious that a library be part of the sisters' welfare bureau, so Mother Faustina appealed widely and successfully for book donations. Tompkins himself gave hundreds of his own books to help form the nucleus of the convent lending library. While Mother Faustina, as founding superior, became more familiar with the people and their needs, she consulted widely and organized services for the area. And as others became aware of the sisters' work there, they generously donated cash, free services, food, clothing, furniture, and transportation. The Sampsons remained especially supportive.[19]

Canso Welfare Bureau, operated by the Marthas from 1933 to 1962.

The four pioneer sisters–Mother Faustina, Sister Maria Concepta, Sister Denis Marie (Mary Margaret) Mulcahey, and Sister M. Vincentia (Eleanor Monica) Doyle–discovered urgent needs in Canso: many people were no strangers to poverty, so material relief was often required; children needed training in Christian doctrine; and the poor (in spirit and possessions) and the sick had to be visited. The sisters worked with youth in sodalities and garden clubs. Then, following the St.F.X. extension department's philosophy of self-help, the Marthas worked to revive traditional home industries so women could improve their material circumstances. Mother Faustina reported in 1936:

Our handicraft work is going splendidly. Nineteen knitting groups functioned regularly all winter, and a great deal of good work was done. Nine looms are now in operation, four in the Convent and five placed in private houses in the surrounding districts. Blankets are being made, also suiting for men and women, and everyone is busy. Our Sister weaver [Sister Vincentia] goes from place to place supervising the working of the looms, as well as keeping the ones going in the house—so there are not many idle moments. We plan on having a large handicraft exhibition in the fall. Our library, too, is growing and is as popular as ever.[20]

Evidently, the sisters Encouraged the women to better themselves and their communitites by offering them the necessary skills, equipment, publicity, and encouragement wherever they could.

The Canso Marthas also undertook choral work and piano instruction in the 1930s. Sister Mary Raphael Watt, who had studied at the Toronto Conservatory of Music and was a licensed music instructor, taught its piano repertoire to interested students. In 1940 and 1941, she succeeded in luring its founder, Sir Ernest MacMillan, on the long adventure from Toronto to Canso, where he examined her students. Hence, Canso became one of the first Maritime centres to offer the Toronto Conservatory program. Even some Protestants, and there were those in Canso who disdained Catholicism, voiced their appreciation for the Marthas' efforts to raise the standards of music in "a culturally impoverished neighbourhood." So when news spread in 1944 of Sister Mary Raphael's impending transfer to another mission, it sparked an outcry and a petition asking the mother superior to reconsider this decision.[21] Remarkably, Sister Raphael would still have music pupils until she was eighty-six years old. Later, in the 1940s and 1950s, sisters such as Sister Margaret Mary (Mary Wilhemina) Hervé,

Sister Mary Raphael (Eileen) Watt giving music instruction.

would teach music, crafts, or academic subjects in the Canso district schools.

While always a small mission of the congregation, usually not requiring more than four or five sisters, the Canso Welfare Bureau was a significant venture in social welfare, parish work, and adult education.[22] In a way, the Marthas laboured there as an arm of the newly established St.F.X. extension department and tried, along with the pastor and extension fieldworkers, to make accessible to all the "good and abundant life." Their resources were meagre, since much of their early work was among the poor. However, the motherhouse, benefactors like the Sampsons, and government agencies did augment local sources of income. In 1934, revenues came from rent, the sale of milk, church laundry, entertainments, donations, sale of goods, sale of a bond, and a loan from the motherhouse. In addition, Mother Faustina occasionally borrowed money from St.F.X., and in 1933 she received a training grant from the Carnegie Corporation of New York.[23] Things were never easy for the sisters in Canso. In 1953 the canonical visitor, delegated by the bishop to visit his parishes and congregations every five years, commented crisply: "Hard mission; heroic sisters. Housekeeper lonesome." In spite of the difficulties, the Marthas went there, at Father Tompkins' urging, to do "anything that needs to be done." For what they did do through the decades, they received praise and admiration from both the community and its observers.

Formal Parish Social Work in Cape Breton

In addition to their community development work, the sisters were drawn in the mid-1930s into more formal parish social work, ministering to the numberless casualties of economic, family, and personal distress. Of course, the congregation already had an admirable track record by 1935 of counselling, helping the needy, visiting families, and assisting orphans and unwed mothers. However, the Great Depression, with its widespread unemployment and crippling financial distress, provoked and heightened family problems. There appeared increased incidents of inadequate diet, poor health, overcrowding, loss of independence and self-respect, indebtedness, eviction, transiency, and loss of faith. The stop-gap, piecemeal efforts of government and voluntary agencies failed to meet the desperate needs of many people, so parish priests and church leaders felt compelled to help fill the void. In Calgary, Bishop Monahan decided to establish a social service centre. He persuaded Mother Ignatius to send two sisters–Sister Baptista Maria (Catherine) Macdonald and Sister Mary Alexandria (Jane) MacKenzie–in 1933 to the School of Social Work at the University of Toronto. Monahan expected them to set up his proposed Calgary centre after the completion of their studies. However, the Vatican interfered; it transferred Monahan to the Archdiocese of Regina in 1935 and so his Calgary plan came to naught.[24]

In Sydney, Cape Breton, Father Ronald C. MacGillivray of Sacred Heart Parish and Father James F. MacIsaac of St. Theresa's Parish were dismayed by the escalating impact of the Depression on families in the steel and coal mining industries. Outmigration was no longer a solution to economic distress and relief from governments in the Maritimes was limited.[25] They concluded that private parish efforts were necessary to supplement the work of the city's relief office. Many people in the urban, industrial area (with its population of about 10,000) and the rural hinterland urgently needed help. Therefore the parish priests and laity cooperated to form, on 10 November 1935, the Catholic Charities and Welfare Association. Thanks to Mother Ignatius, two sisters–Sister Baptista Maria Macdonald, who had recently graduated from Toronto's School of Social Work, and Sister Joseph Helen Mulvihill–started the new agency and established an office in the nurses' residence at the congregation's Sydney hospital, St. Rita. A board of directors composed of the two parish priests, lay people, and sisters administered the new social work agency. Sister Baptista Maria, as the field secretary, reported regularly to the board on her activities, and volunteer collectors made quarterly parish fundraising drives to aid the sisters' work.

Catholic Charities of Sydney tried to encourage "community improvement" and "to assimilate and adapt all the resources within the community for the welfare of the family in order that it may maintain its integrity."[26] Its program was broadly conceived; the board minutes reveal the range of topics discussed–the need for religious instruction in the schools, recreation for young people, youth organizations and summer camps, church attendance, employment opportunities, economic relief, alcohol abuse, and housing needs. The board was the fundamental support for the sisters, providing money, encouragement, and volunteer assistance. And the sisters often worked closely with other groups, such as doctors, lawyers, the parish women's council, priests, the municipal relief office, the Children's Aid Society, the Department of Social Welfare, the Red Cross, the city police, the juvenile court, and Alcoholics Anonymous. In spite of their broad program, they found that material relief was the central issue for many families during the Great Depression. Therefore, satisfaction of urgent needs for clothing, housing, food, and money absorbed most of the social workers' and the board's time. For decades afterward, the public concluded that Catholic Charity organizations were merely private relief agencies. Sister Joseph Helen, who assisted Sister Baptista Maria, reflected years later: "The many hours the social workers devoted to other problems, frequently without tangible results, were scarcely understood or appreciated."[27] Some families never resorted to the agencies for counselling, because they considered them nothing more than organizations that provided "handouts."

The sister social workers travelled by bus or on foot, and, in obedience to their rule, always in twos. Of course, they held regular office hours when clients could visit. After several months, Sister Baptista Maria found the work varied and vast, and it helped that the parishioners were friendly and supportive.[28] When families or old-age pensioners were unable to manage their own financial affairs, she found herself administering their resources. At times she acted as an advocate. For example, in a case where Dominion Steel planned to evict a family from company housing, she arranged a two-month extension. At other times, she was a mediator, trying to salvage a marriage that threatened to fly apart. She was also very frequently a relief agent, for example, to a family when the father had to be hospitalized. Another family who had lost their wife and mother came for her help to find a housekeeper. The sisters regularly supervised children in paid foster homes. They also acted as an employment referral agency, helping unemployed and transient persons to find work. Then there was the religious work organizing parish sodalities, preparing children for first communion, and teaching catechism.[29] The Great Depression did not bring unemployment for the Marthas!

Religious faith inspired and directed the Martha pioneer social workers. The example of Christ, beliefs about the value of each individual being made in the image of God and redeemed by Christ, the membership of each in the mystical body of Christ, and the divinely granted free agency of each person, inspired the sisters to compassion, to respect the worth of all, and to allow each client to determine his or her own future. The Marthas' Catholic convictions about the sanctity of the family, and the importance of devout religious practice and upright morality, compelled them to work to keep families intact and to strengthen their religious commitments and moral standards. They believed that religious-spiritual problems were at the root of many family and individual difficulties. Where families or individuals needed material help, the sisters tried to give relief promptly, adequately, and confidentially.[30] Through counselling about employment opportunities or financial management, they encouraged the indigent to become self-supporting and independent. The sisters gave help based on need, not on the perceived worth of the recipients. One wrote, "We have tried to pattern our methods on those of Christ, Who was after all the first social worker the world ever knew, and whose methods of case work would jolt many a modern mind."[31]

War in 1939 altered the work for the sister social workers in Sydney. It reduced unemployment and therefore the numbers requiring material relief. However, family problems multiplied. Special difficulties were created by hasty wartime marriages, by absent father-soldiers who sometimes never returned home, by the increased burdens mothers faced when they entered the paid workforce and left unsupervised children at home, by the increased number of common-law unions, by infidelity on the part of either partner during the extended separations required by military service, and by children born out of wedlock. In 1944 the sisters' social work caseload in Sydney had mushroomed to the point where St. Theresa's Parish required a separate agency and full-time social worker. Sister Joseph Helen Mulvihill was the pioneer (1944-1948) who established the new Catholic Charities and Welfare Association for that parish.

That same year, Father Leo B. Sears orchestrated the formation of a social work agency in Holy Redeemer Parish, Whitney Pier, called the Family Welfare Association. Since 1935 the sister social workers from Catholic Charities, Sydney, had visited families in Whitney Pier twice a week. "The Pier" was an ethnically diverse urban area close to the steel plant. With the new set-up, Sister John Hugh (Lauretta Mary) Robertson worked out of the church basement office and was assisted by a board of directors and a women's council; she would serve that parish for fifteen years.[32] The staggering burden of work forced the Cape Breton social workers to demand a clarification of their roles within the parishes in 1944. Priests found the social workers convenient sources of labour for help with their many parish duties. Hence, the sister social workers and parish priests, along with representatives of the congregation, met in Cape Breton to clarify and underscore that family welfare–and not sodalities, religious vacation schools, etc.,–was their first responsibility.

The Social Work Scene Expands

From 1935 the congregation's social work in Cape Breton expanded beyond Sydney to the surrounding coal towns where the cycles of employment and unemployment frequently created intense family hardships. Responding to a request from Father Jimmy Tompkins of St. Joseph's Parish, Reserve Mines, and Father Charles W. MacDonald of Immaculate Conception Parish, Bridgeport, in the fall of 1935, Mother Ignatius sent Sister Mary Alexandria MacKenzie, with the temporary assistance of Mother Faustina, to conduct social work in these parishes. Sister Mary Alexandria had recently graduated with Sister Baptista Maria from the Toronto School of Social Work. Copying the agency model already established in Sydney, Bridgeport parishioners formed the Catholic Charities Association in January 1936 with two sister fieldworkers who lived and worked from the sisters' hospital in Glace Bay (St. Joseph's).[33] As in Sydney, the sisters formed sodalities. The young women's Junior Sodality of our Lady became a crucial support for the social workers. Sister John Hugh Robertson described the sodalists' contributions: "Some of their activities were Catholic literature displays, special celebrations for our Lady's feasts, Mother's Day programs, teaching religion during the school year and during vacation, helping with the Gardiner Church fund, assisting with Christmas activities for the poor, money making events for Catholic Charities, helping with summer camps, etc."[34]

As the work mounted and the needs multiplied, "Father Charlie" convinced the congregation to staff a social service centre in Immaculate Conception Parish. Through his efforts, a two-storey convent, situated on Park Street near the main road from Dominion to Glace Bay, came into being in 1938; it was appropriately named St. Charles Convent. Mother Ignatius and her council assigned eight sisters to the new centre. The local press heralded this delightful development as a real boon for the area whose population was gradually expanding. And it was a boon, for under the leadership of Sister Mary Carmelita (Lillian) Brocklehurst (superior, 1938-1944), the sisters continued with social work but also opened a library, gave instruction in handicrafts, organized sodalities, and taught music, art, and domestic science in the local public schools.[35] These sisters made noteworthy contributions to the parishes and schools: Sister Mary Rodriquez (Sarah Anne) Steele (music); Sister Mary Raphael Watt (music); Sister Marie Camilla (Mary Ellen) Saunders (art); Sister M. Winifred (Veronica) Dollard (art); Sister Mary Jude (Jean) Doyle (crafts); Sister Margaret Mary Hervé (music); Sister Edmund Marie (Theresa) Kurtz (art); Sister Mary Edna (Anne Louise) Carey (domestic science); and Sister Mary Henry (Christina) Chiasson (domestic science). Sister Mary Rodriquez and Sister Margaret Mary established the Toronto Conservatory program in the area. The sisters' social service centre and ambitious program, which paralleled their work in Canmore and Canso, drew financial support from private music lessons, teachers' salaries, town grants, parish stipends, donations of cash and services from many local benefactors, and from Bethany. In 1940, after her official visitation and discussions with representatives in the parish, Mother Immaculata concluded, "The presence of the Sisters of St. Martha is considered an absolute necessity in the Parish."[36]

Besides the missions in Sydney and Bridgeport-Dominion, the Marthas also established other Cape Breton social work agencies in the 1930s and 1940s. However, they proved ephemeral. The social work begun in Reserve Mines in 1935, at the request of Father Jimmy Tompkins, was stopped within one year;

he and the social worker disagreed about the means needed to resolve family problems; and some parishioners were unsupportive.[37] In 1938, at the instigation of Father A.J. MacIsaac of Stella Maris Parish, Inverness, parishioners formed a Catholic Welfare Association and hired Sister Rosalia (Katherine) MacNeil to run the agency. Poverty was rife in this mining town (pop. 2,500) on Cape Breton Island's west coast, where the Marthas already operated St. Mary's Hospital. Even though Sister Rosalia mothered into existence a healthy range of parish organizations and activities, and formal social work, financial difficulties forced the agency to shut down in 1943.[38] Finally, from her base at the congregation's Little Flower Institute, Sister Mary Alexandria MacKenzie did social work from 1941 to 1944 under the title of "Parish Visitor" for St. Joseph's Parish, Bras d'Or. Like Sister Rosalia in Inverness, Sister Mary Alexandria provided formal social work services while fulfilling many other parish duties for Father Alexander S. MacKenzie. It was a difficult assignment for her; the parish embraced about nine small, widely separated districts. She found little poverty and destitution, but many other family difficulties, some caused by the war. When Sister Mary Alexandria became ill in 1944, the congregation did not supply another social worker for the parish.[39]

St. Mary's Home/Mercy Hospital, Sydney

The congregation's social work apostolate extended beyond adult education, parish work, and formal social work to institutional care. In 1917 the sisters had established St. Mary's Home in Sydney for orphans and unwed mothers in the Diocese of Antigonish. Then, in 1927 the diocese had built an orphanage in Bras d'Or called the Little Flower Institute; the sisters also staffed it. The congregation explained its rationale for St. Mary's Home in a report to the Vatican: "The Home is a dire necessity of the times, as these mothers were obliged to seek refuge in Protestant homes of this kind and their children were thus lost to the Church and the mothers were not benefited by their stay there."[40] The unwed mothers–most were Catholics–came from all areas of the diocese; some even came from Newfoundland. Usually they gave their babies up for adoption, but sometimes they kept them or had them sent to the Little Flower Institute for longer-term care. The sisters at St. Mary's occasionally gave shelter to homeless girls and infants under one year, too; they had a policy of refusing help to no one.

By the mid-1930s, St. Mary's Home was serving only a small number of unwed mothers. Most were going to other hospitals in the diocese such as St. Joseph's Hospital in Glace Bay, St. Martha's Hospital in Antigonish, or City Hospital in Sydney. The general council assigned Mother Faustina to investigate the declining admissions. She reported that "all hospitals objected strongly to this type of patient, as married women did not care to be placed in the same category as these others; and moreover, practically all these hospitals are determined to take a stand against admitting these patients."[41] A meeting of clergy unanimously supported resolutions for (1) an addition to St. Mary's Home in order to accommodate those unwed mothers who might be barred from other hospitals, and (2) a name change to Mercy Maternity Hospital; they hoped these changes would increase government support for the institution. A new two-storey wing was added at a cost of $35,000. Five sisters and one graduate lay nurse staffed the enlarged institution with Sister Francis Theresa Hergott as superior. The sisters running the Catholic Charities Association of Sydney moved their headquarters from St. Rita Hospital into the expanded Mercy Hospital.

Admissions increased. However, the Mercy continued to struggle with inadequate revenues. Expectant mothers usually stayed for an extended time but then rarely could pay their bills. Because of the stigma attached to their condition, fundraising proved difficult. Low sisters' salaries ($100 annually in 1938), donated medical and legal services, and government grants failed to eliminate the annual shortfall. The sister treasurer heard perennial complaints from Bishop Morrison about the Mercy's financial dependence; regularly he had to bail it out of a deficit position.[42] In 1939, he decided to appoint an advisory board of area clergy "in order to safeguard and promote the interest of that institution."[43] Finances were the central issue, but an agreement between the Mercy Hospital and the Little Flower Institute over the care of infants born elsewhere also had to be settled. Actually, by 1942 the advisory board, whose constitution and by-laws Mother Faustina had drafted, was functioning as a joint board for both institutions. The superiors of the Little Flower

Institute and the Mercy Hospital began reporting annually to the board, and it established policy for their institutions.[44] Two sisters sat as members of the joint board from 1942.

Although admissions to the renovated Mercy Hospital did increase, its financial difficulties continued to plague an exasperated Bishop Morrison. In 1945, he wrote to the beleaguered superior, Sister Margaret Claire (Mary Everett) McAskill, "I must repeat what I said in a former letter, that whatever be the consequences, the number of admissions to the Mercy Hospital must be reduced. I see no way to carry the financial load involved and so the disreputable clientele of girls must be made to understand that they will have to face the real hard way for their perversity."[45] This was not one of the old bishop's finer moments, but his frustration was understandable. Two years before he had been forced to impose an annual diocesan levy of $8,000 for five years to meet current operating deficits and wipe out the capital debt. By 1950 the diocese had given $80,000 to support the Mercy Hospital and only about $3,000 to the Little Flower Institute.[46]

The Sisters of St. Martha could not be blamed for the financial difficulties of their hospital for unwed mothers. Their salaries remained low and administration was efficient. And, in spite of its problems, the Mercy Hospital was a good work, an act of mercy toward young women in distress. Between 1917 and 1951, when the hospital closed, the sisters cared for 686 unwed mothers; most came from the Sydney-Glace Bay urban, industrial area. These women found compassion and support during a dark hour of their lives; they never forgot the Marthas who offered refuge from a harsh, censorious society.

The Little Flower Institute, Bras d'Or

The Little Flower Institute, Mercy Hospital's sister institution in Bras d'Or, had offered a refuge for children since its establishment in 1927. The children's circumstances were often heartrending. For example, two children under three were found wandering on a street in Sydney and needed care; their parents were inebriated. A young widow from Newfoundland sought to place her six children in the Little Flower; her doctor had certified her mental condition to be unstable and a threat to the children's well-being. And the Glace Bay police requested emergency protection for two girls, age five and seven; their parents had separated and the mother was living in an unsuitable building renowned for its excessive drinking.[47] Actually, by the 1940s, children at the Little Flower were only rarely true orphans. Mother Ignatius commented: "About 84 percent of the children come from broken homes. This shows an alarming change in home conditions ... for not so many years ago the majority cared for in this institution were orphans and charity cases."[48] The Little Flower offered a home for about fifty to seventy children annually during the 1940s.[49] Eight to ten sisters were

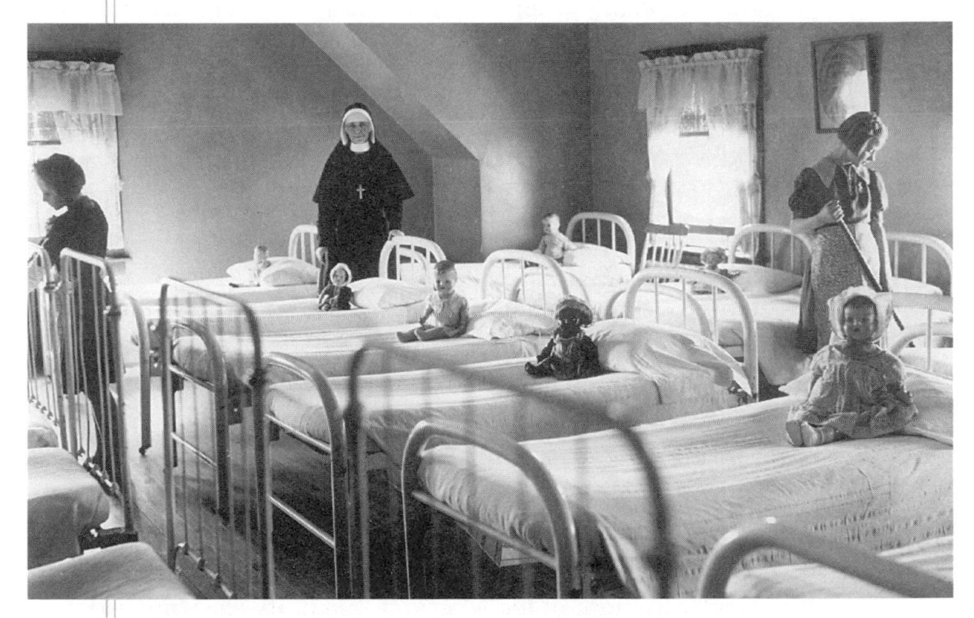

Little Flower Institute dormitory, Bras d'Or, Cape Breton. Sister Jean Carmel (Mary Anne) MacLean is supervising housekeeping.

assigned to the adjacent Sacred Heart Convent, which staffed the "orphanage."[50] A small army of social workers, doctors, lawyers, school inspectors, priests, and Children's Aid workers assisted them.

Life for the sisters at the Little Flower was lived in the fast lane. Energy abounded. Sometimes it was ill-directed. One year several boys slightly damaged a rough box coffin in a nearby cemetery where a deceased parish member awaited burial. A sister reported, "To cure them of this form of amusement, one of the maids enveloped herself in a sheet, feigning the departed spirit of the man who died, and went to the dormitory after the boys had settled down for the night." The maid, speaking in "deep sepulchural tones," interrogated the terrified boys until she found the one responsible for the damage. The frightened boy promised to say beads for the spirit every day for a week, and at once the spirit vanished. After two years the orphanage children still pointed with trepidation to the grave from whence the spirit had originated.[51]

The degree of interest and support from parish and community organizations for the sisters' mission at Bras d'Or was remarkable. Youth groups from parishes came regularly to celebrate birthday parties. Priests gave talks, showed films, and organized sports teams. The Catholic Women's League, the Elks, the Knights of Columbus, the Cape Breton Boxing Commission, and the Sydney Mines Dramatic Club organized special events and outings. The sisters evidently made the religious and cultural life of the institution rich. They organized religious devotions, processions, music festivals, summer camps, handicrafts, and art exhibitions. In the interest of order, discipline was strict and life carefully regulated. Of course, the sisters were very concerned for the spiritual welfare of the children. The house annalist recorded in 1952, "On the spiritual ledger, we had many consolations. A great number of the children who came in were from homes where they were neglected. They learned their prayers for the first time and it was possible to teach them their religion."[52]

The finances of the Little Flower Institute were always stronger than those of the Mercy Hospital. Its residents had no need for anonymity, and the public was always moved by the plight of defenseless children who were innocent victims of fate. The provincial Department of Child Welfare, to which the sisters reported annually, provided support. So did the Children's Aid Society of Cape Breton, parents and guardians, benefactors, district municipalities, local organizations, and the Diocese of Antigonish. From 1929, for ten years the diocese published a periodical called the *Little Flower Messenger* as a means to edify the faithful with "good Catholic reading material" and to raise money for its two welfare institutions, the Little Flower Institute and Mercy Hospital. This periodical was discontinued in 1939 because it proved ineffective as a source of income.

Social Work in Regina, Saskatchewan

The sisters' nascent ministry in social work extended to western Canada, the scene of their new missions in hospital and parish work during the 1930s. Archbishop Monahan of Regina drew the congregation there in 1936. He hoped to realize in Regina the earlier Calgary plan he had for the Marthas to staff a social welfare centre; however, his episcopal transfer had intervened. Regina had been designated the capital city of Saskatchewan when the province had been formed in 1905. In 1931 it was the province's governmental and commercial centre, with a population of 53,209. Its people were highly transient, ethnically diverse, and about 30 percent Roman Catholic.[53] By 1936, Regina had various public and private welfare organizations that its citizens had developed to meet urgent social needs, for example, a Salvation Army home for unwed mothers, a Bureau of Child Protection, a United Church Settlement House, and a Community Clothing Depot. However, these organizations were usually staffed by "non-professional, non-Catholic, and frequently anti-Catholic workers." There were no distinctively Catholic welfare organizations, a situation at least potentially subversive of Catholic principles.[54] Archbishop Monahan believed strongly that the province's capital needed such distinctively Catholic organizations and he hoped that his good friends, the Sisters of St. Martha, Antigonish, would help him as they had before. He wrote to Mother Ignatius in 1935: "From what I see of the City of Regina and the Catholic position, I feel that we are in dire need of laborers to take up the social work."[55]

The archbishop had three schemes in mind: a Catholic home for unwed mothers, a welfare agency, and a hostel for young women. In March 1936, he bought a sixteen-room, solid brick residence as a home for unwed mothers and deeded it to the congregation. It was a large home, in fine condition, and in a good location near the business centre of Regina. Several sisters converged on Regina that spring to prepare the home: Sister M. Immaculata Fraser, superior of St. Michael's Hospital, Lethbridge; Sister Mary Gilbert (Catherine Bernalda) Ernewein, Sister Mary Maurice Brocklehurst; and Mother Faustina. The first resident was admitted at the end of June. Sister M. Clotilda (Bridget) Cadegan, superior (1939-1943), described the plight of the young women: "Most of these girls come to us in the early stages of pregnancy to seek shelter and to be shielded from an unsympathetic world whose ostracism they feel must be faced if their condition becomes known. Very often parents or the immediate members of their own family are not aware of their condition."[56] The sisters offered the same services as those provided by the Mercy Hospital in Sydney, Cape Breton. The "girls" were given shelter, support, encouragement, counseling, legal advice on adoption, medical care before and after their "confinement," and homemaking training and mothering. The Marthas tried to create a homelike atmosphere; they also carefully assessed and nurtured the spiritual well-being of their patients. Conversions and returns to the sacraments were happy developments for the sisters.

The Mercy Hospital for unwed mothers in Regina, Saskatchewan, operated by the Marthas from 1936.

The Marthas' maternity hospital in Regina certainly filled a need. There were sixty admissions and forty-one births in 1936; these numbers had climbed to eighty-one admissions and fifty-five births by 1950. Most women were between seventeen and twenty-five years of age.[57] The sisters had a universal admission policy–neither race, religion, nor financial status barred anyone's admission–and a policy of confidentiality to protect the reputations of the young women. Financial support was forthcoming from the beginning. Of course, the archbishop was a strong supporter, since the hospital was his pet project. But its revenues also included provincial and municipal grants, patient fees, and donations from parishes and organizations. In 1948, local Catholic leaders, at the request of the Co-operative Commonwealth Federation government, formed an advisory board so the hospital would be constituted like others in the province. This board greatly helped the sisters with hospital affairs.[58] The congregation usually assigned five to six Marthas annually to the institution.[59]

Archbishop Monahan's second welfare scheme in 1936 to be undertaken by the sisters in Regina was formal social work. The congregation favoured him with two sisters–Sister Mary Alexandria MacKenzie and Sister Joseph Helen Mulvihill–who began in the fall of 1936 and worked out of the Mercy Hospital. The following spring, the archbishop formed an agency with an incorporated board called the Catholic Welfare Society, a set-up similar to the parish social work agencies being established in Cape Breton. However, his agency served all of Regina's ethnically diverse Catholic parishes; therefore it was financed by the archdiocese and through regular fundraising campaigns.[60] After an organizational shakeup in 1947, when Archbishop Monahan relinquished control shortly before his death, it could also access funds from the city's Community Chest.

The sister social workers' first mandate was family welfare. During the Depression, of course, material assistance was frequently a critical family need in Regina, just as it was in Cape Breton. Among the sisters' common tasks were home visits, interviews, meetings, employment referrals, emergency grocery orders, and the distribution of clothing. The Regina sisters encountered family problems much like those their counterparts dealt with in Cape Breton. The average caseload in 1941 was 80; by 1951 it was 230. By the late 1940s, the Catholic Welfare Society had two sister social workers, one lay social worker, and a secretary. At different times, it offered well-baby clinics, marriage counselling classes, and library services. The Marthas also functioned as attendance officers for the Catholic separate schools.

The sisters at the Catholic Welfare Society, Regina, had their own unique experiences. They were the first ones in the congregation to use a car, a great boon considering the large number of parishes they served. A sister wrote in 1941: "Our car, 'Shirley Anne,' has been behaving very well. We have had no cops after us for some time. She is very sturdy."[61] Sister M. Crescentia (Mary Catherine) Duprey had a gratifying and productive tenure

(1940-1951) as director of the agency. The board was riled to hear of her pending transfer in 1950, and it wrote to Mother Ignatius: "Sister has done much, while Director of our Society, to build up our prestige with both government and civic organizations and of course, it goes without saying, to enhance our organization and inspire confidence in it on the part of our Catholic people."[62] The board was anxious, but failed to retain her services.

Archbishop Monahan's final welfare scheme for Regina that involved the Sisters of St. Martha was a hostel. On 19 January 1938, Sister M. Augustine Kennedy and two other Marthas opened a "fine private residence" rented by the archbishop for the purpose of boarding young working women "of slender means." The hostel's opening was announced in all the city parishes and its fees were nominal. In this way, the archbishop hoped to provide single Catholic women with an alternative to cheap, disreputable boarding houses. Unfortunately, by the summer of 1939, Monahan judged the venture a financial failure and decided to close it in September. He reluctantly informed the mother general, "I know this will be a disappointment to you but the deficits incurred during the two years that this institution has been in operation are such that we cannot possibly carry on and expect our people to give us their money."[63] The women's hostel was the only short-term project Archbishop Monahan got the congregation involved in. By the time of his death in 1947, he had drawn them to missions in Regina, Broadview, and Melville. Sister John Baptist Cameron fondly remembered, "His Grace had sent many good candidates to the Congregation, and was keenly interested in all our undertakings."[64]

Social Work's Meaning for the Congregation

During the 1930s the social work apostolate became an important area of missionary endeavour for the Sisters of St. Martha. It included adult education, parish work, formal social work, and institutional care. In the 1920s, Dr. Coady had been responsible for drawing the sisters into rural education, and in the early 1930s, he was partly responsible for their close identification with adult education. Through his frequent contacts with the congregation, and through the sisters who worked with him in the

St.F.X. extension office, the Marthas imbibed Coady's philosophy of adult education, gained expertise in handicrafts and became involved with the challenges facing rural women.

In the mid-1930s the Sisters of St. Martha also started to gain expertise in methods of formal social work. At the invitation of priests in the urban, industrial areas, such as Sydney-Glace Bay and Regina, where the Great Depression created untold suffering, the sisters entered the relatively new field of social work by cooperating with priests and laymen to establish parish agencies. This was especially important work, since government assistance was still piecemeal and inadequate; Canada's national pension, unemployment insurance, and health care schemes had not yet been introduced. The sister social workers, at considerable personal and congregational sacrifice, became "angels of mercy" for distraught families. Sisters commonly walked long distances, received low salaries and were overworked.

Social work, in its several guises, had important implications for the sisters. Along with teaching and hospital service, it eroded further the semi-cloistered life of the congregation. Martha extension and social workers served in the rough and tumble of secular life and witnessed the socio-economic problems plaguing many families. In addition, they participated in professional associations that influenced and informed their methods of work. The secretary of the Canadian Association of Social Workers wrote to Mother Immaculata in 1943: "You might be interested to know that yours is the only religious order of sisters which has cared to have its members belong to our professional association. We feel proud to have people who are doing such a fine piece of pioneer social work in various parts of Canada belong to our association, and are more than appreciative of your interest and theirs in professional standards of social work."[65] The demand for social workers also impelled the congregation to gain further education for selected sisters assigned to this apostolate. Finally, the broad range of social services offered by the sisters developed an immense fund of gratitude and goodwill among the troubled families, unwed mothers, and parish communities to whom they ministered. Social work strengthened the Marthas' identity as a people's congregation.

The congregation's new missions in social work and hospitals, established in both eastern and western Canada during the 1930s, were very public affairs; developments in the sisters' internal community life were more hidden, yet also important. The periodic general chapters, whose proceedings were secret, were events of first importance, since they were the institute's supreme authority and elected its leadership. The congregation's second general chapter, held in August 1931, was composed of six general officers, ten local superiors, and nine elected delegates. In that year, sisters under perpetual vows, the ones who elected the chapter delegates-numbered 109 and had an average age of forty and ranged in age from twenty-three to sixty-seven.[66] Together they served on twelve missions and staffed the motherhouse.

The chapter elected an administration–Mother Ignatius (mother general, second term), Sister M. Thecla Price, Mother Faustina, Sister Marie Carmel (Sarah) MacKinnon, and Sister Thomas Aquinas (Mary) MacLellan–whose average age was forty-six. With the recent extension of missions to western Canada in Lethbridge (1929) and Banff (1930), the delegates considered the formation of provinces within the congregation; however, they concluded "that the time is not yet ripe for such action, the number of houses not warranting such."[67] However, the delegates allowed western postulants to experience a trial period in one of the western missions before going to Bethany, and urged the exchange of letters between the east and the "far off missions" in order to "keep up a family spirit." The chapter delegates were preoccupied with breaches of discipline–violations of grand silence, teachers keeping late hours, fault-finding and gossip, unsuitable recreations, giving community news to externs, the use of luxury clothing such as silk undergarments, etc.–and predictably censured them. Lack of mutual respect between older and younger sisters, and assumed status distinctions based on a sister's apostolate, were also becoming troublesome. The chapter declared, "All Sisters should show consideration for each other and remember that the work is for God whether it be teaching or scrubbing."[68] However, the congregation overall did accept status distinctions or rank based on seniority and office. Mother

L-R: A professed sister, junior professed sister, novice, and postulant.

Ignatius reported the proceedings in a circular and urged all sisters to follow the general chapter recommendations "for the greater honour and glory of God, for the good of the congregation, and for the peace and happiness of each member."[69]

The only other general chapter held during the 1930s convened in 1937 with twenty-eight delegates present; 175 sisters then under perpetual vows had elected them. Although Mother Ignatius was elected for a third term, she declined; the constitutions prohibited a mother general from serving more than two successive terms. The delegates' second choice was Sister M. Immaculata Fraser, a forty-six-year-old native of Southside Harbour, Antigonish County, who had entered the congregation in 1918. Her forte was hospital work. She had served at St. Martha's Hospital, Antigonish, and had been trained in laboratory work, pharmacy, and nursing; in 1931 she had been the first Martha to earn a bachelor of science degree in nursing. When the congregation extended west in the early 1930s, Mother Immaculata had gained administrative experience as superintendent of St. Michael's Hospital, Lethbridge (1932-1937). Apparently the mother general-elect was "quiet and reserved by nature" but blessed with "a keen sense of financial acumen and administrative ability."[70]

Mother Immaculata, Mother Ignatius, Mother Faustina, Sister Maris Stella MacDonald, and Sister Marie Carmel MacKinnon composed the new general council. By now the average age of the councillors had increased from forty-six to fifty-three. The chapter formulated many resolutions on disciplinary regulations, and recommended the formation of study clubs on various topics, an obvious St.F.X. extension department influence. The chapter also decided to apply for a permission from Rome for certain sisters–those in nursing, food services, and laundry work–to wear white, and for the nursing sisters to be present in the delivery rooms; the permission was granted. On recommendation from Mother Ignatius, the chapter delegates extended the novitiate by one full year and decided to provide more training and supervision for the junior professed (sisters under temporary vows).[71]

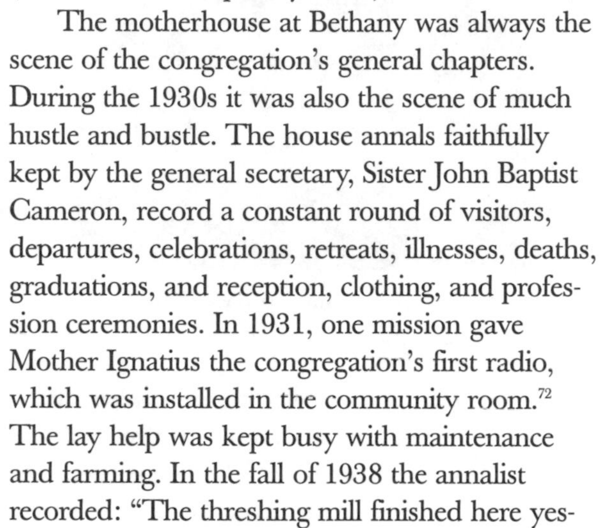

Mother M. Immaculata (Jennie) Fraser, superior general, 1937–1943.

The motherhouse at Bethany was always the scene of the congregation's general chapters. During the 1930s it was also the scene of much hustle and bustle. The house annals faithfully kept by the general secretary, Sister John Baptist Cameron, record a constant round of visitors, departures, celebrations, retreats, illnesses, deaths, graduations, and reception, clothing, and profession ceremonies. In 1931, one mission gave Mother Ignatius the congregation's first radio, which was installed in the community room.[72] The lay help was kept busy with maintenance and farming. In the fall of 1938 the annalist recorded: "The threshing mill finished here yesterday. We have 450 bushels of oats besides green feed. A splendid yield it was. We have abundance of vegetables much of which was sold."[73] Sister M. Columba Bryden remained at full steam in the printing and bookbinding department; so did the Marthas in

Sisters M. Potens Landry and M. Columbia Bryden in printing department at Bethany, 1940s.

the church goods department producing chasubles, dalmatics, copes, stoles, albs, linen surplices, veils, and altar cloths. The liturgical movement of the time recommended a new design in vestments called "ample vestments." Diocesan priests were ordering the new type of vestments, so Sister M. Thecla Price and Sister Mary Leocadia (Evelyn May) LaRusic visited Benedictine Sisters in Minnesota to obtain patterns and gain required expertise. High demand also allowed for no let-up among the Marthas in the altar bread division.

Sisters who visited Bethany in the summer of 1937 discovered that the building had nearly doubled in size. The new east wing, mirroring the brick one on the west side, had been made necessary by congregational growth. The sisters had started planning and fundraising the year before. Sister John Baptist Cameron remembered that Mother Ignatius did all the purchasing for the addition and was most exacting: "There was not a match nor a stick, nor a pound of cement, nor anything else went into the building but she knew the price and this was usually the lowest figure available.... Mother made a special trip to the United States where she got some splendid prices on hardware and plumbing fixtures."[74] Among the new wing's facilities was an "artistic and liturgically correct" chapel,[75] a dining hall, and a kitchen. Two years later the general council could finally afford to renovate the old wing, by then nearly twenty years old. In the interests of efficiency, always a critical concern of the sisters, the "Bethanites" began to hold monthly staff meetings; each department–kitchen, refectory, laundry, chapel, the four floors, library, altar bread, printing and bookbinding, etc.–reported on its affairs and all discussed ways to improve overall operations.[76]

Bethany Motherhouse after 1937 addition.

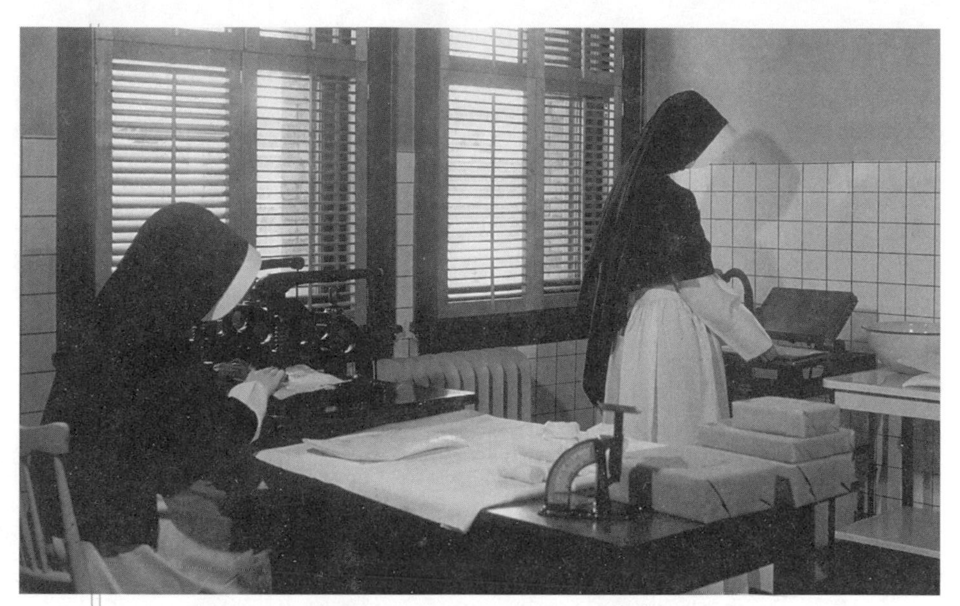

Sisters in the Altar Bread Department at Bethany, 1940s.

The motherhouse also became the headquarters for an important diocesan teaching service in the 1930s: correspondence courses in Christian doctrine. Sister John Baptist gave an account of their origin:

> *In the autumn of 1936, at the earnest solicitation of some of the Priests of the diocese, a catechetical correspondence course was started at Bethany. For a time Dr. Malcolm A. MacEachern and some senior students of [St.F.X.] university examined, corrected and valued the papers that answered the questions, but after the second year this was discontinued and the sisters have since been taking care of the work unaided."*[77]

Sister Mary Colina MacDougall offered the courses. Her students were usually from isolated areas where Roman Catholic Church operations and influences were weak. She continued the correspondence service until 1943, when the need for it had decreased; convents had been established in some of the areas she served. However, Sister Colina would later revive these catechetical courses in the 1950s.

Homemaking in Toronto

Among the many new missions undertaken by the Marthas in the 1930s was a rather intriguing assignment in homemaking that placed sisters close to the centre of Canada's English-speaking Catholic hierarchy. The recently appointed Archbishop of Toronto, Most Rev. James C. McGuigan, received Sister Mary Magdalen (Catherine F.) Cann and Sister Mary Celestia MacNeil in February 1935 to fulfil the domestic duties of his palace located on Wellesley Street, Toronto. McGuigan was from Prince Edward Island where he had first discovered the Marthas as a young priest professor at St. Dunstan's College (1918-1919); the Antigonish Marthas were there, under the direction of Mother Stanislaus, doing housekeeping and training sisters for a new Island congregation.[78] Of course, he had also observed them at St. Augustine's Seminary in Toronto. Among the congregation's incentives to work for McGuigan were a steady, moderate income, without the need for contributed services, and a temporary residence for sisters sent to study in Toronto. After the first sisters reviewed the domestic department, they wondered if the former housekeepers had "lived in the stone age." The annalist penned her first entry on a light note: "Sing a song of sixpence, A can of Gillette's Lye, Two stiff scrubbing brushes, There away we fly."[79] Over the years, the sisters witnessed an endless procession of church and government dignitaries who came to visit the archbishop. For example, in 1936, the annalist wrote: "A high brow banquet was tendered Bishop McNally, with His Grace presiding. The courses were unique and pronounced excellent."[80]

Aside from a financial misunderstanding between Mother Immaculata and the chancellor in 1938, when she threatened to withdraw the sisters' services, the relationship between Archbishop McGuigan's residence and the congregation remained congenial.[81] McGuigan himself sometimes had recreation with the sisters to the "yawning hours" and, among other delights, enjoyed Irish music with them. The sisters were ecstatic when he was raised to the Cardinalate in 1945 and became the first English-speaking cardinal in Canada. Mother Ignatius was not unaware of the strategic value of having sisters serve in his residence. She wrote in her visitation report of 1945, "Be loyal to the

Archbishop. He fills a very important post in the Church, and can do much for the Congregation."[82] Cardinal McGuigan expressed in the mid-1950s his satisfaction with the twenty-year record of the sisters: "We have nothing but gratitude for all that you have done for us throughout the years."[83]

Sisters at Cardinal McGuigan's residence, Toronto, Ontario: L-R Sister Ann Cornelius (Elizabeth) Beaton, Sister Anna Mary (Catherine) Maureen Butlin, Sister Anna Maureen (Lillian Isabel) Chisholm, and Sister Marie Thérèse (Minnie M.) Richard.

Conclusion

The Great Depression of the 1930s, coupled with an absence of adequate state-funded health and social services, created dire social needs that the Marthas were called upon to help meet in both the Maritimes and western Canada. As the sisters responded in the fields of health care, education, social work, and parish activities, they became immersed in the urgent daily problems faced by all Canadians. Here they wrestled to provide ministries directed by their deep Christian convictions as religious sisters, while expanding their range of services to meet basic human needs. In sharp contrast to single apostolate institutes, the Sisters of St. Martha became a people's congregation, one intimately identified with all the essential human needs–spiritual, physical, intellectual, material, social, and cultural. Thanks in part to the Great Depression, human warmth, understanding, and empathy with people facing life crises became ever-stronger features of the Martha character and public image.

Notes

1 Bethany Annals, 10 October 1925, F6,S1,SS1,f11,b106.
2 See James D. Cameron, *For the People: A History of St. Francis Xavier University* (Montreal: McGill Queen's University Press, 1996), chapter 11.
3 Bethany Annals, 10 October 1925, F6,S1,SS1,f11,b106.
4 Ibid., 7 March 1931.
5 Bethany Annals, 8 February 1939, F6,S1,SS1,f5,b107.
6 Ibid., 12 August 1932.
7 Ibid., 28 August 1933.
8 Sister Marie Michael MacKinnon, Speech to the Atlantic Institute, pp. 4-5, 21 July 1982, F5,S34,SS19,f1,b94.
9 Report of Extension, May 1934, Extension Department Scrapbook, July 1930-December 1942, 15, EC, STFXUA.
10 *Casket* article, n.d., F5,S34,SS19,f11,b94.
11 Bethany Annals, 30 April 1934, ibid.
12 Sister Marie Michael, Speech to the Atlantic Institute, p. 6.
13 Interview with Sister Irene Doyle, 24 February 1993, St.F.X.
14 Bethany Annals, 14 November 1932, F6,S1,SS1,f2,b107.
15 *Census of Canada 1971*, 1.1:2-12.
16 Rev. J.J. Tompkins to Bernard Brennan, 7 March 1935, F5,S34,SS19,f4,b94.
17 For an overview of Father Tompkins' sojourn in Canso, see Jim Lotz and Michael R. Welton, *Father Jimmy* (Wreck Cove, Cape Breton: Breton Books, 1997), chapters 3-4.
18 To this point, the sisters' social service work had been primarily within institutions, such as St. Mary's Home for unwed mothers and the Little Flower Institute for children.
19 Canso Welfare Bureau, List of Benefactors, F23,S1,SS2,f2,b195.

20 Mother Faustina to Miss Henry Dexter, 20 May 1936, F23,S2,SS1,f7,b196.
21 J.H. Drover to Mother Superior, 17 August 1944, and Petitioners to Mother Ignatius, 17 August 1944, F23,S2,SS1,f8,b196.
22 Canso Welfare Bureau Personnel List, F23,S1,SS1,f1,b195.
23 President H.P. MacPherson to Rev. Sr. Faustina, 3 November 1933, F3,S1,SS2,f1,b5.
24 Mother Ignatius, Visitation Report, April 1952, Catholic Charities, Sydney, F40,S1,SS1,f7,b237.
25 Forbes and Muise, eds., *The Atlantic Provinces in Confederation*, pp. 273-83.
26 Catholic Charities and Welfare Association, Report for September 1936, F6,S28,SS2,f3,b66.
27 Sister May Mulvihill, "History of the Sisters of St. Martha," II:8:90.
28 Sister Baptista Maria to Mother Faustina, 7 December 1935, F5,S28,SS3,f4,b67.
29 Catholic Charities and Welfare Association, Report for September 1936, F5,S28,SS2,f3,b66.
30 Ibid.
31 Catholic Charities and Welfare Association, St. Theresa's Parish, Annual Report, 1945, F5,S28,SS3,f3,b67.
32 Holy Redeemer Parish, Family Welfare Association, Historical Notes, Statistical Data, and Reports, 1944-1960, F5,S28,SS4,f1,b67.
33 Historical Notes, Catholic Welfare Association, Bridgeport and Dominion, F5,S28,SS7,f1,b67.
34 Sister John Hugh Robertson, "Early History of Social Work, Immaculate Conception Parish, Bridgeport, Cape Breton, 1936-1941," p. 5, ibid.
35 *Sydney Post Record*, 29 November 1938.
36 St. Charles Convent, Visitation Report, 28 February 1940, F27,S1,SS1,f11,b219.
37 CSM, *Sixty Years*, p. 71.
38 Stella Maris Parish, Catholic Welfare Association Historical Notes, F5,S2,SS2,f1,b68.
39 Based on correspondence, reports, and summaries, St. Joseph's Parish, Bras d'Or, 1941-1944, F5,S28,SS6,b67,f1.
40 CSM Quinquennial Report to the Holy See, 1931, F5,S34,SS1,f1,b84.
41 Clergy Meeting Minutes, Sydney Lyceum, 4 May 1937, F19,S3,SS1,f1,b181.
42 Mercy Hospital Financial Reports, F19,S1,SS2,f3,b181.
43 Bishop Morrison to Rev. Father, 28 September 1939, F19,S3,SS1,f1,b181.

44 Minutes of the Joint Advisory Board for the Mercy Hospital and Little Flower Institute, 1939-1950, ibid.
45 Bishop Morrison to Sister Margaret Claire, 9 November 1945, ibid.
46 Bishop John R. MacDonald to M. MacCormack, 17 November 1950, F20,S1,SS2,f2,b190.
47 Report of Admissions and Discharges, Little Flower Institute, 1955, ibid.
48 General Chapter Proceedings, 1949, F5,S8,SS2,f1,b6.
49 Diocesan Charity Report, 30 November 1954, exhibit 4, F5,S27,SS1,f1,b65.
50 Little Flower Institute Personnel Lists, F20,S1,SS1,f1,b190.
51 *The Bethanite*, XI, March 1944, p. 10.
52 Little Flower Institute Annals, 1952, F20,S1,SS2,f1,b190.
53 *Census of Canada 1971,* 1.1:2-90.
54 *The Bethanite*, IV, December 1937, pp. 84-94.
55 Archbishop Monahan to Mother Ignatius, 19 October 1935, F9,S3,SS1,f1,b144.
56 Historical articles, Mercy Hospital, Regina, F18,S1,SS1,b177.
57 Mercy Hospital Statistics, 1936-1984, F18,S1,SS2,f2,b177.
58 Mercy Hospital Advisory Board Minutes, 1948-1959, F18,S4,SS1,f1,b178.
59 Mercy Hospital, Regina, Personnel List F18,S1,SS1,f6,b177.
60 *The Bethanite*, IV, December 1937, pp. 84-94.
61 Sister M. Matthew to Sister Mary of Mercy, 4 November 1941, F5,S31,SS3,f1,b70.
62 H.M. Gough to Mother Ignatius, 22 August 1950, ibid.
63 Archbishop Monahan to Mother Immaculata, 11 August 1939, F5,S34,SS17,f12,b93.
64 Sister John Baptist Cameron, "Brief Outline of the Early History of the Sisters of Saint Martha, 1894-1948" (Bethany, 1948), p. 183.
65 Elizabeth Wallace to Mother Immaculata, 26 March 1943, F5,S27,SS2,f1,b65.
66 List of CSM Sisters Under Perpetual Vows, 1931, F5,S8,SS1,f1,b6.
67 General Chapter Proceedings, 1931, p. 2, F5,S8,SS1,f2,b6.
68 Ibid., p. 3.
69 Circular, 3 August 1931, ibid.
70 Obituary of Mother Immaculata, F5,S33,SS5,f3,b78.
71 General Chapter Proceedings, 1937, F5,S8,SS1,f3,b6.
72 Bethany Annals, 2 January 1931, F6,S1,SS1,f1,b106.
73 Bethany Annals, 9 September 1938, ibid.
74 Sister John Baptist Cameron, "History," p. 140.
75 Sister Irene Doyle made this comment and noted that the sisters' new chapel inspired priests who were building new churches. They

would come to Bethany and discuss the design with Mother Ignatius and Sister Remegius MacGillivray.

76 Monthly Staff Meeting Minutes, Bethany, 1937-1941, F6,S4,SS1,f4,b112.

77 Sister John Baptist Cameron, "History," p. 143.

78 Peter McGuigan, "The Cardinal and the Island," *The Island Magazine* 3 (Fall/Winter), p. 29.

79 Cardinal's Residence Annals, F22,S1,SS1,f3,b194.

80 Ibid., June 1936.

81 Archbishop McGuigan to Mother Immaculata, 28 May 1938, F22,S2,SS1,f1,b194.

82 Cardinal's Residence Visitation Report, 6 May 1945, F22,S1,SS1,f4,b194.

83 Cardinal McGuigan to Mother Ignatius, 17 July 1956, F22,S2,SS1,f1,b194.

Chapter Eight

Marthas in the War Decade: The 1940s

On September 1, 1939, the Bethany annalist tersely wrote, "Great Britain has declared war against Germany. God help us." Shortly thereafter, on September 10, Canada declared war on Hitler's Germany. The war, drawn out for more than five torturous years and causing a staggering loss of life worldwide, quickly pulled Canada out of economic depression and fuelled its rapid industrial growth. Unemployment rates nose-dived, and the federal government established important new social programs as it constructed a welfare state. New military bases were established in the Maritimes, the shipbuilding industry revived, and many country people flocked to the cities for work. Abject poverty declined. Carmen Miller writes, "increasingly the region took on the appearance and feeling of an armed camp; rumors of spies and saboteurs, blackouts, and air-raid drills fed the region's sense of fear and apprehension."[1]

Although the Sisters of St. Martha did not serve overseas, the war and its aftermath deeply affected their congregation. While suffering a shortage of personnel and new vocations, they maintained their commitment to existing missions, now extended across Canada, and even established more. Post-war university enrolment trends severely tested the congregation's largest and oldest mission at St.F.X., and developments in the Canadian hospital field were a challenge to sisters in that important apostolate. However, the stressful war decade closed with a happy celebration as the sisters commemorated their congregation's golden jubilee in 1950.

A Vocation Crisis

The sisters' report to the Holy See in 1931 commented: "No strong measures have been used to draw members into the community."[2] Strong measures would have been unnecessary, especially through the Depression years of the 1930s, for the number of entrants was high. In 1931 the congregation numbered 129 professed sisters; by 1941 this number had more than doubled to 270. The Marthas happily witnessed about twenty-three candidates a year arriving at Bethany to enter the novitiate. This trend permitted general administration to expand rapidly in western Canada and to assign many sisters to new parish and social work missions. The expansion into western Canada itself helped vocations, for more than twenty westerners made the long trek east during the thirties to enter the Bethany novitiate.[3] Finally, the congregation's personnel resources were reduced by only ten deaths throughout the decade, about one each year.[4] For these reasons, the Marthas remained dependent on relatively low key recruitment strategies: the support of parish priests, printed vocational literature, and retreats for girls. Actually, the retreats were a new idea in 1929 when the first were held at the convent in St. Andrews.[5] They would become a more significant undertaking in future decades.

The Second World War quickly damaged the rosy vocation picture of the 1930s. Through the war decade, only about one-half as many new candidates (twelve per year) entered the congregation. Hence, overall congregational growth decreased to 4.8 percent during the decade. As mentioned, in 1941 the Marthas numbered 270 professed; ten years later this number had only grown to 283. Ten sisters had died during the 1930s; during the 1940s, nineteen sisters died. Of course, some candidates always left or were dismissed from the novitiate because of difficulties adjusting to the religious life–isolation from family and friends, loneliness, ill health, and unsuitableness for such a vocation. But in the 1940s, there were just many fewer applicants. Mother

Immaculata thought the decrease resulted from more careful screening of candidates: "We are less because we wish to place our Institute on a firm basis";[6] others believed that God, for His own reasons, was calling fewer women to the religious life. However, the war was primarily to blame for the decrease in vocations that struck most other congregations too. Sister John Baptist Cameron observed: "Owing to war conditions and so many young women having enlisted in the services, and others doing work hitherto carried on by men, there was a general dearth of vocations to the Religious Life."[7]

Postulants at Bethany entrance, 1936.

The "dearth of vocations" led to careful soul-searching among the Marthas. Mother Ignatius, re-elected for a third term by the general chapter in 1943, rang the alarm in 1946. In August she sent an urgent four-page letter to her entire congregation. It opened: "This month we have one novice making Profession, no one taking the habit, and three postulants entering. From almost every mission comes the cry: 'Send us more Sisters, our work is growing.' The situation is indeed alarming and serious. Sisters, what are we as a Community doing together about it?" In her view, God had sent the vocation shortage as a cross for the congregation's ultimate blessing. However, she declared the immediate need for "a long-term program for fostering vocations," and urged more fervent prayers, cheerful acceptance of the increased hardships, organization of study clubs by the superior of each house, and publication of articles in the *Casket* on vocations and the work of the Marthas.[8] She advised: "Pray as if everything depended on God; work as if everything depended on you." She also cautioned her sisters to be more sensitive about public relations. A few years before, Mother Ignatius had warned that sisters who gave "dis-edification" through "sarcasm, cutting remarks, and unkind criticisms" should be removed from contact with externs. "Fine young Catholic girls," she affirmed, "have no desire to enter a Religious Institute where they see Sisters give in to moodiness, bad temper, and incivility."[9]

Novices at prayer.

So, in August 1946, the houses of the congregation did as their leader directed. They each developed a program of study and action designed to deepen their spiritual life and increase their understanding of the religious life. Mother Ignatius also asked each individual sister to send in her own opinions explaining the decline of vocations and the remedy for it. Some blamed "the uncharitable spirit which seemed to prevail in the Congregation."[10] Mother Ignatius also thought the teaching sisters had a poor record of attracting vocations in their schools.[11] More positively, the Marthas held occasional open houses at Bethany in the 1940s, especially for young women, published advertisements in the diocesan paper, the *Casket*, created exhibits for Catholic missionary conferences, distributed vocation pamphlets, and discussed the vocation issue with priests and other congregations who were suffering from the same problem.[12] They also resurrected the practice of holding retreats for girls as they had in the early 1930s. For example, fifty young women attended a retreat held at the motherhouse in July 1945. The annalist commented, "We are hoping St. Martha will win some of the best girls to enter her Congregation."[13] Unfortunately, these efforts paid small dividends; the number of new vocations would not accelerate until the 1950s.

The vocation crisis severely limited the number of new missions the general administrations could establish during the 1940s and forced the congregation to hire more secular help. To add insult to injury, the number of requests Mother Ignatius received for help nearly tripled compared to requests received in the 1930s. The war effort had created a general labour shortage, and most pleas were for housekeepers and teachers, and for the congregation to operate hospitals. The Marthas' reputation had spread with their expanding missions; it was also being broadcast by clergy and laity who migrated from the Maritimes to the "Boston States" or to central and western Canada. The result? Requests for domestic help came from parish priests, bishops' palaces, retreat houses, monasteries, colleges, and seminaries. Catholic school boards lobbied for sister teachers, and many small prairie communities such as Barrhead, Bellegarde, Lebret, Kindersley, Swift Current, and Brandon asked for the sisters' help to set up and operate hospitals.[14] By the end of the war decade, the endless demands and endless refusals, as well as the requirements of her own understaffed houses, caused a frustrated Mother Ignatius to exclaim, "The same old cry: shortage of sisters. I am beside myself at times to know where to turn to answer the constant demands. May God send … the workers we need for the harvest of souls."[15]

Novices at Bethany, 1946.

New Missions: Main-a-Dieu and Eskasoni

In spite of severe sister shortages, the congregation did take on two new missions in the 1940s, both in teaching. In Main-a-Dieu, a fishing village on the southeast coast of Cape Breton, Father A.A. Poirier believed the Marthas could improve the school and the religious tone of the community. People sometimes called Father Poirier "the French edition of Dr. J.J. Tompkins"; he was firmly committed to the cooperative movement and successfully promoted it in his village.[16] He had a fine church, but no convent to offer the sisters. Nonetheless, the general administration accepted his invitation and assigned three sisters to the school in September 1942. The pioneer Marthas in Main-a-Dieu–Sister Mary Regina MacDonnell (superior and teacher), Sister M. Athanasius (Jennie) Smith (teacher), and Sister Mary Louise (Catherine) MacGillivray (homemaking and cooking instructor)–taught in the public school (primary to grade eleven), promoted handicrafts, and helped with parish activities. From a later perspective, their living conditions were rudimentary and rustic; electricity did not reach the village until 1947, and the convent walls in winter feebly checked the onward march of Jack Frost. However, their accommodations and the school facilities improved within a decade. Over the thirty years the Marthas served in Main-a-Dieu, their numbers remained small, at about three to five. In 1955, Mother Ignatius warmly commended the sisters; by then three young women from the parish had entered the novitiate and several other students had gone on to study at Xavier Junior College, Sydney, and St.F.X.[17]

Toward the end of the war decade, in 1947, the Marthas established a fascinating teaching mission on a Native reservation, a congregational first. Cape Breton's *Sydney Post-Record* reported on 8 May 1947: "Believed to be the first social experiment of its kind in Canada, transformation of the Indian village of Eskasoni [Cape Breton] into a model community with a modern general store, new school, nurses' station, saw mill, about 100 new homes, church, and baseball diamond, is now underway." The federal Indian Affairs Branch of the Department of Mines and Resources was following a policy of centralization recommended in 1942, and the Mi'kmaq people on Nova Scotia's nineteen reserves were being encouraged to move to either Shubenacadie or Eskasoni. There, modern facilities and services would raise their standard of living and make them more self-supporting, hoped department officials. As Eskasoni grew, Bishop Morrison had established it as a parish in 1944 and appointed Father Alexander A. Ross parish priest.

The educational plan for the Eskasoni Reserve included the

Sisters of St. Martha, for they were asked to operate the school and to include domestic science and manual training in its curriculum. The general administration accepted and assigned sisters in September 1947 to the convent, or "Teachers' Residence," that was built and maintained by Indian Affairs. The pioneer sisters–Sister Mary Genevieve (Isabel) Gillis (superior, 1947-1953), Sister M. Reginald (Eunice) MacKinnon, Sister Mary Maurice Brockle-hurst, Sister George Marie (Mary Teresa) MacPherson, and Sister Mary Joannes (Margaret Ann) Chisholm–ran the school (enrolment 163, grade primary to eleven), formed a choir and a glee club, a homemakers' club, visited families, organized youth groups, and promoted handicrafts.[18]

The Eskasoni mission was an important and challenging one for the congregation. The sisters were surrounded by several dialects of the Mi'kmaq language and attempted to absorb some basics. They learned of the Natives' plight from first-hand experience, retained close links with the Indian Agent, F.B. MacKinnon (later Regional Supervisor), and participated in conferences and institutes devoted to Native concerns. Financially the mission was a boon; the teachers' salary scale was higher than the provincial one, and care for the Teachers' Residence was the responsibility of the Indian Affairs Branch. The canonical visitor in 1953 summed up the prevailing sentiment of gratitude for the Marthas' work at Eskasoni: "Edifying apostolic work, appreciated also by non-Catholics and officials."[19] Finally, one young Native woman from Eskasoni–Agnes Michael (Veronica) Matthews–entered the congregation. Sister Agnes Michael, Sister Mary Kateri (Dorothy) Moore of the Membertou Reserve, and one other Mi'kmaq, were Native women who became Marthas.

The College Connection Revisited

In 1940, St. Francis Xavier University was the congregation's oldest mission and among its two or three largest ones. Of all institutions external to the order, the college had the most intimate relationship with the Marthas, who were "part of the warp and woof of Xaverianism," claimed one professor. The domestic needs of St.F.X. had been the raison d'etre for establishing the Marthas in the 1890s, the motherhouse had been on its campus until 1921, and the college had controlled important aspects of congregational life until the sisters had achieved independence in 1917. In addition, many sisters served at one time or another at the college, and each year some registered in its programs and special summer courses and conferences. The sisters had gradually expanded their ministry beyond household management, the sacristy, and the infirmary to include extension department work (from 1933), assistance in the bursar's office (from 1935), and the library (from 1942). The college administration, the priest professors, and the students usually recognized the wonderful advantages they enjoyed by having the Marthas so deeply involved in their affairs.

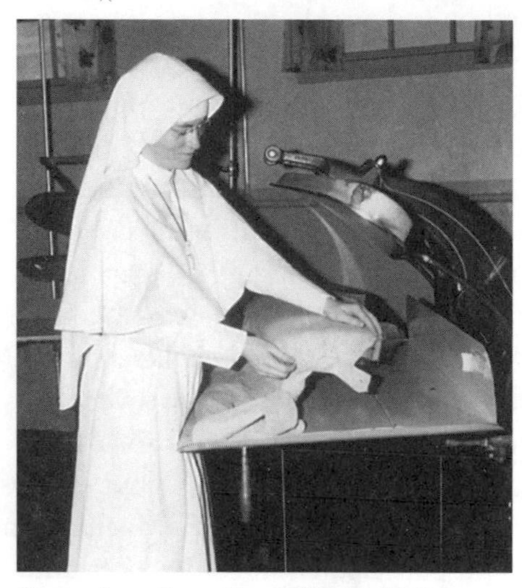

Sister Ann Cornelius (Elizabeth) Beaton in laundry at St.F.X., 1950s.

Occasional strain did occur in the relationship, for example, in 1917, when the Marthas pressed to become independent of the college. And in 1928, Mother Faustina, the "unvarnished woman," frankly urged the "Old Rector," H.P. MacPherson, to correct irregularities there. She stated, "You, reverend Doctor, are not unaware of the fact that St.F.X. has already to its credit, a fair sized procession of

Sister Regina Clare (Madeline Teresa) Connolly, librarian at St.F.X.

both lay and clerical who made, during their stay in the College, either a starting point on a downward career, or an unchecked continuation of the same."[20] She was upset over true reports that a young college priest was given to scandalous drinking binges, and she challenged the rector to quickly resolve the problem. Then, in 1938 the college apparently considered giving its household management to lay people because of dissatisfaction with the sisters' service.[21]

In spite of these occasional stresses and strains, the college connection remained firm. St.F.X. publicly recognized the admirable work of the congregation, both on campus and elsewhere, when it conferred an honorary doctor of laws degree on Mother Faustina in 1937. Also, the sisters living at the original motherhouse, St. Martha's Convent, had the advantage of moving to a modern convent that was part of a major new building completed in 1938 called Morrison Hall. Their convent was overcrowded and St.F.X.'s dining and kitchen facilities were outdated. Sister John Baptist noted that the move was a difficult wrench for some of them: "It was rather with a heavy heart that the Sisters moved from St. Martha's Convent to the commodious new building even if it offered more comfort and better facilities for work."[22]

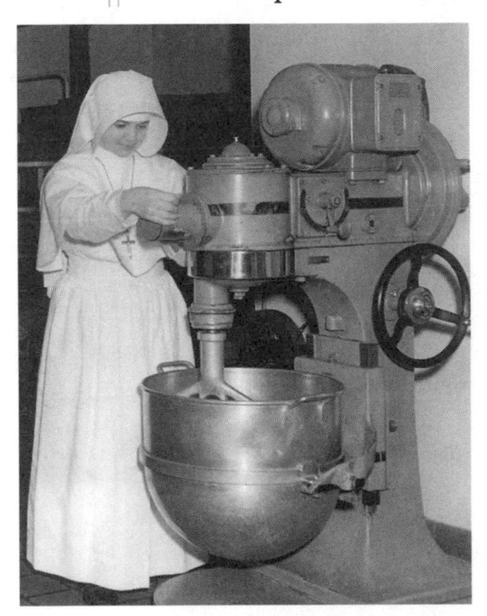

Sister Martina Marie (Pauline) Lichacz in the bakery at St.F.X.

The congregation's vocation crisis during the war decade placed stressful demands on the Marthas' services at St.F.X. In 1940, twenty-nine sisters lived and worked on the campus, and about this same number were there ten years later. However, the college had changed dramatically by then. Enrolments leaped from 359 students in 1939-1940 to 913 in 1949-1950. Part of the growth came from an influx of war veterans immediately after the war. Under its Veterans Rehabilitation training scheme, the federal government offered to finance, through monthly allowances and grants, the studies of ex-service men and women, and many seized the opportunity. Thus, St.F.X. had to enlarge its faculty and build two new residences and a much bigger chapel and auditorium. All these changes affected the Marthas at St.F.X., for they provided the domestic and food services for Xaverians. The shortage of sisters forced them to relinquish some services, for example, the laundry in 1947, and to hire more lay help.[23] Mother Ignatius informed the general chapter which re-elected her for a fourth term in 1949: "In recent years the work has doubled and trebled, due to the increased enrolments of students, and it is no longer possible for the congregation to provide Sisters to fill every department. It is necessary to employ a number of seculars.... There are, nevertheless, many duties the Sisters could fill if we had the numbers."[24] Those many duties would, unfortunately, remain unfilled by the Marthas.

Sisters darning students' socks at St.F.X., 1940s.

Maritime Hospitals

The congregation's vocation shortage during the 1940s had an impact on their hospitals in both Maritime Canada and the west. St. Joseph's Hospital in Glace Bay, Cape Breton, run by the Marthas since 1915 and owned by them since 1930, had expanded during the Depression years, as had the town's population (from 20,706 in 1931 to 25,147 in 1941).[25] A three-storey staff residence was built in 1933, and a TB unit and $251,000 four-storey wing in 1939 that increased the total beds to 144. In 1937, Mother Ignatius had become the hospital's administrator/superior, and she remained so until her re-election as superior general in 1943. She faced dissatisfaction among the district miners who supported the hospital through the check-off system but demanded more say in its operation. They gained increased board representation through a revised constitution; and the long-serving board chair and co-founder of the hospital, Father Charles W. Mac-Donald, resigned and was replaced by Father Michael J. Mac-Kinnon, "the workingman's friend."[26] While the war era increased demands on St. Joseph's Hospital, its sister staff remained at about twenty-six.

Compared to St. Joseph's, St. Rita Hospital (est. 1920) in nearby Sydney was smaller, with forty beds. An average of fifteen Marthas served there annually during the war decade when the city's population expanded by over 2,000 to 31,317 by 1951.[27] The war-inspired crowding had the sister administrators scrambling to find more staff and more room. They understandably felt distress at having to turn patients away because of limited space.[28] Unfortunately, wartime conditions did not permit them to expand. However, they were able to relieve some of the congestion by purchasing the adjacent MacDonald House and making it over as a maternity unit in 1943.

On Cape Breton's west coast, in the mining town of Inverness, a small band of Marthas struggled to maintain adequate services at St. Mary's Hospital. As mentioned, they had taken over the forty-bed institution in 1925. The hospital's finances remained tied to the cycle of mine closures and strikes that beset the town. The parish priest had generously purchased "a large, commodious" staff residence for the hospital in 1933 that was shared by the hospital sisters and lay nurses. A five-bed ward was added in the late 1930s. Each year, through both the 1930s and the 1940s, about seven sisters were assigned to St. Mary's Hospital, where they supervised its several departments. The Marthas were keenly aware of the nursing and maid shortages there, compounded in 1940 by the need to accommodate patients from the town's Memorial Hospital, which was destroyed by fire.

In Antigonish, just below the motherhouse, the congregation's oldest and largest hospital mission, St. Martha's, was experiencing wartime difficulties common to the other Martha hospitals. The hospital had grown since 1930 with the addition of a government-funded, fifty-bed TB annex in 1932.[29] Although plagued by uncollectable hospital bills incurred by patients who lacked cash, it had periodically upgraded its facilities and equipment, and had maintained full accreditation. Thanks to "the greatest friend and benefactor of the hospital," Dr. John L. MacIsaac, St. Martha's had received over $100,000 at his death in 1941. Nonetheless, the sisters' plans to expand the hospital in 1946 had to be shelved, notwithstanding the urgent need for more space. Thirty-two sisters served at St. Martha's Hospital at the end of the war decade. By then, the town's population registered at 3,196, an increase of more than one thousand in ten years.[30]

St. Joseph's Hospital and St. Martha's had well-established nursing schools in the 1940s. For financial reasons, St. Rita Hospital had closed its school in 1933, and it would remain closed until 1955.[31] Tough economic times made nursing schools an attractive labour pool for the hospitals, because student nurses provided free nursing services in exchange for room and board, plus a small living allowance. Salaried graduate nurses could be kept to a minimum. Of course, the Marthas trained some of their own to become nurses, but sisters were also needed by the domestic, teaching, and social work apostolates. So they remained heavily dependent on lay student and graduate nurses. The nursing schools created a more reflective, studied atmosphere in the Marthas' hospitals and sometimes produced vocations for the congregation. On the debit side, they needed a director, made additional budgetary demands, and required release time for a staff qualified to teach.

Sister M. Florence (Mary Ann) MacNeil in hospital lab.

All nurses–religious, student, and graduate–worked long, arduous hours for low pay, and occasionally they were victims of exhaustion and tuberculosis. These were distressing features characteristic of the entire nursing scene in Canada, which was emerging as a major occupational field for women.[32] Nurses began forming provincial and national organizations to improve their conditions and upgrade their training.[33] Nursing school admission standards were low, curricula were poorly designed, and few schools could afford a full-time instructor. The Registered Nurses' Association of Nova Scotia (RNANS), established in 1909, aimed to protect graduate nurses and maintain their honour and status, to unite nurses into one general body, and to set examinations and raise standards. In 1923, Sister Ignatius, then administrator/superior at St. Joseph's Hospital, had been appointed chair of its Standardization of Training Schools Committee. This committee had three major concerns: higher admission standards, common curricula, and the appointment of nursing school inspectors.[34] The committee's work, continued through future decades, stimulated awareness about these issues. Fortunately, the general condition of nurses improved during the war, as demand for their services intensified. Hospitals made more use of graduate nurses, and nursing schools hired clinical instructors.

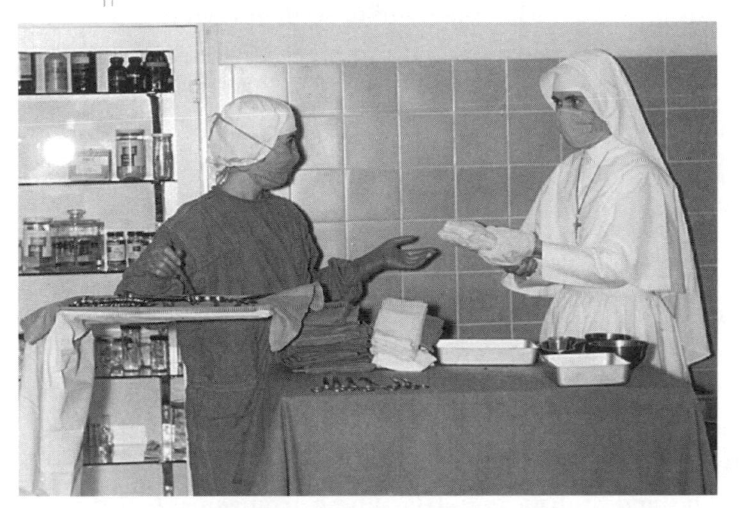

Sister Maria Louis (Mary Bernadette) MacLeod in St. Martha's Hospital operating room, 1960s.

The Sisters of St. Martha shared concerns with others in the hospital field about nursing school standards. Being sisters, they were also concerned about the religious component of nursing education. So, in 1948, when rumours circulated about a possible government-sponsored central nursing school at Dalhousie University, Halifax, representatives from the Marthas' hospitals met with Roman Catholic clergy and other hospital sisters to plan strategies to forestall the move. They passed a motion "that the four Catholic Nurses' Training Schools, St.F.X. University and Mount St. Vincent secure the services of an expert or experts to survey both the work of the schools and their university connections with the view to the adoption of a program designed to strengthen the schools of nursing and secure their permanence."[35] A centralized, government-sponsored nursing school did not materialize in Halifax, but the threat of one impelled the Catholic nursing schools in Nova Scotia to examine their standards, and those in the Diocese of Antigonish seriously considered partial centralization of nurses' training in Antigonish.[36] Sister Clare Marie (Winifred Mary) Lyons, assistant to Sister Mary of Calvary MacDonald, director of St. Martha's School of Nursing, worked for over one year to design a new three-year program in which student nurses from the congregation's two other schools would take about six months training in Antigonish and the remainder at their own hospital schools. However, the entire project was abandoned before the proposed opening date in September 1952. Hospital board members at St. Joseph's and St. Rita were worried about finances, losing the identity of their own nursing schools, and accommodation and tuition expenses in Antigonish.[37]

Another health field issue the Marthas grappled with during the war decade was hospital finance. This issue was a perennial one faced by all eighteen Catholic general hospitals in the Maritimes.[38] By the 1940s, hospital personnel were advocating hospital insurance schemes; many had lived through the financial crisis of the Great Depression and then witnessed the spiralling costs created by the war. Government grants were inadequate, and patients on low or fixed incomes either avoided hospitals or could not pay their hospital bills. The Sisters of St. Martha had used the check-off system and hospital contracts in places such as St. Joseph's and St. Rita hospitals. These arrangements had improved their hospitals' financial stability, but there was still a need for a broader solution.

In 1940 the Nova Scotia and Prince Edward Island Hospital Association appointed Coadjutor Bishop John R. MacDonald of Antigonish, a firm friend of the Marthas and someone deeply interested in health care, to chair a committee on hospitalization. The upshot of the studies, reports, and recommendations was an insurance scheme based on Blue Cross plans developed in the United States. In 1943 the newly formed Maritime Hospital Association (a union of the N.S., P.E.I., and N.B. associations) accepted the plan, and an Act of the Nova Scotia legislature incorporated the Maritime Hospital Service Association or Maritime Blue Cross Plan to administer it. The Marthas fully supported and promoted this insurance scheme, which was open to voluntary participation by any individual, group, or hospital.

Based on the experience of her hospitals, Mother Ignatius, ten years later, judged the Blue Cross Plan a success.[39]

Prairie Hospitals

The Marthas' four general hospitals in the west–St. Michael's (Lethbridge, Alberta), Mineral Springs (Banff, Alberta), St. Michael's (Broadview, Saskatchewan), and St. Peter's (Melville, Saskatchewan)–had serious staff shortages during the 1940s, just as the Maritime hospitals did. St. Michael's was by far the sisters' largest prairie hospital with one hundred beds. In 1949, eighteen sisters formed its Martha community, and worked with over sixty lay staff. For the preceding tens years, the administrators/superiors–Sister Mary Beatrice McMahon (1937–1943), Sister Marie Germaine (Marie Anna) Brassard (1943–1946), and Mother Immaculata (1946-1952)–had often frantically tried to maintain full hospital services in the city.[40] The region's population increased with Japanese evacuees from the Pacific coast during the war, and with displaced persons after the war. The population of Lethbridge itself rose from 14,612 in 1941 to 22,947 in 1951.[41] Annual admissions increased from 3,553 in 1941 to almost 6,000 by 1950, so the building regularly "bulged at the seams." As early as 1941, the advisory board recommended hospital expansion, and the staff residence badly needed improvement; neither problem would be resolved before the 1950s. In March 1945, the hospital was only accepting emergency admissions because of its nurse shortage. It did not have a nursing school and hired only graduate nurses. This policy, along with regular equipment upgrades and frequent staff training, probably accounts for the high accreditation St. Michael's had consistently attained since its opening in 1930. The inspector for the American College of Physicians and Surgeons affirmed in 1950, "This is a very good institution for rendering service to [the region]."[42]

Mineral Springs Hospital at Banff in the Rocky Mountains faced its own stresses and strains throughout the war decade, even though the town's resident population increased only minimally to nearly three thousand.[43] The accelerating demands, especially for arthritic and physiotherapy treatments, required

Mother Ignatius and her general council to increase the six sisters there in 1941 to ten by 1951.[44] Sister Mary Clarissa (Florence) Chisholm, a strong, competent leader, remained superior administrative from 1943 to 1949. Overcrowding forced her to take stop-gap measures and to press for a new hundred-bed hospital. In 1944, her hospital at times had eighty-five patients, and those on the waiting list sometimes stayed at a local hotel. She was able to open a new six-bed ward in 1945, but this was entirely inadequate to meet the demand. Although new hospital plans were approved in 1947 and a site was secured, construction was delayed by high costs, a short-staffed architect, and the difficulty of buying mater-ials. The old, deteriorating hospital facility had become utterly inadequate, staff were hard to find and keep, patients were refused admission, and the medical staff and advisory board members urged the sisters to build. These unresolved problems made Mineral Springs a most difficult mission, in spite of its idyllic mountain setting. And new problems lay just around the corner.

The congregation's two Saskatchewan hospitals were smaller than the Alberta institutions. At St. Michael's Hospital in Broadview, Sister Peter Marie (Alice Marie) Gazeley led the small community of five Marthas from 1941 to 1947. The twenty-bed community hospital experienced some annual increases in admissions through the decade, although the town population remained relatively stable at almost nine hundred.[45] Sister Peter Marie found it a severe hardship to find and keep nurses, a problem compounded by frequent sickness among her own sisters. The proximity of Native reserves allowed her to hire Native women to help with St. Michael's household needs.[46]

The leadership at St. Peter's Hospital, Melville, was much less stable during the difficult war decade than at St. Michael's. Four superior administrators served between 1940 and 1950. Sister Superior Mary Daniel MacLellan, a capable leader, tragically died from a "cerebral hemorrhage" in 1943 at the age of fifty-one after only three years as superior.[47] Her successors faced the central problem of staffing shortages that plagued all the hospitals. Annual admissions to the fifty-five-bed institution increased; but the number of sisters in community there annually remained fixed at about six. Unlike Broadview, Melville's population grew by over 500 to 4,458 by 1951.[48] The shortage of nurses and maids required the Melville sisters to work very long hours. In spite of the sisters' trials, their hospital received strong commendations from external inspectors.[49]

Hospital financing in Saskatchewan took an intriguing turn near the end of the war decade. Hospitals in that province faced the same difficulties as those in Maritime Canada–inadequate government support, uncollectable patient accounts, and expensive facilities and equipment. So hospital insurance schemes had long been discussed in the west and were sometimes established at local initiative.[50] However, on 1 January 1947, Premier Tommy Douglas and his Co-operative Commonwealth Federation government inaugurated the Saskatchewan Hospital Services Plan that introduced mandatory hospital insurance. Suddenly the province's hospitals found themselves in a new ball game.

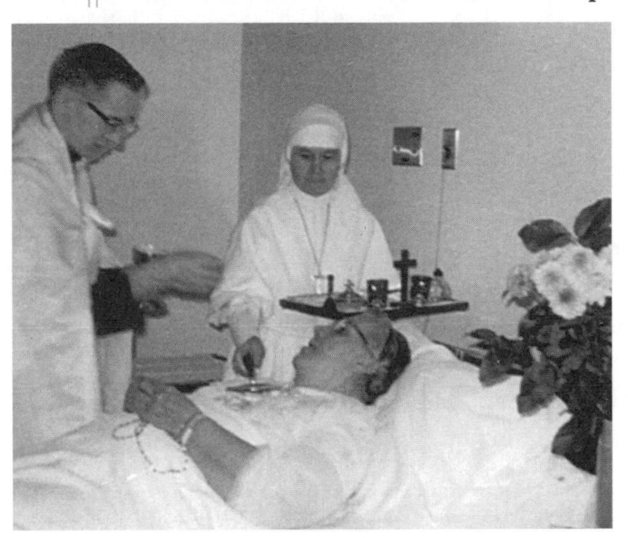

Sister Olivia Francis (Martha Agnes Geraldine) Fodey assisting with communion for the sick at St. Peters Hospital, Melville, Saskatchewan.

At first there was "great fear for the future of Catholic hospitals."[51] The Sisters of St. Martha were definitely worried about a government takeover; in Saskatchewan they owned two general hospitals and a maternity hospital for unwed mothers. Nevertheless, Premier Douglas's socialist government did not nationalize the hospitals. It did, however, announce that it would cover hospital costs, but not the salaries of sisters; instead, hospital sisters would receive only an allowance for food and clothing. The CCF did not want religious congregations siphoning public hospital funds out of the province. For congregations, the minimal income received under this pitiful arrangement would contribute little to liquidating debt or paying interest on loans.[52] So Catholics, especially the Catholic Hospital Conference of Saskatchewan, created a howl and mounted a vigorous lobby to reverse what they judged to be a discriminatory government policy. Mother Ignatius and supporters, such as the CCF member from Cape Breton, Clarence Gillis, joined right in. They were quick to remind the province's CCF government of their pioneering role in Saskatchewan health care, of their heroic war efforts, of their twenty-four-hour-a-day service, and of the millions of dollars they had saved the government.[53] Their campaign worked; the CCF backed down and reversed its position, an about-face that greatly relieved the Sisters of St. Martha. Sisters employed in hospitals would receive the same salaries as their secular counterparts. Although the new plan spawned an army of hospital inspectors and auditors, it did not undermine the congregation's control of its own hospitals; and the funding scheme gave its Saskatchewan institutions a more dependable financial base.

The Marthas and Health Care Associations

While the bulk of the Marthas' work in the health care apostolate was helping local communities meet the health needs of their people, they also contributed to the development and proceedings of Canada's hospital and nurses' associations. The sisters helped usher into being or strongly supported organizations such as the Maritime Conference of the Catholic Hospital Association, the Nova Scotia and Prince Edward Island Hospital Association, the Canadian Hospital Council, and the Maritime Council of Catholic Nurses. The Marthas participated as founders, promoters, executive members, voters, conference convenors, participants, and speakers. They reaped a harvest of benefits from this active participation–knowledge of current health issues and trends, information about developments in nursing education and hospital financing, exposure to diverse viewpoints, contacts with key government and professional people in the hospital field, and periodic injections of inspiration. The ultimate beneficiaries of this broad involvement were the patients they served.

Mother Ignatius, the superior general whose leadership dominated the congregation's life from 1925 to 1961, was especially active in professional associations. In 1922, she had helped Sister Audet of New Brunswick, a Religious Hospitaller of St. Joseph, form the Maritime Conference of the Catholic Hospital

Association (MCCHA).[54] This conference, a member of the parent organization in the United States, included Nova Scotia, Prince Edward Island, and New Brunswick and was the first of its kind in Canada. Speaking as president to the annual convention in 1924, Sister Ignatius, then superior administrator of St. Joseph's Hospital, urged all delegates to strive for "the highest possible standards of hospital efficiency in our respective institutions."[55] She struck a note here that was to inform her congregation's policy toward all its hospitals: to aim for the highest standards and the best methods within the limits of its resources. Other Marthas besides Mother Ignatius regularly participated in the MCCHA. For example, at the annual conference in 1928, Sister M. Jovita MacArthur demonstrated methods of nursing instruction, Sister Mary Elizabeth Ross lectured on dietitics, and Sister Mary Beatrice McMahon read a paper on hospital hospitality.[56]

The non-denominational Canadian Hospital Council was established in 1931 at Ottawa. The MCCHA was invited to join and the Marthas strongly advocated this. Even though the parent organization in the United States opposed the move, Maritime bishops and sisters believed it would help them. Canadian hospital problems were different from those south of the border. Hence, three delegates from the MCCHA attended the founding convention.[57]

The Marthas also supported the formation of a non-sectarian hospital association in the Maritimes. Dr. Harvey Agnew of the Canadian Medical Association, a close friend of Mother Ignatius, urged Maritime hospitals in 1929 to form a regional association.[58] Mother Ignatius was right behind the idea, especially as it promised to spread a "progressive spirit" and help form a united front for lobbying governments to increase hospital grants. Interested hospital people in Nova Scotia started with a provincial organization. Mother Ignatius, as part of the organizational drive, circularized the province's hospitals and collected information on hospital financing in other provinces. Government funding had remained at pre–World War One levels in spite of rising costs. She wrote in March 1929: "The first and most important move after we become organized is to make a strong, united appeal to the Government of Nova Scotia for a higher grant toward our hospitals."[59] Mother Ignatius became the vice-president of the association formed that year. By 1931, Prince Edward Island had joined, to make it the Nova Scotia and Prince Edward Island Hospital Association. Sister John Baptist Cameron wrote a series of newspaper articles for the new association that informed the public of the role and plight of the region's hospitals; her aim was to pressure governments for more generous funding.[60]

Strong support for professional health organizations became a standing policy of the congregation. It supported the MCCHA's sponsorship of a Maritime Council of Catholic Nurses in 1935.[61] The MCCHA also joined with other Canadian Catholic hospital conferences to form a national organization–the Catholic Hospital Conference of Canada. The story of professional involvements was the same for the sisters in western Canada. As associations developed there, both Catholic and non-denominational, the hospital sisters participated. In 1939–1940, for example, Sister Mary Beatrice McMahon, superintendent of St. Michael's Hospital, Lethbridge, became president-elect of the Prairie Conference of the Catholic Hospital Association.[62]

Golden Jubilee and Retrospective

At the conclusion of the trying war decade, the Sisters of St. Martha had reason to celebrate: they had reached their fiftieth anniversary. From this milestone, they looked back with gratitude to God for all they had achieved together. And it was considerable. The congregation had grown to about 283 professed sisters; most of them came from Scottish, Irish, and Acadian Catholic families of the Diocese of Antigonish, but some came from the prairie west and Newfoundland too. Twenty sisters had more than forty years experience in the congregation. Sister M. Dorothy Beaton, age 77, was the longest professed at fifty-two years. Fifty-four sisters of St. Martha had gone to their eternal reward.[63] Overall, the Marthas' educational levels had increased markedly: thirty-three held teachers' licenses, fifty were graduate nurses, twenty-seven had earned bachelor's degrees, and two had masters degrees.[64] Many others had acquired diplomas in health-related fields, social work, art, and music.

By 1950, all this congregational "woman power" and educational expertise was distributed widely. The sisters' "four-fold" apostolate of domestic work, health care, teaching, and social work was by now well established. They had developed twenty-four foundations in all. Most of the sisters, over forty percent, served in the ten hospital missions–five in the Maritimes and five on the prairies. Nearly twenty percent of the congregation lived at the motherhouse in Antigonish, which housed the general administration, the infirmary, and other departments. Forty-one sisters were assigned to three domestic service missions, nine worked at the Little Flower Orphanage, twenty-four taught on four teaching missions, each of which had a homemaker were serving as social workers, and seventeen laboured in parish ministries.[65] The external works of the sisters from Antigonish were indeed impressive.

The development of all these external works created both wealth and debt for the community. Sister Mary Hugh Cameron commented bleakly that it was impossible to "picture any house belonging to the tribe of St. Martha without being deeply in debt." She added, "One thing we should be most grateful to the Almighty for, and that is to be such excellent financial swimmers. There must be a lot of financial cork in our make up, because so far, thank God, we are able to keep floating."[66] Actually, the congregation's finances had improved since the Great Depression years. During the war decade, hospital revenues had increased, and the sisters paid off a considerable amount of hospital debt. Teachers' salaries had also risen, and the motherhouse enterprises–altar breads, bookbinding, printing, church goods, art and handicrafts, and farming–generated revenues too.[67] The war-pumped Canadian economy experienced no precipitous downturn after the armistice in 1945, so the congregation benefited from the healthy economic environment. Despite assets of $2.2 million primarily accounted for in their eleven buildings, including Bethany and the four largest hospitals, and responsible financial management, the sisters' debt load remained at over $1 million.[68]

One of the happy events after the war that gave further cause for rejoicing in the jubilee year was final papal approval of the congregation's constitutions. The sisters had applied in 1931 to become a papal institute, and shortly thereafter the Vatican had awarded them temporary approval. In April 1939, Mother Immaculata, on behalf of the Marthas, had again applied to Rome, this time for final approval. Her agent in Rome was Msgr. William R. Clapperton; so she had prominent Canadian ecclesiastics who knew the congregation send supporting letters to him.

The Apostolic Delegate in Canada informed the general council in 1941 that approval was imminent. However, not until January 1946 did the sisters find out for sure that Pope Pius XII had given their constitutions his blessing three years before, on 3 April 1943; war conditions had delayed the news.[69] Since that time, in 1946, the sisters have held an annual mass of thanksgiving for this blessing. Mother Ignatius declared before the general chapter in 1949: "We should be most grateful to our Archbishop, to the Apostolic Delegate, and to the Archbishops and Bishops who assisted us in placing our congregation on a firm footing. It is up to each one of us to love and cherish our constitutions, to observe faithfully all that it contains, and to guard conscientiously the sacred trust confided to us on April 3, 1943."[70]

Novice and postulant playing baseball.

By their golden jubilee, the Sisters of St. Martha had developed a mature, and successful community life. They had experienced no wrenching schisms that could have threatened the unity of their common life. The congregation reported to Rome, "Religious discipline is observed and the government of Superiors made easy, for the most part, by the docility of the subjects."[71] The heavy regime of work might partly explain the "docility of the subjects," as would the tradition of deference to religious authority. But the sisters also played and recreated together. During daily recreation and other celebrations, they talked, sang, danced, ate, played cards, told stories, swam, enjoyed picnics, and more. There was nothing dour, joyless, or rigid about this side of their common life. In Antigonish it became a tradition at New Year's for the university to open the rink for the local sisters.[72] Sometimes the students invited them to an exhibition game of hockey. By the late 1940s, another tradition was underway: the celebration of sisters' golden jubilees. The congregation's earliest professed were aging. Golden anniversary celebrations came to include the jubilarian's renewal of vows during mass, a special dinner in her honour, opening of gifts, and visits from relatives. Marthas expected the younger sisters to show appropriate deference to their elders. Date of profession in the congregation had become, along with administrative service, a criterion of status and rank.

The New Year's skate at St.F.X.

Sketch by Sister Irene Doyle

Changing times had also wrought alterations in the sisters' common life. As they spread nationwide, the Marthas adopted measures to strengthen "the internal bonds of union." The general secretary required each mission to send in bimonthly news items for *The Bethanite*. In alternate months, the motherhouse sent a newsletter to the missions in the far west, and frequently it circularized all the missions of the congregation. House annals were to be excerpted annually for the motherhouse records.[73] By 1950 the sisters were depending more and more often on cars for transportation. In Regina, during the late 1930s, Sister Joseph Helen Mulvihill became the first sister to drive. In the Maritimes, Sister Aneas Joseph (Agnes Josephine) MacDonald was the first in 1941; she drove the congregation's new nine-seater bus in Antigonish. The Bethany annalist speculated, "We presume there will be some consternation in our small town to see a Sister at the wheel for the first time in the Diocese of Antigonish."[74] Finally, by their golden anniversary, the Marthas were promoting professional development and upgrading among themselves to meet the challenges of their professional apostolates–teaching, health care, and social work. Sisters found themselves more and more often registering in diploma and degree programs, and participating in study clubs, round-table discussions, conferences, and institutes.[75]

A central part of the Marthas' internal community life remained religious ceremonials and practice. Again, by 1950, they had extended, developed and modified their original pattern of religious observance. Their devotion to St. Martha had become richer. In the 1940s, certain sisters, for example, Sister John Baptist Cameron and Sister Joseph Helen Mulvihill, composed St. Martha prayers, meditations, and hymns. In 1949 the Vatican's Sacred Congregation of Rites approved a mass of St. Martha written by four priests at the university (Fathers John Hugh Gillis, George L. Kane, James McMahon, and Jerome C. Chisholm) that could be used on the feast of St. Martha.[76] In 1947 the sisters began study clubs to rework their 1926 *Directory and Book of Customs*, and the mimeographed revision came into use in 1949. It was not substantially different from the earlier directory, covering the means to acquire perfection, the constitutions, congregational government, and regulations for postulants and novices. However, it was more concise than the earlier one and wisely allowed for more flexibility in the sisters' daily house schedules. Finally, the Marthas made two important changes in their prayer book tradition. In 1933, Father Jerome Chisholm helped them compile a new manual to replace their first one produced in 1913. Sisters referred to the new 403-page compilation as the "Good Manual." However, it proved expensive and long, so a 116-page "Everyday Manual," or "Small Prayer Book," came into use after 1943. All the meditations, devotions, customs, regulations, and prayers promoted the life of perfection according to the Catholic model. Furthermore, Marthas believed prayer to be an important means of pleasing God and enlisting His aid for their individual and community projects. Mother Ignatius affirmed: "We are particularly grateful for the generous way in which [the sisters] respond to appeals for prayers for special intentions. We are convinced that any success the congregation may achieve in its various undertakings is due to the earnest prayers of the Sisters, and we humbly acknowledge that without these prayers our material efforts would be of little avail."[77]

In 1949, on the eve of its golden jubilee year, the congregation held at Bethany its fifth general chapter. Mother Ignatius was re-elected; it would be her fourth term as superior general. The delegates were preoccupied with minor breaches of discipline, for example, violations of grand silence, gossip, lack of charity to one another, unworthy reading material, neglect of community regulations, visiting and travelling alone, and the problem of "spiritually lax" sisters. Mother Ignatius reported that she had received dozens of requests for new missions since 1943, but only one had been approved (the school at Eskasoni) because of "the scarcity of sisters." She added that the nursing shortage during and after the war remained "a serious problem."[78] Finally, as the chapter delegates were fully aware of their pending golden jubilee, they decided to honour the late Bishop John Cameron, "the founder of our Congregation." Hence, they designated his patronal feast, 24 June, as "Founder's Day" and declared it a grand holiday. Sister John Baptist was assigned to write a "sketch" of Bishop Cameron's life that was later distributed to all the congregation's houses.[79]

The jubilee year inspired a rush of planning and preparation that culminated with special celebrations on Jubilee Day, August 1, 1950. Visitors galore, some of them high-ranking church leaders, descended on the town of Antigonish. A Pontifical High Mass was held in thc St.F.X. University Chapel, Pope Pius XII sent a congratulatory message, special dinners for clergy and visiting sisters were held, and a portrait of "our revered founder" was unveiled at Bethany. Also, the clergy and laity of the Diocese of Antigonish presented the Marthas with a $9,000 chcque, for the sisters, a "touching" manifestation of "loyal support and good will." The special events continued on 2 August with a Solemn Requiem Mass for the deceased sisters, a procession to the cemetery, a reception at Bethany for family and friends, and a final Solemn Benediction by Bishop Francis P. Carroll of Calgary.[80] A tide of letters, cards, and telegrams from well-wishers, such as sister congregations, expatriate clergy, professional associations, and the Antigonish town mayor also flooded Bethany.

Other honours were also heaped on the Sisters of St. Martha during this special year. *The Casket, Halifax Herald*, and *Sydney Post* printed eulogies under such headings as "East and West Benefitted by Busy Congregation," "Like their Patroness, Sisters of St. Martha Serve True Son of God," and "Xaverian Family Indebted to Sisters, Says Msgr. Nicholson." The Xaverian family (St. Francis Xavier University), one of the major beneficiaries of the Marthas, conferred an honorary degree on Mother Ignatius. President Nicholson wrote to her, "It was felt that such an action would be appropriate at any time, but particularly so because of the anniversary occurring this year, which occasions so much joy to us all."[81] Finally, Edmonton's Archbishop John Hugh MacDonald, a native of Antigonish County who had witnessed the founding of the congregation while a student at St.F.X., sent an insightful tribute: "I wish to congratulate those in charge at different times on the magnificent spirit they have developed in the Community, and which has become so characteristic of its members wherever they are engaged. I sincerely trust that this spirit, with its simplicity, humility, and charity will continue to grow during all the years to come."[82]

As part of its jubilee, the congregation itself honoured Mother Ignatius and her predecessor Mother Stanislaus by sending them on a trip to Rome. An untimely illness kept Mother Stanislaus at home. However, in the fall of 1950, Mother Ignatius and Sister Thomas Aquinas MacLellan visited Rome and interesting stopovers in between. The highpoint of their lengthy pilgrimage was an audience with Pope Pius XII; they asked for and received his blessing on the congregation. The Bethany annalist exulted the day afterwards: "We received glorious news today! In a private audience with the Holy Father he imparted his Apostolic Benediction to all our Sisters and their works, and to the Sisters' parents, brothers, sisters, and relatives! We were certainly delighted, and privileged, and it was surely sufficient reason for *Deo Gratias* all day!"[83]

Bethany hospitality–L to R: Sister M. Bernadette Peters, Sister M. Thecla Price, and Mother M. Ignatius.

The jubilee year aptly marked the conclusion of an eventful fifty years for the Sisters of St. Martha. As a community that had overcome many obstacles and challenges, as well as experienced numberless opportunities and blessings, they had much cause for celebration. The jubilee itself evoked reflections on the path they had traced together. The literary fruits of this reflection included a biography of Bishop John Cameron and a history of the congregation, both written by Sister John Baptist Cameron. These historical musings helped the sisters maintain links with their past, and the presence among them of nine pioneer Marthas who had entered the community before 1901 served as a living connection with their roots.[84] Unfortunately, the oldest living link in 1950, Sister M. Theodore Sampson, age 83, died after being struck by a car in Sydney.[85] That year also marked the end of the stressful war decade when vocations had been few, staff shortages many, and sisters had knitted for soldiers and practiced blackouts to prepare for air raids. The year 1950 also commenced a demanding ten-year period that would begin with Rome's appointment of a new bishop for the Diocese of Antigonish.

Notes

1 E.R. Forbes and D.A. Muise, eds., *The Atlantic Provinces in Confederation* (Toronto and Fredericton: University of Toronto Press and Acadiensis Press, 1993), p. 310.

2 The statistical data in this paragraph and the following one are based on the congregation's Quinquennial Reports to the Holy See, 1931, 1941 and 1951, F5,S34,SS1,f1-2,b84.

3 Vocations from the west would probably have been higher had the motherhouse itself been in the west and the priests and public more aware of the congregation. Young women often considered the motherhouse, where they would be trained, too far away. Sister Francis de Sales to Dear Sister, 14 January 1949, F13,S2,SS1,f1,b170.

4 CSM Register of Deaths, 1899f, F5,S33,SS9,f1,b79.

5 Retreat Register, 1929-1930, F5,S32,SS1,f1,b71.

6 General Chapter Proceedings, 1943, F5,S8,SS1,f4,b6.

7 Sister John Baptist Cameron, "History," p. 178.

8 Mother Ignatius to Dear Sisters, 17 August, 1946, files of Sister Irene Doyle.

9 Mother Ignatius to Sisters, 6 September 1943, F5,S8,SS1,f4,b6.

10 Mother Ignatius, Visitation Report, 8 March 1947, F6,S3,SS2,f4,b111.

11 Proceedings of Teachers' Institute, 24-28 August 1953, p. 19, F5,S25,SS1,f1,b61.

12 Bethany Annals, 9 September 1943, 21-24 July 1944, F6,S1,SS1,f9-10,b107.

13 Ibid., 29 July 1945.

14 Review of Unfilled Requests file, 1930-1960, F5,S35,SS1,f9-11,b95.

15 Mother Ignatius to Mother St. Brigid, 22 July 1950, F5,S35,SS1,f9,b95.

16 *The Bethanite*, IX, November 1942, p. 17.

17 Mother Ignatius, Visitation Report, 20 April 1955, F38,S1,SS1,f6,b235.

18 *The Bethanite*, XIV, 1947, p. 6.

19 Rev. Michael Harding, OFM, Canonical Visitation, May 1953, F5,S34,SS1,f13,b85.

20 Copy of letter in Mother Faustina to Bishop Morrison, 12 April 1928, Incoming Mail, #14968, BMP, ADA.

21 See Mother Immaculata to President D.J. MacDonald, 2 November 1938, F21,S2,SS1,f8,b192.

22 Sister John Baptist Cameron, "History," p. 151.

23 *Xaverian*, 25 January 1947, p. 1, STFXUA.

24 General Chapter Proceedings, 1949, F5,S8,SS2,f1,b6.

25 *Census of Canada 1971*, 1.1:2-11.

26 Bethany Annals, 14 January 1937, F6,S1,SS1,f4,b107.

27 *Census of Canada, 1971*, 1.1:2-11.

28 Mother Immaculata to Most Rev. Ildebrando Antoniutto, 3 April 1943, F5,S34,SS1,f8,b84.

29 Bethany Annals, 4 December 1931, F6,S1,SS1,f1,b106.

30 *Census of Canada, 1971*, 1.1:2-11.

31 Nursing School Statistics, F5,S22,SS12,f1,b57.

32 David Coburn, "The Development of Canadian Nursing: Professionalization and Proletarianization," *International Journal of Health Services*, 18, no. 3 (1988), pp. 437-455.

33 Janet Ross Kerr and Jeannetta MacPhail, *Canadian Nursing: Issues and Perspectives*, 3rd edition (New York: Mosley, 1996), p. 31.

34 "A Brief History of Years from the Beginning of the RNANS in 1909 through 1934," *RNANS Newsletter 1909-1979*, p. 4.

35 Minutes of a Meeting held in Halifax, 15 May 1948, F5,S22,SS14,f3,b57.

36 Meeting of the Committee on the Central School Question, 23 August 1951, F5,S22,SS14,f3,b57.

37 Notes by Sister Antoinette Chiasson, 23 February 1994, F5,S22,SS11,f1,b57.

38 Anon., "The Development of Catholic Hospitals, Maritime Provinces, 1922-1947," F5,S21,SS1,f1,b52.

39 Mother Ignatius, "Blue Cross in the Maritimes," *The Canadian Hospital* (December 1955), pp. 38-39.

40 St. Michael's Hospital, Lethbridge, Personnel, 1929-1988, F9,S1,SS2,f7,b143.
41 *Census of Canada 197*1, 1.1:2-103.
42 Dr. Malcolm T. MacEachern to Mother Immaculata, 28 September 1950, F9,S3,SS1,f2,b144.
43 *Census of Canada, 1971*, 1.1:2-106.
44 Mineral Springs Hospital Personnel Lists, F11,S1,SS2,f2,b159.
45 *Census of Canada, 1971*, 1.1:2-89.
46 St. Michael's Hospital, Broadview, Personnel List and Statistics, F15,S1,SS2,f1-2,b175.
47 Bethany Annals, 10 January 1943, F6,S1,SS1,f7,b107.
48 *Census of Canada, 1971*, 1.1:2-89.
49 St. Peter's Hospital, Statistical Data and Personnel List, F13,S1,SS2,f1,b169, and Record of Standardization and Accreditation of Hospitals Operated by the Congregation to 1960, F5,S22,SS2,f1,b53.
50 Hospital Plans in Western Canada, 1959, F5,S21,SS1,f1,b52.
51 St. Peter's Hospital, Melville, Annals Highlights, 1947, F13,S1,SS1,f6,b169.
52 Sister John Baptist Cameron, "History," p. 184.
53 Mother Ignatius to Clarence Gillis, MP, 10 February 1947, F13,S2,SS1,f1,b170.
54 "Atlantic Conference of Catholic Hospitals," souvenir booklet, 1965, F5,S21,SS6,f3,b52.
55 Sister Ignatius, President's Remarks to the MCCHA, Charlottetown, 1924, F5,S21,SS5,f9,b52.
56 Bethany Annals, 10 June 1928, F6,S1,SS1,f1,b106.
57 Sister John Baptist Cameron, "History," pp. 119-20.
58 Bethany Annals, 20 February 1930, F6,S1,SS1,f1,b106.
59 Mother Ignatius to Sister Mary Carmel, 8 March 1929, F8,S2,SS1,f4,b132.
60 New Brunswick formed its own hospital association that merged with the Nova Scotia-P.E.I. organization in 1943 to form the Maritime Hospital Association.
61 *The Bethanite*, II, May 1935, p. 14.
62 Sister John Baptist Cameron, "History," p. 162.
63 CSM Register of Deaths, 1899f, F5,S33,SS9,f1,b79.
64 These figures are based on annual reports to the Holy See, F5,S34,SS1,f5,b85. Because of changes in methods of reporting, they are approximate.
65 Ibid.
66 Sister Mary Hugh Cameron to Sister Mary of Mercy, 7 February 1951, F15,S2,SS1,f5,b175.

67 CSM Quinnquennial Report to the Holy See, 1951, F5,S34,SS1,f2,b84.
68 Financial Report to the General Chapter, 30 June 1949, F5,S8,SS2,f1,b6.
69 See Appendix III for the final 1943 Decree of Approval.
70 Mother Ignatius, Report to the General Chapter, 1949, F5,S5,SS1,f1,b256.
71 CSM Quinnquennial Report to the Holy See, 1951, F5,S34,SS1,f2,b84.
72 Bethany Annals, 2 January 1940, F6,S1,SS1,f5,b107.
73 CSM Quinnquennial Report to the Holy See, 1951, F5,S34,SS1,f2,b84.
74 Bethany Annals, 9 July 1941, F6,S1,SS1,f7,b107.
75 For an example, see Documents on Institute for Hospital Sisters, Bethany, 16-17 August 1947, F5,S22,SS4,f1,b54.
76 Bethany Annals, 27 and 29 July 1949, F6,S1,SS1,f11,b107.
77 General Chapter Proceedings, 1949, F5,S8,SS2,f1,b6.
78 Ibid.
79 The Marthas would later revisit this question of their founding and would revise their conclusion about Bishop Cameron's role.
80 Bethany Annals, 1-2 August 1950, F6,S1,SS1,f12,b107.
81 President Nicholson to Mother Ignatius, 3 April 1950, F5,S34,SS19,f29,b93.
82 Archbishop John Hugh MacDonald to Mother Ignatius, 12 August 1950, F1,S5,SS1,f1,b2.
83 Bethany Annals, 16 September 1950, F6,S1,SS1,f12,b107 and correspondence re trip to Rome, F5,S33,SS6,f3,b78.
84 Golden Jubilee booklet.
85 Bethany Annals, 10 October 1950, F6,S1,SS1,f12,b107.

Chapter Nine

A Demanding Decade: The 1950s

Starting in their jubilee year, the Congregation of the Sisters of St. Martha shifted to an accelerated level of activity. In their many new endeavours, they would experience the impact of broad Canadian changes: the war had revitalized industry and reduced poverty and unemployment; people often forsook their rural and village homes for anticipated opportunities in the region's towns and cities; MacKenzie King's Liberal government had created new social programs–unemployment insurance (1940), family allowance (1944), and Canada Mortgage and Housing (1946); the civil service at both levels of government expanded by leaps and bounds; and the Canadian population grew by 30 percent to more than 18 million during the decade. Television appeared in living rooms to dispense the culture and ethics of "mainstream North America," and the post-war baby boom brought a massive increase in school-age children. And, in spite of the Cold War climate in East-West relations, the general prosperity created a feeling of optimism and confidence about the future. The 1950s appeared, then, as a dynamic "decade of development" when "the forces of change would sweep away most of the remnants of the traditional way of life and replace it with highly bureaucratised and centralised structures from which few could escape."[1] The Sisters of St. Martha would find this optimistic, expansive decade a most demanding one. Their social work would multiply and even extend into the United States, their teaching assignments would increase, their involvement in the retreat movement would deepen, and their hospitals would undertake expensive building programs.

CHANGE IN DIOCESAN LEADERSHIP

The new Bishop of Antigonish, the Very Reverend John R. MacDonald, was the major source of the accelerating demands placed on the Marthas. His predecessor, Bishop Morrison, had died on 13 April 1950 at age 88; thus had ended a thirty-eight-year, dignified and staid episcopate. Bishop Morrison and the Marthas had enjoyed a positive, fruitful, and respectful relationship since his appointment in 1912. Close to the end of his life, the congregation had expressed its gratitude for "the many favours we have received because of your kind and fatherly interest in our little congregation during the past thirty-seven years."[2] The bishop had supported the congregation's extension of its missions beyond the Diocese of Antigonish, had accepted their bid for independence from the college in 1917 and had affirmed their desire in 1929 to gain the status of a papal institute. Caution, prudence, conservatism, and sober diligence had been his stock-in-trade; during their early years of youthful inexperience and enthusiasm, the sisters had benefited from this approach. On their side, the congregation had been a powerful ally for the bishop in developing and strengthening the Catholic faith and institutions of his diocese. He could not have been blessed with a more loyal and dedicated army of diocesan workers.

Bishop John R. MacDonald, a fifty-nine-year-old native of Port Hood, Inverness County, Cape Breton, and graduate of St.F.X. (1911), first met the Marthas when he enrolled at the college in 1905. For over a decade after 1926, he had remained spiritual director and confessor for their novitiate. His biographer concluded, "During those years he laid a solid foundation of friendship for the congregation that endeared him to the Sisters and, at the same time, made it easier for him to ask for help whenever needed; and the need became constant."[3] The sisters had established a teaching convent in St. Andrews during his pastorate there (1928–1932), and while rector of St. Ninian's

Cathedral, Antigonish (1916–1922 and 1932–1943), he had almost daily contact with the sisters at Bethany. Moreover, Father MacDonald had a keen interest in hospitals and had closely collaborated with Mother Ignatius in that field. At the news of his appointment to the Bishopric of Peterborough, Ontario, in 1943, a sister wrote, "We were thrilled and grieved to hear the wonderful news that a great friend of the congregation–Rev. John R. MacDonald–was appointed Bishop of Peterborough."[4] That "wonderful news" had dashed the sisters' hopes, but only temporarily, that he would succeed the aging Bishop Morrison. Father John R. would return as co-adjutor in 1945. For his part, the young priest admired the Sisters of St. Martha. In 1941, he wrote to Mother Immaculata: "One could not be a regular witness to the unselfish devotion and the beautiful religious spirit of your Sisters, without profiting by the experience."[5]

His appointment as bishop of Antigonish in 1950 inaugurated a new era for all diocesan institutions, and especially for the Sisters of St. Martha. He was a bishop in a hurry, with a lengthy background of broad concern about social issucs; now that the diocesan administrative reins were finally in his hands, after serving as Bishop Morrison's co-adjutor for five frustrating years when he was allowed to do little, he planned to make things happen. The Bethany annalist in January reported the new bishop "really getting into the harness." She commented: "Things are really starting to hum in diocesan ecclesiastical circles. His Excellency is starting to organise."[6] The Marthas had been overjoyed to learn of Father John R. MacDonald's appointment as bishop, but little did they know what he had in store for them. By March, Mother Ignatius began to discover it. She lamented, "Sickness is depleting our ranks–we seem to have so many young Sisters breaking down–and now that Bishop MacDonald has taken over in real earnest, we are just about going around in circles. He wants vacation schools, lay retreats, and a host of other things."[7] Evidently he planned to harness for his diocesan purposes what he correctly recognised as "the wonderful zeal, the devoted service and the unlimited kindness of the Sisters of St. Martha."[8] And Mother Ignatius would be obliging, perhaps too obliging. Bishop MacDonald would exert most pressure in social work and teaching.

New Schemes in Diocesan Social Work

Changing trends in social work, formal surveys, and destructive fires altered the social work scene in the Diocese of Antigonish during the 1950s. Progressive thinkers were highly critical of the institutional care of children. Child welfare leaders favoured instead the nurture of children, especially the very young, within families.[9] The Marthas at the Little Flower Institute, the Mercy Hospital, and in parish social work agencies generally agreed with this approach. Then, in 1950 the new bishop invited his colleague, Bishop J.G. Berry of Peterborough, Ontario, to survey the diocesan social work agencies and he did so in July. He recommended a greater unification and coordination of all diocesan agencies. "Bishop John R.," as he was known locally, presented the report to the Joint Advisory Board of the Mercy Hospital and Little Flower Institute. He then suggested that "this present board constitute a Diocesan Board–which would include–Mercy Hospital, Little Flower Institute, Catholic Charities, and general questions 're' diocesan charities, that is promoting the work in other parishes, etc."[10] Thus was born the Board of the Antigonish Diocesan Charities (ADC). Bishop John R. also followed Bishop Berry's recommendation to appoint a director of Catholic Charities: Father John G. Webb had studied at the Maritime School of Social Work in Halifax and became full-time director in 1955 with an office in Sydney. The Martha social workers cooperated closely with Father Webb and also participated on the new board.

A fire at the sisters' St. Rita Hospital, Sydney, in February 1951 closed the career of Mercy Hospital. During thirty-four years, its sisters had cared for 686 unwed mothers and their infants. However, the fire allowed Bishop John R. to be rid of a financial white elephant and to experiment with a new program for unwed mothers. He offered the Mercy to the congregation as an emergency maternity hospital after St. Rita had been closed by the fire. At the time, seven sisters were working at the Mercy under the superiorship of Sister Mary Albert (Charlotte) Gleeson.[11] The congregation accepted his offer, and from then on, unwed mothers would use this "new" St. Rita Maternity Hospital, or other hospitals in the region, for delivery only. In keeping with trends toward deinstitutionalisation, and with the help of the Sisters of St. Martha, the bishop initiated a foster home program for pregnant single mothers. Sister Mary Rosalia (Katherine) MacNeil was transferred to Sydney from the Marthas' social work mission in Regina. Her assignment was to find good, temporary homes for pregnant single women until their time for delivery. Usually these homes were free and close to the hospitals. Sister Rosalia's assignment was a busy and stressful one. She reported: "In this program the total responsibility of the unmarried mother rests with the Diocesan Social Worker who calls on the other agencies when they are needed." She helped each mother deal with her condition, access appropriate hospital care, decide on the fate of her offspring and their financial support and become re-established afterwards. From 1951 to 1959, she assisted 611 pregnant single women; most were Roman Catholic, and her annual caseload was about 115.[12]

Since many unwed mothers decided to surrender their infants, home care had to be arranged until adoptions had been finalized. Again the Marthas were called on to provide a sister to organize the Boarding Home Program in September 1952. Sister Margaret Claire McAskill identified and assessed potential boarding homes and then placed the babies of unwed mothers with them. Arranging the infants' maintenance and supervising these temporary foster homes was time-consuming work–in 1957 alone she placed fity-two infants in boarding homes.[13]

The new Boarding Home Program was also a means to transfer children out of the diocese's Little Flower Institute and into home care. Actually, in 1950, Bishop Berry's report on diocesan social work had recommended a "foster-home boarding-out plan" for children under six. He had been dismayed by his visit to the orphanage, describing it as "dull", "a maze of corridors," and possibly "a horrible fire-trap." It had too many beds, he concluded, and too little privacy. None of this was news to the eight sisters and their superior, Sister Mary Matthew (Magdalena) Kurtz, who ran the institution; their revenues were inadequate and rooms were severely limited, especially after the influx of young children when the Mercy Hospital closed in 1951. While scoring the building's shortcomings, Bishop Berry had also complimented the sisters' work: "The staff is a good one and through the social work activities of the Sisters in the neighbourhood parishes, the Sisters are alert to some of the things they need to know in this field. Their relationship to the children on short observation seems to be real and happy."[14] To the great joy of the orphanage sisters, in 1952, Bishop John R. initiated a diocesan-wide "Penny-a-Meal Campaign" to finance construction of a new Little Flower Institute. While doing so, he recognized in a speech to the Catholic Women's League Convention the Marthas' sacrificial role in operating the Little Flower. Up to 1945, he announced, the motherhouse had received only $100 annually as each sister's salary, but he estimated their cumulative contributed services to be worth $35,000 and concluded:"So far as the Diocesan Orphanage is concerned, the Diocese has been pretty niggardly with the Sisters."[15]

Again, fire gave impetus to change. Fortunately, none of the seventy-eight children or staff was injured by an alarming blaze that damaged the Little Flower in March 1953. Actually, it brought positive results: many families in the area rallied to offer temporary shelter, while some gave more permanent care for the children. And the financial campaign surged ahead, netting $227,615. So a new Little Flower child care institution opened in June 1956 at a spacious and convenient location in Sydney at a cost of $230,000. A newspaper described it as "a three-storey brick structure including a spacious basement, a lovely chapel, bright cheery dormitories, playrooms for the children, attractive staff quarters, dining room, nursery, kitchen and laundry."[16] Sister Leo Marie (Georgina) McEvoy became the superior and supervised nine other Marthas and seven lay staff. By 1960, admissions, especially of younger children, had dropped dramatically and their stays were shorter; the new emphasis on home care was making an impact. Also, most of the children, in contrast to earlier years, were from broken and troubled homes, and were not real orphans. The decline in admissions created deficits because the size of government grants depended on the number of children at the Little Flower. Nevertheless, the home's busy life continued.

Parish Social Work Agencies

In 1950, Bishop Berry's report on diocesan social work had also assessed the parish agencies. He had praised the contribution of the sisters and lay workers in these "fine establishments," which in his mind, rivalled "any Family case work office in the better-organized and large communities."[17] However, Bishop John R. was not satisfied with praise alone; he wanted expansion. He hoped to supplement the existing agencies in Canso, Sydney, Whitney Pier, and Dominion-Bridgeport with new ones in every possible parish. The findings of his Family Life Commission on family conditions in the Cape Breton industrial area, led by Father F.A. Marrocco in 1952, confirmed him in this design.[18] The rising cost of living and the rising lifestyle expectations driven by television advertising and the spread of consumerism were placing new strains and stresses on families. Now, the Marthas had every intention of continuing their commitment to social work. Mother Ignatius had confirmed this commitment in a report to Rome: "It is the desire of our Congregation as far as possible to meet the many requests for this type of work, for therein, we think, lies fertile field for alleviating the spiritual and bodily ills of mankind, and thus contributing to the glory of God and the welfare of souls."[19] However, the congregation's spirit was willing but its resources were weak. Mother Ignatius complained in 1956: "The demands of our own Diocese have multiplied so rapidly under the energetic zeal of our good Bishop that it is almost impossible to keep up with them."[20]

In the early 1950s the sisters helped to establish a new parish social work agency in the cathedral town itself. In contrast to its stagnation during the early decades of the century, the town was experiencing a steady growth in population through the 1940s and 1950s. The motherhouse already had a long tradition of informal family visitation and material help for the needy in Antigonish. However, in 1952, Mother Ignatius assigned Sister Leo Marie McEvoy to visit needy families, distribute basic foods, call on the aged, and visit inmates at the local jail.[21] Within one year, through the leadership of Rev. W.J. Gallivan, the parish had established the Family Welfare Council of St. Ninian's Parish, composed of representatives from parish organizations such as the Catholic Women's League and the Knights of Columbus. The new organization engaged Sister Leo Marie as fieldworker. The agency's purposes, she stated, were "to promote Catholic social welfare within the parish, to advance the cause of our holy religion among the people, and to do all we can to better their moral, social and economic conditions."[22] Many local individuals and organizations helped Sister Leo Marie as she visited families, conducted casework, distributed relief to the poor and helped the aged. The agency's caseload increased rather dramatically between 1953 and 1960. And that year, three neighbouring parishes–St. Andrews, St. Joseph, and St. Peter's in Tracadie–joined the agency which required the addition of another sister fieldworker.

Without doubt the main social services story in the cathedral town during the 1950s was the congregation's establishment of a home for the aged. As in social work, the sisters had long before established precedents in working with the elderly. They had cared for small numbers of them in two Antigonish locations–Mount Cameron Farm (1907–1928) and the House of Providence (1914–c. 1923). However, since then, little had been done for the aged in Antigonish. While coadjutor bishop in the 1940s, Bishop John R., along with other priests, had discussed this lack with Mother Ignatius. In 1951 the Bethany annalist recorded: "Bishop MacDonald visited Mother in the afternoon–he is agitating for an Old People's Home now!"[23]

Mr. Joseph A. Cesale, the first resident, is welcomed into the R.K. MacDonald Guest House, Antigonish, by Sister Mary Joseph (Anne) MacGillivray, administrator, and Mrs. Mary MacIntosh, receptionist.

Unfortunately, financing any proposal appeared intractable until the death of an "old friend" of the congregation in 1955. Roderick Kennedy MacDonald willed $100,000 for the erection of a seniors' home and stipulated that the Sisters of St. Martha operate it. The congregation was pleased, the demanding Bishop John R. jubilant.[24] On 18 February 1958, a seventy-bed, two-storey brick seniors' home, christened by Bishop John R. as "The R.K. MacDonald Guest House," was opened, with considerable pomp and ceremony, by the congregation at a cost of $450,000. One sister declared: "This was a history-making day in the congregation, for it marked the establishment of a new foundation, and the beginning of a new work–the care of the aged."[25] The new foundation was erected at a desirable location on Pleasant Street in the town of Antigonish. The congregation generously mortgaged its motherhouse to finance the undertaking, delayed a much-needed expansion program there and subsequently met operating deficits at the seniors' home. Mother Ignatius assigned eight sisters to the new mission with Sister Mary Joseph (Anna) MacGillivray as the superior and they cared for about seventy-one seniors that first year.[26] "The R.K.," as it is known locally, would become a mainstay institution for the elderly in the town and county of Antigonish.

Bishop John R. was most anxious to expand the parish social work agencies in the heavily populated industrial area of Cape Breton. In 1954, Mother Ignatius was able to assign two sisters–Sister Mary of Nazareth (Mary) MacDonald and Sister Mary Ian (Jean Therese) Chisholm–to work in St. Joseph's Parish in North Sydney, and in the two parishes of Sydney Mines, Immaculate Conception and St. Pius X. In the early 1950s the combined population of North Sydney and Sydney Mines was over 15,000.[27] The sisters lived with their religious community at the recently remodeled Little Flower Institute at Bras d'Or, now called the Villa Madonna Retreat House. They had the use of a car to do "all the good possible" in the "Northside" parishes. At first, no formal agency boards were set up; instead the sisters worked closely with auxiliary committees of existing parish organizations. In addition to completing a massive survey of the parishes that required over two thousand family visits, the sister social workers dealt with problems common to the other parish agencies. In 1959 the Sydney Mines parishes finally established a formal agency with a board of directors; North Sydney did the same in 1962. The sisters' annual combined caseload for the three parishes ranged from 161 to 254 between 1955 and 1960. Evidently the Martha social workers missioned to the Northside were needed.[28]

Toward the end of the 1950s, demands for social workers reached Mother Ignatius from Canso and the neighbouring

African-Canadian community of Lincolnville. Since 1933, Marthas had done family welfare work in Canso without the help of any formal parish organization. One sister reflected: "It was just a matter of doing everything and anything that could be done to help the people, in any way it could be done."[29] However, for Bishop John R., who sat squarely at the diocesan helm after 1950, the key to success was organization. And social work organization came to Canso in 1958. Over the decades, the Marthas at the Canso Welfare Bureau had become less directly involved in parish visitation and more involved in school teaching. In 1955, Sister Mary Irene (Loretta Teresa) Peck began the work of reviving parish work in Canso. She reported: "The re-establishing of the work of the welfare centre is due to the zealous and energetic Pastor Reverend George MacDonald who sees the need of this medium to aid him in the apostolic work of his parish."[30] Father MacDonald had a board organized in 1958, composed of the sister social worker, the parish priest, and delegates of parish organizations. By 1960, seven Marthas lived at the Canso Welfare Bureau which was renamed Star of the Sea Convent in 1961.

Mother Ignatius had increased the number of sisters at Canso to help with another new undertaking. In 1957 the hurried Bishop John R. MacDonald had asked Father Anthony, an Augustinian brother, to work among the blacks of Guysborough County. The black communities had a long history of poverty and hardship, a result of racial discrimination and inequitable treatment by the dominant whites. In Lincolnville, a community about sixty-five kilometres from Canso, most black families were Baptist or of no religion. Many of the men worked in the woods, housing was deficient, and in the bishop's view there existed moral irregularities–unwed mothers and common-law unions–as well as religious indifference. In 1958, Father Anthony asked Mother Ignatius if the Canso sisters could help him out at Lincolnville. The annalist at Bethany commented: "For a long time they have been a neglected group. Mother General readily gave them her blessing and assent to do so."[31] The pioneers assigned for biweekly visits to Lincolnville were Sisters Matthew (Magdalena) Kurtz and M. Vincentia Doyle. They established a "varied program" that included cooking lessons for girls, entertainment, singing lessons, home visitation, picnics, and handicrafts. Religious instruction and preparation for baptism and first communion were also part of the varied program. Apparently the sisters were well received by the community, which expressed gratitude for their efforts. In their report on year one at Lincolnville, the sisters observed: "Although having little of this world's goods, these people have a happy disposition and are especially fond of music, singing and dancing." [32]

As the Lincolnville work got underway, Bishop John R. was urging the Director of Diocesan Charities, Father John Webb, to expand Catholic social services in Cape Breton; ultimately the bishop forced the hand of parish priests in Glace Bay and New Waterford to establish family agencies. Of course, the Marthas were expected to rally to the cause again. The bishop was troubled by severe family problems in the area, with its population of over 35,000;[33] he was frustrated that earlier meetings of priests had not brought into being any new parish agencies. In 1957, Mother Ignatius sent Sister Mary of Nazareth MacDonald, who had recently helped establish welfare work on the Northside in Cape Breton, and Sister Paul Thérèse (Marie Thérèse) LeBlanc into the district to make a start.[34] They quickly formed agencies to serve the district parishes and began their social work. The separate parish agencies amalgamated in 1959 as the Glace Bay Catholic Family Service, which provided help to families in four area parishes: St. Anne's, St. Leo's, St. John's, and St. Anthony's.[35] After pressing the Glace Bay area parishes to organize social welfare, Bishop John R. encouraged the pastors of New Waterford and district to do the same. The parish priests of St. Agnes and Mt. Carmel (New Waterford), St. Michael's (Scotchtown), St. Joseph's (New Victoria), and St. Alphonsus (Victoria Mines) met in 1958 and forwarded another request to Mother Ignatius for two sister social workers. Father Webb knew that Mother Ignatius was short of trained social workers, so he had been trying unsuccessfully to obtain Sisters of Service and Sisters of Charity social workers for the New Waterford district.[36] However, Mother Ignatius was able, in September 1959, to meet the bishop's demands with two more sisters–Sister Paul Thérèse LeBlanc and Ann Patrick (Evelyn) O'Leary–who established an agency called the Catholic Family Service of New Waterford and District.[37]

Bishop John R. had largely been behind the rather rapid proliferation of Catholic social work agencies during the 1950s. By 1960, nine family welfare agencies operated in the Diocese of Antigonish–seven in the industrial area of Cape Breton and the other two in Antigonish and Canso–serving thirty-three parishes. More than twenty Marthas with varied levels of training were directly involved in serving nearly 1,400 families. As well, sisters ran the Unmarried Mothers Program and the Adoption and Boarding Home programs.

The bishop's demands had strained the resources of the congregation. It had experienced a vocations shortage during the 1940s, but fortunately this changed during the 1950s (282 women were admitted to the congregation, compared to only 121 in the 1940s). However, it took time to properly qualify sisters as social workers. By 1960 the rising qualification levels were apparent: six sisters had master of social work degrees and four held diplomas in social work.[38]

The sister social workers laboured under excessive workloads, low salaries, transportation hardships, and restrictive regulations. In 1959 the diocese doubled the qualified social workers' monthly stipends of $50 plus board. The strongest pressure in the congregation to own cars and learn to drive came from the social workers. Gradually, after 1940, more sisters drove and the parish agencies or the diocese commonly placed vehicles at their disposal. However, the congregation was slow to modify its regulation that each sister had to travel outside her convent with a sister companion. The social workers found this rule a severe inconvenience, especially as caseloads increased. They complained that it was inefficient and inhibited communication with clients. In 1949, Sister Crescentia Duprey and Sister John Hugh Robertson asked Mother Ignatius to grant them an exception from this regulation. The frustration of all the social workers mounted when general administration refused to budge. Their formal request to the council in 1952 warned: "We are so mentally, spiritually, and physically frustrated that we would like to discontinue the work completely."[39] However, in 1953 general administration, with Bishop John R.'s blessing, relented and formulated a cautious permission: they allowed perpetually professed sisters with a minimum of three years experience to work alone if they were on official social work duty. The superior general and council advised: "If all Sisters who have permission to go out alone act religiously and prudently, we do not anticipate any evil effects from this new regulation."[40]

Going South: St. Martha's Catholic Centre, Boston

Until 1952 the Sisters of St. Martha worked exclusively within Canada. However, this changed after an important Bostonian made a short visit in 1950 to receive an honorary degree from St. Francis Xavier University in Antigonish. While there, Archbishop James Cushing of Boston, Massachusetts, discovered the Marthas. Almost everywhere he toured, he met Marthas. He found them serving in the extension department, in the library, and in the faculty dining room; he saw their hospital and school of nursing, and also their motherhouse perched on the hill above the hospital. And at the university convocation, he saw the Marthas' superior general, Mother Ignatius, honoured for the congregation's fifty years of dedicated service to the diocese. After inquiries, the impressed archbishop invited the Marthas to establish a foundation in Boston and indicated the rich opportunities there for recruiting and ministry. The Bethany annalist wrote: "Archbishop Cushing of Boston made an urgent request to Mother for Sisters, during his brief visit here, and Bishop MacDonald is insistent that the offer be accepted!"[40] Shortly after Mother Ignatius visited Boston in June, the general council decided to accept the archbishop's invitation and to establish a foundation "of a social service nature."[42] Archbishop Cushing himself had no definite ministry planned for the sisters. Moreover, he could not receive Marthas in Boston just then, because he lacked an appropriate property for them.

Archbishop Cushing, who would become a cardinal in 1958, was a tall, impressive, energetic, and persuasive fifty-five-year-old churchman of Irish ancestry. He had administered the Archdiocese of Boston since 1944. In the prosperous post-war era, he had orchestrated a rapid, comprehensive building program of diverse Catholic institutions in the huge archdiocese, the second largest in the United States and encompassing over 1.3 million Catholics. Cushing's archdiocese, and the religious congregations he had invited there, built and maintained a vast network of

Catholic institutions and services–parish churches, general and special hospitals, convalescent homes, refuges for the needy and challenged, parochial schools and colleges, and charity and counselling services. Nearly three thousand priests and members of diverse religious orders ministered within the archbishop's expansive orbit.[43]

In May 1952 the Marthas found themselves quite suddenly drawn into Cushing's urban archdiocese. Mother Ignatius received this curt message: "I think I have a place for your Boston foundation. Will you please send a couple of Sisters to me as soon as possible? God bless you for being patient with me. You have a host of friends around here waiting for you."[44] By the end of May, three pioneers–Sister Mary Anselm Doyle (superior), Sister Baptista Maria Macdonald, and Sister Maria Monica (Eileen) Shaw–had moved into a lovely, old six-storey brick residence at 36 Commonwealth Avenue recently vacated by the Irish Medical Missionaries. These sisters were later joined by Sister Georgeanna (Helen Frances) Peck (housekeeper), Sister Joseph Marie (Bertha Johanna) MacDonald (cook), and Sister Frances Joseph (Mary Elizabeth) Williams (secretary). Thus was established the Sisters of St. Martha's first American foundation. The archbishop officially named the new mission St. Martha's Catholic Centre.

Sister M. Anselm (Irene) Doyle at St. Martha's Catholic Centre, Boston. Run by the Marthas from 1952.

Archbishop Cushing supported the Marthas' decision to do social work in Boston. They established 36 Commonwealth Avenue as home base for a family counselling service. Sister Baptista Maria, a trained social worker, began parish family visiting in the South Boston and Roxbury districts. She visited low-income families and established working relationships with helping agencies, such as nursing homes, medical clinics, and child welfare societies. She also organized a very successful Volunteer Friendly Visiting Program aimed at reducing the isolation of seniors, especially of the Catholic aged, who lived in the many small institutions and boarding homes of the greater Boston area.[45] The sisters' work was described in the archdiocesan paper, *The Pilot*, and in brochures that were distributed to the parishes.

A "host of friends"–more than 150 former Nova Scotians–had warmly welcomed the sisters to the city. For many years, Boston, a city of over 800,000, had been a favourite destination for expatriate Maritimers searching for work or adventure or both. In October, Sister Anselm began organizing almost five hundred friends of the Marthas into the Guild of St. Martha to help support their work in Boston. The Guild was "the backbone of the financial resources of the Boston community for many years." Its members were organized as teams, and membership fees were paid to a team captain. The Guild's fundraising events were "mammoth in size."[46] No doubt the presence of such a crowd of Maritimers in the Boston area made it attractive for the archbishop to have a Maritime congregation work within his archdiocese.

The sisters' work in Boston was reorganized twice. In 1954, Sister Baptista Maria became supervisor of the Family Division of the Catholic Charitable Bureau, where she counselled and supervised staff in the department. Two years after Sister Anselm completed her master of social work program at the Boston College School of Social Work in 1956, she and Sister Baptista Maria orchestrated a second reorganization; the result was a casework agency called Catholic Family Counselling. The archdiocesan Catholic Charitable Bureau had a poor reputation, so with prudent diplomacy the sisters convinced Cushing, appointed cardinal that year, to establish an independent, more professional, and specialized agency.[47] Its aims were "to contribute toward strengthening of harmonious inter-family relationships, and to promote healthy development and social functioning of families and individuals."[48] Father Joseph Alves, who was studying social work in Washington, was appointed director of the new agency, which was already in process of being established.

The Boston foundation was a significant one for the sisters involved, and even for the entire congregation. Through their professional work, the sisters at St. Martha's Catholic Centre became immersed in the life of the archdiocese while helping to meet the needs of the elderly and of families in distress. They participated in a three-year interagency action-research project on multiproblem families and participated in national Catholic welfare organizations and conferences. Sister Anselm was a member of the Conference of Religious of the National Conference of Catholic Charities for four years, including two years as chair. Cardinal Cushing and the sisters established a good working relationship. In 1956, he had requested more sisters for social work and declared that he had found the Marthas "exemplary in every way."[49] And at the end of her term as superior, Sister Anselm wrote to the Cardinal, "Your continued fatherly interest in us, and your many kindnesses carried us over the first years which always have their own kind of difficulties."[50]

From the beginning, Mother Ignatius had recognized the potential benefits of the Boston project "because of its central location, and the many advantages available for sisters to study and prepare for the needs of the Institute."[51] Indeed, over the years, many sisters would go to Boston for study, for example, at Boston College; and meanwhile they had the convenience of staying with their own community on 36 Commonwealth Avenue. The Boston sisters also tried to encourage vocations to their community through activities such as car excursions to the motherhouse for the semi-annual reception ceremony. The Boston foundation was really the first Martha mission where sisters were invited to go for their own good and not to meet some urgent and neglected need within the church; however, they soon found themselves ministering to serious needs. The mission paid small financial but worthwhile educational dividends to the congregation as the Marthas served through the decades within Archbishop Cushing's huge network of Catholic institutions.

The Surge in Teaching

Not only did Bishop John R. MacDonald exert pressure on the Sisters of St. Martha for more social workers, but he also expected the congregation to supply more teachers. His episcopate continued through a time when Maritime public education was "revolutionized by dynamic growth, centralization, and bureaucratic organization."[52] The first Marthas had begun teaching in rural schools back in the mid-1920s at the urging of Dr. Moses Coady. From September 1925, they had staffed the school at Margaree Forks, Cape Breton. While living at St. Theresa's Convent, four to six sisters had laboured annually, generally with good local support and satisfaction. Their first male principal–Archie Neil Chisholm–had been appointed in 1957. In addition to regular academic instruction, the sisters had done much with public speaking, 4-H Clubs, dramatics, music, and arts and crafts. The sisters' teaching mission at Little Bras d'Or, Cape Breton (est. 1926), had ended in 1943, for the local school board proved unable to pay regularly the sisters' salaries.[53] However, they returned in the 1950s. From 1928 the Marthas had also maintained a teaching foundation at St. Andrews in Antigonish County that proved of great benefit to the local people. Because of the vocation shortage, only two more teaching missions had been established in the 1940s– at Main-a-Dieu and Eskasoni in Cape Breton.

The congregational pace of creating new teaching missions accelerated during the 1950s. The first one the general administration accepted was quite close to home, less than twenty kilometres to the east, in a community called Heatherton, an old Catholic parish, functioning since around Confederation. In 1951, its pastor, Father Hugh John MacDonald, and his parishioners built an attractive three-storey convent next to Immaculate Conception Church and invited the Marthas to send teachers for their school. In September of 1951, Sister Rose Miriam (Margaret A.) MacKinnon (superior/teacher), Sister Teresa Clare (Teresa Elizabeth) Ryan (high school/principal), Sister Edmund Marie Kurtz (music/art), Sister Marie Therese (Minnie M.) Richard (homemaker), and two young, junior professed sister students moved in. Their convent was christened Our Lady of Fatima, and the teachers taught that fall in the local public school; it included grades primary through eleven. Like other teaching missions, the sisters' activities extended beyond the school to 4-H, music, choir, religion classes, and home visitations.[54]

In the mid-1950s the congregation sent a small army of teaching sisters to various communities in Cape Breton. The first was another old parish: St. Mary's, East Bay, about twenty kilometres west of Sydney. The rural community had built a new school called MacCormick School, and the pastor, with the strong backing of Bishop John R., had requested teaching sisters. The new school opened in September 1953 with 108 students in grades one to nine and teaching Marthas were there. The East Bay sister pioneers were Sister George Marie MacPherson (superior/teacher), Sister Mary Regina MacDonnell (principal), Sister Mary Camillus (Genevieve) MacDonald (homemaker), and Sister Helen Matthew (Ann Marie Catherine) Coady (music). They were soon involved in the busy round of parish life. In 1957, they acquired the renovated rectory, a much more adequate convent, which they called St. Mary's; and in 1960, four more sisters were assigned and Martha teaching duties extended to the nearby communities of Portage and Big Pond.[55]

By the end of 1958 the congregation had taken on six more teaching assignments in Cape Breton. Again, the restless bishop reinforced each request that arrived on Mother Ignatius's desk from the pen of local pastors. Three of these missions were on the rugged northeast coast of the Cape. As the East Bay mission was being established, in September 1953, sisters were also settling into a comfortable former glebe-house-turned-convent in the fishing village of South Ingonish, located on the Cabot Trail nearly a hundred kilometers north of Baddeck. Sister M. Athanasius Smith (grades primary and one), Sister Mary Natalie (Shirley Teresa) Bruce (grades 1 to 4), Sister James Francis (Eleanor Jean) Morrison (superior and principal, grades 7 to 11), Sister M. Teresita (Mary Teresa) Gouthro (music teacher), and Sister Mary Lawrence (Margaret Mary) Poirier (homemaker) composed the community invited there by Father George MacDonald. The convent, situated in Cape Breton Highlands National Park, took the name of the church, St. Peter's. The logistics of transporting the sisters to the several district schools—Ingonish Beach, Ingonish Centre, Ingonish Ferry, and MacDonald Memorial—was simplified in 1954 with the opening of a modern, eight-room consolidated school at Ingonish Beach. School consolidation was an important educational trend in the 1950s. About forty-five kilometres further to the north lay the small community of Dingwall.[56] The supplications of Pastor Francis A. Morley brought four sisters there in September 1955. Bishop and pastor were anxious about the lack of religious instruction for the youth in the district. A small house was renovated as St. Joseph's Convent, and it became home to Sister Mary Bernadette (Gertrude) Peters (superior/music), Sister Mary Prisca (Mary Rita) MacLellan (grades 2 to 4), Sister Mary Alexina (Mary) MacNeil (primary and grade one), and Sister Mary Josita (Sarah Joanna) MacNeil (homemaker).[57] They taught in the four-room school and laboured to upgrade the religious knowledge of Dingwall Catholic youth.

Even further to the north of Dingwall, and isolated on the tip of the Cape, was the fishing district of Bay St. Lawrence. Few teachers hankered to go there. Its suppliant for teaching sisters was Father John A. Chisholm. Again Bishop John R. prodded the superior general and sweetened the prospects, this time with the promise of a renovated rectory for a convent in St. Margaret's Village. Mother Ignatius came through with three sisters for the fall of 1959: Sister Ian Marie (Jessie Margaret) MacFarlane (superior/grades 3 to 6), Sister Ann Catherine (Lucy) MacNeil (primary to grade two), and Sister Patricia Claire (Mary Audrey) Mullins (homemaker). They made the long trek north that fall to teach in an old two-room school with a religiously mixed student body of eighty.[58]

The other three Cape Breton teaching missions begun by the Marthas in the 1950s were located further to the south. Only one required a new convent to be opened and that was at St. Peter's on the southern shore of the Island. An earlier unfilled request for two teaching sisters was renewed by Father Paul MacNeil in 1956 (and seconded by Bishop John R.) when he wrote to Mother Ignatius: "Should we be looking for some teaching Sisters next Sept., have you any available? A new four-room school will be functioning at Lakeside–four miles from here, on the opening of the next school term. The area is 100 percent Catholic and the children are darlings."[59] Mother Ignatius did not have any available teachers for Father MacNeil until September 1958. Then she sent Sister Mary Kateri (Mary Dorothy) Moore and Sister M. Teresita (Mary) Gouthro who lived at St. Paul's Convent and taught at Lakeside School, Sampsonville; Sister Cecilia Joseph (Marion) Gough was superior and Sister Mary Joseph Agatha Hines did the housekeeping; the parishioners were delighted to see them arrive.[60] A few years before St. Paul's Convent had been erected, sisters had been sent to teach at Alder Point, a fishing village and mission of Bras d'Or. Sister Maria Pius (Mary Hannah) Keough and Sister Angela Maria (Catherine Margaret) MacFarlane lived with the Villa Madonna community, Bras d'Or, while teaching from September 1956 in Alder Point. After meeting sisters for the first time, one student informed his surprised mother that the Virgin Mary had taught him that day. Finally, the St. Theresa's Convent at Margaree Forks extended its teaching services to include Captain Allen's School at South West Margaree from September 1958 to 1962.

Bishop John R. was also a strong presence behind the congregation's growing commitment to certain schools within the mainland section of his diocese. In 1956 the Post Road Elementary School trustees, located a little to the west of the town of Antigonish, were pleased to receive for their small rural school two sister teachers–Sister Mary Neala (Kathleen Elizabeth) Campbell and Sister Irene Marie (Audrey Kathleen) Steele–who commuted daily from the motherhouse. A new consolidated school called Saint Andrew Rural High School on the southern edge of Antigonish town asked for and received sister teachers in 1956 to supplement its staff of more than twenty instructors. The general administration assigned Sister Hugh Marie (Sarah Jeanette) MacPherson (chemistry, history, agriculture), Sister Teresa Ryan (English), and Sister Mary Helene (Mary Alberta) Wadden (music). Sister Mary Helene was already employed as music supervisor for the county schools. And, from 1958, two more sisters started teaching there in a section designated for the elementary grades called Antigonish Suburban.[61] Finally, on the local county scene, Father E.J. Nash at Tracadie, a small Acadian community about thirty kilometres east of Antigonish, asked for two sisters to help staff a new school that was opening in 1959. Against her better judgement, but once more in deference to Bishop John R., Mother Ignatius supplied the need, sending Sister Marie Ninian (Annie Agnes) Beaton and Sister Mary Clare (Elma) Roach.[62]

The Marthas were already active in Guysborough County from their base in Canso at the Welfare Bureau. But with the strong support of the bishop, in 1957, Father George B. Stephenson, pastor of St. Ann's of Guysborough, revived an earlier request for sister teachers and parish workers. The general administration made a commitment for September 1958 and sent five sisters under the supervision of Sister John de la Salle Fougere; they lived in a convent eventually given to the Marthas by the diocese and taught in two rustic schools at Intervale and Havendale. Bishop John R. supplied a car, and the parish deeded St. Ann's Convent to the congregation. This deed was returned to the parish when the sisters withdrew. Protestants were strong in Guysborough and some of them opposed the entry of the Marthas, although the sisters observed a gradually mellowing toward them over time. Guysborough was the shiretown for the county and it had prospered in the nineteenth century through the shipbuilding and timber trades. But during the 1950s its population had decreased to less than 8,000.[63]

Protestant-Catholic tensions were certainly a factor in the Marthas' initiation of a mission in Trenton, Pictou County, that year. Trenton, located on the East River and immediately adjacent to New Glasgow, had been incorporated as a town in 1911. Because of the presence of coal deposits, a steel industry had developed in Trenton, whose population numbered over 3,000, about 30 percent Roman Catholic in the late 1950s.[64] The congregation undertook this "foundation which sprang up overnight" at considerable sacrifice. As usual, the bishop's role was central; while he exhorted Mother Ignatius to send teachers, he apparently had two priests praying in the car for her acquiescence.[65] The school crisis had developed this way: In 1953 the first pastor of the new Trenton parish, Father Roderick W. MacPherson, had three classrooms built in the basement of Christ the King Church and opened as a publicly funded school to save Catholic children from the sometimes bigoted Protestantism rampant in Pictou's public schools. The town permitted the arrangement only because of overcrowding at its school. In 1958, shortly before school opening, the Pictou County School Board decided to withdraw funding because it now had room for the children in a local school. Thus, Bishop John R. pleaded that the congregation send teachers, which it reluctantly did. Providentially,

Native children from Pictou Landing started coming to the school shortly after it opened, and this brought in federal funding. Eventually the parish was able to provide a convent for the pioneer sisters stationed there–Sister M. Alexina (Mary) MacNeil, Sister Alice Louise (Mary) MacFarlane, and Sister Ann Carmel MacNeil, who ministered under the superiorship of Sister M. Bonaventure (Genevieve) Gouthreau (1958–1964).

Significance of the Teaching Surge

In 1950 the Marthas had taught in less than ten schools; by 1960 the congregation had teaching sisters in twenty-five schools, and the number of teachers had more than tripled to over sixty regular academic instructors.[66] Although vocations increased in this decade, the rapid expansion stretched personnel resources; sometimes Mother Ignatius even had to withdraw sisters from education programs in order to meet the mounting requests. Of course, the congregation reaped financial benefits from the surge in teaching, especially as teachers' salaries increased.

The expansion in the teaching apostolate also more broadly enmeshed the congregation in rural parish life. When teachers were hard to get, the Marthas tried to fill the gap. Moreover, the sisters not only taught regular academic subjects in the classroom but also became involved in a host of busy parish activities. As well, Marthas such as Sister Mary Rodriquez Steele, Sister Margaret Mary Hervé, Sister Mary Raphael Watt, Sister Mary Helene Wadden, Sister M. Teresita Gouthro, Sister Ann Carmel MacNeil, Sister Edmund Marie Kurtz, Sister M. Vincentia Doyle, and Sister Pauline Marie (Madeline Bell) MacDonald brought the cultural benefits of instruction in art, music, home economics, and handicrafts to many communities. In places such as Inverness and Antigonish counties, sisters travelled a circuit of schools each week to bring instruction in these cultural arts.

Like their hospital, nursing, and social work sisters, the teaching Marthas developed professionally to maintain good teaching standards by joining the Nova Scotia Teachers' Union, by attending teachers' conferences and summer schools, by having a coordinator of schools (Sister Mary Colina MacDougall, 1953–1961), and by forming their own teachers' association. The Teachers' Association of the Sisters of St. Martha was begun in

1947; from the 1950s, it held annual conferences and institutes on issues important to rural school teachers.[67] The Marthas worked to keep pace with the general emphasis in schooling on more highly trained and specialized teachers.

Finally, the Marthas teaching apostolate should be recognized for its contribution to religious instruction in the Diocese of Antigonish. When Bishop John R. gained full control of the diocese in 1950, one of his many new appointments was a director of religious education. Father George L. Kane filled the post, and shortly thereafter revived religious vacation schools and correspondence courses in Christian doctrine. Within ten years, small groups of sisters–often regular school teachers–had taught over thirteen thousand children through their religious vacation schools held each summer in selected parishes. For example, in 1957, twenty-two sisters travelled to eight locations and taught 935 children prayers, singing, catechism, stories, rosary, liturgy, sacraments, and morals. One sister recalled, "This represents a lot of arduous work, preparation of material, travelling long distances, living out of a suitcase, makeshift accommodation in rectories or parish halls, and other inconveniences."[68] In 1952, Sister Colina MacDougall revived the catechetical correspondence courses she had offered in the 1930s "for children in the remote areas of the Diocese."[69] The numbers enrolled peaked at around four hundred in 1956 and thereafter declined as the Marthas established teaching convents around the diocese and bolstered

Sister Teresa Clare (Teresa Elizabeth) Ryan teaching religion.

religious instruction in many local parishes. Overall, Sister Colina's courses, along with the congregation's mushrooming work in schools and parishes, contributed to Dr. Coady's broad program of rural reconstruction in eastern Nova Scotia.

The teaching sisters faced two issues in the 1950s. First, as religious committed to a vow of poverty, should they be involved in strike action for higher salaries and other improvements? In 1952, lay teachers in Cape Breton and Antigonish County went on strike for higher salaries. The cost of living was rising and teachers' salaries were woefully behind.[70] While opening themselves to criticism, the sisters at Heatherton, St. Andrews, and Main-a-Dieu decided to act in solidarity with the striking lay teachers. Second, in 1957 the issue of lay versus sister teaching appointments came to a head. By that year, the Marthas, along with the congregations of the Sisters of Notre Dame, the Sisters of Charity, and the Daughters of Jesus, held teaching appointments in many schools located in the diocese. Lay Catholic teachers expressed deep dissatisfaction at the dominance of sisters in administrative positions and charged that school boards preferred hiring sisters over lay teachers. After being convinced by J. Frank Glasgow, a member of the Nova Scotia Teachers' Union executive, of the seriousness of the issue, Bishop John R. called representatives of the teaching congregations and the lay Catholic teachers to a meeting at Mount St. Bernard College, Antigonish. There the bishop, ironically the one largely responsible for the dilemma because of his desire for strong religious influences in the schools, forcibly stated the facts: sisters taught in sixty-seven schools that employed 695 teachers, 352 sisters, and 343 lay instructors. He announced that forty-eight of these schools had sister principals and seventeen sister vice-principals. The bishop concluded: "It was pretty evident that there was not an equal sharing of principalships." Eventually the delegates agreed that lay and religious teachers should be granted equal employment opportunities; that, where possible, boards should hire an equal number of each; that religious should actively participate in union and professional activities; and that male principals should be hired in schools where boys predominated over girls. The meeting ended cordially. Mother Ignatius had shown sympathy for the concerns of the Catholic lay teachers.[71]

Another Martha activity in the 1950s that garnered enthusiastic support from Bishop John R. was their establishment of formal lay retreat houses. Although the Marthas had held lay retreats before, they resurrected the practice in the mid-1940s as one response to the shortage of vocations. Of course, the sisters were also well aware of the spiritual benefits of retreats for lay people. So, in 1949, the congregation opened Fatima Retreat House at a lovely seaside location called Seabright, several kilometres north of Antigonish. There they had already enjoyed, for many years, a cottage (Silver Haven) as a place of rest and recuperation. Mother Ignatius expressed the hope that "the retreats for girls may be the means of contacting those who have a vocation to the religious life and of attracting them to our Community."[72] From 1949, during the summer months, the sisters regularly offered weekend retreats for young single women, nurses, married women, teachers, and girls. The building was ideally located for retreat work and could accommodate about twenty eight women. Retreatants had to pay for their transportation; the sisters only asked for a voluntary offering to cover food and lodging. From 1954 the number of retreats declined substantially, and in 1959 a sister commented: "Financially [Fatima House] is more or less of a lost venture, but spiritually we hope its benefits are much greater."[73] It closed as a retreat house in 1960.

Actually, a new retreat house in Cape Breton accounted for the declining use of Fatima House in Antigonish County. As mentioned, the old orphanage, Little Flower Institute, had been partially destroyed by fire in 1953 and the children moved into Sydney. Bishop John R. shortly thereafter suggested that the former orphanage be renovated and used as a multipurpose institution for evening classes in cooking, sewing, and childcare, and as a retreat centre for women.[74] Mother Ignatius and her council accepted the proposition and supplied nine sisters who worked under the superiorship of Sister Mary of Nazareth MacDonald. The remodelled building, called Villa Madonna Retreat House, provided sister and retreatant quarters, a chapel, chaplain's quarters, a spacious lounge, and a dining room. The number of Catholic women who took advantage of the retreat centre increased through the 1950s; in 1958, more than one thousand retreatants came and went. Part of this increase resulted from the promotional work of Father Peter A. Nearing, Director of the Villa Madonna Retreat House, who organized the Villa Madonna Retreat League, which appointed "retreat fishers" in the region's parishes to promote the retreat house at the local level.[75] The Marthas offered retreats through 1964, when Villa Madonna became strictly a sisters' residence.

Anyway, the new project was an extremely busy one. Not only did it offer retreats for women, but the sisters also offered day classes in home economics to students in the district schools, and evening vocational classes that the Adult Education Division of the Department of Education sponsored.[76] The first teachers were Sister Marie Monica Shaw and Sister Miriam Vincent MacGillivray. In addition, the social workers serving on the Northside lived there, as did teachers appointed to Alder Point School in 1956. A survey of the house annals reveals a mini Grand Central Station. One sister observed, "During the week the Sisters of the house put in orders for supplies, launder, clean and beautify all for the retreatants, while social service workers and teachers are busy about God's work in their respective fields."[77]

Even though Villa Madonna was expensive and plagued by deficits the diocese had to meet, Bishop John R. was gratified by the sisters' work there. When it opened in 1954, his diocese could boast four retreat centres for men and women: Fatima House and St. Augustine's Monastery on the mainland, Villa Madonna, and Our Lady of the Atonement Retreat House in Gardiner Mines. He stated in a brochure promoting Villa Madonna, "Only through the lay retreat movement can we keep our Christian spirit vigorous in life and stimulate apostolic work."[78] The Sisters of St. Martha heartily supported his conviction; retreat houses for them were also a source of hope for future vocations. By 1955, Mother Ignatius believed that many young women who had made retreats at both Fatima House and Villa Madonna had entered her congregation.[79]

Hospitals East and West

The sisters' health care apostolate did not remain unscathed by the demands of the 1950s, even though Bishop John R.'s influence was not as noticeable there. The Marthas operated nine hospitals throughout the decade–four in the east and five in the west–and had well over one hundred sisters working in them as administrators, nursing superintendents, nursing instructors, nurses, technicians, secretaries, pharmacists, and housekeepers.[80] The hospital apostolate was especially expensive in the post-war era, for workers began to unionize, nurses' salaries increased, and all other costs spiralled. The federal government had made $13 million available to the provinces in 1948 for hospital construction. The money provided more incentive to build, but the grants only met a portion of construction expense. The congregation's St. Martha's Hospital, Antigonish, opened a five-storey, three-wing addition on 17 October 1951 at a cost of about $800,000. Its total bed capacity was then raised to 203, plus a 54-bed TB unit. The school of nursing remained productive, and in 1960 the hospital sisters cooperated to help open a regional mental health clinic in their building. Their hospital in Glace Bay, St. Joseph's, undertook major building repairs between 1949 and 1953 and continued to operate a nursing school. Mother Ignatius stationed about twenty-seven sisters there annually. She also maintained about eight sisters at St. Mary's Hospital in Inverness, where the sisters decided to take over the obsolete TB annex to obtain further space.

Sister John Bosco (Teresa) McAskill in the Pharmacy Department, St. Martha's Hospital.

A major fire on 4 February 1951 complicated the scene at St. Rita Hospital in Sydney. In the late 1940s the congregation had decided to replace the old hospital because of a bed shortage and fire hazards, but obstacles had blocked the way. Delays ceased, however, when the fire forced the general council to build a new five-storey, 162-bed hospital, which opened on 29 April 1953.

For the congregation, the cost of about $1.8 million was "a terrific financial burden."[81] About twenty-six sisters worked annually at the new St. Rita. In 1955, the hospital sisters reopened the school of nursing (which had been closed since 1933) under the direction of Sister Marie Barbara (Sarah Josephine) Muldoon. This health care complex served a city population that had slowly climbed to over 31,000.[82]

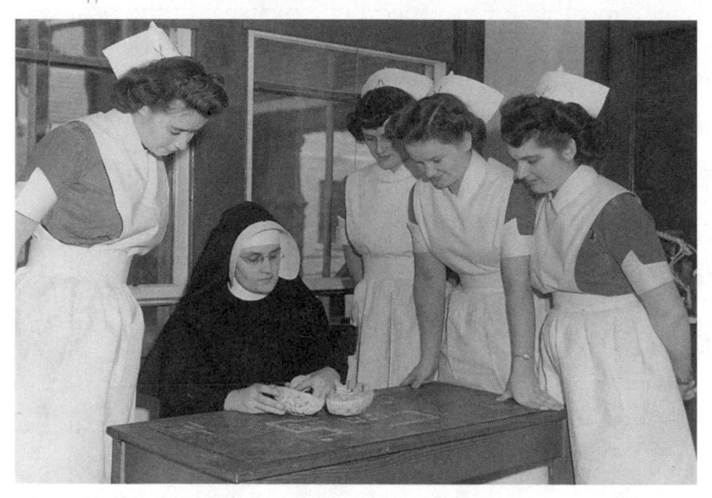

Sister Winnifred Mary (Clare Marie) Lyons teaching nursing students, 1950s, St. Martha's Hospital.

Expansion and upgrading were also central themes for the congregation's hospitals in western Canada. By erecting a new, three-storey, eighty-bed wing at St. Michael's Hospital, Lethbridge, the congregation created the largest medical centre in southern Alberta–total beds reached 203, and forty-one doctors on the medical staff served an ever-growing number of patients. Happily, the sisters replaced the outmoded nurses' residence in 1954; they then opened a new nursing school. By 1955, St. Michael's also offered approved instructional programs in x-ray and medical laboratory technology. In spite of the expansion, the sisters' upgraded hospital facility was overtaxed by the end of the

The new St. Rita Hospital, 1953, Sydney, Cape Breton.

demanding decade. Lethbridge itself grew fast during the post-war era, from 22,947 in 1951 to 35,454 in 1961.[83]

Further west of St. Michael's, the eight sisters at Mineral Springs Hospital in Banff, faced their own peculiar problems: an aging building that urgently needed replacement, and declining revenues. The congregation had already decided during the 1940s to replace the building, but hindrances had delayed construction. Then, in 1949, revenues began to slip; a new cortisone treatment for arthritis became popular, and provincial governments in the west stopped sending their workers compensation cases to Mineral Springs. The embattled superior, Sister Mary Beatrice MacMahon (1949–1952), had to institute painful measures to keep the hospital in business. Since Banff was in a National Park, it was not an incorporated municipality; hence, neither the provincial government nor the town adequately supported the hospital. In 1954 a frustrated Mother Ignatius threatened closure. The residents, fearful of losing their hospital, voted overwhelmingly in June 1955 for a municipalization scheme that assured the hospital more adequate financial support. Therefore, the sisters remained and opened a new forty-five-bed hospital on 26 July 1958, financed by the congregation with a loan of $650,000 and some assistance from government.[84] An observer reported, "The opening on [26 July] 1958 ended fifteen years of disappointments, frustrations, and delays, but was an important milestone for the town of Banff."[85] Like other western Canadian towns, Banff's citizenry grew in numbers during the 1950s to 4,101 by 1961.[86]

Growth and expansion were also themes at one of the sisters' hospitals in Saskatchewan. At St. Peter's in Melville (opened in 1942), the Marthas had in the 1950s contemplated building an addition to the fifty-five-bed facility. In 1954, before any concrete plans were underway, a disconnected exhaust pipe between the gas furnace and the flue in the basement of the convent one night almost ended the lives of six sisters there; the near tragedy was averted when someone discovered the problem and rescued the stricken sisters. A few years afterward, the general council decided to build an addition; so a financial campaign was held and the work was eventually completed in 1961 at a cost of over $700,000. The congregation had nine sisters at the eighty-bed hospital,[87] which served a population of well over 5,000.[88]

St. Michael's Hospital in Broadview, with a bed capacity of only twenty, had been built in 1940; and the sisters made no plans to expand it during the 1950s. The town's population grew very slowly during the decade to only 1,008 in 1961.[89] Only four sisters worked there in 1960. In a remarkably resourceful move, Sister Mary Hugh Cameron, who was on staff in 1955, obtained a fireman's licence so the hospital did not have to hire a second fireman to satisfy government regulations. She wrote, "'I looked after the boiler, or it would be more truthful to say that I visited the boiler room the last thing before going to bed and the first thing in the morning ... Fred (the fireman) showed me what gadgets to pull in an emergency!'"[90]

The small community of five sisters at the Mercy Hospital, Regina, continued with their hidden ministry to unwed mothers.[91] In 1954, grants from the Community Chest supplemented their income from the city and provincial governments. The mothers stayed for shorter periods during the 1950s. Through these years, and even before, the Marthas and their board had discussed the need for a new hospital; hence, the archdiocese mounted a financial campaign in the late 1950s. However, no changes were made until the mid-sixties.

Finally, the congregation's hospitals, both east and west, happily found themselves on a firmer financial base than ever before at the end of the demanding 1950s. After passing the Hospital Insurance and Diagnostic Services Act, the federal government inaugurated in 1958 a national hospital insurance scheme in cooperation with the provincial governments. At first, Catholics were suspicious that the scheme might threaten the independence of their religiously based, voluntary health care institutions. National and diocesan leaders, among them some Sisters of St. Martha, discussed and debated the federal proposals for several years.[92] For her part, Mother Ignatius trusted both levels of government because of their past treatment of voluntary, religious hospitals. Moreover, she believed that the proposed scheme would extend health care to all regardless of economic circumstance and would place all hospitals on a firmer financial basis.[93] The congregation was proud in July 1957, when Nova Scotia's government invited their veteran superior general to serve on the Hospital Services Planning Commission.[94] Then, in 1958, Mother Ignatius was appointed to the permanent commission set up to administer the new insurance plan. Unfortunately, this extra committee work precipitated a stroke, and she had to resign on 2 January 1959, one day after the inauguration of the Nova Scotia Hospital Services Insurance Plan. She later reflected on her excessive workload: "Our good Bishop John R. MacDonald was anxious that I accept the appointment and I could not refuse him."[95]

Community Life

While the sisters rapidly expanded their external works, most remarkably in teaching, during the 1950s, their internal community life also underwent noteworthy changes. The congregation convoked a general chapter in 1955, and thirty delegates assembled at the motherhouse in July. However, the proceedings were interrupted; a large majority vote for Mother Ignatius to serve as general superior for a third successive six-year term required permission from Rome. Bishop John R. strongly supported the request and Rome granted its approval.[96] Mother Ignatius was sixty-three years old, and this would be her fifth term leading the congregation; it was a controversial, and in retrospect, unwise decision to re-elect her. She was advancing in years and church law frowned on a general superior having three consecutive terms. While the delegates waited for a decision from the Holy See, they assessed revisions of their *Spiritual Directory and Book of Customs*, and their two prayer manuals.[97] The subsequent approval of these revisions, along with the re-election of Mother Ignatius, was probably the most significant work of the 1955 chapter. The new 214-page *Spiritual Directory and Customs* (1957), completed after broad consultation and intensive reflection by all the sisters, differed from the former edition "more as to form and arrangement than content."[98] It did permit more flexibility in the daily schedule of teaching sisters, and it confirmed the right of social workers to travel alone under prescribed conditions. Up to 1955 the congregation had used for many years *Jesus the Model of Religious* (two volumes, translated in 1925) for daily points of meditation that were read in common. From then on, the sisters were permitted to make their daily meditation in private. The distribution of the 135-page revised prayer manual in 1956 eliminated the use of two manuals within the congregation.[99]

Conclusion

The Marthas reached their sixtieth anniversary in 1960, which they celebrated with little fanfare.[100] The years immediately before and after were ones of important transition. Sixteen sisters had died during the decade, some of whom had been old stalwarts and guiding spirits of the community, such as Mother Faustina who died in 1954 at the age of eighty-one. In 1959, as mentioned, Mother Ignatius was incapacitated by a stroke, although she made a partial recovery. Close, supportive friends of the congregation were also passing on. Dr. Moses Coady died on 28 July 1959, and then later that same year Bishop John R. MacDonald expired suddenly on 18 December from a heart attack, probably from overwork.[101] By 1959, the sisters themselves were only too aware of the rigorous demands he had placed on himself and those around him. However, the Bethany chronicler, who considered Bishop John R. the congregation's "best friend," remarked, "The shock was a sickening one to all of us, and especially to Mother General."[102]

As the sisters contemplated their achievements in 1960, they were no doubt amazed by the changes wrought through sixty years. Now, with 431 professed members, they were the congregation with the largest number of women religious serving in the Diocese of Antigonish. The total women religious in the diocese numbered 848. Martha entrants during the decade had reached 282, more than double the number who had entered in the 1940s. Some women were possibly being attracted to the religious life because of declining opportunities in the workforce for women during the post-war era; moreover, post-war Canadian society experienced a period of revitalization and growth in church membership and high rates of church attendance.[103] Marthas, in 1960, served on thirty-four missions: twenty-three in the diocese, three in Ontario, seven in western Canada, and one in the United States. They managed the household affairs of three educational institutions and one cardinal's residence; they ran eight general hospitals and one for unwed mothers; they operated a home for the elderly and one child care institution; their teachers worked in nineteen rural, one Mi'kmaq reserve, two city, and two town schools; and they operated two lay retreat centres. Finally, the community had helped establish eleven family welfare agencies that served forty-three parishes, two social service agencies on a parish helper basis which served six parishes, and one child welfare agency that served the Diocese of Antigonish.[104] It was an impressive range of work in diverse Canadian communities.

Although the congregation's finances had been bolstered by teachers' salaries and the national hospital insurance scheme, still,

The novitiate class of 1956, which reveals the large number of entrants in the 1950s.

the demands for expansion, especially in hospital construction, had created an outstanding debt of $3.8 million.[105] In spite of a gratifying increase in vocations during the decade, Mother Ignatius had chosen to refuse eighty-three formal requests for help during the past decade. These refusals had been painful, and some requests had come from captivating places such as Japan, the Scottish Highlands, the Bahamas, Hawaii, and even Rome itself. Her refusals to appeals "from away" during the 1950s had largely been forced by one overriding consideration: Bishop John R. MacDonald's spiralling demands for help in his own spiritual vineyard.

Notes

1 Forbes and Muise, eds., *The Atlantic Provinces in Confederation,* p. 382.
2 CSM to Bishop Morrison, 27 July 1949, F5,S8,SS2,f1,b6.
3 Peter A. Nearing, *He Loved the Church* (Antigonish: Casket Printing and Publishing Co., 1975), p. 48.
4 Bethany Annals, 8 June 1943, F6,S1,SS1,f7,b107.
5 Father John R. MacDonald to Mother Immaculata, 30 January 1941, F5,S34,SS4,f4,b86.
6 Bethany Annals, 25-26 January 1950, F6,S1,SS1,f12,b107.
7 Mother Ignatius to Archbishop M.C. O'Neill, 20 March 1950, F5,S34,SS17,f17,b93.
8 Bishop John R. MacDonald to Mother Ignatius, 28 December 1950, F5,S34,SS4,f4,b86.
9 F.R. MacKinnon, Nova Scotia Director of Child Welfare, to Rev. Michael MacCormack, 14 June 1948, F20,S1,SS2,f2,b190.
10 Mercy Hospital and Joint Advisory Board Minutes, 20 April 1950, F19,S3,SS2,f1,b181.
11 Statistical Reports and List of Personnel, Mercy Hospital, F19,S1,SS2,f1,3,b181.
12 Diocesan Charities Reports, F5,S27,SS1,f1,b65.
13 Ibid.
14 Bishop J.G. Berry's Report, October 1950, F5,S27,SS3,f6,b65. His conclusion about the good standard of child care was confirmed by a confidential report to the Bishop in 1953. See Confidential Report to His Excellency, Bishop John R. MacDonald Re: Proposed Child Care Institution, 10 February 1953, F5,S27,SS6,f1,b66.
15 Bishop John R. MacDonald, Address to the CWL Convention, Antigonish, 2 July 1952, F20,S1,SS1,f1,b190.
16 *The Casket*, 30 May 1957.
17 Bishop J.G. Berry's Report, October 1950, F5,S27,SS3,f6,b65.
18 The Family Life Commission Report, May 1953, F5,S27,SS5,f1,b66.
19 CSM Quinquennial Report to the Holy See, 1951, F5,S34,SS1,f2,b84.
20 Mother Ignatius to Rev. John F. Curran, 8 April 1956, F5, S35,SS1,f10,b95.
21 Bethany Annals, 10 September 1952, F6,S1,SS1,f12,b107.
22 Family Welfare Council of St. Ninian's Parish, First Annual Report, p. 1, F5,S28,SS11,f1-3,b65.
23 Bethany Annals,15 May 1941, 21 and 24 March 1945, and 4 April 1951.

24 Bethany Annals, 17 June 1955, F6,S1,SS1,f14,b108.
25 Bethany Annals, 18 February 1958, ibid.
26 R.K. MacDonald Guest House Statistics, 1958-1960, F29,S1,SS1,f4,b223.
27 *Census of Canada, 1971*, 1.1:2-11.
28 Northside Parishes, Catholic Family Welfare, Historical Notes, Agreement, and Reports, 1954-1960, F5,S28,SS5,f1,b67.
29 Canso Welfare Bureau, Highlights of Social Work, F23,S1,SS1,f8,b195.
30 Canso Welfare Bureau, Annual Report, 1955-1956, F23,S2,SS2,f4,b197.
31 Bethany Annals, 3 June 1958, F6,S1,SS1,f14,b108.
32 Lincolnville Mission Report, November 1958-May 1959, F23,S2,SS2,f5,b197.
33 *Census of Canada 1971*, 1.1:2-11.
34 Bethany Annals, 17 September 1957, F6,S1,SS1,f13,b108.
35 Family Welfare Agencies, Glace Bay, Historical Notes and Reports, 1957-1960, F5,S28,SS8,f1-2,b68.
36 Bishop John R. MacDonald to Father John G. Webb, 23 February 1957, F5,S27,SS4,f5,b65.
37 Catholic Family Service of New Waterford and District, Historical Notes and Statistics, F5,S28,SS9,f1,b68.
38 Statistical Summaries, F5,S29,SS1,f5,b68, and Annual Report to the Holy See, 1960, F5,S34,SS1,f5,b84.
39 Requests from Social Workers for Permission to do Field Work Alone, c. 1952, F5,S27,SS4,f3,b65.
40 Report of the Committee re Social Service Workers, 14 August 1953, ibid.
41 Bethany Annals, 28 May 1950, F6,S1,SS3,f12,b107.
42 Ibid., 17 June 1950.
43 "Archbishop James Cushing," *Current Biography* (New York: H.W. Wilson, 1952), pp. 133-4 and "Boston, Archdiocese of," *New Catholic Encyclopedia* 1967, pp. 722-3.
44 Archbishop Cushing to Mother Ignatius, 7 May 1952, F5,S34,SS17,f5,b92.
45 Social Work Report, 1 June 1953, St. Martha's Catholic Centre, F26,S2,SS1,f2,b215.
46 Recollections of Sr. Irene Doyle, Bethany, June, 1998.
47 Sister Anselm to Mother Ignatius, 23 March 1958, ibid., and interview with Sister Irene Doyle, 24 March 1998, Bethany.
48 Historical Notes, St. Martha's Catholic Centre, ibid.
49 Archbishop Cushing to Mother Ignatius, 27 June 1956, F26,S2,SS1,f1,b215.

50 Sister Anselm Doyle to Archbishop Cushing, 6 September 1958, ibid.
51 Mother Ignatius to Dear Sisters, October 1952, F26,S2,SS1,f5,b216.
52 Forbes and Muise, eds., *The Atlantic Provinces in Confederation*, p. 398.
53 Dan Serroul to Mother Immaculata, 21 July 1943, F20,S1,SS2,f1,b190.
54 Our Lady of Fatima Convent, Historical Highlights, F44,S1,SS1,f5,b239.
55 St. Mary's Convent, East Bay, Personnel List, F41,S1,SS1,f3,b237.
56 St. Peter's Convent, Historical Highlights, F32,S1,SS1,f7,b228.
57 St. Joseph's Convent, Historical Highlights, F33,S1,SS1,f4,b229.
58 *The Bethanite*, XXIV, October 1959, p. 31.
59 Father Paul MacNeil to Mother Ignatius, 3 March 1956, F31,S1,SS1,f5,b227.
60 St. Paul's Convent, Historical Highlights, F31,S1,SS1,f2,b227.
61 Bethany Annals, 11 September 1956, F6,S1,SS1,f13,b108.
62 Bethany Annals, 1959, ibid., f14.
63 *Census of Canada, 1971*, 1.1:2-12.
64 Ibid.
65 Bethany Annals, 26 August 1958, F6,S1,SS1,f4,b108.
66 Data on Schools, 1952-1968, F5,S25,SS8,f1,b63.
67 Correspondence and Minutes re the Teaching Apostolate, 1929-1959, F5,S25,SS1,b61.
68 The Teaching of Catechism, p. 4, F5,S26,SS1,f1,b64.
69 Bethany Annals, 14 January 1952, F6,S1,SS1,f12,b107.
70 Norman H. Fergusson, *The History of the Nova Scotia Teachers Union* (Armdale, NS: Nova Scotia Teachers Union, 1990), pp. 104-110.
71 Resume of Meeting Re School Problems, 23 November 1957, F5,S25,SS5,f8,b62.
72 General Chapter Proceedings, 1949, F5,S8,SS2,f1,b6.
73 Sister to Sister Mary Corona, 12 January 1959, F5,S32,SS1,f2,b71.
74 Bishop John R. MacDonald to Mother Ignatius, 1 April 1953, F5,S34,SS4,f4,b86.
75 Villa Madonna Retreat House, Historical Notes, F5,S32,SS1,f6,b71.
76 Ibid.
77 Villa Madonna Retreat House Annals, 1956-57, F24,S1,SS2,f4,b198.
78 Villa Madonna Retreat House brochure, F24,S1,SS1,f6,b198.
79 Mother Ignatius, Report for the General Chapter, 1955, F5,S8,SS2,f1,b6.
80 Statistics of Sisters Engaged in Hospital Work, 1955-1962, F5,S22,SS2,f1,b53.

81 Bethany Annals, 16-18 March 1953, F6,S1,SS1,f12,b107.
82 *Census of Canada, 1971*, 1.1:2-11.
83 *Census of Canada, 1971*, 1.1:2-103.
84 Mineral Springs Hospital, Banff, anonymous article, F11,S1,SS2,f3,b152.
85 Ibid.
86 *Census of Canada, 1971*, 1.1:2-106.
87 St. Peter's Hospital, Annal Highlights, F13,S1,SS1,f6,b169.
88 *Census of Canada, 1971*, 1.1:2-89.
89 Ibid.
90 Quoted in Sister May Mulvihill, "History of the Sisters of St. Martha," III:10:82A.
91 Personnel List, Mercy Hospital, F18,S1,SS2,f1,b177.
92 Minutes of Meetings, 22 March 1956 and 13 March 1957, F5,S22,SS4,f3,b54.
93 Mother Ignatius, "Health Insurance in Nova Scotia," 1958, F5,S21,SS3,f1,b52.
94 Bethany Annals, 23 July 1957, F6,S1,SS1,f13,b108.
95 Mother Ignatius to Rev. A.L. Denis, 20 April 1959, F5,S33,SS6,f10,b78.
96 Bishop John R. MacDonald to Mother Ignatius, 27 August 1955, F5,S34,SS1,f8,b84.
97 Bethany Annals, 29 July-20 August 1955, F6,S1,SS1,f14,b108.
98 Committee to Dear Sisters, March 1958, F5,S6,SS4,f1,b257.
99 Bethany Annals, 24 July 1956, F6,S1,SS1,f14,b108.
100 The congregation did publish a useful history recording its sixty years of work which it called *Sixty Years-Deo Soli.*
101 Nearing, *He Loved the Church,* pp. 95 and 99.
102 Ibid., 18 December 1959.
103 Murphy and Perin., *A Concise History of Christianity in Canada,* p. 355.
104 Congregational Report to Bishop William Power, August 1960, F5,S33,SS2,f3,b77.
105 CSM Quinquennial Report to the Holy See, 1961, F5,S34,SS1,f4,b84.

Sister Marie Brenda (Ellen) Grant at the Catholic Family Agency office, 1960s.

Chapter Ten

The Last Phase of Expansion, 1960-1966

Although Bishop John R. MacDonald's voice, urging the Marthas on to new missions and greater responsibilities, was stilled by death in December 1959, the sisters continued in an expansive, buoyant, and optimistic mood through the first half of the 1960s. Like other Canadians, they anticipated a rosy future. Living standards continued to rise, governments expanded services, and the federal government transferred monies to the less developed provinces. Della Stanley affirms, "New highways, power plants, factories, and industrial parks sprouted throughout the [Maritime] region. Communities expanded into modern high-rises, sub-divisions, shopping malls, and urban renewal programs. There were substantial improvements in income levels, employment opportunities, municipal services, education, health care, ethnic relations, and interprovincial co-operation."[1] The Marthas busily expanded the Bethany complex, opened eleven new houses and even investigated the field of foreign missions. Growth during the 1950s, strong congregational finances, healthy numbers of entrants, and the congregation's relatively young average age no doubt fed their buoyancy. Their numbers peaked in 1962, when a total of 460 women wore the Martha habit. Moreover, an experienced superior general and council assumed the administrative reins in 1961.

However, the early sixties were, in a way, an age of innocence for the Marthas. Little did they expect that Rome's Vatican

Council II (1962–1965) would unleash massive change within Roman Catholic churches and religious congregations worldwide; nor did they anticipate that new and profound social trends would reshape society and erode their ranks. For the Marthas, both developments would conspire to close an era of optimistic expansion.

New Diocesan Leadership

Bishop John R. MacDonald had suddenly and unexpectedly died on December 18, 1959. Rome replaced him with Father William E. Power, a forty-four-year old, bilingual, Montreal native and graduate of its Grand Seminary. He was installed in style at St. Ninian's Cathedral, Antigonish, on 10 August 1960. Like his predecessors, Bishop Power developed a warm and supportive relationship with the congregation. His "Martha duties" included the appointment of chaplains and confessors to their convents, attendance at special Martha ceremonies, canonical visitations and examination of candidates, and consultation with the general administration about the congregation's diocesan works. For their part, the Marthas administered important diocesan projects and provided household services at Bishop Power's Antigonish residence.

New Congregational Leadership

The first major congregational event to involve Bishop Power was its general chapter held at Bethany from 27 July to 2 August 1961. As usual, all Marthas had been asked beforehand to submit recommendations to the chapter, and the thirty-three sister delegates considered the crucial ones. Mother Ignatius, now broken down in health, presented the motherhouse keys to the presiding bishop, symbolic of her retirement from office. She also proposed a recommendation rooted in her own experience: "That no Sister should be appointed Superior General for a third term. Two periods is [sic] difficult and very tiresome. A third should not be undertaken."[2] Mother Ignatius had served three consecutive terms (eighteen years), the last one with special permission from Rome. In all, she had been superior general of the Sisters of St. Martha for an astounding thirty years, nearly one-half the entire life of the congregation!

The chapter delegates debated and approved other recommendations, for example, that the postulate be extended beyond six months, that the novitiate last two full years, that temporary vows be taken for five years, and that a juniorate program (an ongoing formation program for sisters under temporary vows) be established. They appointed full-time schools and vocation directors, and expressed deepening concerns about keeping up with rising professional standards in hospital work, teaching, and social work; hence the urgent need for upgrading sisters' qualifications. The chapter accepted a memorandum of proposed changes to the constitutions but then directed that a committee be established to revise them again. Televisions and cameras remained on the list of prohibited possessions.

The chapter elected a new administration, which included Sister Paul of the Cross Kyte (superior general), Sister Mary of Calvary (Anastasia) MacDonald, Sister Anselm Doyle, Sister Mary Magdalen Cann, Sister James Francis Morrison, Sister Joseph Helen Mulvihill (secretary general), and Sister Mary Clarissa Chisholm (treasurer general). The councillors, whose average age was 52, represented the four congregational apostolates.

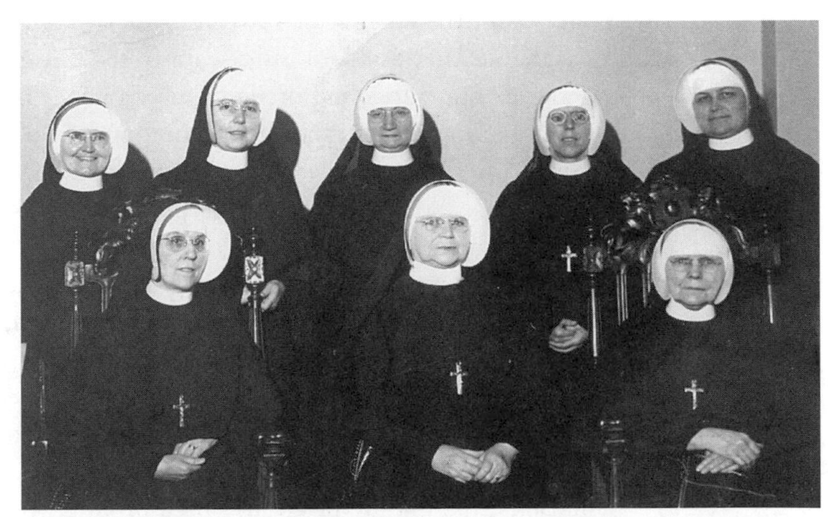

SITTING, L-R: Sister Mary of Calvary (Anastasia) MacDonald, Mother Paul of the Cross (Eunice Viola) Kyte, superior general 1961-1967 and Mother M. Ignatius. STANDING, L-R: Sister Joseph Helen (May) Mulvihill, Sister Anselm (Irene) Doyle, Sister M. Magdalen (Catherine) Cann, Sister James Francis (Eleanor Jean) Morrison and Sister Mary Clarissa (Florence) Chisholm.

Mother Paul of the Cross, age 64, was the oldest and most experienced member of the new administration–she had served as Mother Ignatius's vicar general for two consecutive terms. Her birthplace was St. Peter's, Cape Breton, and the Marthas had trained her at their St. Joseph's Hospital School of Nursing in Glace Bay. In 1928, she entered the congregation, took first vows in 1930, and then went on to serve as St. Joseph's Hospital Nursing School director (1931–1941), next the hospital's administrator (1941–1946), and finally the administrator of St. Martha's Hospital in Antigonish (1946–1961). As well, she was professionally active in hospital associations and had been the recipient of awards from the American College of Hospital Administrators (1947 and 1955). Sisters remember Mother Paul of the Cross as forthright and fair, traditional and conservative, as well as competent and flexible. She was an obedient daughter of the Church; as new congregation leader in 1961, she had little inkling of what that obedience would require of her.

Building at Bethany

The congregation's expansive mood was certainly evident both before and after the chapter of 1961. To ease overcrowding, Mother Ignatius, her assistant Sister Paul of the Cross, and the other general councillors had orchestrated a major, three-phase, $2 million building program at the motherhouse in the late 1950s. First, they located a new gymnasium immediately behind the motherhouse. The Marthas swiftly put it to use as a recreational and conference facility, overflow sleeping quarters, craft school, etc.[3] Next came a large new wing designed like a T and built at the eastern end of the motherhouse; it opened, along with a new boiler house, in 1962. The four-storey concrete and brick structure became home for the infirmary, congregation administration offices, classrooms, sisters' bedrooms, and the altar bread and sewing departments.

The Bethany building program's final product was a beautiful, spacious, octagonal, brick and stone-sheathed, steepled chapel placed at the eastern extremity of the motherhouse and accessible from its new wing through a broad narthex. P.M. Keenleyside of Toronto planned the structure and the Canadian division of Rambusch designed the stained-glass windows and sanctuary furnishings. A teardrop theme throughout symbolizes, first, penance and sorrow, but ultimately the resurrection hope that God will be with his people and will "wipe away all tears from their eyes; there will be no more death, or no more mourning or sadness" (Rev. 21: 3-4). A Casavant organ from St. Hyacinthe, Quebec, was placed within where 360 worshippers could gather. Amidst much congregational rejoicing and elaborate ceremony, Bishop Power blessed, dedicated and consecrated

Bethany, Antigonish, 1963, after the addition of a new wing and chapel.

the new motherhouse chapel before a throng of invited guests on 11 December 1963. This final addition to the Bethany complex cost over $600,000.[4]

The motherhouse expansion was certainly not the only ambitious building project the sisters undertook during the sixties. The congregation also made substantial additions to five hospital complexes: St. Rita, Sydney (1963); St. Martha's, Antigonish; St. Joseph's, Glace Bay (1964); St. Michael's, Lethbridge (1965); and St. John's, Lowell (1966). As well, the Marthas built an attractive new facility for their Mercy Hospital in Regina, renamed Martha House.

New congregational missions established in the early 1960s also revealed the sisters' buoyancy and expansiveness. In their health care apostolate alone, the Marthas assumed the administration of three additional hospitals to the nine they already managed.

Eastern Memorial Hospital, Canso

Canso, a small fishing community on the northeastern extremity of mainland Nova Scotia, had seen the first Marthas arrive in 1933 when social activist Father Jimmy Tompkins had brought them there to open a Welfare Bureau. In 1948, leading citizens had established an eleven-bed outpost hospital equipped and financed by the Red Cross. Actually, the hospital had used rent-free the renovated house belonging to the Marthas and located next to their Welfare Bureau. For financial and religious reasons, the Marthas had refused from the start to assume control of the tiny hospital. However, they had well understood the need for one in Canso, for the sister annalist there had commented on its opening day:

> *For years such an emergency measure was a crying need for the town, especially during the winter months, when isolation by ice and snow made transportation out of Canso almost an impossibility–and it was not uncommon for people to die enroute to St. Martha's Hospital in Antigonish, 75 miles distant.*[5]

Finally, on 1 October 1960, to the delight of board chair John R. Chafe, who had wanted the sisters from the start, they acceded and sent two Marthas, Sister M. Etheldreda (Florence) Brean, administrator, and Sister Joseph Allana (Mary Rita) MacDougall, secretary. The congregation would administer the little Eastern Memorial Hospital for about ten years. It was a difficult task, for the facility was poorly designed for hospital use and its medical services were uneven; the community had difficulty attracting and keeping nurses and doctors. Nonetheless, the hospital provided a key service to the people of Canso.[6]

St. John's Hospital, Lowell, Massachusetts

One year after accepting the management of Eastern Memorial Hospital, Canso, the congregation assumed control of a much larger hospital in Massachusetts. In 1952, Cardinal Cushing had had the Marthas open the St. Martha's Catholic Centre, Boston. Ten years later, he succeeded in luring them into his orbit once again. In 1960 the Cardinal told Mother Ignatius that the Daughters of Charity of St. Vincent de Paul had given him the gift of a profitable, 180-bed hospital in Lowell. The city, about fifty kilometres north of Boston, had been a leader in the nineteenth-century industrial revolution but now shared in the general economic malaise of its region, the Merrimack Valley. The Cardinal continued, "I am trying to find some sisters to staff it. If I find them I will give them the Hospital. Not only that, but over a few years I will probably spend as much as one million dollars in modernising it. The Sisters to whom I give the institution will be obliged to pay back the money to me as they realise the profit. Would you be interested?"[7] Predictably, Mother Ignatius was "definitely interested," and after investigation, her council accepted the Cardinal's challenging offer.

On 1 September 1961, the congregation received the St. John's Hospital assets of $2.6 million, and the Cardinal pledged $1 million for modernization (the hospital had been opened in 1867). The mother general assigned ten sisters to supervise its key departments: Sister M. Consolata MacDonald, superior and administrator; Sister Marie Barbara Muldoon, 1st assistant and

St. John's Hospital, Lowell, Massachusetts.

director of nursing; Sister Mary Frances (Rose Evelyn) LaRusic, 2nd assistant and business manager; Sister Mary Pius (Catherine) MacGillivray, seamstress; Sister Mary Anita Chisholm, sacristan; Sister M. Simone Roach, unit administrator of the affiliated Catherine Laboure School of Nursing; Sister Ann Bernardine (Frances Claire) Butler, dietician; Sister Ann Francis (Jean Patricia) O'Neil, operating room supervisor; and Sister Mary Terence (Mary) McMahon, obstetrical supervisor. The sisters were not to displace lay persons already occupying professional positions at St. John's, and the director of nursing was to cooperate with the affiliated Catherine Laboure School of

Nursing. The modernization program produced a new wing in 1966 that brought the hospital's total beds to 251. St. John's in Lowell was a major new responsibility for the Marthas, and expansion continued under the able leadership of Sister Maria Loyola (Catherine Elizabeth) MacIsaac. The Catholic community, along with the cardinal, joyfully welcomed them and over time they received the support of a host of benefactors. Some sisters also became involved in parish and community activities in Lowell. Happily, they were within striking distance of their Martha sisters working at St. Martha's Catholic Centre in Boston.[8]

New Waterford Consolidated Hospital

Closer to home in Nova Scotia, the Marthas were urged by the town of New Waterford, Cape Breton, to aid its local hospital. Most men in the town (incorporated in 1913) mined coal, the backbone of the economy. Back in 1914 the Dominion Coal Company had converted two company houses into a small hospital; a decade later, New Waterford completed a much more adequate forty-five-bed general hospital. By the 1950s, however, the facility was obsolete, and its finances and administration were in shambles; so, on behalf of the town, a civic commission planned a new hospital and lobbied the Sisters of St. Martha to assume its management. Eventually, Mother Ignatius and her council accepted the request and signed an agreement with the New Waterford Consolidated Hospital Commission to administer but not own the facility.

Builders completed the hospital in September 1961. It had eighty-eight beds plus operating, x-ray, laboratory, and dietary facilities. The staff residence could house thirty student nurses and seventeen sisters. The Marthas, by now experienced and wise in hospital affairs, refused to assume control of the new building until certain structural deficiencies were rectified. Finally they moved in, transferred patients from the old hospital and officially opened on 5 August 1963, the year New Waterford celebrated its golden jubilee. The contingent of pioneer sisters included Sister Ann Romuald (Genevieve) McArthur, administrator and superior; Sister Francis de Sales (Katherine) Gregory, 1st assistant and purchasing; Sister Basil (Theresa) Levangie, 2nd assistant and director of nurses; Sister Frances Theresa Herrgott, pharmacist; Sister Josita MacNeil, dietary; Sister Roberta (Loretta) McGrath, x-ray; Sister Mary Grace MacDonald, dietary; Sister Catherine of Siena (Alexius) MacLellan, operating room; and Sister Mary Fatima (Ethel) Kyte, director of the school for nursing assistants. They worked with a medical staff of five; the total staff numbered over 120. New Waterford Consolidated was a busy hospital. The sisters were well-received in the community, and Sister Ann Romuald and her staff soon demonstrated that the town's hospital could be placed on a sound financial basis and run competently.[9]

St. Pius X High School

In addition to accepting new hospital missions during the early sixties, the Marthas also optimistically and generously acceded to three requests for sisters to supervise institutional domestic work. Their first household management mission since 1935, and the fourth in the congregation's history, came about this way. To increase priestly vocations, the Archbishop of Ottawa, Most Reverend M.J. Lemieux, opened a minor, or preparatory, seminary for anglophone youth in the nation's capital. The archbishop's friend in Antigonish, Bishop John R. MacDonald, sent him two priests in 1958 to help with his new educational project. After being refused by, among others, the Antigonish Marthas, Archbishop Lemieux found an Italian congregation to discharge its domestic duties, but this arrangement proved deficient. Hence, the archbishop travelled to Antigonish in December 1959.

On the seventeenth he went to meet Bishop John R. MacDonald for a scheduled appointment with Mother Ignatius. To his horror, he discovered the bishop dead in his drawing room. In spite of the shock, he convinced the mother general to send four sisters to Ottawa in September 1960; they would replace the Italian sisters who transferred elsewhere.[10] Four sisters, including Sister Mary Magdalen Cann (superior), Sister George Aiden (Catherine) MacLellan and Sister Daniel Theresa (Ada) Fougere, arrived that fall to administer the seminary's domestic affairs for a three-year trial period. By 1961 the archbishop had completed a comfortable new convent for them. His seminary registered about a hundred students, around forty-five of whom were boarders. The Marthas' seminary convent was a convenient residence for sisters sent to study at educational institutions in Ottawa. Marthas would remain at St. Pius X High School for seventeen years.[11]

The Coady International Institute

In 1961 the Marthas expanded their work at St. Francis Xavier University by contributing to a fascinating new project christened the Coady International Institute. Of course, the university was the original work that had called them into being as a congregation in 1900. Since then, through thick and thin, they had tried to maintain a small army of vigorous sisters at St.F.X. (thirty-six sisters lived there in 1961), supplying housekeeping and food services, infirmary and sacristan personnel, and business office, extension department, and library staff. Unfortunately, their working conditions deteriorated swiftly after World War II under the onslaught of rapid university expansion. Mother Ignatius complained in 1957 that the administration knew nothing of the institution's domestic needs and expected "impossible things of the Sisters."[12] Their plight was so deplorable by 1959 that the local superior, Sister Mary Magdalen, and her sisters, with the consent of Mother Ignatius, warned the university's chancellor, Bishop John R. MacDonald, and authorities:

Sister M. Vincentia (Eleanor Monica) Doyle, age 80, mending at St.F.X.

> *We have long borne in silence, and have made innumerable efforts to protest through the ordinary channels. Justice and charity make it clear to us that we should now complain thus. We respectfully wish to serve notice, therefore, that if–before next year–attention is not given to providing Morrison Hall with adequate facilities to enable us to cope with the demands of an ever-increasing student body, we, the Sisters of Morrison Hall Convent, shall ask our Mother General to reconsider our appointments.*[13]

St.F.X. heard the message loud and clear. By 1962, it had made important and expensive extensions and improvements to the laundry and Morrison Hall, acceptable to the sisters.

The university could also reveal a more considerate side without being threatened into action. In 1954, Rev. Dr. John Hugh Gillis, professor of classics, exhorted the students to form a Sisters' Appreciation Society to devise ways and means to show gratitude for the Marthas' contribution to St.F.X.'s welfare. With his thoughtful guidance and support, the Xaverians produced an occasional publication called *X-Owes*, organized an annual "Sisters' Sunday," and, along with other gestures of gratitude, made innumerable small and large purchases for them of statues of St. Martha, a portable organ, and religious pictures. In 1960 they even helped obtain for the convent sisters, again with Father Gillis's behind-the-scenes manoeuvring, a seaside vacation cottage called Alma Mater.[14] In 1964, St.F.X. purchased a new Pontiac car for the university sisters–their first car–to demonstrate its appreciation of their long years of service.

The sisters played a part in the new Coady International Institute. St.F.X. had designed this innovative program, named after the late Dr. Coady, to extend the university extension department's regional work for human betterment to the international level. Students from less-developed countries would study the traditional philosophy and methods of the famed Antigonish Movement. Dr. Hugh J. Somers, the university president, announced the inauguration of the institute in December 1959.[15] Its founding director, Father Francis J. Smyth, was most anxious to have the "motherly presence" of the Marthas, who would help to create a family atmosphere while managing the Coady's domestic affairs.[16] Mother Ignatius assented and assigned three sisters to the institute's new four-storey brick building named after their friend and late bishop, John R. MacDonald. In September 1961, Sister Mary Justina (Margaret Lucina) MacIsaac, superior, Sister Daniel Marie (Catherine Jean) Chisholm, and Sister Donalda Marie (Anna) Beaton moved into a small convent area at the north end of the "Coady MacDonald" building.

Father Smyth also successfully pushed for the presence on his staff of Sister Marie Michael MacKinnon, a former pioneer member of Dr. Coady's extension department staff in the 1930s. As librarian, she became a great asset to the international students during her tenure at the Coady from 1964 to 1971. The Coady Marthas developed supportive, sensitive relations with the students, who came literally from the four corners of the earth and faced, in Nova Scotia, the manifold problems of separation from home and adjustment to the language, food, and customs of the Bluenosers. In 1961-1962, sixty-five students from twenty-three countries studied at the Coady International Institute.[17] Mother Paul of the Cross confided in Father Smyth, "The Congregation as a whole is proud to be able to contribute ... to the fulfilment of Dr. Coady's dream for the Extension work of St.F.X."[18]

Holy Heart Seminary, Halifax

Optimism and a sense of obligation no doubt carried the Marthas, in 1964, to a household management assignment at Holy Heart Seminary, Halifax. Father Patrick B. McCluskey, the rector of this old seminary established by the Eudists in 1895, showed up at the motherhouse door in 1963 with a tale of woe: eight Eudist sisters would be withdrawing from his institution in June 1964 and he urgently needed to replace them. Would the Marthas come? Using his own calculations, he pointedly reminded them that 92 percent of Maritime diocesan clergy and about 85 percent of Antigonish Diocesan secular clergy had received their clerical training at Holy Heart. With the blessing of Halifax's archbishop, Mother Paul of the Cross's council concurred and assigned five sisters to Holy Heart.

Sister Teresa Carmel (Sarah) Gillis, superior, Sister Leo Andre (Kathleen Veronica) Holland, Sister Mary Romuald (Mary K.) MacNeil, Sister Mary Christopher (Ida Marie) Rowlands, and Sister Yvonne Melanson moved into the new two-storey convent attached to the seminary. They began the work, in September 1964, of household management for the sixty-two seminarians and eight priest faculty. The seminary atmosphere was monastic and all but one of the faculty was of French descent.[19] A grateful seminarian wrote after the arrival of the Marthas: "God love the Marthas! Excellent food, lots of it–real butter, real milk at every meal plus a milk cooler in the rec. hall, etc., etc. Besides, they're doing a wonderful job of brightening up the atmosphere–they talk, they smile, they laugh–in short, they add a vivacious touch to an institution which was sorely in need of it."[20] Seminarians were commonly graduates of St.F.X. who knew the sisters. The Marthas at Holy Heart contributed to Halifax parish life and welcomed to their convent sister students assigned to study at Halifax educational institutions.[21]

Teaching Missions in the West

The surge in Martha teaching missions during the 1950s, which had been mostly orchestrated by Bishop John R., did not end until 1962. Indeed, in 1961 and 1962 the Marthas added two more schools to the twenty-four they already served. With the blessing of Bishop Carroll of Calgary, Father William O. MacCallum, the parish priest at Picture Butte, Alberta, wrote Mother Ignatius in 1958, requesting teachers for the new local Catholic school. Dissatisfied with her negative reply, he went knocking at Bethany's door in 1960, when he extracted a promise for two teachers and a housekeeper to begin in September 1961. After overcoming snags about convent living quarters and teacher qualifications, Sister M. Maurice Brocklehurst (superior and teacher), Sister Mary Jude (Jean) Doyle (teacher), and Sister M. Helen Cathcart (homemaker), arrived at Picture Butte in August 1961. This bustling town, located in sugar beet territory, had its own sugar factory. The parishioners, many with European roots, warmly received them and the sisters soon got down to work as teachers, religious education instructors, and parish visitors. Their field of work extended to the neighbouring communities of Shaughnessey, Diamond City, and Turin. For the sake of improved community life and economy, the congregation closed St. Catherine's Convent in September 1965; thereafter, the teaching sisters commuted from St. Michael's Hospital, Lethbridge. At least one sister would remain on Picture Butte's Catholic school staff until 1981.[22]

From further to the west and beyond the Rocky Mountains in Kamloops, British Columbia, an old friend of the Marthas also requested teachers for a new Catholic school. It was located in Our Lady of Perpetual Help Parish. Again the Marthas wanted to oblige and eventually did. Bishop Michael A. Harrington, former pastor of Blairmore (1926–1950), who had invited the sisters to Crow's Nest Pass in 1939, played suitor once again. His overtures, by no means the first to arrive at Bethany from British Columbia, began shortly after he became bishop of the gargantuan Diocese of Kamloops in 1952. He finally achieved success in 1961 after writing to Mother Paul of the Cross:

> *Before things could become forgotten in the rush and detail, I want to renew my humble appeal for the Sisters of St. Martha for Kamloops Diocese. I need teachers and social workers and I have a school, eight rooms, and a convent ready for them. All I can offer, Sister, is work, co-operation from clergy and laity, and I feel the blessing of Almighty God will flow from their sacrifice.... The Spirit, the Work and Sacrifice of the Sisters of St. Martha is what this Diocese needs.*[23]

This gentle flattery helped to win the day; four Marthas arrived in Kamloops for the school opening, in September 1962, and moved into an attractive convent near the church and school. They were Sister Ian Marie (Margaret) MacFarlane, superior and principal; Sister Ann Carmel MacNeil, teacher; Sister Joseph Marie (Bertha Johanna) MacDonald, homemaker; and Sister Mary Elaine (Rosaline) Tynski, parish visitor. Nearly seventy grade one and two students excitedly arrived at school that fall. Higher grades were added in future years and the sisters faced expanding numbers. Our Lady of Perpetual Help School was an independent parochial school that followed the British Columbia curriculum but received, at that time, no government financial assistance. For at least one decade, the sisters survived on little more than the cooperation and moral support of clergy and laity.[24] A deeply appreciative parish would keep the Marthas there until 1998.

Sister Ian Marie (Margaret) MacFarlane, the first Principal of Our Lady of Perpetual Help School, Kamloops, B.C.

THE SOCIAL WORK APOSTOLATE

The social work apostolate was another arena that testified to the buoyancy and expansionism of the Marthas in the early 1960s. However, this was revealed less in the multiplication of their missions and more in their ambitious upgrading of sister social-worker qualifications and increasingly professional counselling services. Social worker numbers and range of work remained essentially static for the decade. Around thirty sister social workers in the Diocese of Antigonish administered the Little Flower Institute for children in Sydney, ran nine Catholic family agencies, and operated two important programs, one for unwed mothers and the second a boarding home program for children. In Regina, Saskatchewan, two Marthas ran the Catholic Family Service Society. About five administered Mercy Hospital for unwed mothers, an institution that changed its name to Martha House and moved to an advantageous new facility in the mid-sixties. At Blairmore, Alberta, the Marthas extended their work in the Crow's Nest Pass area when Sister Leo Agnes (Teresa) Bellefontaine established a family service bureau under the supervision of Father P.B. O'Byrne of the Catholic Family Service of Calgary. Finally, three social workers at St. Martha's Catholic Centre, Boston, worked in several archdiocesan helping programs–the Lay Apostolate of the Aging, and Family Counselling and Guidance Centres.[25]

An accelerated drive to upgrade and advance the professional qualifications of the social workers marked their apostolate in the sixties. Although the social workers began "Sisters' Meetings" in the mid-1950s to discuss common problems, a stronger impetus to higher levels of training began under Sister Anselm Doyle, who became congregational social work coordinator in 1961. A pioneer member of the St.F.X. Extension Department, she was also an experienced social worker and general councillor. Under the auspices of Antigonish Diocesan Charities (ADC), the organization that supervised diocesan social work, she accessed government training grants to improve the qualifications of the Martha social workers. Her staff development program offered the social workers supervision and consultation, training at summer institutes, courses at Xavier Junior College and St.F.X., and participation in social work conferences. In 1960 about twelve of all the sister social workers had virtually no formal training, although some of these had considerable practical experience. By 1970 the fruits of staff development were plain: ten sisters had earned masters in social work and six more had diplomas; the remainder had varied but upgraded professional credentials. In addition to her program of upgrading, Sister Anselm became vice-president representing the Atlantic Provinces for the newly formed Catholic Charities Council of Canada, and she developed briefs to government and fostered positive relations between ADC and the Nova Scotia Department of Welfare.[26]

Foreign Missions

Their keen contemplation of the foreign mission field is one final example of Martha expansionism in the early sixties. Special stimulus arose from two sources: the many requests desperate priests sent from foreign lands, and the Vatican-inspired diocesan interest and involvement in the Caribbean, and in Central and South America. For example, Father Pius Hawley, superior of the Antigonish priests in Honduras, called for the Marthas to join them there. Mother Paul of the Cross took all the foreign mission requests seriously. In 1964, she reminded her sisters about the recommendation of the last general chapter that the congregation move toward opening a foreign mission. Therefore, she called for volunteers for the foreign mission field. The response was swift and enthusiastic across all four congregational apostolates. Mother Paul of the Cross soon had a list of 128 sisters who had expressed interest. One sister wrote to her: "Dear Mother, In response to your request for volunteers to go to a foreign mission, joyfully do I step forward, I realise that all plans are still in the future, and that I do not have a great deal to offer. However, I lay at your disposal my gifts of body and soul to be used in any way, and in any part of God's vineyard which it pleases you, His representative, to send me."[27]

In response to Father Hawley's request from Honduras, the general administration sent two sisters–Sister Anselm Doyle and Sister Marie Michael MacKinnon–there in 1966 to investigate the possibilities for a Martha foreign mission. Mother Paul of the Cross advised the congregation: "I know that all the Sisters will be keenly interested in this project and in the prospect of being represented in the mission fields, even though it may be some time yet before the actual mission can be opened. This is a momentous event in the life of the Congregation and we can all share in it by supporting Sister M. Anselm and Sister Marie Michael with our prayers."[28] Certainly it was a momentous trip for the two sisters, but not so for the congregation; based on their reports, the general administration elected not to establish a Martha community in Honduras. Two formidable obstacles were learning the language and supplying enough sisters. Two decades would pass before the Marthas' dream of their own foreign mission would come true when, in 1986, they would finally establish one in St. Kitts in the Caribbean.

Meanwhile, several sisters individually would accept foreign assignments. From 1968 to 1970, Sister Baptista Maria Macdonald, the congregation's "first missionary sister," worked among Vietnamese refugees in Vietnam as deputy coordinator of social welfare for the American Catholic Relief Services. Sister Joan Fultz, in 1971, helped Our Lady's Missionaries, Scarboro Foreign Mission Society, and the people of the area to establish a hospital in the Philippines on the Island of Leyte. And, from 1977 to 1979, Sister Genevieve McArthur served as business manager of the Hopeville Rehabilitation Centre in Uturu, a small Ibo village in Nigeria.[29]

The Death of Mother Ignatius

Mother M. Ignatius's death in 1964 marked the passing of an era. Furthermore, portents of deep congregational change began to appear on the horizon by the mid-sixties. Such harbingers signalled the end of the Marthas' last phase of expansion. One obituary grasped the importance of Mother Ignatius's passing:

> *A most significant chapter in the history of the Congregation was brought to a sad but triumphant close with the death of Mother Mary Ignatius at the Motherhouse on Sunday, May 10, 1964. The Congregation was sixty-four years old when she died. For almost half of that time she had served as Superior General, guiding it through the precarious years, working towards its expansion and growth, and in the process becoming one of its most beloved and revered members.*[30]

For several years, *The Bethanite* had been tracking the decline of her health from a series of strokes. Her long career had been remarkable, characterized by competence, energy, vibrancy, vision, and firm leadership. Hospital associations had honoured her outstanding work in hospital affairs. In 1962, Pope John XXIII had recognized her contribution to Roman Catholicism by awarding her a papal medal. Her own Martha sisters paid tribute to her stature among them by, among other things, producing a special six-page bulletin describing her final days and the ceremonies following her death.[31]

New Social Trends

New directions in Canadian society, whose population reached over 18 million by 1961,[32] also signalled changes ahead for the Sisters of St. Martha. Social protest, challenge to authority, and lifestyle experimentation, especially among youth, became defining features of the sixties. As elsewhere in the western world, young people, women, Natives, ethnic minorities, labourers, and francophones demanded to be heard and asserted their right to equal treatment in all areas of life. Student protests and appeals for institutional reform frequently convulsed university campuses. It was a decade of "optimistic and egalitarian idealism." Some Canadians discarded traditional moral standards and experimented with drugs, free love, and birth control. There was a marked emphasis on personal freedom and individualism. Canadians challenged institutional authority, vigorously criticized traditional ways, and openly discussed taboo subjects.

These social shifts occurred against a political backdrop that witnessed Lester B. Pearson's Liberals defeat John Diefenbaker's Conservatives in 1963, the Quiet Revolution in Quebec, important royal commissions on bilingualism and the status of women, expanding government bureaucracies, debates about American ownership of Canadian industries, and growing sensitivity to regional disparities. On the cultural front, Canadian governments helped to stimulate a cultural renaissance, and in 1967 the nation celebrated its centennial. As members of a western democracy, Canadians participated in the Cold War but witnessed with horror the arms race and the spread of communism. Many doubted the wisdom of American involvement in the Vietnam War.[33]

The Sisters of St. Martha, through their daily lives in social work, teaching, household services, and health care, witnessed and felt the changes in Canadian society, just as lay Catholics did. They also witnessed the rapid waning of Roman Catholicism in Quebec. However, the general church council convoked in Rome by Pope John XXIII in 1962 unleashed the most profound changes for the sisters.

Vatican Council II

Actually Vatican II was not the Holy See's first postwar initiative to urge the updating and renewal of the active religious life. Until his death in 1958, Pope Pius XII had pressed religious congregations, through public statements and international congresses of religious, to reform themselves, to educate their members to higher levels and to adapt to contemporary life. He had emphasized sound theological formation and higher education that would gain for sisters parity with their secular, professional counterparts. One result in North America was the Sister Formation Movement whereby religious congregations collaborated to examine their lifestyles and plan relevant congregational formation programs.[34] The Sister Formation Conference in the United States spawned colleges, produced a periodical and stimulated among sisters advanced formal educational achievement. Some Canadian congregations participated in the movement. The Antigonish Marthas were not directly involved, although some absorbed the radical thinking of the movement expressed in its publications and at its conferences. Sister Mary Olga McKenna affirms in her recent study of the Sisters of Charity, Halifax, that "Women religious in North America, perhaps more than any other sector of the church in the modern world, were prepared for Vatican II by the groundwork of the Sister Formation Movement of the 1950s."[35]

Pope John XXIII convoked the Roman Catholic Church's twenty-first ecumenical council at Rome in 1962. A council document of central importance for the Sisters of St. Martha, and for all religious congregations, was entitled *Perfectae Caritatas.* In it, the council fathers affirmed the "surpassing value" of the vowed life. As well, they called for a renewal of religious life involving two processes: (1) "a continuous return to the sources of all Christian life and to the original inspiration behind a given community," and (2) "an adjustment of the community to the changed conditions of the time."[36] Such a fundamental call to renewal required religious communities to investigate their foundings and revise their constitutions, books of customs, and prayer life. The council directed that appropriate renewal be initiated by general chapters that would issue norms, pass laws and "allow for a right amount of prudent experimentation, though in all such matters, according to the norm of law [and] the approval of the Holy See."[37] Sister Geraldine Anthony, SC, comments on the response of religious communities: "When Vatican II ended in 1965, it was followed by intense discussion in all religious congregations of men and women on its documents and the changes needed to renew congregations, adapting them to contemporary life."[38]

Intimations of Congregational Change

Even before the council had ended, the Antigonish Marthas began feeling its reverberations, as well as those effects created by the new social trends in western society. Vocations declined, fewer novices took first vows, and more sisters applied to withdraw from religious life. In 1960, thirty-two candidates entered, twenty-one made first profession, and two sisters left the congregation. In contrast, only seven candidates entered in 1966, four took first vows, and ten left religious life. The Marthas began deregulating and experimenting in their community life too. They adopted a more simple head-dress in 1963. The following year, the congregation stopped celebrating the superior general's feast day. A significant change in communal prayer was the adoption of a new prayerbook called *Morning Praise and Evensong*, the liturgical prayer of the Church, based on the Psalms, that replaced the communal book of devotional prayers. That year, Mother Paul of the Cross also decreed the end of refectory seating according to rank and to mail censorship. The Marthas began study clubs and lectures on Scripture in all the houses, and in the new ecumenical climate, they were freed to attend special Protestant church services. Changes in the Church liturgy brought changes in their convent chapels; for example, the priest began facing the congregation and the mass used English in place of Latin. In 1965 about forty Marthas trekked from the motherhouse down to the Antigonish courthouse polling station, being permitted for the first time to vote in elections. The public reaction in town was mixed.[39] Mother Paul of the Cross issued a controversial circular in February 1966 that eliminated certain prayers and afternoon grand silence. The horrified reaction of the older sisters was exemplified by Mother Stanislaus; she affirmed in Gaelic: "We are going to the Devil!"[40]

These were only some of the changes the Marthas instituted to 1966 that intimated a coming revolution for them. At the end of her administration in 1967, Mother Paul of the Cross tried to explain to her sisters what had been happening: "The fresh winds of change left their mark in the dropping of many outmoded customs, in the revision of our daily prayer schedule and recreation, and in general in the desire evident on all sides that the Congregation renew itself as a whole and in the life of each individual member."[41]

Conclusion

The sixties began for the Sisters of St. Martha with buoyancy and expansion but soon produced ambiguity and uncertainty. Through the first half of the decade they rode along on the wave of optimistic expansionism that had gained momentum in the fifties. Their expansion and optimism was revealed by the new diocesan and congregational leadership, the general chapter of 1961, the ambitious motherhouse and hospital complex building programs, the many new missions, the peak in numbers of sisters, the upgrading of their qualifications, and the investigation of foreign missions. Often their new services were provided at great personal and financial sacrifice, as they obeyed Christ's dictum that it is more blessed to give than to receive. But an era ended with the death of Mother Ignatius.

Unsettling portents also began to appear: a decline in vocations, rapid social change, and finally the epoch-making Vatican Council II. These developments brought the congregation's last era of expansion to a close. In 1966 the sisters were on the threshold of a decisive congregational event, indeed the most important happening since their founding in 1900. That decisive event was the 1967 general chapter of renewal.

Notes

1 Forbes and Muise, eds., *The Atlantic Provinces in Confederation*, pp. 421-2.
2 General Chapter Proceedings, 1961, F5,S8,SS4,f1,b6.
3 *The Bethanite*, October 1960, p. 40.
4 *The Bethanite*, January 1964 and correspondence re new chapel, F6,S3,SS1,f3-9,b110.
5 Canso Welfare Bureau Annals, 18 August 1948, F23,S1,SS1,f1,b195.
6 Eastern Memorial Hospital, Canso, Historical Notes and statistics, F17,S1,SS1,f1-3,b176.
7 Cardinal Cushing to Mother Ignatius, 17 October 1960, F12,S2,SS1,f1,b165.
8 St. John's Hospital, Lowell, Massachusetts, Annals, F12,S1,SS1,f1-8,b165.
9 *The Bethanite*, May 1963, pp. 42-3, New Waterford Consolidated Hospital Annals and Statistics, F14,S1,SS2,f1-2,b173.
10 Archbishop M.J. Lemieux to Rev. A.A. Johnston, 11 January 1960, F5,S34,SS4,f8,b86.
11 *The Bethanite*, December 1961, p. 10, and St. Pius X High School Annals and Statistical Information, F36,S1,SS1,f1-3,b233.
12 Mother Ignatius to Sister Anselm Doyle, 8 October 1957, F26,S2,SS1,f3,b215.
13 Sister Magdalen and Sisters to the Bishop and university authorities, 1 May 1959, F21,S2,SS1,f8,b192.
14 Sisters' Appreciation Society Records, BX 4261,M3,R4, STFXUA and St. Martha's Convent Annals, June 1960, F21,S1,SS1,f1,b191.
15 Cameron, *A History of St. Francis Xavier University*, pp. 332-36.
16 Interview with Father Francis J. Smyth, 14 April 1994, Antigonish.
17 *The Bethanite*, October 1961, p. 8.
18 Mother Paul of the Cross to Father Francis Smyth, 27 June 1962, and Memorandum of Agreement between the Coady International Institute and the CSM, 28 October 1961, F5,S20,SS3,f2,b51.
19 *The Bethanite*, September 1964, pp. 9-10.
20 Dan Doucet to All the Sisters, 30 September 1964, F49,S1,SS1,f4,b241.
21 Holy Heart Seminary Convent Records, F49,S1,SS1,f1-5,b241.
22 St. Catherine's Convent Records, F45 and *The Bethanite*, October 1961, p. 7.
23 Bishop Michael Harrington to Mother Paul of the Cross, 10 August 1961, F5,S34,SS17,f7,b92.

24 Sister Mary Adele St. Cyr, CSJ, *A History of the Diocese of Kamloops–The First Fifty Years* (Kamloops: Roman Catholic Bishop of Kamloops, 1996), pp. 20-3, and Our Lady of Perpetual Help Convent Records, F51,S16,SS0,f1-2,b247.
25 Antigonish Diocesan Charities Reports, 1961-1967, F5,S27,SS3,f2-5,b65, CSM Report on the Catholic Family Services Society, Regina, n.d, F5,S31,SS1,f1,b65, and St. Martha's Catholic Family Centre Records, Boston, F26,S1,SS2,f3,b214.
26 Statistical Statements Re Social Workers, F5,S29,SS1,f5,b68 and Sister Irene Doyle, "Report of the Coordinator of Social Work," 1970, Sister Irene Doyle's Personal Files.
27 A sister to Mother Paul of the Cross, 11 November 1964, F5,S32,SS5,f1,b72.
28 Mother Paul of the Cross to Dear Sisters, 24 September 1966, F5,S32,SS3,f1,b72.
29 Interviews with Sister Irene Doyle, 31 August 1998, and Sister Joan Fultz, 26 February 1999, Bethany, *The Bethanite*, March 1968, p. 1, and Bethany Annals, 9 November 1966, F6,S1,SS1,b108.
30 Quoted in Sister May Mulvihill, "History of the Sisters of St. Martha," III:2:47.
31 *Inter Nos*, May 1964.
32 Leacy, F.H., ed., *Historical Statistics of Canada*, second ed. (Ottawa: Statistics Canada, 1983), A184.
33 See Forbes and Muise, eds., *The Atlantic Provinces in Confederation,* pp. 421-32 and R. Douglas Francis et al., *Destinies: Canadian History Since Confederation*, third ed. (Toronto: Harcourt Brace Canada, 1996), pp. 350-71.
34 Sister Mary Olga McKenna, sc. *Charity Alive: Sisters of Charity of Saint Vincent de Paul, Halifax, 1950-1980* (Lanham, M.D: University Press of America, 1998), p. 82.
35 *Ibid.*, p. 97.
36 Walter M. Abbott, SJ, ed., *The Documents of Vatican II* (Piscataway, N.J.: New Century Publishers, 1966), p. 470.
37 *Ibid.*, 470.
38 Sister Geraldine Anthony, SC, *Rebel, Reformer, Religious Extraordinaire: The Life of Sister Irene Farmer* (Calgary: University of Calgary Press, 1997), p. 133.
39 Bethany Annals, 16 November 1965, F6,S1,SS1,b108.
40 Bethany Annals, 15 February 1966, F6,S1,SS2,f2,b109.
41 Mother Paul of the Cross, Report to the General Chapter, 1967, F5,S10,SS3,f1,b12.

Mother Teresa Ryan, superior general 1967-1973

Chapter Eleven

In the Crucible of Renewal

The 1967 general chapter of renewal was a congregational watershed that inaugurated a strenuous period of intense self-reflection and exhilarating regeneration among the Marthas. In retrospect, congregational historian Sister May Mulvihill concluded, "No other Chapter brought such radical and far-reaching changes in the lives of the sisters as did that one."[1]

After expectant and exhausting preparation, the chapter prayerfully convened and elected a new mother general and administration, initiated an examination of congregational origins and goals, and enjoined experimentation with community governance, lifestyle, sister formation, internal communication, and external relations. Innovative emphases surfaced in the delegates' deliberations, such as concerns about openness, personal freedom, individual responsibility, democracy, relevance, and reform. Afterwards, special committees and a general assembly (1970) sustained the renewal process. While the upheaval evoked pain and conflict for sisters, naturally troubled by the loss of traditional ways, others greeted reform with joy and gratitude. Unfortunately, a dismaying downturn in vocations and an unforseen upswing in departures from the congregation dogged the renewal. These developments combined to keenly influence the Martha missions in health care, social work, teaching, and household services.

Mother Paul of the Cross Kyte, a traditionalist who had reached the age of "three score years and ten," conscientiously followed Rome's directives for her congregation's spiritual renewal and updating. She and her councillors, some of whom were enthusiastic supporters of reform, orchestrated a process of chapter preparation unprecedented in Martha history for its comprehensiveness and depth. Their objective was to mobilize all the sisters, junior and senior, "to study questions vital to the welfare of the Congregation."[2] The administration organized an elaborate system of regional committees and subcommittees that prepared and submitted reports to coordinating committees at the motherhouse on community living, apostolate and witness, personnel and government, and administration. The Marthas also canvassed the diocesan priests for an evaluation of the congregation; as well, they had a priest sociologist survey all the sisters about renewal. The diocesan priests expressed great respect for the Marthas, and they also registered many and varied complimentary and critical observations. The sisters warmly thanked the priests for their feedback and requested "their renewed support and constructive assistance as the congregation sallied forth on the road of reform."[3] Overall, the sisters reacted energetically to the call for renewal.

The outpouring of pre-chapter discussion, reports, and questionnaires elicited a novel, frank airing of grievances within the congregation. Many sisters expressed dissatisfaction with excessive workloads, with the lack of free time, with the stress on conformity, with superiors who treated them like children, with communal recreation, and with the absence of personal choice in work and training. A large majority, especially of younger sisters, believed the congregation emphasized trivial and legalistic practices. The community's pollster concluded, "[Ninety percent] of the respondents think that the structure of religious life as it is now being lived in the Marthas needs revamping."[4] Mother Paul of the Cross was shocked, distressed, and certainly enlightened by the response. She had been largely innocent about the depth of dissatisfaction among her sisters. As a final preparatory step for the renewal chapter, she appointed a small chapter committee that produced a near miracle by reducing the nearly 1,100 recommendations to about 200 proposals. Thus was established the general chapter agenda.

Chapter Proceedings

Thirty-eight sister delegates convened at the motherhouse in late July 1967, no doubt sensing that they were about to do groundbreaking work for the congregation. They experienced both excitement and trepidation and, as a community, prayerfully and ardently sought God's assistance. Change was in the air, but the Martha delegates saw through a glass darkly and had to grope their way ahead into uncharted territory. The renewal chapter required two sessions—27 July to 27 August 1967, and 15 to 18 April 1968–to complete its enormous workload. From the start, the delegates jettisoned the old rule of secrecy that traditionally enshrouded chapter proceedings. Indeed, two extra chapter secretaries were commissioned to prepare regular news bulletins for the congregation and occasional releases for the public. The fundamental thrust of the chapter was renewal. The delegates initiated this process by electing an almost completely new administration, by re-examining the congregation's constitutions, rules, and customs, by inaugurating a period of experimentation, and by passing enactments to guide the sisters forward into the new era of renewal.

The general administration election created the following group: Sister Teresa Clare Ryan, mother general; Sister Anselm Doyle, vicar general; Sister Ann Romuald McArthur; Sister Mary Donald (Mary) MacIntosh; and Sister Mary Helene Wadden. This new council of talented, capable, and experienced women had an average age of forty-seven, an average considerably lower than its predecessor. Sister Anselm was the oldest councillor at age fifty-four; from Mother Paul's council, she alone survived the elections for another term in council. Instead of electing the general secretary and general treasurer, the council appointed them. Sister Kathleen Marie (Veronica) Morrison became general treasurer and Sister May Mulvihill remained general secretary until 1969 when she was replaced by Sister Olivia Francis (Geraldine) Fodey.

The new mother general would bear a heavy cross, for she was fated to lead the congregation in directions some would vigorously applaud and others would angrily censure. At her election, Mother Teresa Ryan was forty-five years old and had been professed twenty-seven years. She was a native of Canso, Nova Scotia, and the eighth child in a family of thirteen. After profession in 1940, Mother Immaculata had selected her for a teaching career; eventually she also gained administrative experience as a school principal. As well, she had gained solid academic credentials with both bachelors and masters degrees; shortly before the renewal chapter in 1967, Mother Teresa Ryan had completed a masters degree in religious education at the Catholic University of America in Washington, D.C. Her thesis was entitled "The Role of Work in the Spirituality of Relig-ious Women," and she had described it as part of the search of active women's institutes to make their communities "more spiritually and apostolically relevant."[5] Mother Teresa, therefore, had a rich background in theology and spirituality; she was well read in contemporary Catholic thought, understood the roots of church renewal and enthusiastically embraced it. She was a competent leader who fearlessly confronted issues head-on. The pressure of leadership and her high-strung personality would sometimes force her to the brink; fortunately, she had a strong vicar general and council to lean on, a blessing she herself readily acknowledged.[6] Finally, she had full confidence that the Marthas' deep faith and pioneering spirit would sustain them as they entered the crucible of congregational regeneration.

This was the first general administration to wear contemporary dress– Mother Teresa Clare Ryan, superior general 1967-1973 (front right) and her general councillors: L-R Sister Irene (Anselm) Doyle, Sister Genevieve (Ann Romuald) McArthur, Sister Mary Helene Wadden, and Sister Mary MacIntosh.

Chapter Enactments

Based on the congregation's recommendations, as well as their own deliberations, the chapter delegates approved a host of enactments, some trivial, some consequential. They reduced the number of permissions sisters required from superiors, and permitted some experimentation with personal prayer and the habit. They allowed sisters to own wristwatches, and to travel, drive, and visit alone. Because of its "education and cultural aspects and advantages," they permitted convents to purchase televisions. The delegates abolished the unpopular chapter of faults where sisters confessed their personal shortcomings to one another in small groups. Sisters were also granted more personal responsibility and choice for fulfilling their spiritual exercises. Moreover, the administration began to consult sisters about their own preferences and abilities as it prepared them for congregational service.

The chapter delegates were almost unanimous that new Marthas retain their baptismal names and that current Marthas "have the option of using their secular name, or their profession name, with or without the family name attached".[7] Sister Irene (Anselm) Doyle explained to the public that, "the change of name which in other ages had signified separation from the world seemed to have lost its relevance for contemporary active religious such as the Sisters of St. Martha. In keeping or returning to their own names the Sisters are opening the way to be recognized as persons with roots in the community as well as members of a religious congregation."[8] The new ruling had an immediate impact; the Bethany annalist reported in September 1967: "The change of name project is in full swing at Bethany and every day some new name is announced over the PA. It would appear that all the younger sisters and many of the older ones have decided to return to their secular names. Mother General and most of the General Officers have decided to do so also."[9]

The general chapter passed a multitude of other enactments, too numerous to list. However, two important ones should be noted: (1) that the congregation's "present policies, rules, regulations and constitutions currently operative be set aside [as far as the norms of canon law permit] for an experimental period" and (2) that the general chapter grant its powers of experimentation to the superior general and council, which would be required to convoke a general assembly before the next general chapter. Since the chapter of 1961, a committee had produced a "Tentative Revision of the Constitutions"; the delegates, however, realized that "the tentative revision was out-dated even before the first portion of the Chapter was concluded in August 1967."[10] Hence it was tabled indefinitely. The groundbreaking renewal chapter finally closed on 18 April 1968. Afterwards, Mother Teresa Ryan stated in a follow-up circular to all the sisters: "The work of the Chapter as such is now completed, but for all of us in the Congregation it is only a beginning. I make an earnest appeal for a renewal of enthusiasm and zeal in the work that lies ahead of us."[11]

Renewal in Practice

In late August 1967, Mother Teresa Ryan circulated lists of chapter decisions effective immediately. She observed, "The detailed regulations that are being promulgated at this time are of relatively minor importance, but they do have major implications. They should contribute to permitting the sisters more freedom to be personally responsible for their own personal and spiritual growth."[12] Her general administration also commissioned a range of post-chapter studies of community living, congregational goals, government and administration, personnel and formation, and apostolate and witness. The reports chart the sisters' diverse responses as they wrestled with the principles of renewal and their practical application to personal and community life. Most of the reports reveal the sisters' optimism about change and their conviction that it was essential to personal and communal growth in maturity, responsibility, charity, spirituality, collegiality, and unity.

The chapter delegates had recommended that more Marthas participate in congregational governance and that local communities experiment with different forms of governance. Few houses opted for electing their own local superiors–most retained the tradition of appointment. However, by 1973, fifty-one sisters had first-time experiences as superiors.[13] The congregation organized superiors' institutes to help sister superiors develop their administrative abilities. The general administration enhanced Bethany's administration by appointing an administrator and service department heads. Even more changes in administration were just over the horizon. Overall, renewal brought about broader participation of the sisters in their own governance. Even the superior general's leadership style became more democratic as Mother Teresa Ryan called on the advice of outside consultants, made her councillors responsible for specific apostolates and consulted widely with the sisters about changes and future directions.

Sisters had criticized the lack of communication and openness in the congregation. A communications committee derided the "undue secrecy," the absence of sharing, the "artificiality" in communications, and the unnatural prohibition against interaction between the novitiate and the professed sisters at Bethany. It urged "a more natural and family-like communication between all sisters."[14] Renewal did effect a much freer flow of information among the sisters, as well as greater openness and deeper communication among themselves and toward society. Prescribed periods of silence were repealed; *The Bethanite* started an opinion forum; general chapters issued news releases; and sisters participated in small group sharing. In 1971, Sister Doris (Maria Josephine) McMullin, the new congregational director of communication, established a communications centre at Bethany; she strengthened communications between the motherhouse and the missions, and managed the flow of congregational information to the public. Televisions and radios gradually became commonplace in all the Martha houses, thus channelling popular culture and worldly news into the heart of the convent. New words and phrases even inveigled their way into congregational discourse, some of them borrowed from contemporary humanistic psychology and existentialism, for example, "authenticity," "openness," "dialogue," "personal growth," "self-fulfilment," "human potential," "team," "primacy of persons," "shared vision," "faith journey," and "Gospel values." These revealed the presence of powerful cultural influences and the emergence of new congregational values and priorities.

Sisters' lifestyle was a key area of experimentation and change during the renewal process. The trend was away from regulation, conformity, dependence, and authoritarianism to personal freedom and individual responsibility. The congregation permitted some experimentation with the habit, and also it lifted restrictions on the personal use of watches, cameras, alarm clocks, alcohol, and attendance at public entertainments. More sisters learned to drive. The congregation encouraged hobbies, cultural enrichment, and personal improvement. It also recognized the need for retirement planning and activities for the elderly, and so appointed a director of retirement.[15] In 1970 all the sisters were permitted to develop their own personal budgets, subject to certain guidelines and the approval of the general administration. Many sisters wished to live in more intimate community rather than in large, structured institutional settings. For example, at Bethany, experimentation with small groups eventually led to the entire motherhouse community belonging to seven smaller groups.[16] Some sisters even felt free to demonstrate publicly in support of social causes. About fifteen sisters, armed with Bethany-made placards, travelled by chartered bus to Sydney in November 1967. To demonstrate their solidarity with the working people, they marched shoulder-to-shoulder with them in the Parade of Concern, protesting the closure of the city's steel plant that had been announced on 13 October, "Black Friday." The Bethany annalist exulted, "This was the first time in the history of the Congregation that the Sisters had ever taken part in a public demonstration of this nature. The reaction to their presence was entirely favourable."[17]

Mother Teresa Ryan's administration made personal renewal and educational upgrading a congregational priority. She explained why: "Our sisters needed time and opportunity for new personal and communal experiences before they could risk too many organizational changes."[18] The moves on this front were swift and massive. In October 1969, Sister Genevieve (Ann Romuald) McArthur indicated the dimensions of the project in a remark to Nova Scotia sister students: "We have in our Congregation 430 professed sisters; we have on full-time study this year 47 professed sisters and one novice. This means that over 10 percent of our sisters are studying. We can claim an Apostolate of Study! In addition, we would guess that another thirty or forty percent of the Congregation is doing part-time study."[19] The record of educational accomplishment between 1967 and 1973 was impressive indeed: twenty two sisters had obtained master's degrees, fifty-five had earned bachelors degrees, about thirty-five had gained diplomas, nine had become registered nurses, six were nursing assistants, and fifteen had earned their grade 12 certificate. In their educational pursuits, sisters most commonly, and predictably, studied general arts, home economics, education, social work, and nursing. Some sisters, however, began striking off in new career directions, such as pastoral counselling and psychiatric nursing. In 1970, Sister Marie Simone Roach was the first Martha to obtain a doctorate, a symbol of the congregation's rising academic credentials. The Marthas' ambitious educational program was expensive and time-consuming, and, it reduced the supply of sisters available for service.[20]

The rapid congregational changes required a new formation program for entrants. A committee had already produced a renovated four-year program in the early sixties,[21] but the 1967 renewal chapter required that it be more flexible in length, content, and work opportunities. With the rest of the congregation, the postulants and novices also enjoyed an easing of regulation toward the end of the sixties. In 1969 the general administration announced a new formation program. The eleven-month Bethany postulancy was replaced by individual placements to missions for eight months, followed by three months at Bethany, leading to reception into the novitiate. The new program retained the canonical year for novices, and then required a second year with work experience on the missions. The junior professed were disbanded as a special group at Bethany.[22]

New Missions

Mother Teresa Ryan's administration established few new missions. This was perfectly understandable, given the decrease in vocations, the congregation's heavy debt load, and its preoccupation with internal renewal. Those new missions the sisters did open were directly influenced by the changes taking place within their ranks. After exhortations from Bishop Carroll of Calgary, and other Catholic Albertans, the Marthas built a novitiate house in Lethbridge that they named the Martha Education Centre. There young candidates from western Canada could acquire early formation in the religious life and test their vocations before travelling east to Antigonish. Marthas teaching in Lethbridge and Picture Butte also used it as a residence. Since vocations dried up around the time the Martha Education Centre opened in June 1968 (only two women applied for admission), the attractive new facility, located on Lethbridge's southern perimeter, came to function as a sisters' residence and retreat house instead of a novitiate.[23]

The Sisters of St. Martha undertook three other projects during this period, two short-term and one ongoing. First, in 1970, as a service to the Scarboro Foreign Mission Society, six sisters assumed control of the vacant Scarboro House on West Street, Antigonish, and for one year ran a female residence; here about thirty young St.F.X. college women were able "to encounter the aspect of community living in religious life."[24] The Scarboro Fathers sold the building one year later. Second, in 1972, Mother Teresa Ryan permitted six sisters to experiment in a unique small group living arrangement in an Antigonish residence on Church Street they called House of Hope. This group would have a rotating leadership in place of a superior, and no homemaker, chapel, or chaplain. Although community members changed, House of Hope continued until 1977.[25] Third, the congregation chose, after extensive study, to use the western wing of the motherhouse, formerly the novitiate section, as a congregation and public retreat and renewal centre. The administration had the section renovated to accommodate about fifty people; it then opened as "Bethany Center" in October 1972 under the direction of Sister Paul Thérèse (Paul Thérèse) LeBlanc. An evaluation of the popular centre in 1977 concluded that it had, by then, made a "tremendous contribution to the diocese, religious communities, priests, lay people, youth, and other denominations."[26]

Martha Retreat Centre, Lethbridge, Alberta, opened in 1968.

General Assembly of 1970

The 1967 chapter of renewal had directed that the congregation convoke a general representative assembly before the next general chapter in 1973. Its purpose was "to make an evaluation of the congregation's renewal program, to ascertain present needs of the church and to plan for future experimentation and apostolates."[27] The assembly, a first in the congregation's history, had no legislative power and could only make recommendations to the general administration. Again, the sisters thoroughly prepared through institutes, regional committees, and a major survey of congregation opinion on renewal. Then forty-two delegates convened on the St.F.X. campus from 7 to 21 August 1970. In her opening remarks, Mother Teresa Ryan declared: "We are coming into maturity, a time of fullness, a resurrection." During the sessions the delegates heard and discussed papers, mostly by sisters but several by priests, on topics such as "The Church in the World Today," "Freedom and Responsibility," and the "Goals of the CSM."

The assembly participants agreed overall with the renewal changes implemented thus far. On the emotionally charged question of making the veil optional, the general administration wisely referred the issue to the assembly for a consultative vote. Thirty-eight sisters favoured making it optional and only four voted for retaining it as a requirement. Immediately after the assembly, the superior general and council decreed: "(1) The wearing of the black and white veil is now optional as to: who wears it, when you wear it, and where you wear it; (2) We witness to others by our behaviour regardless of what we are wearing."[28] The assembly concluded with a series of theme proposals for further discussion and study.[29] According to the Bethany annalist, in spite of some sharp controversy, the delegates had experienced overall "a spirit of peace, unity, dialogue, diversity and fellowship."[30] Hence, the congregation partitioned itself into regions and held nineteen post-assembly institutes to "keep alive the spirit of the assembly by having the sisters who participated explain to those who did not ... what had happened and to discuss its implications."[31]

Pangs of Renewal

While renewal offered many rewards, it had its price. The Marthas, like all Roman Catholic religious congregations, found that change generated considerable stress, division, and controversy.

The personal anguish and controversy were rooted in the departure from familiar old ways, increasing personal freedom, the exodus of sisters who returned to secular life, the experience of ferment and uncertainty, and a sense of guilt and insecurity. For example, after the abolition of grand silence and afternoon prayers, a sister mused, "It is still difficult to shake the guilty feeling which persists when conversation is carried on after two o'clock, and even without a bell the urge to kneel down when three o'clock comes is still strong."[32] The passing of the old, highly structured, semi-monastic order and its replacement by a more biblically based apostolic way of life troubled many senior sisters especially. In 1969, Mother Teresa Ryan advised the novices, "You may sometimes be disturbed by the conversations and attitudes of older members of the Congregation. Many are struggling with changes, with inadequate preparation personally and academically. Patience and acceptance are all you can show them at the present."[33] One Martha remembered the sisters' reaction to changes in the dress code: "The habits, yes, we come [*sic*] to Bethany one day and Sister Teresa Ryan was dressed in a suit and high heels and no veil and they were going some place for supper and we nearly died. She was all dressed in secular clothes."[34] Of course, some of the negative reaction, especially to individual excesses, was justified. Sister Genevieve McArthur later reflected, "Our 1967 Renewal Chapter focused on the primacy of the person, perhaps at the expense of our communal character, tradition and commitment."[35] Moreover, many sisters grew weary of the seemingly endless congregational studies, evaluations, re-evaluations, and self-examinations.

Following the new emphasis on openness, general administration provided forums for debate and criticism. Sisters attended meetings, workshops, lectures, discussions, and the 1970 general assembly. The superior general regularly visited the missions and met with each sister. Mother Teresa reflected in her Bethany visitation report (1969): "Particularly revealing to me was to know firsthand the amount of frustration, conflict and feeling there is among the Sisters."[36] Committees also surveyed congregational opinion, and *The Bethanite* started a section called the "Opinion Forum." Here, opinion pieces, sometimes claiming to express the views of an entire mission, debated issues about the habit, authority, the superior's role, interpersonal relationships, individual freedom, work and leisure, spiritual exercises, communication, and equality. Never before had Marthas questioned so openly and deeply, or discussed so intensely and freely, their feelings and beliefs about the religious life and their own congregation.

Fortunately, the Marthas' experience of renewal did not fracture the congregation. Indeed, it would ultimately bring about a deeper spirit of unity based more on shared personal convictions and less on formal institutional structures. Although Mother Teresa Ryan could be blunt and abrasive, she avoided polarizing the community; she consulted widely and ensured that the general assembly of 1970 was widely representative. Moreover, her council solidly supported the renewal agenda. They organized institutes and workshops, often run by prominent experts on religious renewal. And in 1968 the congregation wisely hired two Boston psychotherapists–Father George Carrigg and Archie Zarkadas–to provide counselling services for sisters and groups; their association with the congregation would be long and fruitful. Prudently, the general administration also made many changes optional, so sisters were free to retain some of the old ways, for example, their religious name and the distinctive religious habit.

Many sisters joyfully welcomed the renewal process mandated by Vatican II. Indeed, some sisters were far ahead of Rome and had long been convinced that the Church and its religious congregations needed fundamental reform. In addition, Bishop Power, a participant in Vatican II, strongly endorsed the Marthas' renewal efforts. During one of his occasional "renewal pep talks" at Bethany, he urged all "to be open and ready to accept the changes that were coming."[37] In 1970 he presented a special program for senior Marthas on changes in the world and the church; he pleaded with them to see the necessity for, and valid-ity of, updating.[38] Moreover, traits native to the sisters themselves helped to inhibit permanent division. The vow of obedience required that they defer to religious authority, and religious authority had mandated renewal. In addition, their religious life emphasized communal cooperation in service to others. One consultant remarked on the lack of bruising power struggles and individual competitiveness among the Marthas, features of institutions he had come to expect because of his experience in the business world. Finally, sisters who became fundamentally discontented with religious life usually left the congregation.

Vocation Crisis and Exodus

The stressful side of Martha renewal was heightened by a simultaneous decline in vocations and an upswing in sisters withdrawing. Six candidates entered the postulate in 1967, one in 1970, and none in 1973; three novices made first vows in 1967, but none in 1970 and 1973. For the first time in the congregation's history, its Novitiate-Profession Register reported: "During this year [1972] no one made Final Profession or First Profession, and no one was received into the novitiate."[39] Nothing the Marthas tried–vocation exhibits, "Come and See" weekends, Christian Renewal workshops, retreats for young Catholic women, vocation pamphlets, pageants and slide shows on the religious life–reversed the disturbing trend.[40] Of course, the alarming development was not unique to the Marthas. In the United States, a steep decline in vocations to women religious congregations had begun in 1967. On the Canadian scene, women religious congregations registered novitiate numbers of 1,280 in 1960 but only 223 by 1975.[41]

Obviously, the vowed life of chastity, poverty, and obedience was rapidly losing its appeal. Perhaps this trend was part of the general secularization of Canadian society, or a result of the expanding opportunities available for women in secular life. Within the Roman Catholic Church, the Second Vatican Council's Dogmatic Constitution on the Church had elevated the status and role of the laity in religious affairs. Some Catholics concluded that the religious state was no longer a better and perfect way of life; therefore why make the sacrifices it required?[42]

While Marthas watched with dismay as their novitiate dwindled to nought, they also bade farewell to the escalating number of sisters who chose to leave the religious life. Sixty-one percent (112) of all professed sisters who withdrew from the congregation through its history did so between 1960 and 1980. The exodus peaked in 1969, 1970, and 1972; thirteen professed withdrew in each of those years. Many who withdrew between 1960 and 1980 were younger Nova Scotian women who had entered the congregation of Marthas during the 1950s; their average age was thirty-one years and their average of years professed was nine. More than one-half had high school diplomas alone, but many others had gained further training at the expense of the congregation. Thirty-five homemakers and twenty-four teachers withdrew during this period; the homemakers were the first to leave in sizeable numbers. Many young sisters left at the expiration of their temporary vows.[43] Like the decline in vocations, the exodus from the Marthas was part of a general trend besetting all religious congregations. Departures of women from Canadian religious congregations peaked in 1972 when 823 sisters withdrew.[44]

A sister's decision to leave the religious life was usually reached after deep personal anguish. Some Marthas first requested a one-year indult of exclaustration (permission to live temporarily apart from the community), often to Halifax, before making their final choice. Mother Teresa Ryan encouraged sisters who were unhappy with the religious life to consider returning to secular life, and she offered them counselling and spiritual direction. Also, the congregation helped the departees financially as it was able.

Women left religious life for many reasons: to marry and raise a family, to expand their personal freedom, to register dissatisfaction with recent changes in religious life, or to pursue a new secular career. Some concluded that they had not had a religious vocation in the first place. Mary Ewens explains, "For some their communities were moving too slowly; for others too quickly; in still other cases, there was a dissatisfaction with community life or a realization that they really had a vocation to marriage."[45] Finally, the painful stigma in Catholic circles earlier attached to undoing religious vows had rapidly eroded. Sister Geraldine Anthony, SC, concluded, "In times past, few sisters had ever left, partly because there was such a stigma attached by sisters and lay people alike to someone who would give up her religious vocation." However, by the late sixties, secularized sisters no longer feared being "treated as pariahs" by the Catholic faithful and hence felt no constraint to remain in their religious communities for the wrong reasons.[46]

The decline in vocations and upswing in departures, along with other developments, led to a serious personnel shortage within the congregation and dealt a blow to the earlier Martha expansionism. Mother Teresa Ryan commented on this in 1969: "We are faced with a critical personnel shortage. Sisters are leaving, getting sick, getting old and dying, and of course the numbers entering are radically reduced. As a result of all this we are not even able to keep up with our present commitments."[47] The "critical personnel shortage" had a direct impact on the works of the Marthas. It required Mother Teresa's administration to curtail and, in some cases, even withdraw services. In most places where Marthas were withdrawn, lay people replaced them.

Social Work

The social work apostolate experienced some contraction of services. Marthas had established the Catholic Family Service Society on behalf of the Archbishop of Regina in 1936. Although one sister remained until 1972, the congregation felt compelled to withdraw the executive director, Sister Stephanie (Stephen Marie) MacNeil, in 1969. The board president praised her work: "The acceptance of and contribution to the community and the harmony, cooperation and development of the staff is in no small way due to the professional competence and leadership role exercised by Sister Stephanie."[48] Such warm tributes became a common refrain wherever the Marthas withdrew. Since 1939 the congregation had provided sisters for Blairmore, Alberta, where they had done parish work and run a kindergarten; in 1964 they had added a family counselling service. With much regret, and to the dismay of the bishop and parishioners, the sisters said goodbye to the Crow's Nest people in 1969 and closed St. Alphonsus Convent.[49] Then, two years later, a *Cape Breton Post* headline, "10 Children to be Sent to Foster Homes," signalled the closure of the Little Flower Institute for children in Sydney, Nova Scotia. The Marthas had given tremendous sacrificial service to unfortunate children through that institution since 1917. In 1971, after extensive discussion, the Diocese of Antigonish had reluctantly decided, for financial reasons, to close it; the sixties had witnessed a consistent decline in the numbers of children cared for by the sisters at the Institute.[50]

The general council maintained some social work services. Three Martha social workers were kept at St. Martha's Catholic Centre, Boston; and at Martha House, Regina, four sisters ran the service for unwed mothers. Sister social workers continued to manage the family counselling agencies in the Diocese of Antigonish; however, their presence diminished for two reasons: (1)

declining numbers and (2) the amalgamation, centralization, and expansion in 1969 of the seven existing agencies into a single organization called the Family Services of Eastern Nova Scotia (FSENS). This was the latest undertaking of Antigonish Diocesan Charities to promote the integrity and betterment of family life. It opened a central office in Sydney and appointed a director, Father Vernon Boutillier, who was responsible to a board of directors.[51] The Marthas, in cooperation with parish priests and laity, had established the parish agencies–some as early as the 1930s–and the diocese had become dependent on them to provide social welfare services for bargain-basement prices. For example, in 1966 the sisters' contributed services to ADC was $121,865; this revealed, from the Marthas' standpoint, "an undesirable dependency relationship between the Diocese and the Sisters of St. Martha."[52] After 1969, sisters continued temporarily to play a key role in the branch offices, but FSENS expanded rapidly and became less sectarian. By 1973, only five sisters served on the organization's paid staff of thirty-six.[53]

Health Care

In the health care field the Marthas' shortage of sisters was compounded by a heavy capital debt load, especially in Nova Scotia. The province's hospital insurance scheme inaugurated in 1959 did not yet provide for capital debt assistance. Mother Teresa Ryan lamented the burdensome debt.[54] In 1967 the congregation owned or operated twelve hospitals, including the R.K. MacDonald Guest Home for seniors in Antigonish. Overall, health care was an expensive, inflationary, complex, and rapidly changing theatre of work. In 1966 the Canadian government had passed the Medical Care Act that provided for medical services insurance, provincial governments were seriously contemplating the regionalization of services because of the skyrocketing expense of buildings and equipment, and Catholic hospitals became apprehensive about long-term survival as their financial and personnel resources dwindled.

The Marthas responded to these trends by commissioning studies of their future in health care, by lobbying governments to change their hospital funding policies, and by relinquishing ownership of certain institutions and withdrawing from others. For example, at the request of the Archbishop of Regina, the congregation, in 1936, had opened the small St. Michael's Hospital in Broadview, Saskatchewan. In 1965 the townspeople had fought valiantly and victoriously against government plans to close it. A year later, deteriorating finances forced the congregation to sell the hospital to the Broadview Union Hospital Board. However, the sisters remained to administer it for three more years. Amid fond farewells, the last three sisters withdrew in 1969 because of a shortage of trained personnel. They had given thirty-three years of health and parish service to Broadview and its environs.[55] Sister Mary Eileen (Miriam James) MacIntosh, the last superior, described the public tributes: "The crowd that attended all these sure shows how much they appreciated the Sisters over the years and so many of them were crying when they said goodbye. The Indian Chief spoke and I wish you could hear him. A lot of the Indians were there too."[56]

The congregation also relinquished ownership of the R.K. MacDonald Guest Home in Antigonish that it had opened back in 1958. After lengthy deliberation, Antigonish town and county purchased it in 1971. However, six to eight Marthas remained for many years to manage the Guest Home, to oversee its expansion and renovation, and to serve in important roles under the direction of the new R.K. MacDonald Nursing Home Corporation.[57]

In 1973 the superior general and council withdrew the last Martha serving at Eastern Memorial Hospital, Canso. At the request of com-munity members, the sisters had assumed management of this small hospital in 1960. As in most places where the Marthas withdrew, the laity carried on the work pioneered by the sisters.

Household Services

The constricting supply of sisters affected the Marthas in household services too. The general administration was no doubt relieved in 1970 by the closure of Holy Heart Seminary in Halifax. Mother Paul of the Cross had sent five sisters there in 1964 to manage the seminary's household affairs. In 1969, *The Bethanite* reported, "From a series of meetings with the Bishops of the Maritimes, the Senate of Priests, St. Mary's University, Pine Hill Theological College and King's College, there evolved a plan for a new program of seminarian education and formation in line with the trend since Vatican II."[58] Seminary numbers had consistently declined through the decade as operating deficits inexorably rose. The Martha annalist's final entry described the departure of the six sisters: "Convent at Holy Heart closed on May 31, 1970. Father Comeau said Mass for all the sisters of St. Martha who had worked there during the past six years. Thanked us for all the good we did for the Priests and Seminarians. They gave us money to go to the best restaurant in town for dinner the day we left."[59]

The Marthas' relationship with St.F.X., an institution that grew by leaps and bounds during the sixties, altered during Mother Teresa Ryan's administration. The sisters' commitment to the Coady International Institute made in 1961 was reduced in 1971 when Sister Marie Michael MacKinnon retired and the institute's convent closed. Other adjustments flowed from negotiations with university authorities: in exchange for salaries equivalent to those paid lay staff, the sisters employed at St.F.X. would henceforth pay their own room and board, and sister students would pay their own tuition instead of getting it gratis, compliments of the university. As their numbers dwindled, the Marthas also recommended that St.F.X. contract out the housekeeping and food services. Up to then, the university had enjoyed the better half of the bargain in its relation with the Marthas and acknowledged so by sending the congregation a cheque for $15,000. Sister Irene Doyle commented on the negotiations that led to these changes: "This was the first time in our history that the Marthas met the priests of St.F.X. as equals. They did not talk down to us, and we did not feel that anything was imposed on us."[60]

The congregation certainly did not terminate all of its domestic management assignments at this time. Important missions were retained at St. Augustine's Seminary, Toronto, at Cardinal McGuigan's Residence in Toronto, and at St. Pius X High School, Ottawa. Besides, the Marthas continued to supply housekeeping services for their many teaching convents and hospitals.

Teaching Missions

During the reduction of Martha services between 1967 and 1973, the teaching missions made the most rapid retreat. Of all Martha services, they had most quickly expanded during the fifties under the relentless pressure of Bishop John R. MacDonald. The congregation had about sixty-nine teachers in 1967, but by 1973 it had only forty. Thus, Mother Teresa Ryan and her general council closed six teaching missions during this period, all of them serving rural schools in eastern Nova Scotia. The teaching convents closed were St. Theresa's Convent at Margaree Forks, Inverness County, Cape Breton (1925–1970); Our Lady of Fatima Convent at Heatherton, Antigonish County (1951–1970); St. Paul's Convent at St. Peter's, Richmond County, Cape Breton (1958-1968); St. Ann's Convent at Guysborough, Guysborough County (1958-1973; re-opened 1975–1988); St. Margaret's Convent at St. Margaret's Village, Bay St. Lawrence, Victoria County, Cape Breton (1959–1971); and St. Mary's Convent at East Bay, Cape Breton County (1960–1970). Usually four to six sisters had lived in each of these convents, providing a range of valued educational, cultural, and parish services.

Closing missions, teaching or otherwise, was a painful act for the Marthas, as well as for their host communities. Like the parting of all good friends, it was "sweet sorrow." Both sisters and communities experienced common emotions–sadness, regret, and a sense of loss. As a "people's congregation," Marthas identified deeply with those they served; they were not disinterested, detached professionals. Without exception, they were close to the people and widely involved in community life. They established countless friendships and built up a deep reservoir of goodwill towards themselves. Sister Mary MacIntosh commented, "Withdrawal is a time of suffering and anxiety for sisters residing in the house. Leaving their work in a specific area is painful, especially when sisters still recognize needs that are not being met."[61] However, the sisters bravely faced their impending departures. The annalist at St. Theresa Convent, Margaree Forks, marked the end of forty-five years of teaching service there in this way: "Shortly after 1:00 P.M. we closed the door of our beloved convent. It was an experience we all shall never forget. Then we said 'goodbye' to our neighbours.... Thus ends our final days at Margaree Forks. A priceless memory as we depart in peace to love and serve the Lord in other places."[62]

The congregation's withdrawal from these six rural communities in eastern Nova Scotia during Mother Teresa's administration was a significant reduction of teaching service. Nonethe-less, Marthas remained at their teaching posts in many other places—Canso and Little Dover, Guysborough County; St. Andrews in Antigonish County; Trenton in Pictou County; Dominion, Main-a-Dieu, Eskasoni, Ingonish, Dingwall, all in Cape Breton; and Canada: Picture Butte, Lethbridge, and Kamloops in western Canada.[63]

Conclusion

In the elaborately prepared-for 1967 renewal chapter, the Marthas had ignited a powerful thrust toward renewal in their congregation. Delegates had commissioned Mother Teresa Ryan and her general council to lead the drive; and the sisters had willingly responded to their call for renewal. For leaders and followers alike, the next six years were exhilarating and arduous ones marked by fundamental questioning and restructuring of the traditional Martha way of life. Marthas gained new freedoms, discovered wider opportunities, explored new horizons and deepened their spiritual lives. They were freed to set out and fulfil their role as apostolic women. Plotting a prudent course, they fortunately avoided permanent fracture and schism. The Marthas began to deregulate their own lives, to jettison the conformity, legalism, and authoritarianism of the past, to expand their personal freedoms and to promote individual and communal experimentation. They dialogued at a deeper level than ever before as they sought greater self-understanding and a new consensus about religious life. Their community was becoming more democratic, more open, and freer in its relations with outsiders. Many sisters were grateful for new opportunities to retrain or to pursue further education. While diminishing vocations and an increasing exodus created a Martha personnel shortage that forced the withdrawal of some services, the congregation maintained many important missions. In 1973 the challenge for a new general administration would be to stay the course and carry the renewal program forward.

Notes

1 Sister May Mulvihill, "History of the Sisters of St. Martha," III: 11:35.

2 Mother Paul of the Cross to Sisters, 30 August 1966, F5,S9,SS1,f1,b7.

3 Quoted in *The Bethanite*, November 1967. For the priest survey, see Rev. Edward Boyce, CSSR, "Sisters of St. Martha as seen by Priests of Antigonish," May 1967, F5,S9,SS3,f3,b8.

4 Report on Questionnaire to Sisters, June 1967, p. 11, F5,S9,SS5,f1,b8.

5 Sister Teresa Clare Ryan, "The Role of Work in the Spirituality of Religious Women, " unpublished master's thesis, Catholic University of America, 1967, F5,S19,SS1,f2,b50.

6 Interviews with Sister Genevieve McArthur, 18 September 1998, Sister Joan Fultz, 12 March 1999, and Sister Irene Doyle, 10 April 1997, Bethany, and Mother Teresa Ryan to Sister Rose Miriam MacKinnon, 23 June 1971, F5,S26,SS4,f2,b64.

7 *The Casket*, 14 September 1967.

8 *The Casket*, 14 September 1967.

9 Bethany Annals, 1 September 1967, F6,S1,SS1,b108.

10 Note re Study on Revision of the Constitutions, 20 May 1969, F5,S2,SS3,f1,b256.

11 Mother Teresa Ryan to Sisters, 29 April 1968, F5,S9,SS1,f3,b7.

12 Mother Teresa Ryan to Sisters, 26 August 1967, F5,S9,SS1,f3,b7.

13 Report of the General Administration, 1967-1973, pp. 32-3, F5,S10,SS13,f1,b17.

14 Committee on Communications Minutes, 26 February 1967, F5,S35,SS1,f15,b96.

15 Notes on Retirement, F5,S33,SS10,f1,b79.

16 Steps Leading to the Development of Groups at Bethany, n.d., F6,S5,SS3,f3,b111, and Community Living and Spiritual Life, F25.

17 Bethany Annals, 19 November 1967, F6,S1,SS1,b108.

18 Report of the General Administration, 1967-1973, to the General Chapter, 1973, F5,S10,SS13,f1,b17.

19 Sister Genevieve McArthur, Report of Meeting of Student Sisters of St. Martha, Bethany, 12 October 1968, F6,S3,SS3,f2,b111.

20 Report of the General Administration 1967-1973, pp. 7-14, F5,S10,SS13,f1,b17.

21 Where We Are in Developing a Sister Formation Program for the Sisters of St. Martha, August 1963, Personal Files of Sister Irene Doyle.

22 Bethany Annals, 3 May 1969, F6,S1,SS1,b108.

23 Martha Centre, F51,S14,SS0,f3,b245.
24 *The Bethanite,* January 1971, p. 18.
25 House of Hope, F47.
26 Sister Clare Marie Lyons and Sister Rosemary Rogers, Evaluation of Bethany Centre, F5,S32,SS2,f1,b71.
27 Newspaper clipping, F5,S10,SS10,f1,b17.
28 Mother Teresa Ryan to Sisters, 22 August 1970, F5,S9,SS11,f3,b14.
29 First General Assembly Minutes, 8-21 August 1970, F5,S10,SS8,f1,b12.
30 Bethany Annals, August 1970, F6,S1,SS1,b108.
31 *The Bethanite,* 13 January 1971, pp. 7-11.
32 *The Bethanite,* March 1966.
33 Mother Teresa Ryan, Novitiate Visitation Report, 21-23 April 1969, F6,S3,SS2,f4,b111.
34 Interview with Sister Anne Fougere, Bethany, n.d. tape 2, tran script, p. 40, CSM Oral History Collection.
35 General Administration Report, 1973-1977, n.p., F5,S10,SS21,f1,b22.
36 Bethany Visitation Report, 1969, F6,S3,SS2,f4,b191.
37 Bethany Annals, 2 January 1968, F6,S1,SS1,b108.
38 Ibid., 13 November 1970.
39 Novitiate-Profession Register, General Secretary's Files, Bethany.
40 *The Bethanite,* May 1966, p. 8, June 1973, p. 4, and March 1977, pp. 9-11.
41 *Statistics of the Religious Congregations of Canada, 1981,* Canadian Religious Conference, p. 30.
42 Doris Gottemoeller, RSM, "Religious Life: Where Does it Fit in Today's Church?" in *Review for Religious,* n.d., p. 147.
43 The data in this paragraph is based on a review of CSM Personnel Records, General Secretary's Files, Bethany.
44 *Statistics of the Religious Congregations of Canada, 1981,* Canadian Religious Conference, p. 30.
45 Mary Ewens, "Women in the Convent," in *American Catholic Women: A Historical Exploration,* ed. Karen Kennelly (New York: MacMillan, 1989), p. 42.
46 Sister Geraldine Anthony, SC, *Rebel, Reformer, Religious Extraordinaire: The Life of Sister Irene Farmer* (Calgary: University of Calgary Press, 1997), p. 165.
47 Mother Teresa Ryan to Rev. R. Roberts, SFM, 17 March 1969, F5,S35,SS1,f12,b95.
48 M.H. Rider, Board President, to Mother Teresa Ryan, 14 January 1969, F5,S31,SS3,f1,b70 and Some Considerations re CSM at Catholic Family Service Society, Regina, March 1969, ibid.

49 *The Bethanite*, May 1969, p. 9.
50 Communications Centre Update, 8 June 1971, p. 2.
51 Antigonish Diocesan Charities, Annual Report 1969, F5,S27,SS3,f3,b65.
52 General Administration Report 1967-1973, p. 74, F5,S10,SS13,f1,b17.
53 CSM General Administration Report, 1967-1973, p. 75.
54 Mother Teresa Ryan to Bishop Michael A. Harrington, 27 January 1969, F5,S34,SS17,f7,b92.
55 St. Michael's Hospital Annals, 1966 and 1969, F15,S1,SS1,f6,b175.
56 Sister Eileen MacIntosh to Mother Teresa Ryan, 21 May 1969, F15,S4,SS1,f1,b176.
57 Communications Centre Update, 8 June 1971, p. 3.
58 *The Bethanite*, May 1969, p. 15.
59 Holy Heart Seminary Convent Annals, 31 May 1970, F49,S1,SS1,f1,b241.
60 Quoted in Sister May Mulvihill, "History of the Sisters of St. Martha," III:11:43
61 General Administration Report, 1977-1981, p. 47, F5,S10,SS27,f1,b18.
62 St. Theresa Convent Annals, 1970, F30,S1,SS1,f4,b226.
63 Report on Teaching, Appendix IV, pp. 62-71 in Report of the General Administration 1967-1973, F5,S10,SS13,f1,b17.

Chapter Twelve

Staying the Course of Renewal

The years from 1973 to 1981 were challenging and exciting ones for the Sisters of St. Martha. Their general chapters and administrations advanced the heady program of renewal initiated in 1967. Congregational preoccupations included self-appraisal, consultation, planning, reorganization, spiritual renewal, and recovery of their Martha heritage and identity. In 1975, sisters and friends joyfully celebrated their seventy-fifth anniversary. Although the congregation withdrew some services, it also pioneered new projects and set sail in fascinating new directions. Fortunately, novitiate numbers making first profession increased a little, while departures from the congregation decreased.

Canadian national developments molded the congregation's experience and future. Prime Minister Pierre Elliott Trudeau's Liberals piloted the ship of state through this era of large-scale government planning, worrisome inflation, and occasional recession. The federal government preserved vital national social programs, such as family allowances, employment insurance, the Canada Pension Plan, and Medicare; it also maintained transfer payments and development programs for Atlantic Canada. A Quebec separatist party that triumphed at the polls in 1976 heightened anxieties about the country's future integrity. Natives, ethnic minorities, and women maintained their struggle for just and equal treatment. Canadian women created new organizations such as the National Action Committee on the Status of Women (1972). And more Canadians awoke to the threats industrialism posed for the environment. Finally, the Canadian religious mosaic altered, as Asian immigrants introduced non-Christian traditions, for example, Muslim, Hindu, and Buddhist, more Canadians professed no religious affiliation, and church attendance dropped. For many, faith became a personal affair as Canadians "moved away from religions based on theology and denominational identification, and toward a view of religion as an inspiration for moral and ethical behavior."[1]

General Chapter of 1973

Against this backdrop, Mother Teresa Ryan's general administration prepared for the 1973 general chapter. Planning committees, assisted by the consulting firm of Hickling-Johnston Limited of Toronto, prepared the way for thirty sisters who convened in session at Bethany in March and July 1973. Priest-observers and St.F.X.'s Father R.B. MacDonald, "theologian-consultant," had been invited to the chapter, which centred on the theme, "We Celebrate Your Presence, Lord."

Mother Teresa Ryan opened with a state of the congregation address. She observed:

> *We are struggling to identify ourselves, to clarify our role in the Church, to re-capture the spirit of the first Marthas and to find God in our midst today. The many changes initiated by the 1967 General Chapter have given us the opportunity to make more personal choices, to exercise our freedom, to honestly examine our personal values, to recognize our human inadequacies and our need to find a new way of relating to community.*[2]

Mother Teresa and her council had led the way to invoke these changes. However, by leading the congregation through the crucible of renewal, Mother Teresa had exhausted herself, and the sisters knew it. After prayerful reflection, the chapter conferred the mantle of leadership on another to carry the renewal project forward. Mother Teresa was deeply disappointed, but she and her council could look back with satisfaction on important achievements. As well, she had participated extensively in external organizations–international conferences of women religious, the Canadian Religious Conference, and professional associations–that had given her a broad perspective and kept her in touch with fresh developments. She urged the newly elected superior general to make "even more national and international contacts than I was able to make."[3]

The delegates elected a new administration but reduced its tenure from six years to four. The new general councillors, now expanded from four to six, were Sister Genevieve McArthur, Sister Marie Barbara Muldoon, Sister Marion (Joanne Marie) Sheridan, Sister Theresa (Francis of Assisi) Parker, Sister Catherine (Angela Marie) MacFarlane, and Sister Thérèse LeBlanc. Sister Olga (Margaret Hugh) MacDougall had been appointed secretary general in 1970. The council appointed Sister Elizabeth (Dolorita Marie) Riopelle as treasurer general.

Sister Mary MacIntosh, superior general 1973-1977 (right front) and her general councillors: L-R Sister Genevieve McArthur, Sister Marie Barbara Muldoon, Sister Thérèse LeBlanc, Sister Theresa Parker, Sister Marion Sheridan (centre), Sister Catherine MacFarlane.

The new superior general, no longer using the title "Mother," was Sister Mary MacIntosh. Both she and her vicar general, Sister Genevieve McArthur, had served on Mother Teresa Ryan's council. Sister Mary MacIntosh was a respected, bright, devout, and kindly Martha who had served in the health care apostolate. Although born in Saskatchewan, her youthful years had been spent in Lismore, Pictou County. Before entering the Marthas in 1955 at the age of thirty-one, she had studied nursing at St.F.X., St. Michael's Hospital in Toronto, and McGill University. After earning a master of science in nursing from Boston College in 1961, she had been the director of Sydney's St. Rita Hospital School of Nursing until 1973. At her election, Sister Mary MacIntosh was forty-nine years old. She had embraced renewal and adopted a team approach to leadership.[4]

Sister Mary (Mary Donald) MacIntosh, superior general 1973-1981

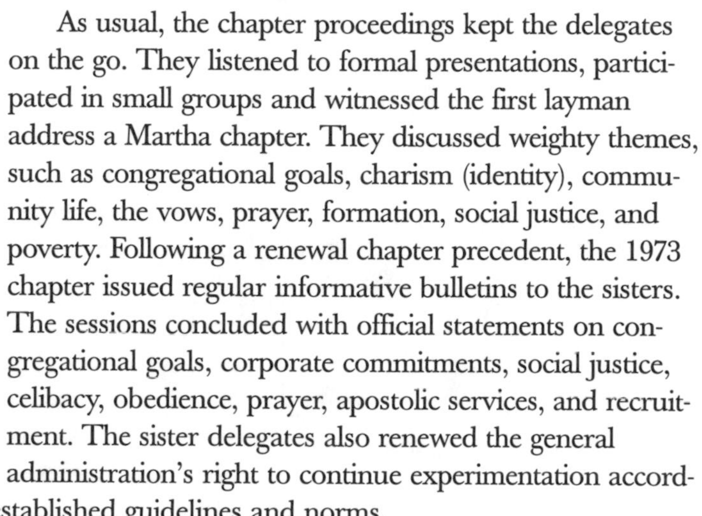

One of her chief concerns was the personal, interior spiritual renewal of each sister.

As usual, the chapter proceedings kept the delegates on the go. They listened to formal presentations, participated in small groups and witnessed the first layman address a Martha chapter. They discussed weighty themes, such as congregational goals, charism (identity), community life, the vows, prayer, formation, social justice, and poverty. Following a renewal chapter precedent, the 1973 chapter issued regular informative bulletins to the sisters. The sessions concluded with official statements on congregational goals, corporate commitments, social justice, celibacy, obedience, prayer, apostolic services, and recruitment. The sister delegates also renewed the general administration's right to continue experimentation according to established guidelines and norms.

From the 1967 renewal chapter, much debate and discussion had swirled around the issue of congregational governance. In consultation with R.A. Dods of Hickling-Johnston, the sisters reformed their governance structures and began experimenting with them in December 1972.[5] The complete congregational restructuring plan was presented to the 1973 chapter. It proposed a degree of decentralization and local autonomy, with communities led by strong leaders, as the congregation's focus of life and mission. The general superior and her council would still formulate general congregational policy within the norms of canon law, chapter directives, and the constitutions. However, a new body was created. An appointed, full-time executive group composed of the superior general, the general treasurer, and apostolate directors would administer the policies formulated by the general council. The elected superior general would be head of the congregation and chair of both the general council and the executive group. A canon lawyer found these administrative proposals to be in harmony with canon law and the thrust of Vatican Council II. The chapter unanimously accepted them on an experimental basis.

Since the renewal chapter of 1967 had begun a reassessment of the congregation's constitutions, spiritual directory, and book of customs, the sisters developed interim guidelines and norms to regulate their experimentations until they produced new constitutions. Successive committees had worked to formulate new guidelines; their final product was a document entitled "Our Way to the Father," which the 1973 chapter approved. It supplied the congregation with temporary guidelines until revised mature constitutions were approved in 1981. "Our Way to the Father", a thirty-six page statement of Martha belief, drew extensively on Scripture and contemporary Roman Catholic theological insights to express the community's basic ideals about call, response, prayer, community life, vows, and service.[6]

Taking Stock

The inception of congregational renewal in 1967 ushered in an era of extensive community self-appraisal and planning. The Marthas followed with a vengeance the Socratic and Platonic dictum that the unexamined life isn't worth living. All dimensions of the congregation–goals, organizational structure, constitutions, community life, spiritual life, personnel, apostolates, finances, etc.–were repeatedly studied. At considerable expense, outside consultants, especially R.A. Dods of Hickling-Johnston, helped the congregation update its organization using corporate planning, information systems, personnel and career planning, marketing systems, cost-benefit analyses, time-use studies, and group problem-solving. In spite of some criticism about this "intrusion from the business world," the Martha leadership found Dods a sensitive and valuable congregational resource person during this time of accelerated change.[7] He also helped the sisters create a much-needed tool of formal evaluation for assessing the effectiveness and future of its diverse congregational services.[8]

Martha self-appraisal and renewal, of course, had a deeply religious dimension more fundamental than the reform of organizational structures. Sister Mary MacIntosh, the superior general, was keenly interested in spiritual renewal of the sisters. One especially significant project of soul-searching was the Martha quest for their unique charism, or identity. The story of this lengthy quest has several parts, including the Vatican II directive for religious communities to return to the original inspiration of their founders; Sister Irene Doyle's study–"The Heritage of the Sisters of St. Martha" (1967)–which historically examined the spirit and character of the sisters; Sister Mary Jane (Christopher Marie) Carew's major study (1973) on the Marthas' charism; and the congregation's late-seventies charism discernment workshops. The culmination was a definitive statement of Martha charism adopted by the general chapter of 1981 and then incorporated into the new constitutions. It declares:

> *We Sisters of St. Martha are called to a deepening faith relationship with God and to a realization of our gift of life nurtured in a community of caring women. Moved by our pioneering spirit, and by our hospitality, simplicity, humanness and celebration, we respond in loving service to present needs in the mission of the Church and continue our tradition of concern for priests.*[9]

This succinct conclusion to the Martha quest for their unique identity issued in greater congregational and individual self-awareness. It was an especially valuable part of congregational stock-taking during the renewal years.

Diamond Jubilee, 1975

The Martha joy in celebration–part of their charism–was happily though modestly indulged in 1975, the congregation's diamond jubilee. After extensive planning by the "Martha Committee '75," 348 sisters then living in twenty-nine different communities were joined by numerous admirers and supporters to commemorate and give thanks for seventy-five years of accomplishment. All the houses held their own celebrations, but the main events were held in Antigonish, the congregation's birthplace. Appropriately, St.F.X., the cradle of the congregation, hosted opening events on 16 July that included the unveiling of a plaque at the original motherhouse on campus.[10] Its eloquent inscription reads, "Here in the original motherhouse of the Sisters of Saint Martha founded at Antigonish in 1900, Saint Francis Xavier University proclaims profound gratitude to a valiant company of religious women for their gracious presence and selfless service to its priests, professors and students." Busy Bethany witnessed receptions, barbecues, masses, ceremonies, an open house, and a variety concert, while congratulations poured in from countless friends, sister congregations, and distinguished members of church and state.[11]

Reflection on the Martha pilgrimage was an important part of the diamond jubilee celebration. The sisters made special efforts to preserve their documentary heritage and history by appointing Sister M. Reginald (Eunice) MacKinnon first congregational archivist in 1974, and by commissioning in 1975 Sister May (Joseph Helen) Mulvihill, then the secretary general, as congregational historian. Through a drama-documentary entitled "Thecla's Choice," written by Dr. Patrick Walsh of St.F.X., acted by Marthas and friends, and filmed by the National Film Board, the sisters also grappled with both their origins and contempor-ary challenges.[12] After the jubilee, senior Marthas of selected classes experienced the nostalgia and memories of earlier years through homecoming celebrations. *The Bethanite* announced the first in September 1978: "Ten sisters from the classes of '38 and '39 participated in the first home-coming celebration of the Congregation in August." These celebrations of personal history and pilgrimage became a regular event at Bethany thereafter.

General Chapter, 1977

Shortly after the diamond jubilee celebrations concluded, a chapter planning committee began the formidable task of gearing up for the next general chapter. Well-briefed through institutes, reading materials, and regional study groups, thirty delegates eventually convened at Bethany for the sessions held in March and July. In keeping with the chapter theme, "We Serve in the Mission of the Church," the congregation involved lay people. For example, two professors from St.F.X. made contributions–Dr. Patrick Walsh as the first lay chairperson, and Father R.B. MacDonald again as the theologian-consultant. In her report to chapter, Sister Mary MacIntosh outlined the congregation's achievements of the last four years and identified promising advances: deeper penetration into Martha history and spirit, greater respect for Scripture, more knowledge about people, a global perspective, and greater use of outside resource people.[13] The delegates re-elected Sister Mary MacIntosh as general superior and brought in a mostly new slate of general councillors: Sister Theresa Parker, vicar general; Sister Marion Sheridan; Sister Joan (Ann Martin) Fultz, Sister Ann (Ann George) MacKenzie; Sister Rosemary (Philip Marie) Rogers; and Sister Josephine (Martin de Porres) Keyzer. Sister Jean (John Brebeuf) Harris, appointed in 1976, was secretary general, and Sister Elizabeth Riopelle remained as treasurer general.

General Council 1977-1981–FRONT, L-R: Sister Joan Fultz, Sister Mary MacIntosh, superior general; Sister Theresa Parker. BACK, L-R: Sister Rosemary Rogers, Sister Ann MacKenzie, Sister Marion Sheridan, and Sister Josephine Keyzer.

The chapter heard a host of proposals and papers on diverse topics. It confirmed the new organizational structure instituted in 1972–1973, but called for its ongoing assessment. Dods' influence was clear in the chapter's heavy emphasis on corporate planning. Indeed, the chapter considered fourteen corporate plans, including ones on the spirit-ual development of persons, on social services, and on missions at Ingonish and Eskasoni. It also commissioned sisters to formulate new constitutions to be reviewed by the next general chapter in 1981. Finally, the delegates urged greater Martha involvement in social justice issues and an expansion of pastoral care services in Martha hospitals.[14] These last exhortations denoted new congregational emphases and directions. However, the traditional Martha apostolates were alive and well, though undergoing modification.

Household Services

From 1967, successive chapters and administrations had carefully appraised the Marthas' traditional works–household services, social work, health care, and education. Domestic service–foods, housekeeping, laundry, and sewing–had been the congregation's founding raison d'etre. The apostolate, however, had rapidly changed in recent decades. From 1961, coordinators and, later, apostolate directors–Sister Mary Magdalen Cann (1961–1967), Sister Irene Doyle (1967–1973), Sister Clotilda (Mary Joanna) McIntyre (1973–1978), and Sister Marie (Blaise Marie) Kelly (1978–1981)–had assisted the Marthas active in household services. They organized useful homemakers' institutes with demonstrations and discussions about cooking, sewing, table setting and waiting, renewal, upgrading, and the value and future of Martha homemaking.[15] Some homemakers attended summer schools of renewal for homemakers and discovered that homemakers in many other congregations enjoyed fewer benefits than the Marthas. In 1977 the homemakers formed the St. Martha Household Services Association with seventy-four members. Until it disbanded in 1992, the association provided the homemakers with mutual support and occasions for vocational development.[16] In 1980, its members even produced *The Martha Cookbook*, a popular 214-page collection of their "most prized recipes" that went into its third printing in 1994.

From the sixties, the Martha homemakers were plagued by a mounting crisis of morale. Its roots were several. Canadians generally had devalued the domestic arts and considered homemaking a menial task of drudgery requiring little in grey matter and training. Some Martha homemakers deplored these attitudes, mirrored, they believed, in the congregation; their apostolate seemed to rank lowest. To them, assurances that domestic service was important and the congregation's first work had a hollow ring. One homemaker concluded, "The Home Making Apostolate has been almost totally neglected in the past with the exception of a lot of talk.... It is no wonder younger sisters look down on it, for it has been ill-treated."[17] An outside observer, the Archbishop of Toronto, G. Emmett Carter, who knew the congregation through its work at St. Augustine's Seminary, feared the Marthas were forgetting their "famous" tradition of personal service. He wrote, "I would hate to think that your Community now considers itself in some way too advanced for personal service. For my part, I see nothing demeaning in the service of others and no essential difference between teaching and counseling and helping others to be fed or housed."[18] The homemakers' morale crisis was also related to their lower educational levels, the disinterest in homemaking shown by new entrants, and plummeting numbers. In 1967, there were 152 homemakers, but by 1973 only 91, and only 38 were in active service by 1981. This numerical slide forced the congregation to reduce its household services.[19]

Although the Marthas had occasionally signalled their intent to withdraw from Cardinal James McGuigan's Toronto residence, the final decision was made for them in 1974 when the aged cardinal died after a lengthy illness. His biographer writes, "In July 1965, he suffered a massive stroke from which he never recovered. Rendered speechless and immobile, McGuigan lingered for nine years before being freed from his bodily imprisonment by a heart attack on 8 April 1974."[20] Sister Margaret (Mary Amelia) Landry and Sister Rita Marie (Frances Elizabeth) Wachtler were with him at the end. A few years before, a sister had witnessed his retirement from the office of cardinal: "The Papal Nuncio to Canada, Archbishop Pocock, and their secretaries were here for lunch. The Cardinal received a letter from the Holy Father informing him of his retirement from office. Father Wall read the letter for him but there was no response."[21] The Marthas had undertaken this housekeeping mission in 1935. By the time it closed, McGuigan had enjoyed the devoted services of a total of thirty-eight sisters. Many found it a challenging, isolated mission; then in later years there had been the cardinal's depressive mental and deteriorating physical health. Moreover, sisters had had to meet high standards, for they served an august parade of visiting dignitaries. After McGuigan's death, the sisters remained temporarily to help Father Leonard Wall finalize the cardinal's household affairs.

The congregation also withdrew housekeeping services from St. Pius X High School in the 1970s. What had been a small, male pre-seminary in 1960 when the Marthas arrived, had become a large, co-ed Catholic high school of about 1400 students by 1977. At the announced withdrawal after seventeen years of service, the Archbishop of Ottawa thanked the Marthas for "the making of a home for the priests and their contribution of a warm and friendly spirit among the teachers and students."[22]

The Marthas still maintained household services at a range of institutions during the seventies. These included Bishop Power's Antigonish residence, as well as the congregation's many houses and hospitals. Two large missions of longstanding were St. Augustine's Seminary in Toronto, and St.F.X. University in Antigonish. At both, the sisters' work had diversified beyond domestic management. Twelve sisters worked at St. Augustine's Seminary in 1980; recent evaluations had recommended the sisters remain, for they made a valued contribution to institutional economy and the formation of priests.[23] Rector John A. O'Mara paid warm tribute to them: "They put heart into these massive buildings and all of us, priests and students, are deeply indebted to them for their constant assistance, co-operation and good example."[24]

The Marthas' quiet but vital labours at St.F.X. had diversified and their household services diminished by the seventies. About thirty sisters filled a variety of roles–domestic supervisors, librarians, professors, chaplains, students, sacristans, and infirmarians. Their bustling convent shared in the university's rich cultural, spiritual, and intellectual life. The St.F.X. sisters had witnessed student unrest in the sixties and a major student strike in the spring of 1971. The annalist described an hospitable gesture the St. Martha's Convent sisters extended to the students in 1979: "At the beginning of the college year, the three front rooms on the ground floor were made available to the St.F.X. students who would like a quiet place to study, chat, read, pray, get acquainted, etc. This area of the house is known as Martha Place."[25] University president Father Malcolm MacDonell praised the warmth Marthas brought to St.F.X. and the powerful sermon preached by their lives.[26] Between 1970 and 1982, his university gratefully conferred honorary degrees on four esteemed Marthas–Sister Marie Michael MacKinnon (1971), Sister Rodriquez Steele (1974), Mother Paul of the Cross Kyte (1979), and Sister Irene Doyle (1982). The tributes notwithstanding, both congregation and university recognized that the Marthas' declining numbers would require a change in their relationship. Sister Mary MacIntosh observed: "There does not seem to be a clear definitive answer to the form this relationship should take, but Council continues to explore and question."[27]

Although some Martha homemakers harboured doubts about the value and status of the domestic arts and household services, their work was essential. Even though people do not live by bread alone, neither can they survive without the fundamentals of food, shelter, and clothing. Moreover, this "first work of the congregation" brought the Marthas into close contact with people and made them countless friends; their thoughtful, kindly, and humble service, modeled after that of their Biblical patron-ess, St. Martha, inspired gratitude and love for them. Martha homemakers were frequently creative, capable sisters and widely involved in parish activities. Overall, their contributions were an integral part of the congregation's work and identity; they reinforced the Marthas' beloved traits of simplicity, hospitality, warmth, and sacrificial service.

Social Work

The Martha social worker ranks diminished in the seventies, yet they also remained an active apostolate. Twenty-eight social workers were employed in 1973; fifteen carried the torch forward in 1981. That year they worked in the diocesan family agencies, drug or alcohol dependency programs, unwed mothers and child welfare programs, mental health care, and support services.[28] Their laudable efforts were strengthened by successive coordinators–Sister Irene Doyle, Sister Clotilda McIntrye, and Sister Stephanie MacNeil–as well as by the Social Workers' Association conceived in 1970 to foster mutual support and professional development. The congregation administered Martha House in Regina, Saskatchewan, missioned sisters at St. Martha's Catholic Centre, Boston, and supplied sisters for Family Services of Eastern Nova Scotia (est. 1969), which it also supported financially. The Martha social workers, though the congregation's smallest traditional apostolate, made substantial contributions to those facing personal troubles–marital discord, substance abuse and addictions, single-parent pregnancies, lack of social and emotional support, economic hardship, and child neglect. They also ministered to the aging and became advocates for the needy. Within their means, the Marthas helped all those who turned to them in need, regardless of sex, class, race, religion, and age. In this difficult, draining work, the Marthas strove to reveal the compassionate face of Christ to troubled individuals and families.

Educational Services

The Marthas' teaching apostolate stretched back to 1925. Teaching assignments had expanded rapidly during the fifties and then contracted through the late sixties and early seventies. As with its other apostolates, the congregation witnessed the number of teachers decline from about sixty-nine in 1967 to around twenty-six by 1981. Nevertheless, teaching remained an employment of vital Martha activity, with an active teachers' association and rising levels of professional qualification shown by the upgrading of class licences, the significant number of Martha principals, and Sister Mary Roderick (Mary Cecilia) MacMullin's doctorate in education (1978). Overall, the teachers warmly embraced congregational renewal, a sentiment disclosed by the former teacher Mother Teresa Ryan's congregational leadership from 1967 to 1973. Teaching Marthas were academic instructors, educational specialists, administrators, and arts instructors. Sister Stella (Shaun Marie) Chafe, Sister Yvonne (Mary Cyril) Vigneault (future congregation leader, 1994–1999), and Sister Genevieve (Ann Ronald) MacDonald are examples of teachers who worked in leadership roles during the seventies.

Sister Marie (Ann Zita) Smith with students.

Through these years, the congregation closed one teaching mission in Cape Breton and established a new one in western Canada. From 1942, Marthas–usually three or four–had been present in the fishing community of Main-a-Dieu; regretfully, inadequate personnel resources required them to withdraw in 1975. Nonetheless, the congregation acceded that year to a request from G.A. Heck, superintendent of separate schools in Fort McMurray, Alberta, to supply Marthas for Catholic schools there. Fort McMurray, situated about four hundred kilometres north of Edmonton, had mushroomed in size because of the Athabasca Tar Sands Project. The pioneer sisters who opened the mission there–Sister Stella Chafe, superior, Sister Jean Harris, and Sister Mary Eileen (Mary Noella) McEachern–contributed stability, continuity, and experience to the Catholic school system and to the youthful and transient population. Fort McMurray Catholics welcomed the sisters, who became widely involved in parish and civic affairs until their withdrawal in 1994.[29]

The Marthas retained several small but important teaching missions and placements through the seventies. In the west, sisters taught at Catholic separate schools in Kamloops, British Columbia, and in Lethbridge and Picture Butte, Alberta. Marthas remained active in the classrooms of rural eastern Nova Scotia communities, such as Ingonish, Dingwall, Canso, St. Andrews, and Guysborough. They were also a presence in Trenton, Pictou County, on the Cape Breton Native reserve of Eskasoni, and in the town of New Waterford. At their teaching stations, sisters confronted contemporary educational trends, such as single-grade classrooms, school consolidation, higher teaching standards, specialization, and school board amalgamation. School consolidation brought greater denominational mixing in Nova Scotia and made it awkward to have religious education in the regular school program. And amalgamated school boards did not always want to hire sister teachers.

By 1981 the Marthas' extensive legacy of educational work with Canadian youth included classroom instruction, formation of character, and training in art, music, drama, and home economics. As well, they had richly contributed to school and parish extracurricular activities. Some sisters had pioneered innovative teaching programs. To boost student motivation, Sister Maria Lawrence (Helen Marie) O'Keefe's Marine Science Program in Main-a-Dieu had male youth learn boat building, navigation, sea safety, and trap construction from local volunteer experts.[30] Sister Shirley (Mary Natalie) Bruce's successful Joy Program, in New Waterford, had seniors share their skills and talents with special-education youth. And in Heatherton, Antigonish County, Sister Sylvia (Maria Bernadette) MacDonald's activity centre for the mentally challenged included a program of social activities, arts, crafts, and music.[31] The teaching sisters also, of course, made a substantial intellectual and financial contribution to their own congregation. In 1981, one Martha, contemplating the teaching needs of the future, concluded, "the magnitude of the challenge lying before us now is no less than that offered the Marthas when they were invited to enter the field of education by Dr. M.M. Coady in 1923."[32]

Health Care Services

The Marthas' health care apostolate provided vital health services to the public in several Canadian regions. On the congregational side, it employed the largest number of sisters, produced the highest revenues and debts, required the most diverse range of skills and represented the biggest chunk of congregational assets. To ensure high standards of care, the health care sisters took degree and diploma courses, organized institutes and attended conferences. They likewise supported professional hospital and nurses' associations, and even created their own Nursing Sisters' Association in 1969. From 1968 the hospital Marthas enjoyed the aid of coordinators and apostolate directors, such as Sister Genevieve McArthur, Sister Ann MacKenzie, and Sister Marie Raymond (Martha) MacDonald. The seventies, an era of "tempestuous seasons" for Martha health care, saw the sisters adjust to altering circumstances and curtail their services. The apostolate had 103 sisters in 1967, but only 55 by 1981, and its hospitals–owned or managed–dropped from eleven in 1960 to seven in 1981.[33]

The sisters transferred ownership or withdrew from three hospitals between 1975 and 1981. In Inverness, Cape Breton, the Marthas had run, but not owned, the small (c. thirty-eight-bed) St. Mary's Hospital since 1925. By the seventies, the facility badly needed replacement. Since two hospitals existed in the town, governments and citizens advocated a single, new non-denominational hospital. Planning began in the ecumenical sixties; the final result, in 1977, was the Inverness Consolidated Memorial Hospital. When the last four Marthas withdrew from St. Mary's, the congregation informed the public: "It is the hope of the Sisters of St. Martha that their service in Inverness will expand as they explore new ways of serving and have the resources to meet these new challenges and opportunities. The Sisters are grateful to the people of Inverness, the Board of the hospital, and lay and medical staff for their friendship and support over the years."[34] As usual, the Martha withdrawal was gracious and charitable.

The transfer of St. Joseph's Hospital, Glace Bay, in 1977 was a landmark event in the Marthas' health care apostolate. The congregation had a presence there from 1902, took control of the hospital in 1915 and assumed its ownership in 1930. Only eleven sisters worked at the 140-bed facility in the seventies, down from the nearly thirty sisters in 1960. As in Inverness, governments and community members advocated that the two local hospitals–St. Joseph's and the Glace Bay General–amalgamate. This sentiment was a product of ecumenism, an oversupply of hospital beds, and financial constraint. After evaluations by the congregation and briefs to government, the Marthas transferred St. Joseph's to the provincial government. A shortage of personnel had dictated the decision. Two Marthas continued on staff. Eventually, St. Joseph's and the Glace Bay General did amalgamate to form the Glace Bay Integrated Health Care System.[35]

Three years later, the congregation transferred ownership and withdrew from St. Peter's Hospital in Melville, Saskatchewan. As with St. Joseph's Hospital, a shortage of sister personnel forced the painful choice. Sister Mary MacIntosh explained to the hospital board: "The Congregation deeply regrets having to leave St. Peter's, but given our present resources, there does not seem to be an alternative."[36] In 1980, five sisters worked in the eighty-bed facility. The congregation, anxious to ensure a Catholic influence in St. Peter's future operation, transferred ownership to the Catholic Health Council of Saskatchewan. A sister described their withdrawal: "Recognition and appreciation functions and presentations to the Sisters for the forty years of service given by the Sisters of St. Martha were arranged for us at Civic, Parish, Hospital and Board levels and by health-related groups and friends."[37]

Withdrawal from these expensive hospital complexes, reduced the Marthas' onerous financial and personnel commitments. Nonetheless, seven other health facilities remained in their care. In eastern Nova Scotia, they were the New Waterford

Consolidated Hospital (c. 88 beds); St. Rita Hospital, Sydney (c. 178 beds); St. Martha's Hospital, Antigonish (c. 190 beds); and the R.K. MacDonald Guest House and Nursing Home, Antigonish (c. 110 beds). In Lowell, Massachusetts, the Marthas operated St. John's Hospital (250 beds). And in the Canadian west, the sisters still owned and operated St. Michael's Hospital, Lethbridge (c. 207 beds) and Mineral Springs Hospital, Banff (c. 50 beds). The Martha presence in Canadian health care remained a substantial onc.

Sister Caroline Lahey with guest at the R.K. MacDonald Nursing Home, Antigonish.

During the seventies, the sisters judged it necessary to study, closely and repeatedly, their commitments in the challenging and changing health care apostolate. A 1978 report entitled "The Future Role of the Congregation in Health Care," recommended that the congregation continue in active treatment hospitals, that renewal programs be developed for hospital staff, that sisters be placed in strategic positions to influence hospital policy, and that the congregation devise an orderly plan for gradual withdrawal as resources dictated.[38] The Vatican II definition of Church as the entire people of God–laity, clergy, and religious–doubtless helped the Marthas realize that their future health care responsibilities would be evermore shared with lay Catholics. To foster lay leadership in eastern Nova Scotia and to discern the future mission of the Church in health care, the Marthas and the Diocese of Antigonish established the Diocesan Health Care Council (DHCC). This Council provided a structure for Catholic hospitals to consider transfer of their ownership to a Roman Catholic foundation and to stimulate parish interest and responsibility for the health care ministry. The memorandum of association was dated 22 July 1981 and the Sisters of St. Martha, with the diocese, financed the Council until 1998.

In addition to congregational anxieties about personnel resources and financial strain, Marthas also faced medical moral issues that disturbed them–abortion, birth control, and depersonalization. These trends increased their resolve to ensure a continuing Catholic influence wherever they withdrew.

The preparation of nurses remained a vital area of Martha service. The congregation had established hospital schools of nursing at St. Martha's in Antigonish, St, Joseph's in Glace Bay, St. Rita in Sydney, and St. Michael's in Lethbridge. St. Francis Xavier University, following its announcement in 1926 to establish a "Department of Nursing and Health," had offered a BSc in Nursing in affiliation with St. Martha's School of Nursing. The program became an integrated four-year program in the mid-sixties and was formally established as a nursing department at the university in 1970, with Sister M. Simone Roach, Chair; Sister Loretta Gillis (later replaced by Sister Peter Claver (Stella) McNeary. At St. Joseph's Hospital in Glace Bay, authorities decided to phase out the School of Nursing beginning in 1968.

Sister Agnes (Gabriel Marie) McCrossin with students in the library of St. Martha's Hospital, Antigonish.

Overall, the Martha nursing educators maintained high achievement standards in the apprenticeship model of hospital programs, gradually reforming them with a more sound educational base. Nursing service, provided in great part by nursing students, certainly reaped the rewards of these improved educational standards. From the 1930s on, the congregation had sisters prepared for nursing service in post-diploma certificate courses, and in basic degree and graduate programs at Canadian and American universities. The nursing Marthas explored nursing education and practice models, including a Central School of Nursing (Sister Clare Marie Lyons), and a block system of teaching and clinical practice (Sister Marie Barbara Muldoon). They also provided leadership in the evaluation and accreditation of nursing programs, and were active in professional associations on the provincial and national levels. Their study of associate degree programs influenced the development of two-year hospital diploma programs under the leadership of Sister Mary MacIntosh in Nova Scotia. Sister Clare Marie Lyons served for ten years as nursing education consultant with the Registered Nurses' Association of Nova Scotia. Martha nursing programs were committed to the students' total needs–practical, intellectual, spiritual, social, and cultural–an approach expressed by the motto of all Martha diploma schools of nursing, "Science, Service, Sanctity."

The Marthas' health care apostolate required of them a colossal commitment in human and financial resources. Its purpose was to provide a Christian ministry of compassionate healing to the sick. The Marthas' healing ministry was stamped by their own ideals and practices, and they maintained high standards of hospital care and nursing practice. They believed in caring for the whole person–physical, emotional, and spiritual–were sensitive to moral issues and provided principled care based on the sanctity of human life and the dignity and value of each person made in the image of God. In healing, as in all their work, the Marthas served everyone, regardless of race, class, religion, or sex. While recognizing the mystery of human suffering and death, their practice witnessed to the reality of a loving Creator. These convictions marked Martha service in health care, whether it was in hospital administration, pharmacy, pastoral care, medical records, the business office, admissions, x-ray, nursing care, nursing education, or household support service.[39]

The Motherhouse at Bethany

The congregation's renewal agenda of the seventies certainly included Martha life at Bethany, Antigonish. About a hundred sisters made Bethany their home through the decade. The administration increased their personal freedoms, formed small groups, improved communications and established Bethany Centre. In consultation with Dods, the general council also reorganized the motherhouse administration. Bethany was departmentalized, and assigned a coordinator, an administrator, and an apostolate director. A management service board was formed (1977), and shortly thereafter a director of physical facilities was appointed. The church goods department, where several sisters made such remarkable contributions, closed in 1969, and in 1970 the unprofitable farming operation was shut down.[40] Bethany also made increasing use of lay staff. In 1964 the all-male lay staff numbered only fourteen–a plant superintendent, a fireman, a chaffeur, a chef, a grounds keeper, kitchen helpers, janitors, laundrymen, and farmhands. Women came on staff in the later sixties, and the entire support staff unionized in 1975. Six years hence, forty-one people worked for the sisters at Bethany, which became a major employer in the town of Antigonish.[41]

Martha musicians–Sister Margaret Mary Hervé at the piano, Sister Ada Fougere and Sister Mary Donalda MacDonald on violins.

Bethany supplied the Marthas with vital services: general congregational government, varied employment opportunities, a place for retirement, a retreat/renewal center, infirmary care, and a final resting place. In 1976 a new novitiate residence called Marian Community was constructed on the Bethany grounds, and in 1980 a new home for the congregational administration called Mount Carmel. Bethany remained the congregation's central home, rich in cultural, educational, recreational, and spiritual activities. The chapter of 1977 called the congregation to maintain Bethany as "a home for all Marthas, a sign of welcoming hospitality to others, [and] a source of prayer and renewal for the Sisters of St. Martha, for other religious, clergy and laity."[42]

Martha Spiritual and Corporate Life

The individual and communal spiritual life of the Marthas remained at the heart of congregational experience for each sister. Sister Mary MacIntosh's administration made significant efforts to promote spiritual renewal. Of course, the communal practices had continued–daily personal and corporate prayer, celebration of the eucharist and feast days, spiritual readings, meditation, days of recollection, and monthly and annual retreats. However, the general administration also encouraged sisters to study scripture, theology, liturgy, and spiritual direction. Sisters were given the opportunity to apply for a sabbatical year of renewal somewhere in Canada, the United States, or overseas, and many took advantage of this. Some even made pilgrimages to Rome or the Holy Land. Marthas attended weekend spiritual workshops, some local and others in distant cities; and at retreats they had well-qualified spiritual directors. Many sisters made the Ignatian Forty Day Institute in Guelph, Ontario, or other Jesuit institutions. Bethany Center, Martha Centre, and the Galilee Renewal Program provided rich opportunities for personal and communal spiritual growth and renewal. Sisters learned to share on the level of faith more commonly than ever before.

The general administration arranged a fascinating, and for the congregation, historic "meeting of Marthas" in November 1976. Then, the entire congregation, with missions in Nova Scotia, Ontario, Saskatchewan, Alberta, British Columbia, and Massachusetts, met together through a national-international telephone conference hookup to participate in an institute on apostolic spirituality presented by Father George Aschenbrenner, SJ. In the closing sessions, the sisters sang together the hymn to St. Martha. Sister Thérèse LeBlanc concluded that the experience "has given a major thrust to our continuing growth in spirituality" and provided "a real sense of unity."[43] The immediate purpose of the weekend conference was preparation for the 1977 general chapter.

The spiritual life of the Marthas strengthened their common life. Like many congregations, the Marthas experienced some weakening of communal commitment early in the renewal process. Some sisters, perhaps intoxicated by the expansion of personal freedom, placed their own will and discernment of spiritual guidance above the directives of the larger community. Sister Mary MacIntosh observed, "Early in [the renewal] we passed through different degrees of personalism, individualism, doing our own thing–call it what you wish. With the passing of the 60's and early 70's personalism seems to have lessened. We are now reaching a balance."[44] The Marthas recovered a strong sense of communal identity, of "We Sisters of St. Martha," and thus resisted the atomism that permanently weakened the corporate character of some other congregations. This corporateness was rooted in a common mission and a common, renewed spiritual life.

From the sixties, the sisters became more conscious of the role of women within the church and more willing to minister directly to their needs. Of course, the Roman Catholic tradition had for centuries provided space for celibate women to pursue careers other than marriage and motherhood. From their founding, the Marthas had followed careers alternative to marriage as part of their religious vocation and within the constraints imposed by society about the appropriate roles for women. They had also ministered to women in their homes for unwed mothers, in their social work, and in their hospitals. Generally, the Martha relationship with males was cooperative and mutually respectful. They had long worked with males, lay and ecclesiastical, on boards and in the parishes. They also had a tradition of special solicitude for priests and often ministered to them in times of personal extremity, such as illness. At times, however, their relations with males did become rocky, for example, when the sisters pushed for independence from St. Francis Xavier University. Priests and bishops were also not above bullying and acting in a paternalistic and condescending manner toward the sisters.

In 1981, Sister Mary MacIntosh concluded that the Marthas had a new appreciation of their role within the church. She stated, "Our growth in this area has been low key but persistent."[45] Marthas were more willing to make themselves heard and less willing to defer to male authority. The range of careers Marthas could follow expanded into areas that had for centuries been the exclusive preserve of men, such as canon law, theology, and spirituality. Certain forms of their ministry were directed specifically toward women, for example, retreat work and addictions counselling. Sister Mary reminded the congregation, "The work of building church includes us, and can benefit through our contributions."[46]

New Horizons, New Directions

Through the seventies and beyond, Martha ministries diversified in fascinating new directions. These new directions and new horizons sprang from congregational renewal, sisters' changing interests, their commitment to meet urgent human needs, and their pioneering tradition. The spiritual development of persons was not entirely new to the Marthas, but they became more deeply involved in it. Martha Centre had been established at Lethbridge in 1968, Bethany Centre at the motherhouse in 1972, and some revival of retreat work in the late seventies at Villa Madonna (the former Little Flower Institute) in Bras d'Or, Cape Breton. In 1975, Father Roy Boucher, a former student of Sister Teresa Ryan, invited her to work with the Oblate Galilee Community at Arnprior, Ontario. It had recently become a renewal centre, house of prayer, and novitiate for English Canadian Oblates. The Galilee Community was "attracted by [the Marthas'] special spirit."[47] The congregation accepted Father Boucher's invitation and the Marthas established a small community at Arnprior and became part of the Oblate renewal team. The first sisters assigned, in 1976, were Sister Teresa Ryan, superior, educator, and spritual director; Sister Mary Patrice (Mary Alice) LaRusic, receptionist and coordinator of retreat programs; and Sister Rosalie (Mary Martha) Lavallee, sacristy and food services. The congregation would remain at Arnprior until 1994, contributing to its diverse spiritual development ministry and sending Marthas there for personal renewal.[48]

The 1970s also witnessed the Marthas opting for small-group rather than large institutional living experiences. Historically the congregation's smaller missions had afforded the sisters experiences of intimate community, but, in the seventies, small groups became the norm at the motherhouse. House of Hope existed in Antigonish from 1972 to 1977. Moreover, three small communities were established in Sydney, Cape Breton. In 1974, seven Marthas moved from St. Rita Hospital and formed a small community called Martha Community on Whitney Avenue.[49] St. Rita Convent, on Bentinck Street, was opened in 1975 as a residence for sisters and a place for prospective candidates to experience the Martha way of life.[50] Two years afterwards, seven Marthas opened Emmanuel Community on King's Road as a residence for working sisters, and for semi-retired sisters who preferred to remain in Cape Breton.[51] Finally, after the closure of St. Mary's Hospital, Inverness, the congregation opened St. Mary's Convent as a residence for sisters who, with the pastor, formed a team ministry in Stella Maris and St. Margaret's parishes.[52]

One new direction or experiment the Marthas did not affirm in the seventies was the proposed formation of a contemplative community. In the fall of 1973, several Marthas had entreated the general administration to establish such a community. However, it decided against the proposal and reported to the congregation: "After much prayerful search and consultation it was refused because it could not be reconciled with the present understanding of our charism, nor discerned as God's plan for the Marthas at this time.[53] Nonetheless, three sisters pressed for the experiment and were granted the right to live temporarily in established contemplative communities.[54] Afterwards, in 1976, and with the blessing and sponsorship of Bishop William Power, these three sisters did establish a contemplative community at Ironville, Cape Breton, that was entirely separate from the congregation.[55]

Sister Sandra Cooke, second from right, with Martha Associates at St. John's Hospital, Lowell, Massachusetts.

In contrast, the Sisters of St. Martha, after initial experiments, did fully support a new form of congregational association for interested lay people. Both general chapters–1973 and 1977–had called for the examination of a new type of association. After consulting with other congregations and experimenting at three convents, the Marthas commenced a form of commun-ity affiliation called Martha Associates. Its purposes were to enrich mutually the sisters and the associates, and to share the vibrant tradition of Martha spirituality. Associates, either men or women, took no vows and incurred no legal or financial obligations; that is, they did not become members. They participated with the sisters in activities, such as monthly meetings, prayer and worship, retreats, days of recollection, and recreation.[56]

The Marthas became increasingly involved in pastoral service and religious education in the seventies. By 1981, twelve sisters provided hospital pastoral care in certain Martha hospitals, such as St. Rita in Sydney, St. John's in Lowell, St. Martha's in Antigonish, the New Waterford Consolidated, and the R.K. MacDonald Guest House and Nursing Home in Antigonish. About five sisters had received specialized training to prepare for this valuable new field of Martha service.[57] Such a ministry in health care institutions had roots in the congregation's spiritual caring tradition, and it allowed the sisters to maintain a spiritual presence in hospitals they relinquished.

Religious education and parish work were not virgin territory for the Marthas, but they became more extensively and formally involved in them during the 1970s. Parishes began contracting their services full-time as the supply of priests dwindled. For example, in 1977, parishes in Canmore and Exshaw, Alberta, hired Sister Margaret Mary Hervé as religious education coordinator and parish worker, and Sister Edna (Mary of the Sacred Heart) MacDonald became religious education coordinator for Immaculate Conception Parish in Bridgeport, Nova Scotia. By 1981, twelve sisters, most of them qualified teachers with further training in religious education, had been hired for this type of work. Moreover, the Diocese of Antigonish appointed Sister Joan Fultz (future congregation leader, 1989–1994) diocesan coordinator of adult religious education (1977–1980), and then director of the office of religious education (1980–1986). Through religious education and parish work, the Marthas promoted religious renewal at the parish level, prepared children in the basics of Catholicism and helped adults deepen their faith.

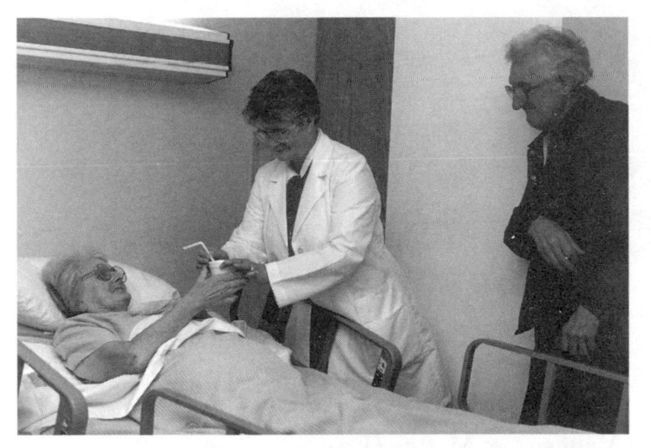

Sister Sylvia MacDonald in hospital pastoral services.

Finally, the congregation pioneered an estimable new direction in health services: home care and support for the elderly. In 1978, following the Martha tradition of seeing an urgent need and then responding to it with deep commitment of sisters and finanical resources, it established and financed two demonstration projects in Antigonish town and county for persons age 60 and over. With the collaboration of lay people, Martha Home Health Care provided home nursing care, and the Antigonish Home

Care Task Force supplied non-medical needs using local volunteers. The founding directors were Sister Hugh Teresina McNeil, Martha Home Health Care, and Sister Baptista Maria Macdonald, Antigonish Home Care Task Force. The initial staff was Sister M. Georgeanna (Helen Frances) Peck, home health care aide, and Anita Driscoll, home health care nurse. An evaluation, in 1980 found the programs to be effective and valued services. Eventually Martha Home Health Care and Antigonish Home Care Task Force acquired some government assistance and became the responsibility of independent boards of local citizens and Marthas.[58] An enthusiastic media report in 1991 affirmed, "Over the past thirteen years, the program has been a godsend to thousands of people in town and country to patients and families alike.[59] Significantly, Martha Home Health Care became the model followed in Nova Scotia home nursing care.

Sister Veronica (Agnes Michael) Matthews, of Martha Home Health Care

Conclusion

Under a new administration in 1973, and again in 1977, the Sisters of St. Martha had stayed the course of renewal that had commenced in 1967. They found it a massive task that demanded constant study, detailed planning, expert advice, comprehensive evaluations, and prayerful trust in God. Flexibility, toleration, creativity, and maturity were also required, as sisters discarded time-honoured ways of living and charted alluring future directions. The results were exciting: large-scale administrative reorganization, a heightened awareness of their own charism, deeper faith, invigorated commitment to the Martha community and mission, greater individual freedom and responsibility, new and more varied apostolates, and finally, in 1983, new constitutions and general directives approved by Rome.

Notes

1 R. Douglas Francis, Richard Jones, and Donald B. Smith, *Destinies: Canadian History Since Confederation,* third ed. (Toronto: Harcourt Brace Canada, 1996), pp. 490-92.
2 Communications Centre Update, 23 March 1973, F5,S35,SS2,f35,b101.
3 Report of the General Administration, 1967-1973, p. 41, F5,S10,SS13,f1,b17.
4 Interviews with Sister Mary MacIntosh, November 1998, Bethany.
5 Mother Teresa Ryan to Sisters, 21 December 1972, F5,S9,SS8,f3,b9.
6 "Our Way to the Father," September 1974, F5,S9,SS13,f1-2,b15.
7 A *Financial Post* article entitled "All Dods' Children" expressed surprise at finding a forty-two year old non-Catholic, non-religious Toronto management consultant working with a Roman Catholic women's religious congregation. See Hickling-Johnston materials, F5,S9,SS11-12,f1-10,b14 and 15.
8 Evaluation of Apostolic Services, 1971-1979, F5,S19,SS1,f3,b50.
9 Sister Mary MacIntosh, Development of the 1980 Statement of Charism, Sister Irene Doyle files.
10 The original motherhouse now accommodates the Department of Geology and is called Augustine Hall.
11 See the special seventy-fifth anniversary edition of *The Bethanite* and a booklet recounting the jubilee celebrations in F1,S5,SS3,b2-3.
12 See "Thecla's Choice" materials in F1,S5,SS3,f3-4,b2.
13 General Administration Report, 1973-1977, F5,S10,SS21,f1,b22.
14 Proceedings of the General Chapter, 1977, F5,S10,SS18,f1,b20.
15 Reports and Presentations on the Household Apostolate, 1950-1972, F5,S20,SS2,b51.
16 *The Bethanite*, May 1978, p. 13.

17 Homemaker Questionnaire, 1968, F5,S20,SS2,f6,b51.
18 Archbishop G. Emmett Carter to Sister Mary MacIntosh, 4 May 1979, F5,S34,SS17,f18,b93.
19 Report of the General Administration, 1967, Appendix II, p. 46, F5,S10,SS13,f1,b17 and General Administration Report 1977-1981, p. 33.
20 McGuigan, "The Cardinal and the Island," p. 34.
21 Cardinal's Residence Annals, 27 March 1971, F22,S1,SS1,f2,b194.
22 St. Pius X High School Annals, February 1976, F36,S1,SS1,f1,b233.
23 Committee Report, Evaluation: St. Augustine's Seminary Convent, Scarborough, Ontario, March 1979, b244.
24 Rector John O'Mara to Mother Teresa Ryan, 12 July 1972, b244.
25 St. Martha Convent Annals, September 1979, F21,S1,SS1,f1,b191.
26 Rev. Malcolm MacDonell, homily, 16 July 1975, F1,S5,SS3,f7,b3.
27 Sister Mary MacIntosh to St. Martha's Convent Sisters, 5 December 1978, F21,S2,SS1,f9,b192.
28 General Administration Report, 1977-1981, p. 37.
29 Interview with Sister Stella Chafe, 13 May 1999, Bethany, and St. Paul's Convent, F35,S1,SS1,f4,b232.
30 Reports, F5,S25,SS7,f4,b63.
31 Joy Program Tenth Anniversary Report, 1972-1983, Heatherton Activity Centre Reports, F5,S25,SS7,f1 and 3,b63.
32 General Administration Report, 1977-1981, p. 31. Important sources on the teaching apostolate include "History of the CSM Teaching Sisters" and "Rememberings: Reflections of Teaching Sisters in 1978," both compiled by Sister Josephine (Aneas Joseph) MacDonald, F5,S25,SS9,f1-2,b64.
33 General Administration Report, 1977-1981, p. 32.
34 News Release, 6 July 1976, and St. Mary's Hospital House Annals, F16,S3,SS2,f1 and 5,b176.
35 Minutes of CSM Corporation Meeting, 22 April 1977, F7,S4,SS2,f14,b122 and St. Joseph's Hospital Annals, 1970s, F7,S1,SS1,f3,b118.
36 Sister Mary MacIntosh to R. Kawecki, 13 July 1979, F13,S5,SS1,f1,b172.
37 St. Peter's Hospital Annals, 1980, F13,S1,SS1,f6,b169.
38 See the entire report in F5,S22,SS6,f2,b55.
39 Mother Teresa Ryan to Sister Stephanie Cormier, 27 October 1969, F6,S3,SS3,f2,b111, and Sister Kathleen Morrison to Sisters, 1 April 1970, F6,S3,SS2,f8,b111.
40 General Administration Report, 1977-1981, p. 28.
41 Quoted in Ibid., p. 11.
42 CSM General Administration Report, 1973-1977, p. 8.
43 General Administration Report, 1981, p. 5.

44 Ibid., p. 7.

45 Ibid.

46 Rev. J. Roy Boucher to Sister Mary MacIntosh, 19 March 1976, F28,S1,SS1,f4,b221.

47 Galilee Community Annals, F28,S1,SS1,f3,b221.

48 Sister Mary MacIntosh to Dear Sisters, 21 November 1973, F51,S1,SS0,f2,b273.

49 St. Rita Convent Records, F51,S2,SS0,b274.

50 Emmanuel Community Records, F51,S4,SS0,b276.

51 St. Mary's Convent Records, F51,S17,SS0,b252.

52 CSM General Administration Report, 1973-1977, p. 8.

53 Bethany Annals, September 1975, F6,S1,SS1,b108.

54 Bethany Annals, F6,S1,SS2,f4,b109.

55 Sister Michelle MacDougall, Report-Associate Membership Experiment, 31 May 1981, F5,S32,S6,f3,b73.

56 General Administration Report, 1977-1981, p. 34.

57 *The Bethanite*, January, May and September 1979.

58 *The Casket*, 23 January 1991.

The 1981 general chapter participants in front of Bethany.

Epilogue

The Sisters of St. Martha held their eleventh general chapter at Bethany in 1981. Its theme was "We welcome your presence, Lord, in all of life." Sister Mary MacIntosh, the general superior, presented her general administration report to the thirty sister delegates. That year, the congregation had 332 sisters, with 243 giving full-time or limited service at the motherhouse and on twenty-nine missions. The congregation's average age was 60, the age range from 20 to 91, and the retired sisters numbered forty-three. Eight novices were in formation.[1] The chapter's central event was the presentation, review, amendment, and approval for submission to Rome of the Marthas' new draft constitutions. In her closing remarks, Sister Thérèse LeBlanc, the newly elected general superior, declared the chapter a historic one, "for we have completed the re-writing of our Constitutions which is a refounding of the Sisters of St. Martha."[2]

The original founding of the Sisters of St. Martha had happened, of course, eighty-one years before at the fateful retreat in Halifax on 12 July 1900. There, at the Mount Saint Vincent motherhouse, thirteen young Marthas, followed by two more shortly thereafter, then serving in the Sisters of Charity auxiliary order, had answered the call by courageously standing up and committing themselves to establish a new, independent congregation in Bishop John Cameron's Diocese of Antigonish. Thus began the odyssey of a new Canadian Roman Catholic religious congregation. Since then, the Marthas had grown and had established missions providing household, health care, social work, educational, pastoral, and spiritual development services. Through time, they had opened missions far beyond the Diocese of Antigonish, gained their independence from St. Francis Xavier University, built a new motherhouse at Bethany, won approval as a papal institute; extended their work into western Canada, and even started a work in Boston, Massachusetts. Their external works manifested a vigorous work ethic. The Marthas had also forged a vibrant common life rooted in the ancient Roman Catholic tradition of vowed religious living. Starting in the 1960s, their community life had been renewed and transformed through the stimulus of Vatican II and by influential trends in western society. The sisters, as an apostolic community, had shed monastic practices that hindered them, and thus became more openly engaged in the world around them. They also faced declining vocations and an exodus of professed sisters that marked the end of their last phase of expansion in the mid-sixties. However, their religious life deepened and they were called to more varied forms of ministry.

What the Marthas had done for others, by 1981, on their pilgrimage toward the City of God had created a vast reservoir of gratitude and goodwill among the people they had served. They had ministered to countless individuals, contributed to the work of educational institutions, extended and strengthened the network of Canadian Catholic institutions, and helped build the nation at the grassroots level, especially in eastern Nova Scotia and the prairie west. Religious and political leaders were quick to recognize the economic advantages of appropriating and "subsidizing their disciplined and self-sacrificing...services."[3] Bishops and priests were especially thankful to the Marthas for their moral support, friendship, contributions as co-workers, hospitality, and convalescent care given in times of personal need.

What the Marthas became, on their journey toward the Celestial City, and how they served other people is also noteworthy. Most Marthas came from economically modest and devout Catholic homes in eastern Nova Scotia, Newfoundland, and the prairie west. Their backgrounds in rural and urban working-class life, their Roman Catholic faith, their devotion to St. Martha, and their first work–household services–forged a unique congregational identity: strong communalism or corporateness, radical religious commitment, and a spirit of pioneering faith, simplicity, humanness, hospitality, joy in celebration, and solidarity with people. This congregational ethos led them to identify closely with people and their basic needs, making the Marthas of Antigonish truly "a people's congregation," known for their service to God and others.

In 1999–2000, the Sisters of St. Martha joyfully celebrate

their centennial, which comes at the end of one millennium and the beginning of another. Since 1981 they have achieved Vatican approval of their revised constitutions and general directives (1983). They have also launched successful new missions, for example, in parish administration and pastoral services at St. Paul's River, Quebec (1983) and St. George's Diocese, Newfoundland (1993). The congregation also established a varied ministry of pastoral, health care, educational, and social services in Basseterre, St. Kitts, West Indies (1986). However, like most other Roman Catholic congregations in North America, they are, of course, aware of their diminishing numbers (224 at the end of 1998), advancing age, and lack of new candidates. In weaker moments, some Marthas are no doubt tempted to believe that Jo Ann Kay McNamara's prophecy will be fulfilled: "[With] no new generation of recruits in sight, the death of the feminine apostolate … seems inevitable."[4] However, the Sisters of St. Martha are still alive, vibrant, and optimistic, with many active sisters who remain surprisingly productive well into their seventies and eighties. Moreover, the Marthas are practiced at celebrating the past, and enjoying the present. And they have always believed that the future is in God's hands.

Notes

1 General Administration Report, 1977-1981, p. 26.

2 General Chapter Proceedings, 1981, F5,S10,SS25,f1,b22.

3 Jo Ann Kay McNamara, *Sisters in Arms: Catholic Nuns Through Two Millennia* (Cambridge, Mass: Harvard University Press, 1996), p. 574.

4 Ibid., p. 631.

APPENDIX I

Copy of the circular letter sent out by Bishop John Cameron to his diocesan clergy, "recruiting" the first novices for the Sisters of St. Martha–22 May 1894

To the Reverend Clergy:

Dear Reverend Father

The need of a change in the domestic service of St. Francis Xavier's College has long been felt and steps have of late been taken to supply it in a permanent way. After much casting about we have at length, through the large-hearted and broad-minded kindness of the Reverend Mother M. Bonaventure, Superior of the Sisters of Charity, settled upon a plan that, with God's blessing, will answer our purpose most satisfactorily. At our suggestion and with the ready approval of His Grace, the Archbishop, the Reverend Mother has under-taken to found in connection with her own flourishing Institution an order of auxiliary Sisters to be known as the Sisters of St. Martha, whose chief object will be to help each other to advance in the work of their own sanctification so as to become worthy spouses of Jesus Christ, the "meek and humble of heart," and, for this end, to perform the domestic duties of educational and charitable institutions,–our College to be given a preferential place. Two years hence we are to receive here a colony of the Sisters of St. Martha duly trained for every kind of domestic service, and under the charge of one or more Sisters of Charity so long as this may be required. Under these circumstances, the least that can be expected of us is to earnestly co-operate with the excellent Mother Bonaventure and her Council in order to procure novices for the new Sisterhood. We therefore ask you, dear Reverend Father, to look through your congregation for such persons as may be fit to join the new order, and to point out to them the great spiritual and even temporal advantages of the life to be led by the Sisters of St. Martha. All the recruits must be virtuous young women of robust health and industrious habits and, as a rule, not over 26 years, nor under 18. Each desirable candidate for the new institute will, as soon as she expresses her willingness to enter the order, put herself in communication with Mother Bonaventure, Mount St. Vincent, Halifax, from whom she will get all the detailed information she will require. The novitiate will be open for postulants the first of next September: it will last for about two years from that date, during which time novices will have to supply themselves with wearing apparel and bedding and pay their doctors' bills.

Trusting that in so laudable an undertaking you will show your well known zeal, we remain, dear Reverend Father, very faithfully,

Yours in Christ,
JOHN CAMERON
Bishop of Antigonish.
Antigonish, May 22nd, 1894.

APPENDIX II

The fifteen founding Sisters of St. Martha who volunteered at Mount St. Vincent for Antigonish and arrived in July-September, 1900

Sister M. Benjamina (Mary Bell) Beaton
Black River, Inverness County
1880-1934

Sister M. Dorothy (Isabel) Beaton
N.E. Mabou, Inverness County
1870-1949

Sister M. Marcella (Leah) Beaton
Black River, Inverness County
1878-1957

Sister Mary Ninian (Agnes) Beaton
(1912-to Poor Clares)
Black River, Inverness County
1876-1956

Sister M. Thecla (Bridget Ellen) Chisholm
Glasburn, Guysborough County
1872-1902

Sister Mary Potens (Mary Anastasia) Landry
Afton, Antigonish County
1870-1967

Sister M. Anne (Katie) MacAdam
West River, Antigonish County
1871-(withdrew 1907)

Sister M. Francis (Elizabeth) MacAdam
Eskasoni, Cape Breton County
1869-1942

Sister M. Faustina (Mary) MacArthur
Pine Tree, Pictou County
1873-1954

Sister M. Jovita (Margaret) MacArthur
Pine Tree, Pictou County
1878-1957

Sister M. Remegius (Laura) MacArthur
Pine Tree, Pictou County
1875-1927

Sister M. Andrew (Margaret) MacDonald
Boisdale, Cape Breton County
1873-1937

Sister Joseph Agnes (Janet) MacDonald
Arisaig, Antigonish County
1877-1929

Sister M. Innocentia (Caroline) MacNamara
Lower River Inhabitants, Richmond County
1871-1909

Sister M. Theodore (Julia) Sampson
Petit de Grat, Richmond County
1867-1950

APPENDIX III

English Translation of the CSM Decrees of Papal Approval

A. TEMPORARY, 1931:

In the Diocese of Antigonish, through the efforts of the Most Reverend Bishop John Cameron, Ordinary of that diocese, the pious Institute of the Sisters of Saint Martha was founded in the year 1900. The Motherhouse was soon afterwards established with due ceremony in the same town. In addition to the general purpose of seeking their personal sanctification, these Sisters consider as their specific work: caring for the sick, aged, and orphans, training youth, and managing the household in colleges of clerics. All members of the Institute lead a life strictly in common under the rule of a Superior General who is to be elected every sixth year, and they profess at the end of their novitiate, first temporarily but later perpetually, the vows of obedience, poverty, and chastity. Since furthermore, Divine Grace continuing to favour them, and the number of Sisters having grown in no mean measure, they have established thirteen houses in several dioceses, the Bishops consenting, nay rather rejoicing, because of the abundant fruits that thus followed for the salvation of souls, recently the Superior General with her Councillors humbly petitioned His Holiness that He would deign to approve with Apostolic Authority this Institute and its Constitutions. In an audience given on December 22, 1931, to the Reverend Father Secretary of the Congregation for Religious, while heeding the favouring letters of the Bishops in whose dioceses there are houses of the Institute, and especially after hearing the favourable vote of Their Eminences, the Cardinals, who had weighed the matter with mature judgement in a plenary session at the Vatican on December eleventh of this year, His Holiness Pope Pius XI deigned to extol and commend with bounteous praise this Institute as a Congregation with simple vows. Temporarily for a period of seven years, He kindly approved and confirmed its Constitutions, written in French, as attached hereto, the autographed copy of which is preserved in the Archives of this Sacred Congregation, and as is clear from the tone of this decree, both the Institute itself is praised and commended, and its Constitutions as above, are approved and confirmed, without prejudice, according to the Sacred Canons, to the jurisdiction of the Ordinaries concerned.

Given at Rome from the Secretariate of the Sacred Congregation for Religious on December 22, 1931.

ALEXIUS HENRICUS M. CARD.
LEPICIER, O.S.M. Prefect.
VINC. LA PUMA, Secretary.

B. PERMANENT, 1943:

On December 22, 1931, the Congregation of the Sisters of Saint Martha of Antigonish, whose Motherhouse is in the diocese of Antigonish, received from the Holy See temporary approval of its Constitutions.

In as much, however, as the same Congregation across the years has flowered rich in fruit for the good of the Church, the Superior General with her Council humbly begged from the Holy See final approval of the Constitutions.

In an audience granted on April 3, 1943, to His Eminence Vincent Cardinal La Puma, Prefect of the Sacred Congregation for Religious, while heeding the favouring letters of Their Excellencies, the Ordinaries, in whose dioceses there are houses of the Institute, and after hearing also the vote of the Commission of Reverend Consultors, His Holiness by Divine Providence Pope Pius XII, has kindly decreed finally to approve and confirm the Constitutions with some changes and additions, a copy of which is preserved in the archives of the said Sacred Congregation, and as is clear from the tone of this decree these same Constitutions are approved and confirmed, anything to the contrary notwithstanding.

Given at Rome from the Secretariate of the Sacred Congregation for Religious, on the day, month, and year mentioned above.

For His Eminence the Cardinal Prefect
F. S. M. PARETTO, Secretary.
V. PADORANI, Under-Secretary.

C. REVISION, 1983

Prot. N. A 66 - 1/81

DECREE

This Sacred Congregations for Religious and Secular Institutes, by virtue of the authority to erect, guide, and promote institutes of the consecrated life, after careful examination of the constitutions presented by the Sisters of St. Martha, Antigonish, Nova Scotia, acceding to the request of the Superior General and her Council, herewith approves, within the limits of common law, these same constitutions as amended according to the observations of this Sacred Congregation. May the generous living of these constitutions encourage all the Sisters of the institute to an ever deeper commitment to their consecrated life in the spirit of St. Martha and under the strong and tender protection of the Mother of God.

Given in Rome, July 29, 1983
Feast of St. Martha.

Map of CSM Mission Locations

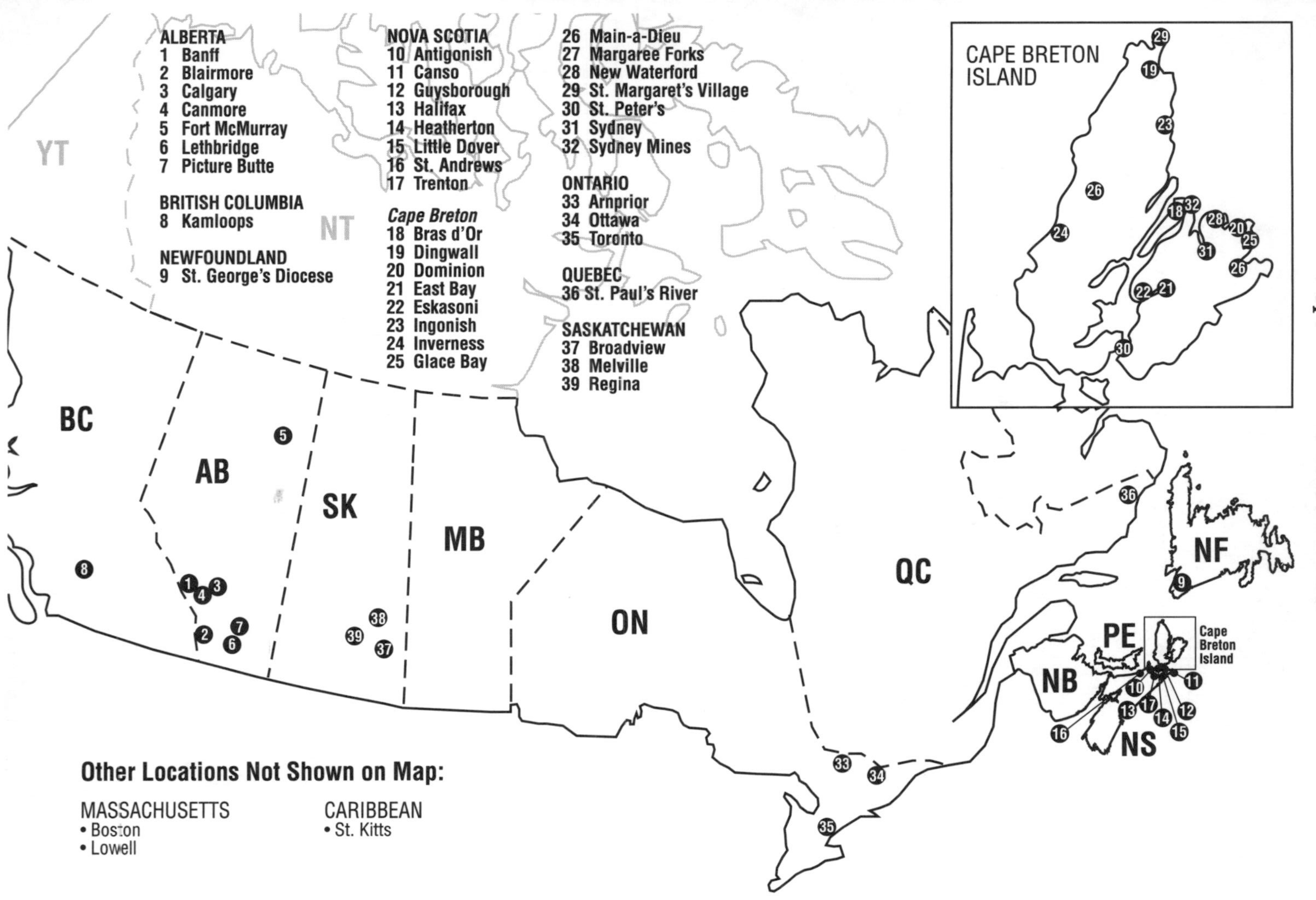

APPENDIX IV

Chronological List of CSM Missions

Note: *The "Type of Apostolate" entry does not convey the rich complexity of work undertaken by the sisters in each locale.*

Name: St. Martha's Convent
Type of Apostolate: Motherhouse 1900-1921; household, office, extension, library; educational, infirmary and pastoral services
Location: St. Francis Xavier University, Antigonish, NS
Dates (start–end): 1900–1994

Name: Wellspring Centre
Type of Apostolate: Pastoral services
Location: St.F.X.
Dates (start–end): 1994–Present

Name: St. Joseph's Hospital
Type of Apostolate: Household services
Location: Glace Bay, NS
Dates (start–end): 1902–1908

Name: St. Joseph's Hospital
Type of Apostolate: Health care and educational services
Location: Glace Bay, NS
Dates (start–end): 1915–1977

Name: St. Martha's Regional Hospital
Type of Apostolate: Health care, educational, social, and pastoral services
Location: Antigonish, NS
Dates (start–end): 1906–Present
*Ownership relinquished 1996

Name: Mount Cameron Farm
Type of Apostolate: Household services and care of retired priests
Location: Antigonish, NS
Dates (start–end): 1907–1928

Name: St. Augustine's Seminary Convent
Type of Apostolate: Household, educational, library, faculty, and counselling services
Location: Toronto, ON
Dates (start–end): 1913–Present

Name: House of Providence
Type of Apostolate: Care of the aged
Location: Antigonish, NS
Dates (start–end): 1914–1924

Name: St. Dunstan's College
Type of Apostolate: Contribution to founding of new congregation
Location: Charlottetown, PEI
Dates (start–end): 1916–1921

Name: St. Mary's Home/Mercy Hospital
Type of Apostolate: Social services (unwed mothers/child care)
Location: Sydney, NS
Dates (start–end): 1917–1951

Name: Ross Memorial/ St. Rita Hospital
Type of Apostolate: Health care and educational services
Location: Sydney, NS
Dates (start–end): 1920–1988

Name: Bethany
Type of Apostolate: Motherhouse services
Location: Antigonish, NS
Dates (start–end): 1921–Present

Name: St. Mary's Hospital
Type of Apostolate: Health care services (parish social services, 1938-1943)
Location: Inverness, NS
Dates (start–end): 1925–1976

Name: St. Theresa's Convent
Type of Apostolate: Educational and pastoral services
Location: Margaree Forks, NS
Dates (start–end): 1925–1970

Name: Sacred Heart Convent
Type of Apostolate: Educational services
Location: Bras d'Or, NS
Dates (start–end): 1926–1943

Name: Sacred Heart Convent
Type of Apostolate: Residence for Little Flower Institute sisters
Location: Bras d'Or, NS
Dates (start–end): 1927–1953

Name: Little Flower Institute
Type of Apostolate: Social services in child-care; (parish social services, Bras d'Or, 1941-1944)

Location: Bras d'Or, NS
Dates (start–end): 1927–1953
Location: Sydney, NS
Dates (start–end): 1956–1971

Name: St. Andrews Convent
Type of Apostolate: Educational and pastoral services
Location: St. Andrews, NS
Dates (start–end): 1928–Present

Name: St. Michael's General Hospital
Type of Apostolate: Health care and educational services
Location: Lethbridge, AB
Dates (start–end): 1929–Present
*ownership relinquished 1985

Name: Mineral Springs Hospital
Type of Apostolate: Health care services
Location: Banff, AB
Dates (start–end): 1930–1988
*ownership relinquished
Type of Apostolate: Pastoral services
Location: Banff, AB
Dates (start–end): 1985–1997

Name: Canso Welfare Bureau/Star of the Sea Convent (renamed in 1961)
Type of Apostolate: Pastoral, social, educational, and health care services
Location: Canso, NS with outreach to Little Dover and Lincolnville
Dates (start–end): 1933–1984
Type of Apostolate: Health care services
Location: Canso, NS
Dates (start–end): 1960–1971

Name: Mount Carmel Convent
Type of Apostolate: Pastoral and educational services
Location: Canmore, AB
Dates (start–end): 1934–1961

Name: Cardinal's Residence
Type of Apostolate: Household services
Location: Toronto
Dates (start–end): 1935–1974

Name: Mercy Hospital/Martha House
Type of Apostolate: Social services—care of unwed mothers and family agency (1936-1972)
Location: Regina, SK
Dates (start–end): 1936–1984

Name: St. Michael's Hospital
Type of Apostolate: Health care services
Location: Broadview, SK
Dates (start–end): 1936–1969

Name: St. Martha's Hostel
Type of Apostolate: Young women's residence
Location: Regina, SK
Dates (start–end): 1938–1939

Name: St. Charles' Convent
Type of Apostolate: Social, educational, and pastoral services
Location: Dominion, NS
Dates (start–end): 1938–1988

Name: St. Alphonsus Convent
Type of Apostolate: Social, educational, and pastoral services
Location: Blairmore, AB
Dates (start–end): 1939–1969

Name: St. Peter's Hospital
Type of Apostolate: Health care services
Location: Melville, SK
Dates (start–end): 1940–1980

Name: St. Alexander's Convent
Type of Apostolate: Educational services
Location: Main-a-Dieu, NS
Dates (start–end): 1942–1975

Name: Bentinck Street Convent
Type of Apostolate: Social services through parish family agencies
Location: Sydney, NS
Dates (start–end): 1944–1956

Name: J.L. MacIsaac Memorial Home
Type of Apostolate: Health care services (care of the aged)
Location: Antigonish, NS
Dates (start–end): 1944–1946

Name: Teachers' Residence
Type of Apostolate: Educational, pastoral, social and health services
Location: Eskasoni, NS
Dates (start–end): 1947–Present

Name: Fatima Retreat House
Type of Apostolate: Spiritual development services
Location: Seabright, NS
Dates (start–end): 1949–1960 *closed as retreat house

Name: Our Lady of Fatima Convent
Type of Apostolate: Educational services
Location: Heatherton, NS
Dates (start–end): 1951–1970

Name: St. Martha's Catholic Centre
Type of Apostolate: Social services; residence for CSM students
Location: Boston, MA
Dates (start–end): 1952–1987

Name: St. Mary's Convent
Type of Apostolate: Educational services
Location: East Bay, NS
Dates (start–end): 1953–1970

Name: St. Peter's Convent
Type of Apostolate: Educational services
Location: Ingonish, NS
Dates (start–end): 1953–1986

Name: Villa Madonna (formerly Little Flower Institute)
Type of Apostolate: Spiritual development services; residence for social workers & teachers
Location: Bras d'Or, NS
Dates (start–end): 1954–1985

Name: St. Joseph's Convent
Type of Apostolate: Educational services
Location: Dingwall, NS
Dates (start–end): 1955–1986

Name: R.K. MacDonald Guest Home
Type of Apostolate: Health care services (care of the aged)
Location: Antigonish, NS
Dates (start–end): 1958–1991
*ownership relinquished 1971

Name: St. Paul's Convent
Type of Apostolate: Educational services
Location: St. Peter's, NS
Dates (start–end): 1958–1968

Name: Christ the King Convent
Type of Apostolate: Educational, social and pastoral services
Location: Trenton, NS
Dates (start–end): 1958–Present

Name: St. Ann's Convent
Type of Apostolate: Educational and pastoral services
Location: Guysborough, NS
Dates (start–end): 1958–1973; 1975–1988

Name: St. Margaret's Convent
Type of Apostolate: Educational services
Location: St. Margaret's Village, Bay St. Lawrence, NS
Dates (start–end): 1959–1971

Name: St. Pius X Seminary Convent
Type of Apostolate: Household and educational services
Location: Ottawa, ON
Dates (start–end):1960–1977

Name: Coady International Institute Convent
Type of Apostolate: Household and library services
Location: Antigonish, NS (St.FX)
Dates (start–end): 1961–1971

Name: St. John's Hospital
Type of Apostolate: Health care & pastoral services
Location: Lowell, MA
Dates (start–end): 1961–1992

Name: St. Catherine's Convent
Type of Apostolate: Educational services
Location: Picture Butte, AB
Dates (start–end): 1961–1965
Location: Commute from Lethbridge, AB
Dates (start–end): 1965–1981

Name: Our Lady of Perpetual Help
Type of Apostolate: Educational and pastoral services
Location: Kamloops, BC
Dates (start–end): 1962–1998

Name: New Waterford Consolidated Hospital
Type of Apostolate: Health care and pastoral services
Location: New Waterford, NS
Dates (start–end): 1963–Present

Name: Holy Heart Seminary Convent
Type of Apostolate: Household services
Location: Halifax, NS
Dates (start–end): 1964–1970

Name: Martha Centre
Type of Apostolate: Spiritual development services and residence
Location: Lethbridge, AB
Dates (start–end): 1968–Present

Name: Scarboro House
Type of Apostolate: Student residence
Location: Antigonish, NS
Dates (start–end): 1970–1971

Name: Bethany Centre
Type of Apostolate: Spiritual development services
Location: Bethany, Antigonish, NS
Dates (start–end): 1972–Present

Name: House of Hope
Type of Apostolate: Residence
Location: Antigonish, NS
Dates (start–end): 1972–1977

Name: Martha Community
Type of Apostolate: Residence
Location: Sydney, NS
Dates (start–end): 1974–Present

Name: St. Paul's Convent
Type of Apostolate: Educational services
Location: Fort McMurray, AB
Dates (start–end): 1975–1994

Name: St. Rita Convent
Type of Apostolate: Residence
Location: Sydney, NS
Dates (start–end): 1975–Present

Name: Galilee Community
Type of Apostolate: Spiritual development services
Location: Arnprior, ON
Dates (start–end): 1976–1994

Name: Marian Community
Type of Apostolate: Novitiate and then Residence
Location: Bethany complex
Dates (start–end): 1977–Present

Name: Emmanuel Community
Type of Apostolate: Residence
Location: Sydney, NS
Dates (start–end): 1977–1998

Name: Martha Home Health Care
Type of Apostolate: Health care services
Location: Antigonish, NS
Dates (start–end): 1978–1997

Name: St. Mary's Convent
Type of Apostolate: Pastoral services and residence
Location: Inverness, NS
Dates (start–end): 1978–Present

Name: Mount Carmel
Type of Apostolate: Governance community
Location: Bethany complex
Dates (start–end): 1980–Present

Name: St. Agnes Convent
Type of Apostolate: Pastoral services
Location: Dover, NS
Dates (start–end): 1984–1992; 1993–Present

Name: Sienna House
Type of Apostolate: Spiritual development services
Location: Kamloops, BC
Dates (start–end): 1984–1990

Name: Shalom Home
Type of Apostolate: Residence
Location: Antigonish, NS
Dates (start–end): 1985–1989

Name: St. Clare Convent
Type of Apostolate: Residence
Location: Sydney Mines, NS
Dates (start–end): 1985–Present

Name: St. Elizabeth Convent
Type of Apostolate: Spiritual development services and residence
Location: Calgary, AB
Dates (start–end): 1985–1998

Name: St. Therese Convent
Type of Apostolate: Pastoral services and parish administration
Location: St. Paul's River, PQ
Dates (start–end): 1985–Present

Name: Christopher Community
Type of Apostolate: Pastoral, health care, educational, and social services
Location: Basseterre,St. Kitts, West Indies
Dates (start–end): 1986–Present

Name: St. Monica Convent
Type of Apostolate: Health care & pastoral services; residence
Location: Lethbridge, AB
Dates (start–end): 1988–Present

Name: Adsum Community
Type of Apostolate: Residence and novitiate
Location: Lanark, NS
Dates (start–end): 1991–Present

Name: Sisters of St. Martha
Type of Apostolate: Parish administration and pastoral services
Location: St. George's Diocese, NF
Dates (start–end): 1993–Present

Name: Xavier Community
Type of Apostolate: Residence
Location: Antigonish, NS
Dates (start–end): 1994–Present

Name: Faustina Community
Type of Apostolate: Residence
Location: Antigonish, NS

APPENDIX V

CSM Congregation Leaders, 1900 to 2004:

1900-1901: Mother M. Innocentia (Caroline) MacNamara

1901-1910: Mother M. Faustina (Mary) MacArthur

1910-1916: Mother M. Stanislaus (Mary A.) MacDonald

1916-1922: Mother M. Faustina

1922-1925: Mother M. Stanislaus

1925-1937: Mother M. Ignatius (Mary Catherine) Floyd

1937-1943: Mother M. Immaculata (Jennie) Fraser

1943-1961: Mother M. Ignatius

1961-1967: Mother Paul of the Cross (Eunice Viola) Kyte

1967-1973: Mother Teresa Clare (Teresa Elizabeth) Ryan

1973-1981: Sister Mary (Mary Donald) MacIntosh

1981-1989: Sister Thérèse (Paul Thérèse) LeBlanc

1989-1994: Sister Joan (Ann Martin) Fultz

1994-1999: Sister Yvonne (Mary Cyril) Vigneault

1999-2004: Sister Mary (Alice Louise) MacFarlane

APPENDIX VI

Congregational Hallmarks

PATRONESS: ST. MARTHA

Martha lived during the time of Jesus in the village of Bethany, two miles from Jerusalem. She was the sister of Mary and Lazarus, whom Jesus miraculously raised from the dead. Martha welcomed Jesus and his disciples into her home, and he loved her just as she loved him.

The evangelists, Luke and John, portray Martha differently. Luke depicts Martha as distracted and apt to complain about her active role of service; he presents her sister Mary as having chosen the "better part," according to Jesus, and suggestively, the only part necessary (10:42). John, on the other hand, paints Martha in a much more positive light, recording that she rushed to meet Jesus just outside of the village once she heard of his visit; in contrast, Mary remained at home (11:20). In both Luke and John, this contrast between Martha and her sister Mary emphasizes the different choices each made in her apostolate. Martha chose a servant role. She used the term "Master" (Jn. 11: 29) to refer to Jesus and "waited" on the guests at the dinner party given for him (Jn. 12:2).

Most notably, Martha demonstrated faith and hope in Jesus as Messiah, a faith divinely revealed to Martha and elicited by Jesus (Jn. 11: 21-22, 24, 27). Her profession of faith parallels the Petrine confession recorded in Matthew 16:16.

LEGENDS OF ST. MARTHA

Through medieval times, many versions of a story circulated which tell of Martha, her family, Mary Magdalene, St. Maximinus, and others being forced from Palestine after the death of Jesus, and set adrift on a boat with neither rudder nor sail, so they would perish. Providence, however, guided the boat to Marseilles, France. Then, in the region of Aix, Martha preached, converted followers to Christianity and performed miracles. The townspeople feared a firebreathing beast, so Martha tamed the beast using a cross and holy water. She was gentle with the creature and mastered it through her faith in God; however, when she brought the transformed beast into town the emboldened townspeople killed it with stones and spears.

CULT OF ST. MARTHA IN THE MIDDLE AGES

Religious cults of special devotion to Martha, Lazarus, and Mary Magdalene existed during the Middle Ages. Martha cults, however, were more popular than the others because she was considered by many as a mature woman of beauty; moreover, less moral controversy surrounded her than Mary Magdalene. *Comments:* Martha has been very important in the Christian tradition as a womanly symbol of the active apostolate whereas Mary has symbolized the contemplative apostolate. Martha is the patroness of many Roman Catholic women religious congregations. Her feast day is celebrated on 29 July.

BIBLICAL SOURCES (*The Jerusalem Bible*)

Luke 10: 38-42:
In the course of their journey, [Jesus] came to a village, and a woman named Martha welcomed him into her house. She had a sister called Mary, who sat down at the Lord's feet and listened to him speaking. Now Martha, who was distracted with all the serving, said, "Lord, do you not care that my sister is leaving me to do the serving all by myself? Please tell her to help me." But the Lord answered: "Martha, Martha," he said, "you worry and fret about so many things, and yet few are needed, indeed only one. It is Mary who has chosen the better part; it is not to be taken from her."

John 11: 1-6, 17-41:
There was a man named Lazarus who lived in the village of Bethany with the two sisters, Mary and Martha, and he was ill. It was the same Mary, the sister of the sick man Lazarus, who anointed the Lord with ointment and wiped his feet with her hair. The sisters sent this message to Jesus, "Lord, the man you love is ill." On receiving the message, Jesus said, "The sickness will end not in death but in God's glory, and through it the Son of God will be glorified."

Jesus loved Martha and her sister and Lazarus, yet when he heard that Lazarus was ill he stayed where he was for a few more days.

On arriving, Jesus found that Lazarus had been in the tomb for four days already. Bethany is only about two miles from Jerusalem, and many Jews had come to Martha and Mary to sympathize with them over their brother. When Martha heard that Jesus had come she went to meet him. Mary remained sitting in the house. Martha said to Jesus, "If you had been here, my brother would not have died, but I know that, even now, whatever you ask of God, he will grant you." "Your brother," said Jesus to her, "will rise again." Martha said, "I know he will rise again at the resurrection on the last day." Jesus said: "I am the resurrection. If anyone believes in me, even though he dies he will live, and whoever lives and believes in me will never die. Do you believe this?" "Yes, Lord," she said, "I believe that you are the Christ, the Son of God, the one who was to come into this world."

When she had said this, she went and called her sister Mary, saying in a low voice, "The Master is here and wants to see you." Hearing this, Mary got up quickly and went to him. Jesus had not yet come into the village; he was still at the place where Martha had met him. When the Jews who were in the house sympathizing with Mary saw her get up so quickly and go out, they followed, thinking that she was going to the tomb to weep there.

Mary went to Jesus, and as soon as she saw him she threw herself at his feet, saying, "Lord, if you had been here, my brother would not have died." At the sight of her tears, and those of the Jews who followed her, Jesus said in great distress, with a sigh that came straight from the heart, "Where have you put him?" They said, "Lord, come and see." Jesus wept; and the Jews said, "See how much he loved him!" But there were some who remarked, "He opened the eyes of the blind man, could he not have prevented this man's death?" Still sighing, Jesus reached the tomb: it was a cave with a stone to close the opening. Jesus said, "Take the stone away." Martha said to him, "Lord, by now he will smell; this is the fourth day." Jesus replied, "Have I not told you that if you believe you will see the glory of God?" So they took away the stone.

John 12:1-2:

Six days before the Passover, Jesus went to Bethany, where Lazarus was, whom he had raised from the dead. They gave a dinner for him there; Martha waited on them and Lazarus was among those at table.

OTHER SOURCES

Irene Doyle, csm, *The Search for St. Martha.* Antigonish, N.S.: Sisters of St. Martha, Bethany, 1993.

MOTTO AND COAT-OF-ARMS

Mother M. Ignatius requested a Rev. R. McGuinness of Raymond, Alberta, to design a coat-of-arms for the Sisters of St. Martha. The design incorporated both traditional and legendary accounts of the life of St. Martha, as well as the inscription, "Deus Solus," the same inscription found on the congregation's official seal. The completed coat-of-arms was presented to the congregation on 16 March 1936.

For undocumented reasons, a few years later the motto was changed from "*Deus Solus*"–"God Alone" to "*Deo Soli*" ("For God Alone.") In 1938, Sister Remegius MacGillivray designed a new coat-of-arms which incorporated the new motto, but outside of minor changes, preserved essentially the same original design. This became the official coat-of-arms.

The arms of the Sisters of St. Martha are made up of two shields: the first, an escutcheon bearing the Constantine monogram, the most ancient symbol of Christ, the one borne by the soldiers of Constantine on their helmets, as their crest. The field of the escutcheon is gold, to show the wealth that has flowed from the martyrdom of, and the shedding of the Precious Blood of Christ, and red, as Jerusalem was the scene of Christ's life and death, and his friendship for St. Martha. His shield is therefore surmounted by the Cross crosslet, the Jerusalem Cross.

The shield of Christ supports as a charge a lozenge escutcheon of Pretence. This proclaims a union between Christ and a maiden lady who has a right to arms because she is an heiress. (St. Paul, "Heirs and joint heirs with Christ"). The colour of her shield (silver and blue) and its form (lozenge) proclaim that she is the pure (vow) bride of Christ and yet remains a maiden always.

Her shield is parted at the honour point of the escutcheon and the chief battlemented to show that she fought against the enemy of Christ (the dragon) and by the use of holy water overcame and bound him. And the base shows on the silver field of purity the dragon bound by chains and powerless beneath the holy water and in the face of purity. The red of the dragon shows the spilling of blood.

The supporters, the prows of the trireme, show that she was cast adrift on a sailless boat, the only mark of identification of which is the Cross of Christ, which is her honour and glory. The Cross chosen is the St. George, because St. George, too, slew a dragon. The prows of the trireme may show the nearness of her home and place of origin to the sea. All that the Sister of St. Martha does and all that she aspires to is summed up in her motto: "*Deo Soli*–For God Alone."

Sources: Sister May Mulvihill, "History of the Sisters of St. Martha" II:7:12-13 and *Sixty Years.*

OFFICIAL SEAL

When the congregation gained legal incorporation in 1907 as the Corporation of the Sisters of St. Martha, it needed to make certain congregational documents official. As a result, the general administration decided in 1912 to obtain an official seal of the congregation to be used on all official and legal documents. Representations of our Lord, St. Martha, and St. Mary are present on the seal, along with the inscription "*Deus Solus*" ("God Alone"). The seal of the corporation, of course, continues to be in use.

Source: Sister May Mulvihill, "History of the Sisters of St. Martha" I:3:9.

MEDAL OF ST. MARTHA

The congregation obtained a medal of St. Martha from the Sisters of St. Martha of St. Hyacinthe, Quebec. Its inscription, translated from the French, is: "Holy Hostess of Jesus, obtain for us your zeal. Love of him banishes trouble." When the rosary beads were no longer a part of the Martha habit, a sister could wear either the Martha medal or the silver crucifix.

Source: Sister Irene Doyle, csm, *The Search for St. Martha*. Antigonish, NS: Sisters of St. Martha, Bethany, 1993, pp. 52-53.

CRUCIFIX

Originally the crucifix was attached to the rosary as part of the Martha habit. Later, it was replaced on the rosary by the Martha medal, and the crucifix was then worn around the neck on a black cord (later on a silver chain). With the change to contemporary dress, the crucifix or the medal could be worn.

RING

From 1905 to 1967 the Martha ring was conferred on all sisters when they made perpetual profession. After 1967 sisters obtained the ring at first profession. An unsigned and undated historical article on the congregation states, "It may be said here that the first rings were made at Eastwood's, New Glasgow. After consulting the sisters, Mother [Faustina] asked to have the letters I.H.S. engraved on each ring."

MARTHA HABIT

The congregation altered the distinctive Martha costume at successive stages of their history. See the photographs of general superiors for changes in headdress especially. Their page references can be found in the List of Illustrations.

PRAYER TO ST. MARTHA

O Blessed St. Martha, who had the happiness of serving the Divine Master in your own home at Bethany, obtain for us the grace to serve God with love and fidelity. May we share in the faith which enabled you to recognize Christ as the Son of God. May our hope be as strong as yours when you trusted him, even though he seemed to fail you. And may our love of God grow and be expressed, as was yours, in loving service of others. St. Martha, model of all who desire to serve God in faith, hope and love, obtain for us the grace of final perseverance. Amen.

EVENING HYMN TO OUR LADY

1. Softly and still as night comes stealing,
   We sing our vesper lay;
   Silvery chimes of eve are pealing,
   It is the end of day

Chorus:
O Holy Queen of Heav'n,
O Star of hope so fair
'All grace to thee is giv'n,
Hear thou our evening prayer.

2. Guard us with love until the morrow,
   And keep our hearts from pain
   Give us thy peace and banish sorrow,
   Renew our strength again.

HYMN TO ST. MARTHA

1. Humble servant of Christ the Lord,
   Hail to Thee in glory bright.
   From our full hearts we sing to Thee;
   Hear thy children, heed our prayer.

2. Careful handmaiden of the Lord,
   Virgin wise with thy lamp alight.
   May our hearts be aflame with zeal,
   Serving Him with love like Thine.

3. Be for us a star to guide;
   Comfort us in life's deep woes.
   May we mirror your love of Christ,
   Seeking solace in Him alone.

Chorus:
Re-sound then our hymn of praise,
Lauding our patroness,
Martha in splendor now in Heaven above.
Hostess of Bethany,
Serving the Son of God,
We greet you, our Mother and model blest.

Source: Father L.E. Sendoya. Adapted by Sister May Mulvihill and set to music by Sister Helene Wadden.

APPENDIX VII

Congregational Statistical Charts and Tables

CHART 1
Total Professed Sisters, 1900–1998

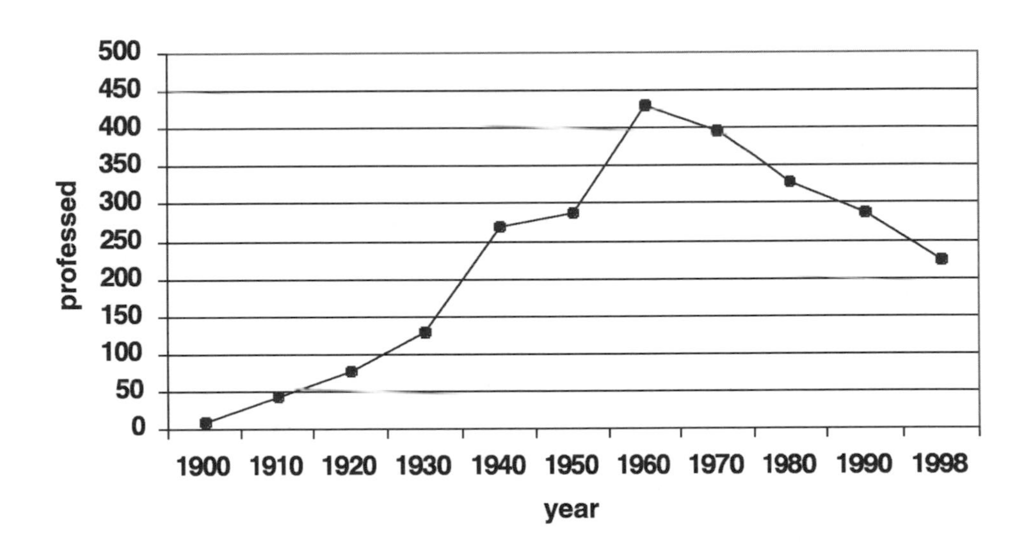

Note: Totals for 1910-1930 are estimates. The peak number of professed was recorded in 1962, when 460 sisters made up the congregation.

Sources: Sister May Mulvihill, "History of the Sisters of St. Martha," I:1: appencies A and B; CSM Quinquennial Reports to the Holy See, 1931-1961, F5,S34,SS1,f1-4,b84 and congregational registers.

CHART 2
Totals Entering and Departing from the Congregation by Decade, 1900–1980

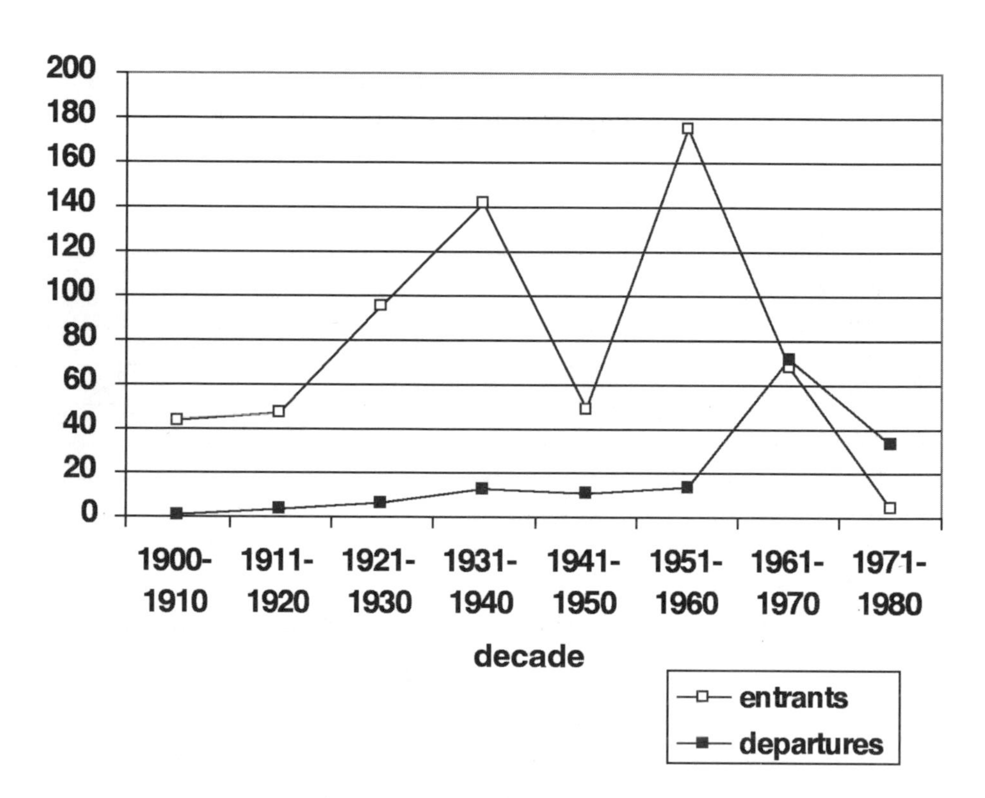

Note: The totals entering include only those who became professed members of the Congregation. The total members departing does not include the deceased.

Source: "Statistics of Numbers Entering, Making Profession, Leaving and Deceased and Exclaustration," F5,S33,SS2,b77,f1.

CHART 3
Congregational Profile, 1910-1998

Total professed sisters: 640

Source: CSM Nominal List, 1998.

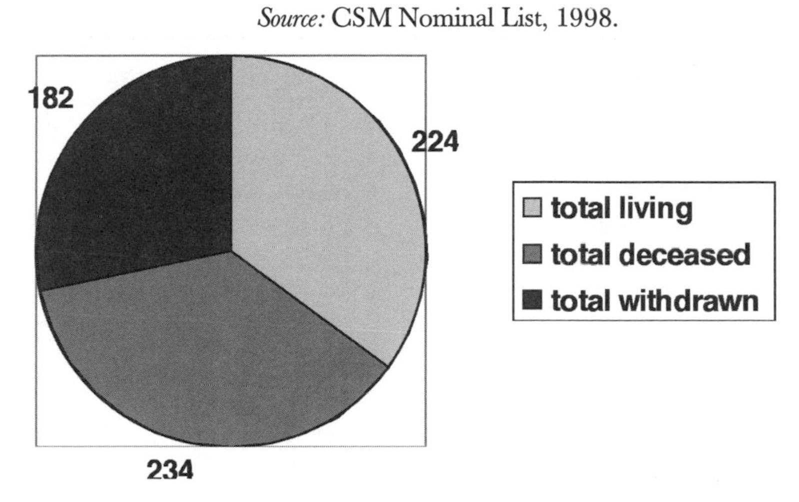

CHART 4
Deaths and Average Age at Death by Decade, 1889–1998

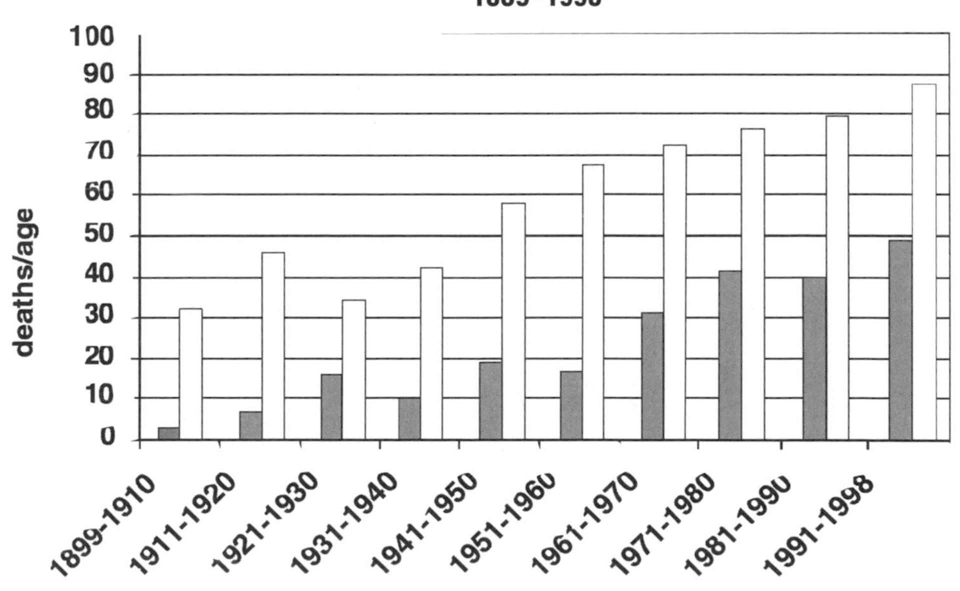

Source: CSM Register of Deaths, 1899-1998 inclusive, F5,S33,SS9,b79,f1.

CHART 5
Geographic Origin of Sisters Making First Profession by Decade to 1980

Place of Origin	1894 – 1910	1911 – 1920	1921 – 1930	1931 – 1940	1941 – 1950	1951 – 1960	1961 – 1970	1971 – 1980	Total
Nova Scotia	42	39	79	69	48	135	57	3	472
New Brunswick	-	-	-	1	2	4	-	1	8
Prince Edward	-	1	-	-	-	1	-	-	2
Newfoundland	1	3	14	16	2	4	-	-	40
Ontario	-	3	4	1	-	-	3	1	12
Quebec	-	-	-	-	-	-	1	-	1
Saskatchewan	-	-	-	9	5	3	2	-	19
Alberta	-	-	-	13	2	1	1	-	17
British Columbia	-	-	-	1	-	-	1	-	2
Manitoba	-	-	-	-	-	-	-	-	-
USA	-	-	-	-	-	3	2	-	5
Other	-	-	1	-	-	-	2	-	3
Total	**43**	**46**	**98**	**110**	**59**	**151**	**69**	**5**	**581**

Note: Total entrants are somewhat lower than actual entrants because the geographical origins of pre-1960 entrants are not always known.

Source: General Superior's Report to General Chapter, 1961, p. 3, F5,S8,SS4,f1,b1 and congregational registers.

APPENDIX VIII

CSM History: Key Events

1894
- Bishop Cameron announces a plan to form, in collaboration with the Sisters of Charity, Halifax, an auxiliary order to be known as the Sisters of St. Martha

1897
- Ten Marthas and three Charities begin a household management mission at St.F.X.

1900
- July 12: Marthas at Mount St. Vincent retreat are given the choice to remain with the Charities or to form an independent congregation in Antigonish;
- July 16: first group of Martha volunteers for Antigonish arrive at St.F.X.
- July 29: the Feast of St Martha; Mother M. Innocentia MacNamara is elected first superior of the new congregation

1902
- Marthas establish their first mission beyond St.F.X.: household management at St. Joseph's Hospital, Glace Bay, Cape Breton

1906
- Marthas open their first hospital: St. Martha's Hospital, Antigonish

1911
- Marthas open their first school of nursing at St. Martha's Hospital, Antigonish

1913
- Marthas begin first mission outside the Diocese of Antigonish: St. Augustine's Seminary, Toronto

1915
- First general council of four elected sisters is formed

1916
- Marthas help to found a new congregation: the Sisters of St. Martha, Charlottetown

1917
- The Congregation gains independence from St.F.X. University
- Marthas establish first mission in institutional social work: St. Mary's Home, Sydney, for orphans and unwed mothers

1921
- The Congregation opens a new motherhouse at Bethany, Antigonish

1925
- Dr. Moses Coady succeeds in urging the Marthas into teaching at rural schools;
- First general chapter of the congregation;
- Mother M. Ignatius Floyd elected general superior;

1927
- Marthas enter the field of adult education by offering short courses in home economics;

1929
- The Congregation opens its first mission in western Canada: St. Michael's Hospital, Lethbridge, Alberta

1931
- Marthas temporarily approved as a papal institute;

1943
- Marthas receive permanent approval as a papal institute;

1950
- The sisters celebrate the Congregation's golden jubilee

1952
- First mission established outside Canada, with the opening of St. Martha's Catholic Centre in Boston, Massachusetts

1967
- General Chapter of Renewal initiates the process of congregation renewal;
- rapid decline in vocations and upswing in sisters leaving the religious life

1975
- The Marthas celebrate their diamond jubilee

1983
- Revised constitutions approved by the Vatican;

1999-2000
- The Sisters of St. Martha celebrate their centenary;

APPENDIX IX

Contributors to the History of the CSM Project

The persons listed below generously granted me interviews, donated documents, or contributed in some other way to the History of the CSM Project.

Sister Anna Beaton, St.F.X.
Sister Shirley Bruce, Bethany
Sister Stella Chafe, Bethany
Sister M. Clarissa Chisholm, Bethany
Sister Stephanie Cormier, Bethany
Sister Irene Doyle, Bethany
Sister Crescentia Duprey, Bethany
Sister Marianne Exner, Bethany
Sister Joan Fultz, St. Martha's Hospital
Sister Margaret Gillis, Bethany
Sister Lillian Gaudet, Bethany
Sister Mary Gouthro, St.F.X.
Sister John of the Cross Hanrahan, Bethany
Sister Josephine Keyzer, Bethany
Christa King, St.F.X.
Sister Clare Marie Lyons, Bethany
Frank Maas, Antigonish
Sister Genevieve McArthur, Bethany
Sister Jean Alexius MacArthur, Bethany
Sister Marie Raymond MacDonald, Bethany
Rev. Malcolm MacDonell, St.F.X.
Sister Margaret MacFarlane, St.F.X.
Anthony MacGillivray, Lanark
Sister Mary MacIntosh, Bethany
Kathleen MacKenzie, St.F.X.
Rev. Dr. Gregory MacKinnon, St.F.X.
Sister Mary Roderick MacMullin, Bethany
Sister Rose Carmel MacMaster, Bethany
Sister Katherine MacNeil, Bethany
Sister Teresina McNeil, Bethany
Sister May Mulvihill, Bethany
Sister Marie Reine Murrin, Bethany
Sister M. Simone Roach, Bethany
Jerome Sullivan, Antigonish
Sister Sandra White, St.F.X.

BIBLIOGRAPHY

A. PRIMARY RESOURCES

1. Manuscript Sources

Congregation of the Sisters of St. Martha Archives (CSMA), Antigonish:
Fonds 1-51
General Secretary's Office: selected registers, lists, and associated materials

Antigonish Diocesan Archives (ADA), Antigonish:
Most Rev. John Cameron Papers
Most Rev. John R. MacDonald Papers
Most Rev. James Morrison Papers

St. F.X. University Archives (STFXUA), Antigonish:
Selected Presidential Papers
Father Peter Nearing Papers

Archives of the Archdiocese of Halifax:
Archbishop Gerald Berry Papers
Archbishop James M. Hayes Papers

Archives of the Diocese of Calgary
Bishop John T. Kidd Papers
Bishop P.J. Monahan Papers
Bishop Francis P. Carroll Papers

Archives of the Archdiocese of Ottawa
Archbishop M.M. Lemieux Papers
Archbishop J. Aurele Plourde Papers

Archives of the Diocese of Kamloops
Assorted materials

Archives of the Archbishop of Regina
Archbishop P.J. Monahan Papers
Archbishop M.C. O'Neil Papers
Archbishop Charles A. Halpin Papers

Public Archives of Nova Scotia
Library Collection: selected items
School Collection

2. **Printed Sources**
The Bethanite
The Casket
Marthas in Mission
St. F.X. Calenders
Xaverian

3. **Government Documents**
Canada *Census*, 1901-1981

B. SECONDARY SOURCES

1. Congregational

Cameron, Sister John Baptist. "Brief Outline of the Early History of the Sisters of St. Martha, 1894–1948." Bethany, 1949.

_______. "Most Reverend John Cameron, D.D., Founder of the Congregation of Sisters of St. Martha," Bethany, n.d.

Congregation of the Sisters of St. Martha (CSM). *Sixty Years, Deo Soli.* 60th anniversary booklet. Bethany, 1960.

Doyle, Sister Irene. "The Heritage of the Sisters of St. Martha." Antigonish: Sisters of St. Martha, 1967.

_______. "My Experience as an Extension Worker Over 50 years Ago." Speech given to the Antigonish Heritage Association, 8 March 1993.

_______. "Young Women from Newfoundland in the History of the Sisters of St. Martha." 1999.

______. *The Search for St. Martha.* Antigonish: Sisters of St. Martha, 1993.

Fultz, Sister Joan. "The Marthas: A Story of Pioneering Faith. A Presentation on an Aspect of the Diocesan History of the Sisters of St. Martha." Paper presented at the Reverend A. A. Johnston Memorial Conference, St. Francis Xavier University, 19-20 August 1994.

MacDonald, Sister Josephine, compiler. "History of CSM Teaching Sisters." N.d.

Lyons, Sister Clare Marie. "History of Nursing Education in Nova Scotia." 1979.

MacKinnon, Sister Marie Michael. Speech to Atlantic Institute, 21 July 1982.

MacPherson, Sister Sarah. "Religious Women in Nova Scotia: A Struggle for Autonomy. A Sketch of the Sisters of St. Martha of Antigonish, Nova Scotia, 1900-1960." CCHA *Study Sessions* 51 (1984): 89-106.

______. "The Struggle Gives the Meaning: The Contribution of the Sisters of St. Martha to Health Care in Sydney, Nova Scotia, 1920-1980" N.d.

Mulvihill, Sister May. "History of the Sisters of St. Martha, 1894-1969." 4 vols. 1980.

2. Women's History

Constance, Maria, SC. *Mother Mary Bonaventure*. Wellesley Hills, Mass.: Mount Saint Vincent, 1972.

Danylewycz, Marta. *Taking the Veil: An Alternative to Marriage, Motherhood, and Spinsterhood in Quebec, 1840-1920.* Eds. Paul-Andre Linteau, et al. Toronto: McClelland and Stewart, 1987.

Ebaugh, Helen Fuchs. *Out of the Cloister.* Austin: University of Texas Press, 1977.

McGahan, Elizabeth W. "The Sisters of Charity of the Immaculate Conception: A Canadian Case Study." *Historical Studies* 61 (1995): 99-133.

McKenna, Mary Olga. "Paradigm Shifts in a Women's Religious Institute: The Sisters of Charity, Halifax, 1950-1979." *Historical Studies* 61 (1995):135-151.

________. *Charity Alive: Sisters of Saint Vincent de Paul, Halifax, 1950-1980.* Lanham, Maryland: University Press of America, 1998.

McNamara, J.C. *Sisters in Arms: Catholic Nuns Through two Millennia.* Cambridge, Mass: Harvard University Press, 1996.

Muir, Elizabeth Gillian, and Marilyn Fardig Whiteley, eds. *Changing Roles of Women within the Christian Church in Canada.* Toronto: University of Toronto Press, 1995.

Neal, Marie Augusta. *From Nuns to Sisters: An Expanding Vocation.* Mystic, Conn.: Twenty-Third Publications, 1990.

O'Gallagher, Marianna. "The Sisters of Charity of Halifax: The Early and Middle years." CCHA *Study Sessions* 47 (1980): 57-69.

Ryan, Eileen. *Mother Mary Fidelis Eustace*. Dorval, Quebec: Saint Veronica Convent, 1972.

Sister Maura. *The Sisters of Charity, Halifax*. Toronto: Ryerson Press, 1956.

3. Local History/Diocesan History

Butts, Peggy, CND. "Pilgrimage from France to Montreal to Antigonish: Living the Visitation Mystery of the Virgin Mary." Paper presented at the Reverend A.A. Johnston Memorial Conference, St. Francis Xavier University, 19-20 August 1994.

Cameron, James D. *For the People: A History of St. Francis Xavier University*. Montreal and Kingston: McGill-Queen's University Press, 1996.

Johnston, Rev. A.A. *A History of the Catholic Church in Eastern Nova Scotia, 1611-1880*. 2 vols. Antigonish: St. Francis Xavier University Press, 1960 and 1971.

_____. *Antigonish Diocese Priests and Bishops 1786-1925*. Ed. Kathleen M. MacKenzie. Antigonish: The Casket Printing and Co., 1994.

McGowan, Mark G. "Conspicuous Influence: The Diocese of Antigonish and the Development of the Canadian Catholic Church, 1844-1994." Paper presented at the Reverend A.A. Johnston Memorial Conference, St. Francis Xavier University, 19-20 August 1994.

McKenna, Mary Olga, SC. "The Sisters of Charity, Halifax: Their Legacy of Service to the Diocese of Antigonish, 1882-1994. "Paper presented at the Reverend A.A. Johnston Memorial Conference, St. Francis Xavier University, 19-20 August 1994.

MacKenzie, Kathleen M. "Deo Soli–For God Alone: The Sisters of St. Martha, 1892-1921." *St. F.X. Alumni News* (Spring/Summer 1988), pp. 4-6.

_____. "The Development of a Permanent Public Health Care System in Industrial Cape Breton 1880-1930." MA thesis, St. Mary's University, 1991.

MacLean, R.A. *Bishop John Cameron: Piety and Politics.* Antigonish: The Casket Printing and Publishing Co., 1991.

_______. *The Casket, 1852-1992: From Gutenberg to Internet. The Story of a Small-Town Weekly.* Antigonish: The Casket Printing and Publishing Co., 1995.

_____. "An Outline of Diocesan History." In *The Casket*, Diocesan Anniversary Supplement, 26 April 1995.

4. General History

Forbes, E.R. *Maritime Rights Movement, 1919-27: A Study in Canadian Regionalism.* Montreal and Kingston: McGill-Queen's University Press, 1979.

Forbes, E.R., and D.A Muise, eds. *The Atlantic Provinces in Confederation.* Toronto and Fredericton: University of Toronto and Acadiensis Press, 1993.

Francis, R. Douglas, et al. *Destinies: Canadian History Since Confederation.* Third edition. Toronto: Harcourt Brace Canada, 1996.

McGuigan, Peter. 'The Cardinal and the Island." *The Island Magazine* 3 (Fall/Winter 1994), pp. 27-34.

Murphy, Terrance, and Gerald Stortz, eds. *Creed and Culture: The Place of English-Speaking Catholics in Canadian Society.* Montreal: McGill-Queen's University Press, 1993.

Theriault, Michel. *The Institutes of Consecrated Life in Canada.* Ottawa: National Library of Canada, 1980

C. SURVEYS AND ORAL SOURCES:

1. Oral Interviews (see list of contributors in Appendix IX)
2. St. F.X. Faculty Alumni Survey, 1992. Author's files.
3. St. F.X. Student Alumni Survey, 1992. Author's files.

INDEX

C=Congregation C.B.=Cape Breton X=St.F.X.